Praise for *Search and Social*

Search and Social

Search and Social

The Definitive Guide to
Real-Time Content Marketing

Rob Garner

WILEY

John Wiley & Sons, Inc.

Senior Acquisitions Editor: WILLEM KNIBBE
Development Editor: DAVID CLARK
Technical Editor: NICK ROSHON
Production Editor: ERIC CHARBONNEAU
Copy Editor: KIM WIMPSETT
Editorial Manager: PETE GAUGHAN
Production Manager: TIM TATE
Vice President and Executive Group Publisher: RICHARD SWADLEY
Vice President and Publisher: NEIL EDDE
Book Designer: FRANZ BAUMHACKL
Compositor: MAUREEN FORYS, HAPPENSTANCE TYPE-O-RAMA
Proofreader: CANDACE CUNNINGHAM
Indexer: TED LAUX
Project Coordinator, Cover: KATHERINE CROCKER
Cover Designer: RYAN SNEED
Cover Image: © LOGORILLA / iStockPhoto

Copyright © 2013 by John Wiley & Sons, Inc., Indianapolis, Indiana

Published simultaneously in Canada

ISBN: 978-1-118-26438-6

ISBN: 978-1-118-28721-7 (ebk.)

ISBN: 978-1-118-28341-7 (ebk.)

ISBN: 978-1-118-28467-4 (ebk.)

For general information on our other products and services or to obtain technical support, please contact our Customer Care Department within the U.S. at (877) 762-2974, outside the U.S. at (317) 572-3993 or fax (317) 572-4002.

Wiley publishes in a variety of print and electronic formats and by print-on-demand. Some material included with standard print versions of this book may not be included in e-books or in print-on-demand. If this book refers to media such as a CD or DVD that is not included in the version you purchased, you may download this material at http://booksupport.wiley.com. For more information about Wiley products, visit www.wiley.com.

Library of Congress Control Number: 2012947716

Dear Reader,

Thank you for choosing *Search and Social: The Definitive Guide to Real-Time Content Marketing*. This book is part of a family of premium-quality Sybex books, all of which are written by outstanding authors who combine practical experience with a gift for teaching.

Sybex was founded in 1976. More than 30 years later, we're still committed to producing consistently exceptional books. With each of our titles, we're working hard to set a new standard for the industry. From the paper we print on to the authors we work with, our goal is to bring you the best books available.

I hope you see all that reflected in these pages. I'd be very interested to hear your comments and get your feedback on how we're doing. Feel free to let me know what you think about this or any other Sybex book by sending me an email at nedde@wiley.com. If you think you've found a technical error in this book, please visit http://sybex.custhelp.com. Customer feedback is critical to our efforts at Sybex.

Best regards,

Neil Edde
Vice President and Publisher
Sybex, an Imprint of Wiley

This book is dedicated to Carla, Sarah, Steven, Mom, and Dad.

👁 Acknowledgments

While my name is on the front and spine of this book, getting it edited, printed, and marketed has certainly been a team effort the whole way through. There were also a lot people who influenced my view of Internet marketing going back many years before I ever thought I would be writing a book. Many others provided great food for thought, discussion, and great thinking about online marketing across a wide variety of disciplines. Many others are inspiring just on their commitment to their professions and their passion alone.

First and foremost, I would like to thank Don Scales for his support since my earliest days in the agency business and for providing the opportunity to work in a position that has offered such a unique lens into online marketing and strategy. Also special thanks to Brian Powley, Tari Haro, Colin Turney, Adam Lavelle, Marlin Jackson, Dave Johnson, Mike Jackson, Peter Randazzo, Matt Schultz, Chris Wallace, Jessica Burdman, Amanda McElroy, Lisa Ponte-Fazio, Pat Stern, Rod Lenninger, and the entire executive team at iCrossing. I would also like to thank all of my colleagues at iCrossing and Hearst (in the United States and abroad), as well as the search-media teams, the natural-search team, creative, and the strategy group.

I was most fortunate to have worked with an amazing team at Wiley and Sybex. Willem Knibbe guided this process the whole way through and has been a true partner from my first correspondence with him to the final print and beyond. Special thanks to the entire team, including Pete Gaughan, Eric Charbonneau, Jay Lesandrini, Candace Cunningham, Chantal Kowalski, Neil Edde, and David Clark. Huge thanks are also due to my technical editor and colleague, Nick Roshon.

I would also like to thank the many people who have provided feedback and support throughout the development and editorial process of this book, including Carla Garner, Collin Cornwell, Tarah Feinberg, Brian Haven, Dana Mellecker, David Deal, Christiana Henry, Kristen Deye, Devin Downey, Dr. Karen Pate, Lori Wilson, Constance DeCherney, Eric Cano, Kent Milton, Doug Lay, Jon Maxson, Mike Grehan, Stan Pugsley, Mike Arceri, Doug Platts, Caitlyn Todd, and Jay Chapman.

Thanks also to the current and past boards and members of DFWSEM, DFWIMA, and SEMPO. Special thanks to Dan Sturdivant, Tony Wright, Mark Jackson, Sean Jackson, Bill Hartzer, Mark Barrera, Christine Churchill, Pete Lerma, and Derek Schafer. Also, thanks to everyone at MediaPost, ad:tech, SES, SMX, Pubcon, Content Marketing World, the ANA, and SXSW.

A special thank-you goes out to the following people as well: Bruce Clay, Matt Cutts, Matt McGowan, Brett Tabke, Chris Boggs, Jeff Pruitt, Barbara Coll, David Berkowitz, Aaron Goldman, Gord Hotchkiss, Duane Forrester, Ryan DeShazer, Janel Landis Laravie, Kaila Colbin, Janet Driscoll-Miller, Bob Birch, Josh Alan, Edmund Wong, Kristján Hauksson, Kevin Ryan, Jonathan Allen, Jill Whalen, Jorie Waterman, Gary Stein, Shoshana Winter, Noah Elkin, Dana Todd, Rachel Pasqua, Richard Zwicky, Danny Sullivan, Giovanni Gallucci, Dave Feldman, Laurie Sullivan, Jeff Herzog, Ryan Utter, Matt Grzyb, Allison Sackett, Patrick Lopez, Rebekah Thomas, all MediaPost writers, Alisa Leonard, Michael Insuaste, David Lindemann, Todd Polk, Mark Beekman, Kevin Lee, Frances Krug, Kevin Gold, Frank Lee, Joe Laratro, Sara Holoubek, Edward Lewis, Steve Plunkett, Mike Gullaksen, and the entire team at Virtual Management.

About the Author

Rob Garner is a speaker, educator, strategist, and renowned expert on the topic of online marketing, search, social, and content. In addition to client work and strategic development as VP of strategy at iCrossing, a Hearst Company, he speaks regularly at many industry events, including SXSW, ad:tech, Search Marketing Expo, SES, WebmasterWorld/Pubcon, and OMMA, and has guest-lectured at NYU on graduate-studies topics in marketing.

Rob was featured on the cover of the Spring 2012 issue of *Search Marketing Standard* and has been interviewed and quoted by many top business and news publications. Some of these include the Dow Jones, Reuters, Mashable, MediaPost, *Adweek*, *AdAge*, *Direct Marketing News*, *Mobile Marketer*, *Smart Business Magazine*, Search Engine Watch, Clickz, CNNMoney, and the Dallas Morning News.

Additionally, he has written for MediaPost Publications' Search Insider since 2006, providing insight into search and social management and best practices. Rob is a cofounder of the Dallas/Fort Worth Search Engine Marketing Association, served as its president from 2006 to 2008, and serves on the SEMPO board of directors as-vice president. He also served on the DFW Interactive Marketing Association board of directors in 2006.

Contents

Chapter 11   **Video and Images**   **261**

Chapter 12   **More Considerations for Real-Time Content Marketing,**
Search, and Social   **279**

Foreword

Building a digital brand has never been so easy or difficult.

On the one hand, you can launch a brand literally in minutes and on the cheap thanks to media platforms like Facebook, Twitter, and WordPress. Just download a few SlideShare presentations on search marketing 101 for a self-tutorial while you're at it, and you're on your way.

But creating an enduring brand that resonates with people—a connected brand or a close relationship with your audiences—now that's hard. (And I have the battle scars working with Fortune 500 firms for 25 years to prove it, including my current role as president and CEO of iCrossing.) Building a digital brand in the social world alone means competing with more than 180 million blogs and 40 million Facebook pages. And 72 hours of video content is uploaded on YouTube every minute. How do you break through that kind of clutter?

But dealing with the proliferation of media channels is a cakewalk compared to figuring out how to build a relationship with the always-on consumer. When I say always-on, I mean people who really do interact with your brand—no, shape your brand—24 hours a day, 7 days a week. She is increasingly savvy in the way she uses search tools and a network of digital media platforms and devices to understand who you are and how you compare against your competitors. And she's not shy about telling the world what she thinks of you. In real time.

Consider a mom planning a family vacation. She might use specialty apps and search tools on her mobile device to find lodging options. When she's ready to book a room at a place that looks appealing, she either relies on a self-service travel booking site or visits your website to find the best rate. If you give her a great deal, she lets you know about it on your Twitter account and Facebook wall. Then when she's on vacation at your hotel, she posts pictures of her vacation in real time on her Instagram and Pinterest accounts—or sends you an angry tweet if she's having a bad time and you have something to do with it. After her vacation ends, she reviews your resort on TripAdvisor and Yelp for good measure.

You had better be present when she's talking about your brand and interacting with you. Failing to respond to her when she has a concern can mushroom into a customer service nightmare. On the positive side, her happy Instagram and Pinterest photos create opportunities for you to do some real-time marketing with your own presence on Pinterest and Instagram.

It's no wonder the leading brands have let go of the mentality that "getting the word out" on as many channels as possible constitutes effective digital marketing. Instead, the leaders are acting more like content publishers for the always-on consumer. Savvy marketers use rigorous research to understand who their most important audiences are (ranging from digitally savvy moms to young professionals planning their finances) and then plan thoughtful calendars to publish marketing content (whether tweets, blog posts, video, or images) on places where brands and audiences can find and engage with each other.

Smart brands are doing what Rob Garner advocates in the book you are about to read: using meaningful content to interact with the always-on consumer in real time. As Rob writes in *Search and Social: The Definitive Guide to Real-Time Content Marketing*, "A marketing strategy is only as good as it is 'right now.' It requires full participation from brands, marketers, and business proprietors acting as publishers and media creators, in a world of search- and socially driven content."

Search and Social will help you figure out how to develop a real-time marketing program with a special focus on applying content marketing, social media, and search. Rob will give you the right tools to become an effective publisher of marketing content, using key search and social strategies to extend the reach of your content.

Rob applies his 18 years of experience in the digital world, including his role as an iCrossing strategy executive helping clients in the United States and Europe build digital brands. I'm excited for Rob and proud of what he has accomplished. I'm also excited for you, the marketer, as you read this book and build a more connected brand in real time.

—*Don Scales*
    iCrossing president and CEO

Introduction

Picture two circles overlapping each other, like a Venn diagram, with one circle titled search *and the other titled* social. *The area in which the two circles meet is vast and complex, to the point that this joined area has become one. This book focuses on this area right in the middle, where search and social overlap, with its inherent real-time characteristics. This book is designed to help marketing practitioners, marketing organizations, and CMOs understand the new and complex real-time marketing and publishing landscape, as well as the emerging interdependency of search and social tactics and technologies. It provides simple and actionable steps toward becoming an effective real-time content marketer by using the basic integrated principles of search marketing, social-media marketing, and content publishing to develop a real-time content marketing platform.*

While some of the concepts presented are not new and in fact date back to the earliest days of the commercial Internet, we have reached a critical mass of adoption in a world where society as a whole in now networked. A collective digital consciousness has manifested itself through networks, and businesses must engage in order to thrive, or risk losing out to the competition altogether.

This book is not a cookbook full of digital-marketing "recipes," and no single book is going to present a complete digital-content marketing approach. The concepts discussed will provide an approach that may even take years to fully mature and will teach you how to think about new media. Sybex has other books that also delve into some of the individual subjects listed, and throughout the book, I call out other titles that I recommend for further review and reading. If you think any single book will solve all of your marketing problems, then you will likely be disappointed with everything you read. If you want to learn about how the new-media landscape works and how to make your business thrive in this landscape, then keep reading. Getting to where you want to go doesn't take a single book; it takes a library, in addition to real practice and real-world experience.

Real-Time Content

Marketers and publishers are witnessing a unique moment in the history of information distribution. As the speed of content dissemination and propagation advances to the point of *real-time* with the advent of real-time search and networked sharing services, traditional publishing and marketing practices are challenged with stepping up to compete and engage. Online networks are inherently real-time, and marketers must increase the velocity of participation and production in order to meet the full opportunity, in a human way. Only marketers who understand how to interact with the always-on consumer in real-time will succeed.

The bottom line is that networks are always active and alive, and a marketing strategy is only as good as it is "right now." It requires full participation from brands, marketers, and business proprietors acting as publishers and media creators, in a world of search- and socially driven content. This book will show you how it works and how to participate.

A major focus of this book is to show you how to establish your presence where content connections and flows are occurring in real-time. Connected conversations are occurring in social and search on a real-time basis, and as every relevant opportunity occurs, *being present* will allow you to potentially have a stake in that conversation. In social networks, this could mean that there are conversations and questions arising about your company specifically or conversations that fall into your own general area of expertise. If you approach them in the right way, you have the opportunity to *become a part of that conversation* rather than being outside of the conversation. The good news is that being part of the conversation increases your footprint in search and social spaces. *Live participation is optimization.*

This book will also help in answering the tough questions that lead to an effective fluid and real-time approach and also to reduce some of the common fears about getting started. In addition, it will spell out some of the predicaments and realities of the new marketing landscape and how "not participating" could have a devastating effect or become a competitive disadvantage.

The first two chapters are designed to provide an overview of the key concepts of search and social together with real-time marketing. Reading these chapters may spark ideas for your strategy and illuminate how content is connecting and flowing all across the Internet. Subsequent chapters will focus on the objective topics of real-time content marketing but also provide key questions that you will need to answer directly for your business. These topics range from the highly strategic and long-term to the hour-by-hour management of your tactical execution.

Later chapters focus on the hands-on development of building your own real-time content marketing platform. They will cover the key networks, tools, tactics, technical implementations, and measurement parameters needed to build platform.

I have used full-path URLs throughout the book, which I realize can be a pain to type in. Search terms and results are not always stable, but you, of course, may use your own keywords to search in Bing or Google for the documents. But as a source for my intended citation, the exact-path URL is the best way to clarify where I intended for you to locate a particular asset, without relying on a third-party URL system.

A New Marketing Discipline Emerges: The Interdependency of Search and Social, with Real-Time Content at the Core

Overall, this book will help search pros see the search engine optimization [SEO] parallels in social networks and help social pros understand how their efforts impact search and how to become literate in search speak. As much as it emphasizes both tactics and strategies, this book teaches a way of thinking. It should spark a new sensibility in marketing in terms of how to think about digital in a new search and social landscape that has come of age.

In today's digital publishing landscape, content is still king, whether it is in the form of an article, conversation, application, video, like, comment, or share. This book will also focus on the creation, development, and distribution of the most common types of real-time content, with a highlight on using interdependent search and social tactics to extend the reach and returns of your efforts. Real-time content marketing is also about using search and social technologies to strike with a message or interaction like lightning. The Internet has always been real-time; it is people who are slow to keep up with its pace.

In the first chapter, I have provided a very high-level introduction to the thinking of Dr. Manuel Castells, with an added bit of philosophical pondering and illustration from Sir Tim Berners-Lee. In the mid 1990s, Castells' work served as my early inspiration for going into Internet marketing, and I hope my short mention will point you toward additional reading.

In many ways, the interdependency and connectedness of search and social are ultimately about people, places, and things becoming nodes in a network. This is the ultimate form of social search, and this foundation is being used as a framework for a form of future artificial intelligence. The search and social worlds are also beginning to enter into our everyday lives in the physical world.

Who Should Read This Book

This book is for the following people:

- Business owners, marketing executives, and CMOs who want to better understand the impact of real-time content marketing on their businesses

- SEO practitioners and strategists who want to employ modern techniques for better natural search-engine performance and a broader strategy

- Social-media practitioners and strategists who need to become more familiar with how traditional SEO techniques can extend the opportunities in their own social efforts

- Online-content creators and publishers who want to better understand how content travels throughout real-time networks
- Any marketer who wants to take advantage of a new opportunity in search and social media and also develop a real-time attitude in their day-to-day marketing efforts

What Is Covered in This Book

Search and Social is designed for front-to-back read-throughs and also as a reference book. Although you may read it all the way through to gain a sense of both "search and social" and real-time content marketing, you will also want to keep it handy as a reference for many common aspects of online marketing. Here is chapter-by-chapter overview of what you can expect to learn:

Chapter 1: Real-Time Publishing and Marketing covers the key thinkers and concepts in real-time marketing, advances in real-time marketing, and the impact of real-time on marketing as a whole.

Chapter 2: Understanding Search and Social explains how search and social approaches have merged together as core drivers for search and social entities and provides new ways of thinking about and acting upon this emerging discipline.

Chapter 3: Ramping Up for a Real-Time Content Marketing Strategy includes considerations and a framework for developing your content and engagement strategy, with search, social, and real-time at the core. Content is the foundation of a modern earned online-marketing approach, and this chapter focuses on strategy, evaluating what you have, and identifying areas for development.

Chapter 4: Market Research and Content Types digs deeper into a search and social approach to real-time publishing and lays out a foundation of content types for your strategy, as well as considerations for where your content will reside in the new publishing landscape. Market research is a key component, and this chapter will also feature key tools and approaches for identifying your audience and producing resonant content.

Chapter 5: Content Strategy: Auditing, Assessment, and Planning focuses on finding out what you already have and what you don't have in order to set the course for your approach. It also covers key SEO considerations so that your social efforts don't fall into a search trap.

Chapter 6: Creating Effective and Engaging Content shows you how to write and develop content and messaging that resonates and engages with both machines and your human audience.

Chapter 7: Social-Network Platforms lays out a basic platform of popular social-media sites in order to build networks, converse, engage, and share content. It covers the interdependent search and social elements of four of the top networks (Facebook, Twitter, LinkedIn, and Google+) and offers a quick guide for optimizing these social spaces for search-engine performance.

Chapter 8: Blogs, Google News, and Press Releases helps you get started with other key areas of real-time content distribution and creates a new channel to get your messaging out fast via search and social strategies. This chapter will show you how to set up a blog, how to optimize for Google News, and how to optimize a press release for search and social spaces.

Chapter 9: Developing and Engaging in Real-Time Communities shows you how to get started with engaging in forums, wikis, and answer sites and also how to build your own. Communities have long been a foundational element of the Internet, and their real-time characteristics make them a strong platform for your own search and social strategies.

Chapter 10: Technical Considerations and Implementation covers other areas of online marketing that are crucial to interacting in real-time, including RSS feeds, URL shorteners, sharing buttons, microdata, and more. It assumes that your existing website assets are already optimized, crawlable, and indexable.

Chapter 11: Video and Images demonstrates how to set up and optimize video and image strategies, using the core principles of search optimization and social-media marketing.

Chapter 12: More Considerations for Real-Time Content Marketing, Search, and Social highlights other core areas of search and social and real-time content marketing: social link development, bookmark sharing, reverse triggers, Creative Commons, and more.

Chapter 13: Social-Media Management outlines the key considerations of audience outreach and covers tactics and strategies for engaging across a wide variety of situations. The chapter emphasizes how to use a search mind-set to extend your visibility in social spaces and become a curator for the living keyword language of your audience.

Chapter 14: Metrics and Measurement shows you some of the popular tools used to measure search and social and real-time content marketing efforts, plus presents some key metrics and goals to consider.

Appendix: Additional Reading and Resources provides a list of further resources for review, and includes links to relevant conferences, blogs, tools, and more.

Overall, this book will provide the complete elements of a real-time marketing approach to content, including a high-level strategic approach and understanding of "how it all works" and a platform for you to distribute your communications in real-time. The term *real-time marketing* certainly covers a wide range of business applications, but here I focus on applying a real-time content approach to a hands-on strategy with tactical application in search and social spaces.

I hope you find this book to be useful and enlightening and that it provides a framework of "how to do it," in addition to sparking many creative ideas that will allow you to take your online marketing efforts to the next level.

Disclaimer and Credits

This book is based on many columns I have written for MediaPost Search Insider and Social Insider since 2006. Many of the chapters and sections include whole and near-whole columns or contain sections that have been edited for this book. Many thanks to MediaPost publisher Ken Fadner and editor Phyllis Fine for allowing me to contribute for so many years and for allowing these columns to be republished and edited for this book.

This book is also based on white papers, blog posts, speaking engagements, hands-on work, and strategic development since 1994. I have written this book independently of my work with iCrossing, and it does not reflect the opinions of iCrossing or the Hearst Corporation.

Please also note some of my other industry and company affiliations:

- Hearst Family of Companies
- SEMPO
- DFWSEM Association

Considering my experiences and longtime affiliation with these groups, you will see references to some of them throughout the book, because they form a key part of my frame of reference. These references are balanced by many other companies, individuals, and organizations that I am not directly affiliated with in any type of business relationship.

This book also represents my views on Internet marketing based on experience and does not contain any direct endorsement or verification from search engines, social networks, or any other publishers. It is based on my experiences over the last 18 years and also on relating the experiences of other successful marketers.

This book was written for many different types of search and social marketers at varying levels and from different backgrounds. It is not intended to be "all things to all people," but I believe there is something here for everyone, in terms of the way you think about online marketing. It is also designed to provide common language and discussion points to help search and social marketers elevate their conversation and knowledge on the topic of the interdependent search and social discipline. It is very advanced in some ways and very simple in others. It assumes a background in SEO but also provides critical tips along the way (the Google starter guide for SEO provides a good foundation; visit this URL to download the guide: `http://static.googleusercontent.com/external_content/ untrusted_dlcp/www.google.com/en/us/webmasters/docs/search-engine-optimization- starter-guide.pdf`).

I would love for you to share your thoughts, opinions, and ratings on Amazon. com, BarnesandNoble.com, and Goodreads. I encourage you to start a conversation about these book concepts online, at a conference, in a classroom, on a network, or wherever your online marketing efforts take you. We are at a point in time where people are still becoming digitally literate, and if you agree with some of the new concepts presented in this book, then please help share them with and teach them to others.

How to Contact the Author

If you read the book or have another type of inquiry, Rob would like to connect with you. For LinkedIn and Facebook connection requests, please be sure to mention that you read the book and would like to connect.

- Follow him on Twitter: @robgarner.
- Read and follow his presentations and documents on SlideShare: www.Slideshare.net/robgarner1.
- Connect with him on LinkedIn: www.LinkedIn.com/in/RobGarner.
- Be friends with him on Facebook: www.fb.com/Garner.
- Circle him on Google+: http://gplus.to/RobGarner.
- Read and comment on his columns at MediaPost: www.mediapost.com/ publications/author/2719/rob-garner/.
- Visit the official website for this book: www.searchandsocialbook.com.
- Email him: rgarner1@gmail.com.

Real-Time Publishing and Marketing

Welcome to the world of real-time marketing, real-time publishing, search, and social. In this chapter, I will begin discussing some of the primary meanings of real-time and also lay a foundation for the definitions, strategies, and tactics covered throughout the remainder of this book. I will also discuss some of the forerunners to real-time marketing in this chapter. Here are some of the topics you can expect to learn about in this chapter:

1

Chapter Contents

The state of the current Internet publishing landscape

Terminology, definitions and history

The fundamental tenets of a real-time marketing approach

Integrating search, social, and publishing into a real-time approach

Introduction to Real-Time Content Marketing

In the new world of real-time information-sharing, there are many new concepts that businesses must embrace in order to be successful in their Internet marketing efforts. At the root of this revolution are the following basic elements:

- Seeking and finding behaviors
- Real-time interaction and active participation
- Consideration for both audiences and individuals
- Social-network distribution
- Instantaneous information-sharing, collaboration, and engagement
- Content promotion

Real-time information-sharing demands a more finely tuned approach from marketers, one that includes a redefinition of the word *publishing* and also brings a business alive on a 24-hour, seven-day-a-week basis.

 Note: The changing landscape is not so much about social networks as it is about *society being networked, in real-time.*

The emergence of the commercial Internet in the mid-1990s presented a new publishing paradigm that forced marketers to rethink their approaches, in terms of the ability to connect one-to-one and many-to-many with their core audience. Today, eMarketer reports that two out of every three Americans engage in social networks, so a more accurate characterization of *social networks* is that society as a whole is almost fully networked. When including search and email usage in overall network participation statistics, as many as 92 percent of all people are networked in some form, according to the May 2011 Pew Internet and American Life survey.

With the adoption of status-updating and sharing, a message can spread around the globe within hours, minutes, and even seconds. If marketers and brands are not part of the content conversation in either their own brand space or the broader category space, they might as well not exist to a certain degree.

Although more companies are becoming increasingly connected, the concepts of being *present* and *active* most often fall by the wayside. Many companies spend years redesigning their websites. Others look at social media in a start-and-stop manner, and by doing so they are allowing social networks to fully control their marketing conversation by simply ignoring it. Marketers and enterprise brands are also finding that the barriers built to protect themselves in the old media world have now become the very obstacles that prevent them from being effective in this new environment. The good news is that by knowing the problem, you can start to address the solution. The solution for marketers is all-encompassing and will require the following:

- Organizational shifts from passive to real-time engagement
- A redefining of *audience*
- A redefining of *brand* to include the audience
- In some cases, a redefinition of business practices
- A greater commitment to sincerity
- A reworking of the definition of *social media* to become more inclusive of search principles
- A deep understanding and executional capability in search and findability issues
- A deep understanding of building out earned attention in social networks
- A redefinition of the word *publishing*
- A commitment to being a "marketer as media publisher"

Another major shift is in the way content is found. Now more than ever, publishers and marketers must label content and make it shareable so that it can be found at the most granular level of search or social relevancy. The process of finding might involve a search engine, social or popularity-based results list, discovery streams, or network sharing. Each of these aspects presents new challenges for marketers that must be addressed in order to properly maximize the opportunity of marketing on the Internet and networks.

The greatest difference between marketing efforts of today and pre-Internet is the rising importance of being *present* and *always-on*. This new landscape—one that has really achieved a new level of fluidity and agility only in the mid- to late aughts through the rapid adoption of social- and network-based content-sharing sites—creates a new urgency for marketers to be part of an "in-the-moment" conversation that occurs 24/7 about their brand or company and about the general consumer conversation at large. Ultimately, the sum of many missed moments in this new landscape will be the death of some companies, and this embracing of "right now" will be the ascension of many others.

What Is Real-Time Marketing?

Real-time marketing is a way of thinking and philosophy that requires businesses to meet the demands of an always-on digital world, and includes production, communication, organization and infrastructure. In is not necessarily prescriptive, but rather refers to being present and fluid in your marketing and business efforts, which means being part of the ongoing conversations that exist around your vertical space and brand, as they happen. In the context of content marketing, going "real-time" requires businesses to redefine themselves in the digital realm through participation and connections through content. Throughout the entire approach, search and social principles are at the core. Real-time marketing is about time, existence in time, and using search and social technologies to interact and strike with lightning speed and laserlike efficiency. Real-time marketing will take on an even greater influence in future society as its digital layer starts to overlap into the physical world.

An active and alive real-time content marketer must do a lot planning and preparation and also be aware of the intricacies of search and social media in order to capture the full opportunity. Because the more up-to-the-moment aspects of the online experience have been largely innovated in the search and social-network realms, an effective marketer must thoroughly understand these channels in terms of the way connections and communications flow and how digital assets best travel between search engines and networks. Real-time content marketing is all-encompassing and includes research, content production, community management and outreach, customer-relationship management, analytics and measurement, and real-time response and interaction through a variety of methods.

Although it could be said that talking on the telephone or speaking in person is the total realization of "real-time" marketing, this definition refers more specifically to *engagement* in the digital realm and connecting with your audience—one-to-one, one-to-many, or many-to-many—in a meaningful way that ultimately serves your own business goals and serves the needs of your audience.

In a broader sense, the definition of *real-time content marketing* is still evolving, but it has been largely adopted by a social-marketing audience rather than a search-marketing audience. *Real-time content marketing is not complete without a deep strategic and tactical understanding of search and social together*, because the two become more intertwined from the marketing and user perspectives. In effect, real-time content marketing is about embracing audiences in a human way, but also recognizing the technical drivers of content through networks. This book will show you the exact nuances and interplay between search and social in various real-time scenarios and how you can master the two together as a single unique discipline.

A full definition of real-time marketing would not be complete without mentioning two pivotal thinkers. One of the key thinkers in real-time and social network theory is sociologist Dr. Manuel Castells, whose key philosophies will be covered briefly in the second chapter. Castells' writings cemented my intentions of a career in Internet marketing in the mid-90s and have driven my strategic perspective ever since. I will show you how his insight and thinking can elevate your own strategies as well.

One other key contributor to the definition of real-time marketing is legendary Silicon Valley marketer Regis McKenna, who planted the first seeds of its meaning in the mid-1990s. In an article titled "Real-Time Marketing" published in July 1995 in *Harvard Business Review*, McKenna described the future elements and approaches of marketing in a world that is fully synaptic and connected and functioning in real-time. Though some of the descriptions outlined an approach to more-traditional marketing and business processes, he hit the nail square on the head by predicting many facets of a real-time content approach that will be developed in other parts of this book. Here are a few direct quotes from his article that you would be well-served to know as you begin using this book:

- "To build customer loyalty...companies need to keep their customers engaged in a continuous dialogue."
- "Companies must keep the dialogue flowing and also maintain conversations with suppliers, distributors, and others in the marketplace."
- "[Real-time marketing must replace] the broadcast mentality."
- "[Real-time marketing must focus] on real-time customer satisfaction, providing the support, help, guidance, and information necessary to win customers' loyalty."
- "Real-time marketing requires...being willing to learn how information technology is changing both customer behavior in marketing and to think in new ways about marketing within the organization."
- "[Real-time interaction] allows the customer and the producer to learn from each other and to respond to each other."
- "The customer still does all the work, hunting and pecking for information. But a real-time marketer would bring the information to the customer."

Again, all of these statements were written in July 1995 by McKenna, but it is only today that marketers and businesses are able to better justify going real-time, because of the greater adoption of the Internet medium by a majority of Americans (this is, of course, also true for many readers outside the United States). So, what are you waiting for?

Other contributions to the real-time conversation include Monique Reece, who in 2010 wrote *Real-Time Marketing for Business Growth*, which outlined traditional marketing and business practices in real-time scenarios, and David Meerman Scott, who in 2011 wrote *Real Time Marketing & PR*.

Other definitions exist on the technological side, as technologies are moving from a "ping" or "pull" method to a push retrieval method. Overall, it is not the terminology that is important. What is important is that marketers understand the existential real-time shift occurring in digital spaces. Marketing terminology is currently in flux, and whether or not the phrase *real-time marketing* is used in the future is irrelevant. The point is that marketers must become active and participatory to fully realize the opportunity of the digital medium, with search and social technologies residing at the core.

What Is Real-Time Publishing?

Real-time publishing is the process of creating and distributing content across networks, including search engines and social media. This term refers not only to the speed at which content can be created by individuals or groups but also to how quickly new content can be distributed and shared globally between networks of like-minded individuals. It also includes the latent effect of leaving behind a digital conversational footprint and trail that can be retrieved at a later interval based on keyword search and community memory. Real-time publishing involves digital asset optimization, traditional SEO principles for hosting and labeling content, active community management and outreach, and the buildup and maintenance of a publisher's network distribution channels. While effective real-time publishers are active and present, it can take months and years of preparation and expertise to do real-time publishing effectively. In the context of real-time, the term *publishing* can be as simple as updating a Twitter account with less than 140 characters at a time, starting an online library of shareable content, creating a video channel, or, more often, publishing a combination of various asset types.

Apply Immediacy to Your Approach

In a word, becoming an effective real-time marketer adds the element of *immediacy* to marketing strategy or, in other words, being relevant to your audience within a certain frame of time. At the basis of this publishing shift are the core principles of search-engine optimization, social media, active social-media participation, audience engagement, and network content distribution. But traditional publishing elements are also still key to this approach, because the distribution of content through search and social channels is also highly connected to fundamental marketing engagement strategies and principles.

Be As Fast As Your Audience

While many brands and marketers have increased their connectivity points in social spaces, current approaches to enable a live digital marketing existence are severely lacking. Average consumers on a social network have no problem speaking their minds in a fluid and active way. Marketers and businesses as a whole do not have a parallel voice that exhibits this same kind of independence.

This problem generally falls into the categories of organizational dysfunction, protectionism, and improperly allocated marketing and IT budgets. What marketers need to do now is to realize the gap that exists between their active presence and the connectedness with the audience and begin a flow of information to the consumer through conversation, outreach, content publishing, listening, and research.

A Real-Time Approach

The following list serves both as a hint at what you will be learning throughout this book and as a high-level framework for real-time marketing and publishing, with search and social residing at the core:

Act "In the Moment," and Be Fluid in Your Online Presence Because your audience is always online and active, it is only common sense that marketers should also be present in their online efforts. It is the difference between existence and nonexistence in a world where conversations come and go if one is not there to be part of them.

Act as a Publisher and Media Provider in Order to Connect Through Content Because digital touch points occur through content (as defined by a wide variety of content types), there is an increasing imperative for marketers to embrace new forms of publishing. The definition of *publishing* and *content* is broad and nuanced in the real-time landscape, and various content types may include images, video, conversation, status updates, applications, and articles, among many others. A real-time digital strategy may include all of the content types mentioned earlier, or a combination thereof. The challenge for marketers is to become comfortable with their own real-time publishing framework and platform and begin to publish on a massive scale in order to take advantage of the opportunities that exist in real-time publishing.

Enable the Spirit of the Audience into Your Online Content and Voice To be effective with a real-time publishing and conversational approach, a marketer must put their spirited and sincere voices on the front line of their real-time presence. Connecting with your audience in a way that they naturally speak and interact is the best way to spread your messages through the digital consciousness. Your audience already has a distinct say in how your marketing efforts and company are perceived, so making the audience a co-partner in your real-time efforts will allow them to resonate in a more synaptic way. Enabling voices means projecting this spirit in your own content and providing a way for users to generate their own content, as well providing insight to help inform how you develop your own products and services.

A Company's Real-Time Search and Social Identity Is Both "What It Says" About Itself and "What Others Say" About the Company The reality of the current state of online marketing is that brands and companies can project only so much about how they want to be perceived before audiences provide their own perception of a company the way they see it. Your real-time marketing identity is a combination of what you write, what you say, and how you conduct your business. Your identity will be ultimately defined by the trail of conversation and content in your real-time marketing efforts and by the consumer trail of conversation and content, for better or worse. To a large extent, your marketing efforts are being judged more by what you are doing *right now* than ever before.

Reach Out to Audiences and Networks in Real-Time, in a Sincere and Present Manner Whether it is connecting with your audience through conversation and outreach, sharing and curating assets, or creating active and passive content for both networks and search engines, the activity must be defined, sincere, engaging, and committed for the long term.

To Be Effective, a Business's Primary Networks Should Be Acknowledged and Developed The fundamental network audiences of a business should include both their own organization (the people working for a company) and their targeted network audience that will be directly interacting with the company. This expansion of the definition of social networks speaks to cultivating social participation, presence, and content development within your organization. Whether you are part of a small company with two or more people or the CMO of a large company with thousands of people, careful study, strategy, and a set of rules to play by will be part of your real-time marketing strategy.

Marketers and Companies Are Obligated to Listen and Interpret Their Data into Meaningful Content and Experiences for their Audience Analyzing your company's data should no longer be an *option but rather an obligation and commitment* to your audience. Your data, and other third-party data, reveals what your audience desires, what they may not be able to find in your network or any other network, and many opportunities for engagement through content and real-time interaction. Your audience tells you what they want in search and social; and as a real-time marketer with a defined strategy, you will be in a position to give back to them in a way that will allow for participating in the conversation on a large scale.

Setting the Stage for a Search- and Social-Enabled Real-Time Publishing Platform

A sizable part of this book is dedicated to enabling you to develop a place to distribute and share content directly with your audience, but you must go into your strategic planning and execution with a key foundation for what is inherently different about today's Internet world. In addition to understanding the foundation of a sound real-time marketing strategy, understanding the core principles of search marketing and social-media marketing is also crucial. The following sections discuss the basic strategic cornerstones of approaching search and social marketing in a real-time landscape.

Dr. Manuel Castells and the Space of Flows

One major work that documented and predicted the impact of the Internet on modern society and economies is called *The Rise of the Network Society*, the first part of a trilogy written by sociologist Dr. Manuel Castells (Figure 1.1), published in 1996. In the book, Dr. Castells forecasted and documented the impact of networks as they created connections that transcended traditional geospatial boundaries and borders. In addition to outlining the global economic and sociological impact of the Internet, he touched on one of his key theories, called "the space of flows." Castells described how networks broke down the traditional forms of communication that had previously inhibited everything from relationships to group organizations to economies on both a massive and a granular scale. He further differentiates the space of flows as a phenomenon of being present in the network in time (and real-time) and apart from the "space of places," which relies on the proximity of physical location.

Figure 1.1 Manuel Castells

The space of flows concept provides a practical basis for defining fundamental social interactions within a global network, which transcends places, and allows for a constant flow of information through people connected as nodes. It is as true and valid today as it was when he first wrote about it. While Castells' writings further address the philosophical and economic implications of a digitally networked society, a fundamental understanding of this concept serves as an invaluable strategic foundation for real-time marketing strategy.

Dr. Castells was one of the first sociologists to publish a significant analysis of networks on economies, world societies, and politics, and predicted their impact on the world at large.

The concepts outlined in Castells' work are extremely intricate, and this short section here does it little justice, other than to call out its meaning toward the premise of this book. In addition to *The Rise of the Network Society*, I also recommend the book *Conversations with Manuel Castells*, if you prefer a more casual take of his theory on the space of flows.

The "Resource-Discovery Problem"

In addition to understanding the philosophical basis for network interaction in real-time marketing, one other key observation about the importance of search to the real-time Internet was posited by World Wide Web inventor Sir Tim Berners-Lee (Figure 1.2). In one of his early FAQs posted on the W3C website in 1992, he explained the huge opportunity for a search engine to come into play and help organize all of this new information and connective structure that was developing at a rapid pace.

As you can see, the web is sufficiently flexible to allow a number of ways of finding information. In the end, I think a typical resource discovery session will involve someone starting on their "home" document, following one to two links to an index, then doing a search, and following several links from what they have found. In some cases, there will be more than one index search involved, such as at first for an organization, and having found that, a search within it for a person or document. We need to keep this flexibility, as the available information in different places has such different characteristics.... In the long term, when there is a really large mass of data out there, with deep interconnections, then there is some really exciting work to be done on automatic algorithms to make multi-level searches.

Sir Tim Berners-Lee; May 14, 1992. www.w3.org/History/
19921103-hypertext/hypertext/WWW/FAQ/KeepingTrack.html

Figure 1.2 Sir Tim Berners-Lee

In the spirit of Dr. Castells, Regis McKenna, and Sir Berners-Lee, the core marriage of the search, social networks, and real-time behavior dates back to the beginnings of the Internet, even before the rise of the commercial Internet. With this statement from Berners-Lee, we see the early framework of the Internet in place, with his crystal-clear observation that one other major need is a search engine to sort and organize it. I would posit that it has been only since 2007–2010 that a tipping point has occurred, with search and social becoming fully interdependent on the other. The interdependence is so strong that the game to watch is not which search engine or social network is bigger, but rather which web property will combine the most robust algorithm with the best human social layer.

The Web Gets a Robust Search Engine and Network Map

While a number of universities and companies had begun developing directories and search engines to help users better find the information they were looking for, it wasn't until Google launched in 1998 that a superior and robust approach to crawling, indexing, and retrieving Internet information began to emerge. Google's approach to crawling all of the Web's content, as well as analyzing the link structures and weighted authority of those sites and individual pages, was a landmark event on the Internet as it began to assemble a structure of the entire Web and its linkage as a network of influence.

Even in their earliest stages, search engines were based on core network principles, and they were developed by humans. It is worth noting that early search engineers constantly fought with publishers in terms of optimizing their content. The search engines wanted to capture the Web as an observer and to rank those pages in order as they saw it. Of course, not every web publisher agreed with their results and some began to reverse engineer the process through what is now known popularly as *search engine optimization* (SEO), a term coined simultaneously by Bob Heyman, John Audette, and Bruce Clay. What the engines did not consider as closely at the time was that their data was an almost living and breathing corpus. The corpus was interactive, and this caused the engines to innovate in ways they had not previously considered. I believe it is unfortunate and misplaced that many people still perceive search-engine algorithms to be purely technical. The more accurate picture is that search is created and edited by people, consisting of content created by people (even if they use technical tools). Links are created by people. The analysis of relationships between links and sites is *network analysis*. In this sense, search has always been "social" and "networked."

Social Emerges as a Description of Network Behavior

A popular description of networks and the Web becoming inherently "social" began to emerge from the O'Reilly Media Web 2.0 Conference in 2004. Users began to more directly associate their online identities via networks and content sharing, and information flowed through one's own personal networks of connections, and that information in turn could be shared more quickly with other networks. In effect, content and conversations could be spread quickly, if not instantaneously, around the globe to audiences of like-minded interest.

While the word *social* became a popular way to describe what was previously known as standard network effects, this word adoption did not necessarily negate the fact that the Internet was already "social" prior to 2004. Many forms of online media were redubbed as being social, when nothing had really changed about them prior to this word adoption. Message boards and forums had been well established, and "social content" in the form of user-generated content and collaboration had also been around since the earliest days of the commercial Internet. Even email—one of the earliest forms of networked media and communication—sometimes falls into the category of social media.

Whether the word *social* tells us anything new or not, it has been embraced by a new generation of Internet marketers as a way of talking about standard network effects. There have been calls by many veteran digital marketers and thinkers to kill the term altogether, but for all practical purposes, it looks like it will remain for at least the foreseeable future.

Engage One Bird, and You Might Attract the Whole Flock (and Flocks of Flocks)

One other core tenet of real-time content marketing involves the effects of *networks of networks*. In the one-to-many scenario, a content creator can publish their work to a network, and in effect, a chain reaction can occur from one like-minded individual in a network to cross over into another network. It extends the concept of one-to-many to *many-to-many*.

By establishing your own primary network, you are providing a launch point for your own content to begin this cascading effect of distribution across the Internet. The quality and size of your distribution network can determine how well your content travels through the networks of those people with their own network influence. This is why a well-thought-out strategy is required for your own search and social platform in order to determine the amount of network influence you want to achieve. In other words, if you have a limited content strategy and limited time for engagement, you should not expect domination of your relevant network channel through these efforts alone. But if you see a huge network and search opportunity in your channel, then you may realize that a robust content strategy is needed to meet the search and social demand, to the point that your efforts are viewed as a hub of leadership in your industry. These hubs of influence tend to spread and disseminate their own messaging, and search engines and social communities reward them for it with a greater mindshare of the conversation and ultimately help you achieve your desired business goals.

Connectedness

The implication of a world society being connected via networks is that marketers and businesses must also be connected in the same one-to-one, one-to-many, and many-to-many sense with their core audiences and customers. *One-to-one* means a direct connection and conversation with individuals, *one-to-many* means connecting to your group or network, and *many-to-many* means being connected and communicating with extended audiences and groups. Not being connected, whether in listening, conversation, transaction, or participation, means that a marketer does not effectively exist in those conversations and economic opportunities afforded in networks. The marketing imperative is to establish these connections in a meaningful way, and this book is designed to show you just how to do that.

Flows

Once you have started to establish your network audience of groups and individuals, you should be managing and stoking the flows of communication. Because information is flowing in real-time, a live presence is required, either as an individual or as an organization. *Network flows* and *search flows* consist of conversation, content publishing, content promotion, content stewardship, curation, and sharing through a variety of methods.

Although a substantial part of this book is dedicated to showing you where to find and establish your social network and search presence, an even greater part of the book will show you *how to maintain the flows of communication* via strategic and tactical content development, community management, search engine optimization, digital asset optimization, and a real-time mentality.

Universally Identifiable, Shareable, and Networked Content

To be successful in the digital publishing landscape, you must ensure that content is readable by both humans and machines. Here, a core understanding and capability in search engine optimization, the principles of community management and engagement, a real-time attitude, and network sharing are in order.

At a high level, your content must be *understood*, by both people and algorithms, in order to get the most out of your online publishing efforts. It must also be inherently capable of being *disseminated* or distributed by people and algorithms to spread your content beyond your hard efforts alone. Being "understood" by people and algorithms means both that it must resonate in way that is readable by algorithms and technology and also that your points are clearly articulated in what you are trying to communicate to humans with influence across networks.

Making It Easy for People to Distribute Your Content via Networks

People in networks can quickly make a judgment about whether your content is of importance to them. This means being clear in your points, utility, usability, design, format, and messaging. Making it "shareable" is also of critical importance in networks and makes a great difference in whether your content is linkable, has the proper sharing buttons, is capable of publishing directly to a share network, or is easily downloadable.

Social and Search Algorithms

Being understood on an algorithmic level requires a literal approach in describing and marking up content in a way that it can be understood and retrieved by machines. Content tagging and labeling via keywords, page elements, and making assets indexable extends the shelf life of your content and conversations and increases the opportunities for that content to be found in both networks and search engines. Making an asset "crawlable" means that it may essentially be copied by automated software to become a freely indexable and shareable object between databases where search or other processes may occur.

It is also important to note that the definition of *search engine* does not just mean a traditionally understood engine such as Google or Bing but includes any site that may crawl the Web or any network with its own search or algorithmic functionality, including Twitter, Facebook, LinkedIn, eBay, or Amazon. In addition to sharing across networks, a large majority of the Web's content is surfaced to consumers via algorithms, whether it is in the form of a search engine, discovery, push notifications, popularity lists, personalization, or other types of technology that show content based on similar interests.

Universal Search and Digital Asset Optimization

In 2007, search engines Google, Yahoo!, Microsoft Live, and Ask each introduced a new search-results concept that has since changed the search marketing landscape as we know it. The "universal" search approach involved not only retrieving the 10 best website result links but also promoting results from vertical engines into the "prime-time" web results area of the page. So, now searchers would see photos, videos, news, blog posts, and other vertical content interspersed into the results page based on its importance and relevance to their query. The days of optimizing for the "10 blue links" alone were officially gone. If you cared about the health of your natural search programs, then the time had come to start venturing off into other areas of content beyond text, and into these verticals, if you had not already done so.

While search professionals had long understood these innovations both conceptually and in practice, it was search and social marketer Lee Odden who coined the phrase *digital asset optimization*. Digital asset optimization implies that it is no longer enough just to optimize your web pages and that a full optimization approach to content creation and strategy is in order. If your audience is searching for images, then you would be wise to consider a content play involving the use of images and optimize them appropriately. If your audience predominantly consumes video, then you need to fire up your digital video cameras and optimize. The same can be said for consumer usage of forum dialogue, news, social status updates, PowerPoint slides, PDFs, and white papers, among many other asset types. Digital asset optimization is not just a search tactic. If executed properly, it will also lend itself to shareability and readability across social networks, in real-time, and this is one of the core tenets of marketing with a search and social frame of mind.

Understanding Delivery Frameworks Across Multiple Platforms

It is also imperative for marketers to understand the platforms and devices that deliver their content and how their audiences consume this content. Search and social tactics are quickly spreading from the desktop and into the physical world in the form of mobile devices, kiosks, RFID, voice activation, voice search, touch screens, and myriad other applications. If you look closely, most of these new digital applications have some function of search and/or social at the most basic level. Studying this landscape as it evolves will help you become a more effective marketer, help you spot new emerging opportunities, and help you plan and execute on strategies for the future. For these new areas of innovation, you may even have to invent optimization techniques of your own.

The Power of Reciprocation

Reciprocation is another fundamental element of search and social marketing in real-time and is apparent in many different forms. In real-time content marketing, there are two basic rules you need to know in order to have an effective strategy and platform.

The First Rule of Reciprocation: You Give, and You Get

The first rule of reciprocation, one that should be central to any agile and real-time frame of mind, is that *you give away a lot in order to earn what you receive*. This takes on many forms:

- Gaining knowledge, expressed in the form of content
- Answering questions in real-time
- Building useful applications in anticipation that they will be used widely
- Providing a voice or point or view to further a conversation
- Volunteering and helping to "crowd-source" online projects

- Sharing the content of others in your community, in hopes they will reciprocate
- Speaking at and documenting industry events and conferences
- Volunteering and participating with industry or consumer associations

As a marketer who has done all of these tasks for many years, these activities have paid immense dividends for the companies I work for in gaining new business, raising awareness, making useful connections (who in turn also reciprocate), and elevating the online conversations that occur in my business, both at the brand and general conversation levels.

The most successful real-time publishers are providing content, coverage, online help, and useful information on a steady basis and allowing this content to travel so that a greater community can receive the benefits as well. In turn, marketers are reciprocated by receiving broader consideration, direct business sales and leads, brand awareness, better collaboration with partners, offline word-of-mouth, assistance in sharing your own content, and general goodwill from their industry and community at large. If your real-time marketing strategy is really amazing, your audience has an ongoing expectation of quality that you must continue to live up to in your content, products, and services. Consistently meeting these expectations can cement your place as a hub in the conversation and content of your industry.

The Second Rule of Reciprocation: Search and Social Are Interdependent

A second type of reciprocation occurs in networks, and it is between search and social. While search and social have many independent elements, they have become interdependent in many ways. Search engines look to social signals to rank content and provide an edge of freshness to their results, and social networks are becoming more algorithmic and also reliant on search engine traffic to build communities. This interdependency creates wider visibility and extends reach to new and recurring audiences.

"Search and social" is quickly evolving into its own discipline. Search and social are often viewed by marketers as opposing entities, but the real-time reality is that they are constantly giving to and taking back from each other. It's not a question of whether search or social will cannibalize each other, but more a question of how they work together to extend the opportunities of real-time marketing and content publishing. This book is also designed to show the key correlations between search and social and how, together, search and social is a guiding marketing discipline unto itself.

Social "signals" are most often just traditional SEO signals. As content passes through networks, new pages and links are created all along the way. Considering that links are one of the main elements of how search engines rank content, social distribution of content is fundamentally connected to basic SEO principles. New links may come in the form of connections, status updates, and shared links in many different formats. At the end of the day, likes, tweets, and +1s are still links.

In addition to the links created by social network distribution, user-generated content can create a massive symbiotic effect between search engines and social discussion spaces. When communities are properly managed and formed, they create new content in real-time, using language that would be impossible for marketers to develop on their own. This content is indexed by search engines and matched to new audiences at the keyword level. The traffic of these like-minded individuals has then found a relevant social network of interest and often becomes part of the community as either an observer or a content creator, which starts the social and search cycle all over again. By properly engaging in communities, a marketer is able to capture both search and social benefits as they grow in real-time and require a hands-on and active presence to maintain and develop.

These are just a few examples of the benefits of real-time search and social reciprocation, and many more will be covered in later chapters. The closer you get to acting in the moment in terms of your online content–publishing strategy, the more you can expect to receive the benefits.

Trust and Authority in Search and Networks

Bing real-time search engineer Paul Yiu describes the process of filtering search and social status updates as dealing with a "tsunami of spam." One of the key problems for Bing, Google, Twitter, and other search and social engines is dealing with the onslaught of spam and filtering it out in order to provide users with a relevant and useful experience.

The spam problem is a major issue that search engines have dealt with since they first began. The fundamental issue for search and social providers delivering results in real-time is that they must trust a content provider to determine whether it is "spammy" or a reliable source of content. Although search engines have gotten very good at studying the signals of trust that point to high-quality content, the imperative for marketers is to cultivate trustworthy websites, content, and a social-network presence that shows it is backed by a real content producer, used by real people.

Marketing at the level of a highly trusted resource means you should always be sending signals of trust to search engines and networks. This includes providing fresh content, attracting links and citations from other trusted sources, and expanding the depth of your content. If you study the top 100 websites that rank for any given set of keywords, you will find that they have many unique pages of content, have a large number of authoritative links, and have long passed all of the basic tests that search engines put them through algorithmically to determine whether they are a site to be trusted. This is why sites like Wikipedia, TripAdvisor, and BankRate, among many others, rank for a wide group of terms within their respective themes of focus.

Social Relevancy

While different search and social spaces have individually had their own methods of determining trust and authority, there is a new and emerging area where relevance, authority, and velocity can be determined by analyzing all as one signal. In 2008, I coauthored a white paper with Gabe Dennison called "Integrating Search and Social Media" and first discussed the concept of *social relevance*. Social relevance takes both search and social signals into account, as well as other key aspects of real-time marketing, to provide a more relevant result. Social relevancy incorporates some of the traditional methods of search algorithms and applies them to the faster-moving world of real-time marketing and social media. It looks at the velocity and speed of shared digital assets, status updates, and keyword search velocity in order to determine what is going on with the real Internet at the speed of "now."

The release of Google+ in June 2011 introduced a new kind of social relevancy, and this time it was not about social signals on search but rather on search signals to improve the social experience. By placing more emphasis on relevancy within social networks through segmentation, Google+ proved that the social experience could be enhanced, not by shouting out to the entire world but by speaking to only the most relevant audience within your network. With the concept of "circles," Google+ users are able to more easily share messages within the relevant context of their network, and this concept is quickly being adopted by other major social networks such as Twitter and Facebook.

In the greater discussion of *social-media optimization* (SMO), a phrase coined by marketer Rohit Bhargava in 2006, social relevance could be considered the "thing" you are optimizing for. My intention for the phrase is to make it easier to describe SMO and SEO together conceptually, in the sense that search and social are one discipline.

Gaining Trust and Authority with Your Audience in Real-Time

Again, the imperative for marketers is to apply what they have already been doing with traditional common-sense SEO principles and extend this method of thinking to the management of networks and content development and propagation. It involves creating relevant networks and attracting followers and friends of like-minded groups, creating content that gets shared by these groups, attracting and promoting citations of your content, and optimizing assets in a way that will extend their shelf life beyond using either social or search tactics alone.

Beyond just search and social, the practice of *being present in your marketing efforts or otherwise having an alive presence that is as active as your audience* will send the strongest signals that your content is backed by a real person of group of people and is not spam. Of course, there is another level of trust and authority that good content providers should be seeking at a very strategic level, and that is with the audience. Building trust and authority with your audience means the following:

- Creating engaging content
- Creating knowledgeable and expert content

- Creating content so good that your audience would be inclined to share it with other like-minded people or groups in their own networks
- Helping your readers and people in your network with their problems and concerns
- Conversing with your audience through passive content or direct interaction
- Writing clearly and communicating effectively
- Keeping a clean and consistent web appearance with your website and digital assets
- Enabling your assets to be easily shared

These approaches require a constant real-time presence and in turn will earn the trust of the audiences you serve, which will ultimately translate into achieving your designated business goals.

Listening to Your Audience, Data, and Your Competition

One of the other biggest, but perhaps most overlooked, opportunities in real-time content marketing is the ability to use data to help inform and build upon your own strategies. When starting off with a real-time content marketing strategy and tactical plan, you may feel overwhelmed by the constantly changing landscape. But knowing that the answers to your big questions lie in both your own data and third-party data should provide you with some relief. A typical problem is determining where to start or determining which conversations are of most importance to your audience. Here, keyword and conversational data can help. Reviewing keyword popularity helps you determine which themes are of most interest to groups of searchers and can provide key direction to start your content-development process. Reviewing common questions in Q&A sites like Yahoo! Answers and Answers.com can also show social popularity of different topics across a wide range of categories. Studying the overall web space can help you find the areas of focus for your own strategy, and later chapters in this book will specifically show you how to do this.

Real-time content marketers should get their data from a number of sources on a timely basis. New content opportunities constantly arise, and if you or your organization are not paying attention, then a major opportunity to become part of the conversation may come and go without you even knowing it.

Google is a great example of a company that makes the best use of its data to create new products and also help expand future strategies. In June 2007 I attended a panel discussion on personalization at the SMX Advanced conference in Seattle. Google engineer Matt Cutts provided an interesting revelation that gave the audience key insight into the way Google's chief strategists think. In a response to a question by one attendee, Cutts effectively stated, "You give us your data for free, and we feel we have an *obligation* to use it."

By "obligation," he meant that users had given Google their data through its search queries and other measured behaviors and that the company had a responsibility to use this data to make their products even greater. So in this case, the end result was personalization of search results, which meant that about 20 percent of a person's search results may be changed based on their own biases taken from prior search, recently viewed or clicked web pages, and geographic locations, among many other factors. Google continues to invest in areas informed by keyword demand and user data. It is also active in promoting Google+ data into many other products and services Google offers.

But the story here is not about Google; it is about you and your business. Consider the following questions with regard to how well you are currently using your data to inform your strategies and tactics in a world of search and social:

- How is your company using its internal site search data to find out what people are looking for but can't find?
- Why are people abandoning your website pages?
- What are the most common questions asked offline about your business?
- Do you have a frequently asked questions (FAQ) page to answer those questions?
- Do you effectively address those questions in your site content and community-management strategy?
- Does the content you publish on your site reflect these questions as a whole?
- What does your competitors' data tell you about what they have and what you lack, and is this something you should address?
- How do people react to your products and services online?
- What suggestions do they make or what changes do they wish for, and how can you implement them or make sure your organization is aware of these suggestions?

Keep in mind that more likely than not, your audience wants you to weigh in online about your relevant areas of expertise. So, in addition to the basic questions about your business, are you chiming in to give that extra level of insight, once the questions go a little bit deeper about your company or respective general conversation area? If a question were to come up publicly right now on a social network, would you be ready to answer it right now or in a timely manner that shows you are active while the conversation is still in the social spotlight?

Real-time search and social data is not just for identifying strategies directly for your own company or brand, but also for comparing how others in your competitive space are doing. What do people like or dislike about your competition? What are they doing right or wrong, and how can you best capitalize on this data with your own strategy? Is there a huge opportunity, or does your company just have a lot of catching up to do in order to remain relevant in search and social spaces?

Brands and Marketers As Real-Time Content Publishers

These are just a few of the questions that will be addressed in the subsequent chapters, and there are so many more you need to answer in order to prepare for acting in the moment, with a real-time frame of mind. Real-time marketing is about interaction and online publishing at its core and about businesses and marketing practitioners embracing real-time content publishing as the *new marketing*. Get ready, because in order to fully understand and develop a real-time marketing and publishing platform, you need to better understand how search and social work together. Chapter 2 will explain exactly how these two are working together to form the foundation for real-time marketing.

Understanding
Search and Social

The distinction of "search and social" together has taken on a deeper meaning as the Internet and other networks have become more sophisticated. Search is becoming more reliant on the factors of trust and relevancy within social networks, and social-networks are leveraging some of the lessons learned in search in order to improve the social network and sharing experience. Now that search and social are more connected than ever, a separate discipline has emerged in terms of understanding how the two work together. This chapter will explore the dynamic interdependency between search and social, and how they are impacted by real-time technologies and participation.

2

Chapter Contents

Definitions of *search and social* and *sharing*

A definition of natural language, and how it connects search and social together

The algorithmic and network synergies between search and social

Social signals in search

The share graph, link graph, and social graph

Networked links and social linking

Active and passive content distribution in networks

Recency and relevancy in search and social

Defining Search and Social

Fundamentally, *search and social* is a real-time Internet marketing mind-set and philosophy that helps your content and conversation gain additional visibility through both search retrieval and network dissemination and consumption. Taking a search and social view of your real-time publishing efforts can extend the reach of your content to the widest audiences, both directly and indirectly through various channels. The combined synergies of search and social represent gaining better social experiences, informing algorithmic progresses with a real-time social layer, and using search data to inform social processes, among many other elements that will be covered in-depth in this chapter. It is real-time in the sense that the synergistic benefits of social and search are combined at the moment content and conversation are created, published, and disseminated, even though it may be consumed long past the period of time in which it was created and distributed.

The phrase *search and social* has been utilized since the popular usage of the term *social* began in 2004, and over this time it has come to have several different meanings. While this book focuses on the interdependency of search and social channels in the context of real-time information-sharing and distribution, let's go over some of the other historic meanings to gain a full picture of what search and social mean together.

- User-generated content (forums, reviews, and so on)
- Tagging (user-facing keywords on blogs and other social content-management systems)
- Social search (Twitter, Google+ Your World social results)
- Search engines that allow direct human input of the results (Google+, Wikia, and so on)
- Any search function that can be edited by a user for use by other users (Wikipedia, Google+, and so on)
- Discovery engines (StumbleUpon, eBay, Amazon, and so on)
- Results and information that is crowd-sourced, like Mahalo or Wikipedia
- Real-time-status networks like Facebook, LinkedIn, Google+, and Twitter, where recent conversations and network status updates can be searched at the keyword level
- Any process that allows social networks or media to influence natural search-engine results
- Social bookmarking
- Digital asset optimization—using basic principles of "crawlability" and "indexability," where an asset may travel across networks of networks (YouTube, Facebook, Google+, and so on)

While there are many different definitions of what is meant by search and social, this book focuses on the content-publishing aspects of search and social, the impact of social signals on search-engine results, the elements of real-time and content velocity, and the algorithmic implications of content distribution through networks.

Natural Language Connects Search and Social Together

One of the fundamental, but perhaps most overlooked, connective elements between search and social is the use of natural language by your audience. Natural language as it relates to search and social is just like it sounds—it reflects the keywords, tone, content, conversation, and tastes of your audience, as they project and reflect them in search and social channels. Whether your audience is using a keyword in a search engine, dictating commands with their voice, or writing down their thoughts in the activity stream of their favorite social network, the language they utilize tells a lot about them, and about what they are seeking. Accepting the natural language of your audience is a critical aspect of succeeding in modern online marketing, from either a search or social perspective, and marketers must strike a balance between what they say about their company and how others perceive businesses, in their own words.

Observing and using the natural language of your audience is a way of enabling the *spirit of your audience* into your brand conversation. Simply put, the effectiveness of your strategy and tactical execution is in many ways proportional to how well you use and understand the language of your audience. For a search marketer, this means that understanding the keyword and content tastes of your audience is critical to success. Social marketers must also have a similar grasp of language, in terms of the way a company communicates and how it creates content. To an even a greater degree, understanding natural language helps you find your audience when they don't know where to look for you.

Throughout this book you will encounter the phrase "keywords are connections to people," and this is for a good purpose. Audience language is tremendously overlooked by many Internet marketers, but the good news is that I will be outlining some of the key tools and approaches for online natural-language study in the following chapters. Keywords are not just for search marketers, and serious social marketers should have masterful command of keyword research as well. In addition to these elements, I will also illustrate how the understanding of natural language contributes to the interdependent success of a search and social strategy.

Interdependent Search and Social Strategy Is a New and Evolving Discipline

While both search and social are highly developed disciplines in their own right, the overlapping aspects of each are evolving a major discipline unto itself. While many of these aspects are tactical in nature, the overarching concept is highly strategic, and a masterful understanding of the synergies is critical for those who want to elevate their online marketing approach. Marketers who have mastered either search or social independently will have to attain the other skills they might be lacking. The job descriptions for these two different areas are also changing in a way that makes them more inclusive of each other. As you will see throughout this chapter and throughout the book, search and social are married together, and those who practice either one individually will need to become effective at both to perform their existing jobs well.

Internet marketing strategy is also impacted by the interdependency of search and social in a big way. Web design, content strategy, user experience, architecture, and even paid media are all impacted by interdependent search and social technologies in some way. In order to be an effective strategist, a full understanding of search and social concepts is critical to get the most out of your budget, and also to ensure that you are capturing the full opportunities that these channels have to offer.

Social Signals and Search

Algorithmic search engines like Google and Bing are increasingly utilizing social signals to help rank content and make it more visible at the keyword and site levels. Social sharing of content creates many signals that may become visible in search engines, including the following:

- Increase in the number of links to your own content and website domain, both from direct sources and citations and from increased activity in social channels

- Creation of pages within networks, such as profile pages, tweets, and forum discussion threads, which rank with your message in the search results

- Comments, which are a signal that people are reading content and which indicate social activity around a particular discussion or asset

- Likes on Facebook, which are used by Bing to help rank content

- Views, which help search engines like YouTube determine the relative popularity of a particular asset within their network

- Status updates (sites like Twitter, Google+, and Facebook), which help search engines determine the velocity of sharing popularity toward an asset, which can allow for quicker ranking in search

- Keyword and URL sharing velocity, a type of analysis performed by Google and Bing and other buzz-monitoring algorithms, which can determine the trending popularity of a particular keyword or topic as it happens in real-time (For example, Twitter Trending Topics show only the themes and keywords with the highest-rising velocity of keyword mentions and retweets.)

How Traditional SEO and Social Signals Are Very Much Alike

With all of the commentary and buzz around social as a search-engine signal, there is one fact that must be clearly understood by real-time content marketers. Yes, different assets may be shared, tweeted, liked, or emailed, but the fact is that the world of social sharing still revolves around the *link graph*. The link graph is a cornerstone measurement of citations of links toward a web page or other digital asset, and in short, the relative quantitative and qualitative scores from the link graph have a high bearing on how web pages are retrieved and ranked in keyword-based search algorithms. Use of the link graph is a fundamental element of Google's patent and use of PageRank, which effectively considers the network relationships of links as weighted citations toward a particular document. The quality and authority aspects of your link graph are cornerstones of how search algorithms measure the quality of content at the page and domain levels and are fundamental to how well your assets will rank in search.

Take a look at the social networks that you use every day, and you will see that while you are still acting in a social environment, your activity leaves a trail of newly created web pages and links. It is the aggregate algorithmic analysis of these effects that increases the authority placed on your website by search engines in order to help increase your content visibility in search-engine results.

Still, there are many different characteristics of social effects on search, apart from just creating links and additional web pages that are not located on your own domains. As a separate cornerstone that is emerging parallel with the link graph of the web, the *social graph* has gained increasing prominence in helping search engines rank results. The social graph is the structure of relationships within a person's network of connections, both within a specific network like Facebook or Twitter and from network to network (for example, think of a subset of nodes between one's Facebook friends and their LinkedIn connections). The weight of a social graph looks not only at the quantity of connections but also at the relative authoritativeness and theme of those connections. Analysis of the social graph allows search engines and other algorithms to study various relationships between active and real-time network users and applies these effects to a variety of uses. These uses may include identifying people in a network who are content creators, influencers, active sharers, or passive consumers of content. This analysis of a social graph has many parallels in the way that search engines have historically used the link graph to measure network influence on web pages and to rank them accordingly by level of network link influence, among many other factors.

Bing real-time search director Paul Yiu outlined this search view of social networks in a March 2012 interview with noted search and social marketer Eric Enge (read an interview with Eric in Chapter 12, "More Considerations for Real-Time Content Marketing, Search, and Social"). In the interview, Yiu described how Bing is taking an algorithmic view of social networks and data in a way that utilizes a traditional search sensibility. In effect, Bing looks at a user as a node, just as it might view a web page or site node in search. It looks at the theme of a person's content and conversation. It looks at the relative quality of the people you associate with in networks, just as Bing looks to the relative quality of the sites that you may link to or that may link to you. In the interview, Yiu also provided a few other key insights that reveal how intertwined search and social have become in the Bing search experience, in this case how they view Twitter data from an algorithmic perspective.

Eric Enge: *Can you outline a bit about how you determine the value of a tweet?*

Paul Yiu: *One metric is how many people follow you, but that can be gamed a little bit. We can actually analyze the follow graph and tell if you are trying to game the system, because your network on Twitter looks disjointed. The typical network on Twitter has characteristics that are hard for people to emulate artificially. These are unnatural, and when we see networks like this you can tell these people are trying to sell teeth whitening or whatever. We look at the way people are connected, and often we correlate that to the quality of a Tweet. We can also analyze the content the Twitter account links to. What does that mix look like, and how do people interact with the content you are tweeting. That's just on the Twitter side of things. On the Facebook side in a way we are still working on it; with Facebook most of the time it's your true identity. On Facebook right now is just stuff from your friends, so it's a different problem.*

For more information from this insightful interview, visit `www.stonetemple.com/author-authority-and-social-media-with-bings-paul-yiu/`.

Sharing

Sharing is one of the most fundamental and widespread activities online. Sharing activities include "liking" a link or other digital asset on Facebook, sending a link via email, tweeting a link, "+1-ing" a link to Google+ networks, sharing a link within LinkedIn, adding links to a favorites list, or working collaboratively on a shared document such as Wikipedia. Ultimately the benefits of sharing allow your content to travel quickly to networks of networks, allow content consumers to create many of the signals that search engines use to help rank your content, and make your content visible to other information-seekers at the algorithmic and keyword levels.

How Social Sharing Democratizes the Link Graph

So, what's the big deal with this shift in the way search engines view links? Links are just links, right? Not necessarily. In the early days of search engines, and particularly with Google, links were considered citations from a source, and the authoritative link networks of those sites were also considered. The early Web skewed generally toward a more technically inclined audience because of the need for more hard-coding skill sets and also a lack of user-friendly open content-management systems. As a result, those gatekeepers of the links tended to have more of a voice with Google algorithms than nontechnical users. This meant that a webmaster or marketer in charge of a website could specifically engineer the links on their sites to influence search results. So in effect, those who held the File Transfer Protocol (FTP) power generally held more of the search-engine voting power in terms of the way links were counted.

With social networks and media, there is a much lower barrier to entry and much more democratization of links via the social graph. A novice Internet user can go to WordPress.com and easily create a blog that has many links in minutes. A Facebook or Twitter user can have more of a say by creating a network and simply publishing links via status update, in a way that can have an equal or greater influence in search. In creating or leveraging a real-time content platform, it is imperative for publishers to understand how to distribute content for the benefit of their users and also extend the life of their content online (see Figure 2.1).

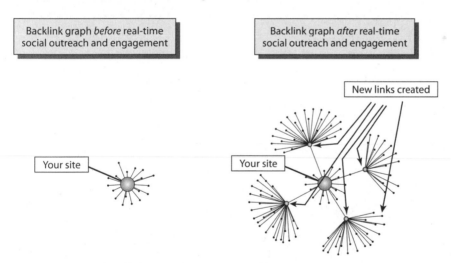

Figure 2.1 The view of a backlink structure for a new blog, before and after social outreach

While link development has been a traditional SEO practice of asking for links, submitting links to directories, attracting links, and creating links, Figure 2.1 displays a different approach to link-building through blogger outreach and social engagement. While link-building campaigns are designed to engineer this type of link growth through planned activities, Figure 2.1 shows actual sharing through social outreach and how social signals can stoke the flows of information to provide a social parallel to the link graph. In Chapter 12 we will cover this type of social linking promotion in more detail, in a way that you can also achieve the same effects for your own digital assets.

In August 2010 at the SES Conference in San Francisco, I participated as a speaker on the "I Want It Now" panel with real-time search and social engineers from the major search engines. On this panel, engineers from Google and Bing both acknowledged that they treated *status updates with links* in social networks differently in terms of how these common social behaviors could have a direct impact of search algorithms. In effect, their statements confirmed that activity streams had finally become a signal that could no longer be ignored, and that links in status updates were being recognized as a search signal. At the time, Bing and Google were tapped into the Twitter fire hose directly to help identify potential signals for search in real-time. Most notably, start-up real-time search engine OneRiot was the first to use the network effects of Twitter, because its results showed links to content based on the popularity of retweeted links alone. So, rather than showing you 100 duplicate retweets of popular content (as Twitter search did at the time), OneRiot compressed these duplicated shares into an aggregate signal and ranked results by Twitter popularity. It was this innovation that both Bing and Google later adopted in their own Twitter Search and Real-Time Search products, respectively. In terms of innovation, the case could be made that Google was doing the same thing with massively duplicated content (think press releases or other syndicated content that is highly replicated), but this was never confirmed as overtly as OneRiot's algorithm.

Google has since created its own proprietary social network called Google+, which will be covered in more detail later in the book, but fully incorporates its stand-alone Real-Time Search product as part of its search algorithm. Bing also utilizes real-time status updates and streams to inform search algorithms, because it currently has exclusive licensing with both Twitter and Facebook status updates to inform its algorithms in both real-time and other parameters of *recency*, which will be discussed at greater length in this chapter.

We now have a space race going on with network information-sharing with the likes of Twitter, Google+, Facebook, LinkedIn top sites, and other networks that use network effects to rank and also push content. With regard to ranking documents in search, it is this *aggregate network sharing effect* of both links and keywords that is having the most impact on search. While links between search and social have been largely observed by experienced search-marketing professionals, it is only since the late aughts that search engines like Google and Bing have expressly confirmed that these social signals are indeed having a critical impact on your search visibility. Just do a search on Google's Matt Cutts (www.youtube.com/watch?v=ofhwPC-5Ub4) or Bing's Duane Forrester (www.bing.com/community/site_blogs/b/webmaster/archive/2011/12/22/the-future-of-search-amp-social.aspx) on the topic of search and social signals, and you won't have to look far to see that they are recommending serious search marketers get active with creating engaging and robust content strategies and propagating this content online in a meaningful way.

The Share Graph Is the New Link Graph

While the social graph is having an impact on search, it is the intersection of socially shared links and keywords and the networks-on-networks effect that is causing search engines to begin to look at the social graph in a different way. In making the distinction between the social graph and the core differences as it relates to search-engine optimization and marketing, I have been referring to this concept as the *share graph* in order to help better educate about how search engines view signals across the social graph. One of the great benefits of publishing my opinions in MediaPost is that I often get instant feedback on my columns. After I published a column outlining the concept of the share graph in September 2011 (www.mediapost.com/publications/article/158563/), I had a chat with RadiumOne's Doug Chavez, and he had some similar ideas on subsets of the social graph that RadiumOne had been developing since 2008. I sensed clearly after our discussion that this view of the social graph is useful not only for looking at how search engines can use these signals for search but also for how ad networks use the concept to create greater relevancy for ad targeting and relationships based on network interactions. Considered together, the two definitions refer to parallel views of the link graph and the social graph, first as it relates to social signals in search and second as it relates to sharing activities across networks to create a more relevant social experience and content-delivery experience. Figure 2.2 shows a RadiumOne share graph segmentation for auto enthusiasts within the greater social-graph context of a sample individual's network.

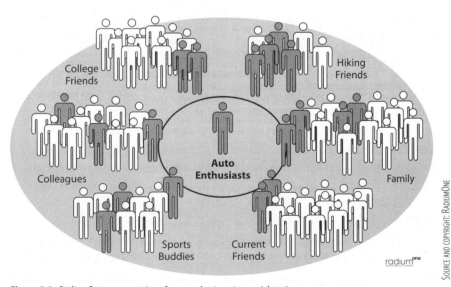

SOURCE AND COPYRIGHT: RADIUMONE

Figure 2.2 RadiumOne segmentation of auto enthusiasts in a social setting

While the share graph is a subset of the social graph, as well as a social parallel to the link graph, search engines are revealing that shared assets in social networks are increasingly influencing how they view the link graph. The share graph becomes particularly important when a ranking may be more relevant over a period in time, particularly in real-time. Taking the social graph and the link graph into consideration, it is also fair that the share graph has characteristics of both and is gaining in prominence to improve the experiences of both. Overall, the implications of the share graph are tremendous in the context of extending the life and opportunities of your content online, and addressing the share graph should be a primary concern as part of your online publishing strategy. This is another easy way to think of the share graph: your site's *link graph* is to the *web graph* as your *share graph* is to the *social graph*.

Here are a few attributes that make specific links and keywords resonate more in a share graph scenario:

- Authority of the network sharer
- Theme of the user or related concepts of the network sharer
- Depth of the network sharer's network and the authority of those in the network
- Trustworthiness of the network sharer (in relation to the likelihood that they produce spam or low-quality content)
- Velocity of keyword usage across a network and the spreading of that keyword or phrase over time though shared networks
- Velocity of a link being shared, over time, based on time frequency, volume, and the level that it cascades through various networks

Overall, understanding the concept of the share graph helps search and social marketers think strategically about the social impact on search and, conversely, the search impact on networks.

How Search Impacts Social

Google's cofounder and coinventor of its algorithm, Larry Page, had spoken of his real-time search vision to the company's engineers in the early 2000s. One day, he said, Google would index the Web *as content happens in real-time*. In an article written by Greg Sterling at Search Engine Land (http://searchengineland.com/larry-page-embraces-real-time-search-19579), Sterling quoted Page's recount of his team's reaction when he expressed his ambition toward a real-time information algorithm and crawler.

I have always thought we needed to index the web every second to allow real time search. At first, my team laughed and did not believe me. Now they know they have to do it. Not everybody needs sub-second indexing but people are getting pretty excited about realtime.

Considering that in the early 2000s Google was refreshing its index every few weeks, this presented a considerable challenge to the company's engineers. Google strived to provide the freshest results from the Web in the ensuing tweaks and updates, each time getting ever closer to crawling, indexing, and retrieving the Web as it was happening *right now*.

By 2008, Google had become very adept at indexing the Web up to the hour, and even up to the minute. But no matter how quick it became at showing the "up-to-the-minute" Web, Google was still falling behind Twitter, Facebook, and other status networks in terms of surfacing content that was happening *right now*. This presented a problem in search and social that would impact all future networks. To have a full robust search and social experience, for both networks and search engines, the following must be attained at a highly sophisticated level:

- A robust crawling, indexing, and retrieving method for distributing information, all across the Web
- A real-time active human social layer

Clearly, Google was at an advantage with its proprietary algorithms, as well as its dominant share of the search market. But it did not have a viable social layer that could detect information velocity and sharing within the freshest real-time edge. In December 2009, it obtained that human edge by licensing Twitter's open data stream to help form its search results (notably, Bing was the first to sync up a deal with Twitter to utilize in its own real-time search offering, which also occurred in December 2009). Now Google could track the velocity of content sharing and keywords in real-time and apply it to its own Real-Time Search vertical search engine. Though the engine itself wasn't widely used, the technology behind it was used to help propagate content using social signals to the mainstream web results page of Google, when query deserves freshness (QDF) parameters were met. In addition to absorbing social data in real-time to inform the algorithm, Google had also updated its crawling platform (called Caffeine) to better determine which sites could be more trusted in a real-time information scenario. But Google's Real-Time Search product acting as a stand-alone engine was drawing to a close, though the technology was being increasingly utilized in the main web search results in a big way. In effect, the adoption of a human-social edge was helping to provide freshness to the results that was not possible to achieve through the crawling and retrieval processes alone.

Google also upped the social stakes by proving that algorithms were more important to the social networking experience with the release of Google+. When considering the broad spectrum of real-time content dissemination, networks like Twitter and Facebook have the human social layer down pat but are lacking in terms of any type of robust technology that would improve the social networking and sharing experience. This is a story that is still being written in social and search and will likely continue in the foreseeable future. Facebook currently utilizes its EdgeRank algorithms to determine which content is shown in Facebook user streams, and it is expected to continue investing in this area.

As the approach of integrating both algorithms and human social layers is more embraced by search engines and social networks, businesses will need to follow suit in order to stay in the game and keep their marketing approaches at the cutting edge. This means taking on a robust approach with SEO efforts and striving to provide a proprietary real-time human outreach layer in order to provide the signals that engines and networks are looking for. This book will show you how to accomplish just that.

Recency Is the New Relevancy

Up until 2008, the search experience was largely focused on providing searchers with what the engines thought was the best result for your query, based on all of its results over *all time*. When search engines did not take historical segmentation or a "what is the best timeline" approach for your query result, it created irrelevant results for a wide range of queries.

Looking for the *best answer* over the *best period of time* is a segment of relevancy. Imagine searching for a coupon or discount code only to be served up a result that was long out-of-date. Imagine searching for the current sports schedule for your favorite sports team only to be served up a result that was from several years back. Imagine searching for current events happening in your town only to find listings that were several months or years old. These are just a few of the problems when search engines show results over "all time."

Real-time search and social sharing are often generally perceived as being about "what is happening right now," but they actually have much broader implications with how content consumers may find, share, and consume your content. Within the context of *relevancy*, what ultimately distinguishes real-time from a traditional "best result over all time" or "the newest result is best" view of information is in terms of *recency*—in other words, content that is sourced by fresh and timely signals, either algorithmically, socially, or both. *Recent* could mean right now, in the last hour, in the last three days, in the last two weeks, in the last month, and so on, as it best suits the query. Search with a view on recency provides more consideration to a timeline view of data, which is a major shift from retrieving just "anytime" search results over the entire history of the assets that it may have in its data corpus.

OneRiot released a study in 2009 that found as many as 40 percent of all search queries may have some level of recency. To show how attributes of a relevancy timeline may better serve a user's search intentions, consider the following recency attributes of search within a selected timeframe, rather than just "all history" (as also informed and reciprocated by social networks):

Last Month, Last Year Coupons and deal-related searches are great examples of commercial search with a high volume but are more suited toward parameters of recent weeks or months, or as long as the deal is valid. Let's face it—an expired coupon or deal is not a deal at all, but current coupons and deals are an amazing find.

Yesterday, Last Week, Today, and Tomorrow   While still not being in the timeframe of "right now," many searchers seek out information that is still recent and is relevant to a current experience. They may be looking for things to do in a particular locale, looking for recent reviews, or monitoring the ongoing the conversation of a current event.

Right Now   Sometimes the real-time element of recency is so spontaneous, readers may not even know the event is happening yet. When Osama bin Laden was found in Pakistan, the news was first reported on Twitter by Sohaib Athar, who was a next-door neighbor to bin Laden. As Athar tweeted about helicopters near his house, he was the first to report on one of the biggest world stories in 2011, though he didn't know the implications of the disturbance at the time (`http://wqyk.cbslocal.com/2011/05/03/bin-laden-neighbor-unknowingly-tweets-raid/`).

While it has taken some time for search engines to achieve the level of "right now," they have certainly come full circle with the implementation of social sharing and conversation as a search signal. While Google does not currently license the Twitter stream for real-time search, it is integrating similar findings from its new Google+ social layer, and it is already impacting Google+ results and other Google services. Whether Google+ reaches 50 million users or 5 billion users, it has become a critical cornerstone to its algorithm, especially for surfacing new content at different levels of recency.

How Search Algorithms Are Upping the Game for Social Networks

We know about how social's recency contribution has improved the experience and relevancy of search engine results. Considering that the winner in the search and social space race is the one that has both the best algorithm and the best human social layer, what does this mean for social networks?

With the release of Google+ in June 2011, the company proved it could create a more robust and relevant approach to the social networking experience by applying a higher level of algorithmic intelligence to people in its networks, fundamentally in the form of better segmentation via Google Circles. Facebook currently has a very simple algorithm for determining what content is seen in its social stream on the news page. At this writing, Facebook has been making more comments in the press that it is getting into the search game. While the question used to be, "How are search engines becoming more social," it is morphing into the reverse, or *"How are social networks going to become more algorithmic?"*

Understanding Velocity in Real-Time Search

Velocity is another aspect of real-time search that is critical to your content-publishing strategy. Because search engines are tapped into the share graph through a variety of networks, they can see how fast a keyword has increased, spikes in usage over a given timeframe, and how quickly a link or other asset spikes in shares across a network or networks.

When velocity between keyword and shared asset occurs, Google promotes links from a variety of its vertical search engines (YouTube, Google News, Blog Search, and so on), into the prime-time real estate of its web search results (best result out of everything). Google refers to this analysis process as *query deserves freshness* (QDF). When a particular keyword or link is tracked, it can be promoted quickly to the front page of the results, based on accrued social and SEO factors of trust and authority or simple propagation by sharing activities.

The Value of Approaching Social with a Search Frame of Mind

When approaching a content strategy in real-time, it is important to weigh the value and differences of search and social in order to make the case for doing them together. Typically, a fresh content piece has a relatively short life of spiking traffic that may last seconds, minutes, hours, or a day. But once that traffic drops, a good article still might receive little to no traffic over the rest of its life. Conversely, a page that is well-written for both search engines and people might not have the same traffic spike from social, but it does better over the long term by matching keyword queries that are constantly referring traffic from search engines.

In Figure 2.3, notice that Pattern 1 reveals a traffic spike in the initial launch, because the link was shared quickly across networks.

Pattern 1: Content with social visibility

Pattern 2: Content with natural search visibility

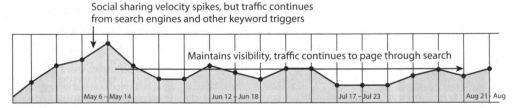

Figure 2.3 Comparing blog content with social traffic spikes only vs. a blog post with both a social and search return

Pattern 2 shows the same social spike, but it has a tail of long-term referral traffic and ultimately allows the page to perform better than approaching from a social perspective alone.

The power for a real-time content marketer is in combining these two principles together to get the benefit of both the social traffic spike and the long-term search-engine returns. A good real-time content marketer must build up relevant networks to distribute content in order to get not only the spike in traffic but also the links and ranking pages that come along with it. As social activity is detected by search engines, social signals are applied algorithmically and the content has a longer shelf life in search. Using a search frame of mind also means optimizing your initial page and using the right keyword triggers that will allow it to be better understood by search engines.

The Power of the Networked Link

While links have long been the cornerstone of natural search algorithms, social provides an opportunity to grow link strength in numbers. A link having a "social" or "network" attribute may include any of the following scenarios:

- Link duplication in status updates (retweets or likes)
- Any link or URL that contains a popularity vote
- Any link that displays quantitative data (number of ratings, number of reviews, number of comments, and so on)

Google and Bing also look at links in terms of the velocity that it is being shared across a network. If there is a breaking news story about a Justin Bieber appearance in Manhattan, the speed of sharing over a given time will utilize these social-network link effects to push it into the main web search results pages for the Justin Bieber keyword space. Networked links can have both an immediate impact on the links and traffic to the page being shared and a long-term impact by leaving a trail of links that increase the trust in the site at the domain level.

It is the combination of sharing, popularity, and velocity that ultimately distinguishes a network link from what we might refer to as an *individual link*, or a link that is placed within a web page. There is a synergy between the two, and ultimately static links are measured by the other links that point to them as well. Understanding how a networked link works is fundamental for any social-network linking strategy. Figure 2.4 shows an example of how Twitter has promoted a highly networked link on *The Wall Street Journal*. In effect, the more the link is shared, the more visible it becomes in a Twitter search. This same effect occurs in Google+, Facebook, and LinkedIn.

Figure 2.4 When a link or status update attains a substantial number of retweets, it is promoted over other content in a Twitter search.

A Second-Tier SERP Strategy for Increasing Your Visibility

Most search-engine optimizers are concerned fundamentally with getting pages to rank for their owned digital assets (their primary website, videos, and so on). But the main problem with optimizing one site is that its search visibility may be limited to only one or two results, because both Google and Bing typically limit the number of visible listings to two per domain (with the exception of navigational links below a main listing, also known as *site links*). So, once you have optimized your primary assets, where do you take your search-optimization strategy from there?

The answer is in allowing social networks and other well-optimized websites to help pull in some of that extra traffic for you, ultimately creating indirect SEO traffic to your site or digital asset. Not only does this connect your social assets in the search engines at the keyword level, but often these second-tier sites may be linked directly to your website. Figure 2.5 illustrates the flow from the search engine to social networks and other websites and how it connects to your owned assets online.

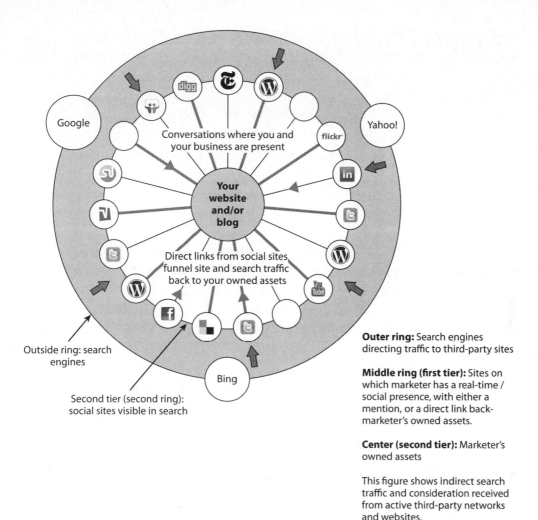

Conversations where you and your business are present

Your website and/or blog

Direct links from social sites funnel site and search traffic back to your owned assets

Outside ring: search engines

Second tier (second ring): social sites visible in search

Outer ring: Search engines directing traffic to third-party sites

Middle ring (first tier): Sites on which marketer has a real-time / social presence, with either a mention, or a direct link back-marketer's owned assets.

Center (second tier): Marketer's owned assets

This figure shows indirect search traffic and consideration received from active third-party networks and websites.

Figure 2.5 Having a robust social presence can enable your business to become visible in search engines, outside of your owned assets.

First-Tier Visibility Any proprietary digital asset in the search-engine results pages, or SERPs, (for example, your website).

Second-Tier Visibility Any other website that ranks in the same keyword space and either mentions your company or links to your proprietary digital assets. Your site or brand is essentially two tiers away from the original source, but you still have the visibility and also links (for example, social-media site, blog, or forum).

The great thing about second-tier visibility is that stoking the flows of conversation and content leaves a trail of visible web pages for search engines to follow, and these pages become visible in SERPs. This can ultimately help you "own the results" for terms and phrases by being highly visible in multiple areas of the SERP.

The following are categories of second-tier visibility:

Pages That Rank for Generic Terms and Phrases That Include a Mention of Your Company or Area of Specific Expertise Having your company name or personal name mentioned prominently on another website or digital asset puts you into the search consideration set. You get the value of an introduction direct from a generic keyword search from someone else's site. All you had to do was become part of the conversation.

Direct Links or Calls to Action from a Second-Tier SERP That Sends a Searcher Directly to Your Page In this scenario, you happen to be mentioned or featured on a site with good search-engine visibility. Not only does the visitor find out more about you and your company's services, but they can also click through directly to your website. *Voilà.* You just received direct traffic from another website and indirect traffic from a search engine based on that site's search visibility.

Proprietary Content and Messaging Hosted on a Site Other Than Your Own Syndicating and releasing your own optimized content for distribution on other websites can help increase your SERP shelf space by getting it placed on other well-optimized websites. Content-syndication networks, PR wires, and guest blogging are just a few ways to achieve this type of visibility.

Interaction with Visitors Who May Be Entering a Social-Media Page or Asset Directly from a Search Results Page Answering questions directly and direct community outreach are great ways to become highly visible in a second-tier SERP strategy. Assess and determine which sites are the big players in terms of their search visibility and amount of the conversation that they own, and then add these sites to your overall community-management strategy. Answering questions and engaging with your audience not only puts you top of mind with people who read you on a network, but also makes you visible to searchers who arrived at those pages via search-engine results.

Understanding the benefits of second-tier visibility can help inform both your social-engagement strategy and your natural search marketing strategy. Doing it effectively requires a marketer to understand how the two work together, and this will be discussed in more detail in later chapters.

Active and Passive Distribution in Networks

As we talk more about how information and content are shared across networks, it is important to understand how different types of sharing and spreading of content occur. I prefer to describe these differences as *passive* and *active*, in terms of how and where a piece of content propagates across the Internet.

Figure 2.6 shows how passive distribution scenarios typically involve the primary networks where your content is syndicated and shared by you. Examples of your passive distribution network include your Twitter followers, your friends on Facebook, your email subscribers, and your RSS subscribers. In a passive scenario, the message can be readily shared though the distribution network, crawled and ranked in search engines, and read by consumers over and over without being shared. But in most information-sharing flows, sending engaging content over a passive network is only the beginning of the process.

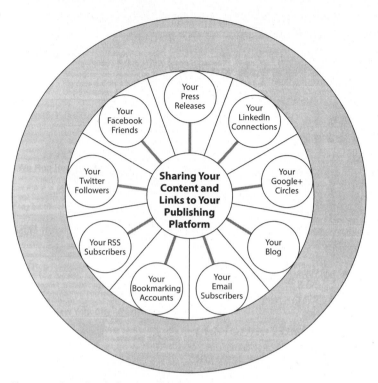

Figure 2.6 A visualization for passive distribution of a digital asset across a network

Once your message is sent out, it may then become active based on how interesting or engaging the message or content is and be spread organically (or actively) from that point, proportional to the level of interest. This expands from one-to-many (passively, from you to your networks) to many-to-many (actively, by sharing from networks to networks).

Figure 2.7 shows *active distribution*, or the process of sharing links across the Web, and may begin passively with your own networks of individuals who subscribe to your content. By enabling the sharing of content with embeddable RSS widgets, retweets, likes, and so on, your own proprietary content may be shared in status updates across networks and consumed directly via the social stream. It is the actual act of sharing across networks to networks by the people who consume it that makes content inherently *active*. The outside ring of this figure shows a variety of actions that can occur to help actively extend your content to networks of networks.

Active and passive distribution are very much interdependent, but understanding how they work together enables a content strategist to better stoke the flows of interaction in networks.

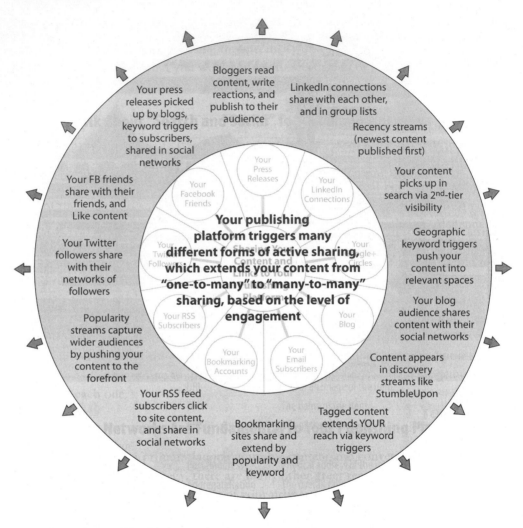

Figure 2.7 Visualization of active distribution or shared content across networks

As a real-time content marketer, building up your own following in social networks is what helps set off the chain of distribution and sharing in the active sense. It is not enough to be just a static web publisher. Your subscribers are networked, and you must attract these like-minded audiences to help both consume and share your content. You must also be aware of the places where content can be syndicated and picked up passively, by either earning it or paying for it. Understanding passive and active distribution is critical to getting all of the benefits of a connected search and social strategy.

List of Social and Search Signals and Synergies

Social media has quickly become an integral part of search-optimization strategy and tactical execution. To end this chapter, here are some key ways that social media influences search-engine visibility (many of these concepts ways will be cited throughout the remainder of the book):

Likes, Retweets, and +1s Likes and retweets form a signal, particularly in Bing, that has access to this raw data. Google also utilized Twitter data for a one-and-a-half-year period between 2009 to 2011 but has since moved to +1s and Google+ shares to provide aggregate social signals that inform fresh search.

Tagging Keyword meta tags are far from dead; they've just moved to the body of the viewable page. Tags are essentially keyword descriptions of the content and used in a variety of applications. The act of *tagging* refers to assets that are given keywords based on what audiences and content creators think of the content and provides a general indicator to search about what a page is about. There are even entire networks like Delicious where tags serve as a primary content source and are searchable based on the popularity of the individual tags.

User-Generated Content (UGC) UGC captures new links, second-tier SERP visibility, and the living keyword language, which would be impossible for a marketer to do independently in real-time. This reciprocation between social communities attracting more content producers and users from search is considered a major component for building a successful and profitable digital marketing strategy. UGC communities are a major segment of the Web, and participation as a real-time content marketer is critical in terms of engaging with other content creators and sharers and creating your own content. Examples of user-generated content include forum discussions, blogs, reviews, comments, and wikis, among many other types.

Keyword Triggering and Keyword Streams in Social A simple innocuous post on Twitter or Facebook might find itself in Google search results or other keyword-discussion streams, provided that the right keyword was used. While this can sometimes be predicted, it is often achieved by just acting naturally. The bottom line is that keywords are connections to people, in both search and social networks, and expert keyword-research skills are a must-have for good search and social marketers.

Digital Asset Optimization (DAO) DAO is about applying standard SEO principles to shareable digital assets and other common social activities. Taking DAO into consideration when acting in either search or social can extend the opportunities in both.

Reinforcement of User/Searcher Language One of the most interesting interplays between search and social is how user-driven language can attract other like-minded audiences. Social content promotes natural-language usage in communities and greatly expands your reach through keyword research, engagement, and network reach. A search and social view of the *living language* of your audience also helps the marketers capture a much greater share of overall visibility, through content and interaction.

Third-Party Site Visibility in Search Results (Second Tier) One other great core effect between search and social is how social pages and other UGC begins to rank in search, thus attracting more like-minded users through search.

RSS Feeds RSS (which stands for "really simple syndication") is critical for pushing your content into various scenarios, as well as setting up your own internal site experience. Feeds become a direct signal in Google whenever it can determine the popularity or relative quality of a feed through its own FeedBurner service or through subscriptions in iGoogle. RSS also allows you to push your content outside of your domain and get it flowing in social networks, static websites, and other real-time streaming applications.

Ratio of Followers to Those Followed Having a higher number of people following or friending, as opposed to how many follow you, indicates a higher level of trust in search and social and is parallel to measurement of inbound vs. outbound site links in search-engine optimization.

Sharing Links via Network Status or Shared Resource with Others in a Network Sharing is one of the most social activities on the Internet, because it allows a link to quickly propagate throughout a network and drive traffic to your original assets. It is also helpful in creating various signals of link and keyword velocity, which can help both the short- and long-term presences of your digital assets.

Real Names The use of real names, as opposed to anonymous, made-up usernames, have come into full acceptance with LinkedIn, Facebook, and Google+ in recent years. Overall, this helps increase trust and quality in search and social, because users tied to their real names are much less likely to say and share things that might be considered spammy. It is a human and algorithmic indicator that content generated from trusted real-name profiles is likely to be from a real person and be potentially more engaging.

Embeds Webmasters and content consumers who place the video code of Google-hosted digital assets (particularly YouTube) on their own sites and social spaces can provide a signal of relative popularity. Think of embeds like reverse links to the original YouTube site, SlideShare site, document hosts, or image hosts.

Personalization Personalization of your Internet experience occurs when data is modified based on your previous behaviors or preferences. This becomes a more social experience when these profiles shift from one user profile to the next, because it then becomes "discovery" (think about how your Amazon shopping experience may have changed based on what you and others have previously bought).

Voting and Ratings Tools from Trusted Sites When a site becomes trusted and the voting system is trusted as well, then votes begin to attain the power of a single networked link. Google in particular counts votes and ratings for videos in YouTube as a vote for its quality in search, and scoring systems like Digg can also achieve this effect (more quality votes = higher indication of trust). Of course, many voting systems can become overly gamed, and they sometimes fall by the wayside in terms of overall search strength when the credibility of the system becomes corrupted.

Freshness of Content Search engines have always devoured fresh content as a signal of trust, especially when it feeds on an ongoing basis. Taking a real-time and participatory approach is a natural way to engage with your social networks and also provide content for search engines.

Widget Creation and Promotion Widgets include basic RSS feeds of recent content to small, modularly coded applications and functions that can be embedded into the sidebar of a blog or personalized page like iGoogle or Netvibes. Useful widgets that provide value to readers and users create a great opportunity to extend the visibility of your content and also create new links back to your assets from other high-quality sites. Creating widgets and making them available to bloggers and other webmasters is a great way to get categorywide and sitewide links from other quality sites.

Schema.org is a set of standard definitions for website code that enable page data to become more portable in search engine results, and other third party applications. Microdata enables search engines to grab parts of your content and data in order to port them into other functions. This extends the visibility of your data and in some cases allows data to be utilized from your site in a social situation. Sample schemas include calendars, events, people, ratings, votes, keywords, offers, and other data that has real-time implications for both search and social networks.

Ramping Up for a Real-Time Content Marketing Strategy

3

This chapter is about setting a foundation for your real-time publishing strategy; it emphasizes the elements of market research, content planning, publishing strategy, and community-engagement strategy. Getting into a real-time frame of mind requires a lot of tactical plan and a solid strategic plan, and that is exactly what this chapter is all about. We will also discuss how to think about the big picture for real-time publishing, and how to prepare yourself and your organization for a more "in the moment" and connected marketing strategy.

Chapter Contents

The basic elements of your real-time content marketing strategy
Formulating your real-time search and social strategy
Developing your market-research strategy
Developing your content strategy
Developing your platform strategy
Developing your outreach and engagement strategy

Answering the Question "Why?"

Why should you engage in a live online marketing and publishing strategy anyway? This is a question you should ask yourself over and over again, right now and in the future. In the absence of asking "why?" or determining the purpose for strategy, discussions about the "how," "when," and "where" inevitably lose their usefulness, because the conversations venture into solving problems that may or may not actually exist.

Before going down any path of execution or tactical planning, seriously ask yourself the following questions about the nature of your business to help guide your strategy and planning:

- Why are you in business?
- What is the purpose of your business at the end of the day, at the end of the year, and at the end of the decade?
- Where do you want your business to be, and why?
- Why should your business be involved in a content strategy?
- Why is connecting with your audience important to your business?
- Why does your business exist in the marketplace, and how does it translate in the digital realm?

This book does not claim to be a "one-size-fits-all" solution to your problem but rather presents a view of how things have changed in marketing and the potential opportunities that exist. These questions are also not meant to be discouraging. This question of "why?" is the most strategic question you can ask, and it must be answered to guide you effectively into any strategy you pursue. Start by asking broadly, but get specific as well, and relate to the core values of what you are trying to achieve. As part of answering the "why?" question, be sure to identify your primary strategic problems, assess current and past strategies and programs, and consider your financial position and possible constraints and strengths.

Basic Elements of Your Real-Time Content Marketing Strategy

Fundamentally, developing a real-time content marketing strategy requires you to delve into the purpose for undertaking this type of approach, finding your audience and voice, and creating a cohesive strategy for content, platforms, and community management. At the core of your overall real-time publishing and marketing strategy are four areas that will be addressed throughout the remainder of this book:

- Market-research strategy
- Content strategy

- Platform strategy
- Social media-management strategy

All of these elements must be synthesized early on to help develop your foundational strategy. Because real-time content marketing involves both publishing and participation, each has its own *independent* considerations, but they are also *interdependent* in today's real-time publishing landscape. While you are working toward creating an ecosystem for real-time marketing, it will be an adaptive and iterative process. Getting into a real-time frame of mind not only includes publishing but also requires participation, as well as careful selection and attention to the networks and channels in which you want to participate.

The previous chapters have provided you with highlights of the tremendous opportunity for businesses to earn their way through the new real-time publishing medium. To get you started with the strategic reasoning behind a real-time search and social strategy, let's review the core steps and considerations for your own real-time content marketing strategy, some of which are covered in more detail later in the chapter.

Evaluate Past and Current Marketing Programs Your marketing history and current programs are a symbol of where you are right now and where you have been. Take a deep look at what has worked and what has not worked. Think more about how successes can be leveraged and how past lessons can improve your new future strategy.

Perform SWOT (Strength, Weaknesses, Opportunities, Threats) Analysis SWOT analysis can be helpful in seeing where you need to do some work and where you have some leverage in a real-time marketing plan. As you consider the questions throughout this chapter, determine whether each one reveals a potential or existing strength, weakness, opportunity, or threat to the success of your real-time marketing strategy, and work toward striking the right balance to make it successful.

Set Goals A strategy without a purpose is meaningless, so different goal levels must be established. Establishing goals early on in the planning process is critical to developing a well-thought-out real-time publishing strategy. Setting realistic goals that align with your objectives enables you to plan according to those goals and keeps you on a defined path. Your goals may even change during the course of execution, and that's OK. The main point is that you are operating with a defined purpose and not just trying to offer a solution to a problem that may or may not actually exist.

Identify Primary and Secondary Metrics The spectrum of metrics can generally range between direct transactions, engagement metrics, and ROI metrics, among many others that will be defined later in the book. Are you measuring based on revenue generated, or do you apply value to individual actions? High-level metrics should be established early on in the strategy process and can be refined all the way through execution and development.

Establish Guidelines for Real-Time Engagement Whether you are a self-proprietor or the CMO of a large enterprise, basic rules of engagement will need to be established before interacting in social and search spaces. A set of guidelines will not only reinforce your goals but will reinforce your purpose for interacting in Internet spaces and how to best engage those people you want to interact with.

Perform In-Depth Keyword and Market Research At the top of any real-time content strategy, there is a primary focus on search-based and audience-targeted market research. Keyword research is a core element, because it reveals both the content and search demand. Market research helps you better understand your target in both search and social and helps you develop personas in order to produce content that is highly engaging. If the content does not pass the market-research test, then it may fail or not do as well as it could have otherwise in either search engines or social networks.

Analyze Market Research and Identify Opportunities Information without translation by a knowledgeable marketing strategist or analyst is practically worthless to your real-time strategy. The research performed in the preceding step must be interpreted and applied to your strategy. This step is critical in synthesizing the data into the actionable pillars of your content, platform (where you plan to publish and converse), and audience-engagement strategies.

Develop a Detailed Content Strategy and Publishing Plan Once your research is compiled and analyzed, the picture for your content strategy is quickly becoming clearer. With the end goal of engaging your audience, it is important to create a scalable publishing strategy in a way that the overarching themes are clear. Publishing without a well-thought-out content strategy only creates a content dumping ground, but translating your data and insights into engaging content opportunities extends the impact of real-time marketing strategy. In this stage, you should be determining themes and topics, depth of strategy, and how to push the right buttons of your audience in the right way.

Create a Plan for Different Areas of Your Business to Cross-Communicate Develop how SEO teams work with social teams and how audience and community managers will inform other areas of your business about what conversations are occurring in real-time. Create points of contact, introduce various teams, explain the real-time strategy, and set guidelines to help determine when to engage internally.

Evaluate and Customize Dashboards and Analytics Platforms to Accommodate New Metrics Once key metrics are determined, analytics and dashboards must be enabled to measure and trend your goals effectively. Start working on your analytics and measurement as soon as possible so you will have the benefit of measuring performance over the entire history of the engagement. If your analytics platform does not measure what you need, start looking for a new analytics package that does.

Create an Agile Publishing Environment That Replicates a Live Newsroom As you begin to see some of the tremendous opportunities for publishing that exist across a wide variety of topics of interest, it will become clearer that real-time publishing is more like a traditional newsroom or magazine. In a live scenario, there should be a sense of urgency to be aware of the current topics of interest as they arise and to publish fluidly and frequently. Taking this live approach to content publishing is one of the key factors that will enable your program to succeed.

Determine Who's Going to Do It and How You Are Going to Pay for It It is important to start thinking about your writers and live-social-media managers early on. Depending on the size of your effort, it may take either a small team or a whole army, but early planning and attention to this detail will help ensure success later.

Prepare and Educate Your Organization Early On, and Throughout the Development Process Large and mid-size organizations should not wait until the last minute to tell the sales, legal, compliance, product-development, and IT teams of their roles in your real-time content marketing strategy. Bring them into the earliest discussions and strategy sessions, and let them know their part, and also the value of your strategy toward your business goals. They are all a critical part of your team, and you need their buy-in and participation to make your content-marketing platform a success. You will need fluidity in understanding and execution to make real-time content work, and you will need to educate along the way.

Considering the Real-Time User Experience As Engagement and CRM Strategy

If you stop to think about it, search and social marketers who advocate for relevant and authentic experiences are actually advocating for the consumer on behalf of your business, as well as the searcher, the social-network user, and their audience in general. Traditionally, the user experience in Internet marketing design tends to apply toward the website experience in a "top-down" approach, meaning that site users enter the site from the home page and work their way through the site. But the reality is that the user experience begins before they enter the website, from wherever they search or wherever they seek information outside of your owned assets. A real-time search and social mind-set takes part of the experience *to the user*, in addition to providing a basis for the audience to interact with your own assets, and this also provides a function of customer-relationship management (CRM). Fundamentally viewing real-time marketing in this way will help shape your overall approach and help guide everything you do to build a real-time method of interacting online.

Thinking about the search and social user experience also changes when viewed in terms of *engagement*. Engagement is as much about advocating for a searcher or network audience as it is about optimization. By advocating for the searcher or user, you must perform market research and keyword research and create personas with the search experience in mind. You must seek them out in a meaningful and nonintrusive way, and you must do so through tools and through real human interaction (more on tools in later chapters).

Website and network experiences may also be thought of as "relational" in the sense that they are starting from the "outside in" as well. *Outside in* means that the user experience starts before your audience enters your site or social space. With an overwhelming majority of Internet users utilizing search and social networks, this experience must become foundational to your marketing strategy. The challenge for user-experience groups is rooted in the question about "what is being done for a person entering your site from a search engine or social network," especially when this initiating experience may begin with 20 to 75 percent of all site traffic and drills down into every part of the site. If your design does not address this problem, then the full picture has not been considered for user experience. Conversely, the user experience must also be considered completely off-site and off-asset, because a large part of the experience is in social spaces not owned but you or your business.

Ultimately, real-time user-experience strategy is about solving a problem for individuals, solving a problem for your audience as a whole, or satisfying search intent in some way. It goes beyond real-time content and into real-time interaction and participation. If the solution does not present itself and become self-evident to the consumer at the point of consumption, then real-time interaction on behalf of your business can also provide an alternative form of relevancy to the audience experience. The difference is that the experience requires a human and conversational touch, while still solving a query intention or a problem. Again, this is major strategic consideration and retooling of marketing philosophy, and even an understanding of "selling in" this concept may be required to enable your organization to make the transition to real-time marketing in a world of search and social.

Developing a Real-Time Presence Online

If there is one consideration that can help guide your strategy, it is recognizing that your audience consists of *people*, not algorithms, robots, or network nodes. *Your customers* are *real people* with a variety of real problems that need to be solved in real-time. Some people may seek to solve an intermittent problem, and others may even seek to resolve a life-threatening need. It is important to get beyond the last search-click attribution mentality and realize that real-time content marketing is the ongoing process of live interest-seeking and problem-solving, and there are multiple opportunities to interject into that conversation in a relevant way through content. It ultimately requires a human touch, not a technical solution.

Marketers often get so caught up in the mechanical aspects of online marketing that we sometimes forget that there is a real person behind the computer or mobile device. We sometimes see customers as a "conversion," a "click," or a number in a log file. Your customers are quantified in every possible way. But as stated in the first chapter, there is a much bigger opportunity to connect and engage with your audience on a true "one-to-one," "one-to-many," or "many-to-many" level and to put a face to your business or company. In terms of your marketing strategy, connecting directly with your audience in real-time raises a few questions that you should be asking right now.

- Who is your audience, and what are they searching for right now?
- What language do they use to find information about their problems (in other words, what keywords do they use, how do they say it in their own words, and how do they linguistically perceive your products or services)?
- What are their key problems, and how might you help solve them as a marketer?
- What various stages of information-seeking occur to help them solve these problems?
- How can you address and solve their problems through content and outreach?
- Does your own body of content represent the answers to the problems and language that they use to seek out information?
- How do you find out what new language is being used to describe a problem or need?
- Where does your key audience congregate, and is your business part of the conversation going on right now?

Again, this is not just a search or social problem, but the power of real-time marketing can be used to help solve these problems for them right now, in both search and social, as they seek it. Because your brand and business theme are being searched for and asked about right now in both search and social, additional questions arise.

- Are you active enough online to identify a question or problem as it occurs?
- Have you planned ahead to create the content that answers the common questions people have right now?
- Do you have places to put content relevant to daily social conversations and keyword searches that are happening right now?
- Are you fluid enough to produce content in a timely manner that will enable you to be part of the greater conversation that is happening right now?
- Are you networked enough in your relative business space that your new content can spread quickly while the conversation is still alive?
- In a simple phrase, are you acting "in the moment," or are you simply being reactive and missing the greater opportunity?

Bringing Consistency to Your Engagement Strategy

As you will see in this chapter and subsequent chapters, there are many moving parts in an effective real-time marketing and publishing strategy. You may already have a presence on one or more social networks, and you may already run one or more websites. One of your key roles as a real-time strategy creator is in making it come together with cohesive execution and voice.

In this chapter, I'll talk about content, audiences, goals, and platforms, among many other elements of real-time content marketing strategy. As you go through each area, ask some of these key questions to help tie in your overall plan to be consistent and not disjointed:

- Is your message consistent between networks? Should it remain consistent, and is it OK to serve different needs and audiences?

- Is there consistency between visual aspects such as avatars, logos, and other images? Is the look and feel between networks consistent whenever possible?

- Will the same content be distributed to all of the same networks?

- Will the same audience managers be communicating between networks?

- How much overlap exists between audiences in different networks (in other words, are the people in your Twitter and Facebook networks the same, or are they different)?

Much of this consistency can be achieved by tying together real-time audience management and content planning, in addition to maintaining a consistent look and feel with visual elements. It will never be 100 percent consistent, because the look, feel, and engagement rules may change from network to network. But striving toward consistency should be part of your strategy for real-time user experience.

Establishing Your Goals

First you must establish objectives and clearly define what you are trying to accomplish in the early stages of formulating your real-time marketing strategy. Establishing goals can sometimes be an iterative process, and you will likely find some of them change as new opportunities arise in the real-time world and as new research findings become available. Start by considering the following goals in terms of defining what you are trying to achieve:

- Increase or introduce awareness of your company to new audiences and markets.

- Increase market share through greater exposure and presence of your business in live conversation and content consumption.

- Help clarify any misperceptions about your business that may be occurring in various forms of online conversation.

- Reengage with current or returning customers.

- Change or shift perception about your company or the way you do business.

- Increase the potential for a transaction, be it a sale, lead, booking, or other type of conversion.

- Enhance the customer-service experience by solving problems through content, both inside and outside of your website.
- Solicit customer feedback to inform products, processes, and services.
- Retain and drive repeat customers.
- Create and enable your own advocates.

Valuing Real-Time and Social-Media Efforts

Real-time publishing and marketing strategy is a long-term commitment and proposition for your business. By going into outreach and engaging with your current and future customers, you are building relationships for the long haul. Just as in life, building relationships takes time, and a real connection must be earned. Your relationships are building through direct connections, content, conversation, and participation. It is important that you should have this expectation for the short and long term, just as your bosses and other key stakeholders in your business should have this expectation.

In addition to taking the time to build your platform and connections, allow for some time to begin seeing returns. Engaging in real-time is fundamentally considered "earned" media and attention, just as SEO is earned. Just as in SEO, you will receive benefits not just for a week, month, or day, but rather for years to come if you continue to engage. As time rolls by, you will begin to grow much more in terms of size of network, reach, top-of-mind consideration, number of shares, and volume of direct traffic.

One of the major hang-ups many marketers have about going all-in with a real-time strategy (or anything "social," for that matter) is that it is often hard to attribute direct return on investment (ROI). Much like search, social touches many different aspects of your business, though it might not be measured the same way. Here are some examples of the ways that a real-time marketing and social strategy can help contribute to the bottom line:

Real-Time Social Signals Are Critical to Maintaining a Leadership Position in Your SEO Visibility Search marketers must face the fact that there is no turning back: both social and content are a direct influence on how well you perform in the natural search channel. Many marketers can realistically attribute 15 to 20 percent of natural search ROI to the social channel when a robust publishing program is in place.

Real-Time Engagement Provides an Avenue for Customer Relationship Management and Reduces Costs in Other Areas of Your Business Ensure that a dollar value is placed for every person served, and attribute this value to every customer served in real-time, either directly to individual interactions or by passive interactions and exposure to content. Real-time engagement and publishing can help decrease costs in other areas of customer relationship management, particularly in-store, call centers, and other areas.

Social Is an Effective Way of Finding and Recruiting New Employees and Talent The costs of finding new employees and talent can be greatly offset or reduced with a solid real-time marketing platform in place. You may want to consider establishing dedicated channels for recruitment, and when you do, be sure to tag individual URLs or job codes to job listings placed in social to help with tracking performance.

Social Works as an Effective Focus Group and Sounding Platform for Your Products and Services Consider your current costs for research and how moving these analyses to social and search data can save money or increase the research value of what you are currently getting. Also consider how social feedback may influence product or service offerings, and attribute value to the social channel in comparison to other areas where you may be spending your budgets to improve products and services.

Social and Search Provides a Front Line for Brand Management and Can Help You Find and Appropriately Address a Problem or Crisis Before It Gets Out of Hand Having a solid network in place can prevent a major digital public-relations catastrophe if your organization is fluid enough and can solve a problem or straighten out any misperceptions or misunderstandings. Unfortunately, some companies find out the hard way what a proactive approach could have saved them from, because getting a real-time strategy together during a crisis is costlier from both a monetary standpoint and a public-relations standpoint.

Real-Time Social Interaction Increases Consideration and Awareness Again, this comes back to placing a value on brand and engagement metrics and on increasing consideration and awareness toward taking a definitive business-positive action.

I would also challenge marketers who insist on placing direct ROI metrics on social actions to also put a monetary value on various actions in their branding campaigns. Because search has typically been very easy to measure, it has been held to higher standards, and as an extension, many marketers also put high expectations on social and real-time engagement. Ironically, these same marketers might spend the lion's share of their yearly budget on TV or radio advertising, never knowing exactly what they got for their money from a direct ROI perspective. The solution for this is simple: if you are an astute marketer who does not spend money blindly, then you should be placing a monetary value on all metrics for every dollar you spend, including branding and engagement metrics. Still, the standards for social ROI should be relaxed a bit, in a way that is consistent with more traditional brand and awareness metrics and measurement.

Setting ROI for direct sales is easy, but assessing and assigning digital engagement and branding metrics is much harder. How much are you paying for someone to walk through a door? How much do you pay for awareness and increased consideration? These are questions that should be answered not just for real-time but for your entire branding ad spend, both online and offline.

Formulating Your Real-Time Search and Social Strategy

We've covered a lot of the "how to think about real-time strategy" concepts so far in this chapter, so now it's time to start homing in on the core elements of real-time strategic development. They include the following:

- Market research
- Content-strategy development
- Network-publishing-platform development
- Community-management development

While subsequent chapters of this book will go into more detail about the tactical approaches for each element, the remainder of this chapter will focus on the high-level considerations for each one.

As you go through each of the elements, keep in mind that you will need to process and synthesize each element both independently and interdependently. So, for example, there will always be consideration for content strategy on its own but also for content within the context of market research, platform development, and community management. The same applies to the other elements as well.

Developing Your Market-Research Strategy

One of the key elements that will help drive content strategy, platform selection, and community outreach is market research. In a way, market research sits at the top of your real-time platform, because your findings will help drive the cornerstones of your strategy. Market research should be produced in varying forms and should be viewed both strategically when considering your results and insights as a whole and tactically, because the same insights can drive specific content themes and outreach strategies. So, before I cover the high-level considerations for content, platform strategy, and community management, let's review some of the key ways you can perform market research to inform your strategy.

Online Focus Groups This type of market research typically involves in-person review and analysis, though many of the benefits of a traditional live focus group can now be achieved online at a much lower cost. Live participants may review products or services, answer direct questions from an objective third-party researcher, or both, among other potential activities. If you have the budget for conducting a focus group, ensure that you are able to monitor Internet behavior and consumption (with the understanding and permission of the user, of course), and focus on identifying the language they use to search and to share or create content. Ask them what they like, but also observe what they do. As more marketers create their own networks and brand pages on Google+, they are finding that the Hangouts video-conferencing feature is a handy way to conduct inexpensive live online focus groups across many different interests within their business. Your followers, friends, and connections in a variety of social networks also serve as an excellent sounding board to help inform your engagement and content strategy.

Internal Intelligence You may already have much of the research you need in another area of your company, so it might just require some digging around to get some key insights to help inform your strategy. If you have ever performed any research to try to understand your customer or audience a little better, take another look and see whether it will help inform your strategy. Don't forget to review your website log files and keyword searches within your internal site search functions, and interview internal stakeholders, among many other potential activities.

Surveys Surveys are a great way to solicit quick feedback on different areas of your website, blog, or on another social network. SurveyMonkey can help you conduct free surveys on your website, the WordPress plug-in community offers many free survey plug-ins for WordPress blogs, and you can create informal polls with your followers on Twitter or friends on Facebook. Google also has a new fee-based service called Google Consumer Surveys that offers marketers the opportunity to ask a single question from the entire U.S. population or within a specific demographic, and surveys are not just for external audiences (www.google.com/insights/consumersurveys/home). And of course, don't forget to use your own networks to see what they think.

Keyword Research A deep understanding of keyword research should be developed in order to get the most out of your real-time marketing strategy. Keyword metrics are like markers for the demand of content in an engine and strong indicators of content interest on social networks. Understanding keywords can also help you think more like a search engine in social networks to find the conversations that matter the most. While the goal of this book is not to make you a keyword-research master, you will have all the tools you need to get started. One great book you should check out is *Keyword Intelligence: Keyword Research for Search, Social, and Beyond*, by Ron Jones; it contains a treasure chest of information about keyword research and finding conversational demand.

Social-Network Analysis Analyzing the buzz in social networks can help you quickly determine what topics are resonating and worthy of current conversation and content. Study the language used in networks, what is trending, and what is on people's minds.

Developing Personas One of my favorite search and web design–integration projects was developing marketing and search personas in the early aughts with Dr. Karen Pate, Adam Lavelle, and Lori Wilson. Personas are fictional characterizations representing the type of people you are trying to reach in your marketing efforts. Personas are often created using one or more of the methods previously listed and show the character and traits of the people you are trying to attract. To be more useful in real-time marketing, personas should focus on the digital behaviors of their targets, particularly with the language they use to seek out information and converse online. Personas are helpful in identifying your target audience and also in internally identifying the type of social media personality you want to be talking to your audience. Remember the first chapter—companies must embrace the spirit of their like-minded audience, and this is also one way to help identify those authentic inside your organization (or outside). For more information, check out Vanessa Fox's *Marketing in the Age of Google* for developing personas with a search and social linguistic emphasis.

Developing Your Content Strategy

While the overall facets of real-time publishing and marketing start to sink in, it is time to start developing a more refined picture of what your content strategy and publishing plan will look like. You can go through each of these step by step or create more-detailed plans for each item as you carry out each task within your organization. The following items will be addressed further in the next two chapters:

Refine Your Content Goals Based on Your Broader Real-Time Marketing Goals While your broad goals and purpose have been determined, specific content goals must be refined in the context of your overall purpose for creating content.

Synthesize Your Research Findings into Content Opportunities Once information is captured and culled, careful analysis must be performed to translate the data into actionable content strategy and goals. Use this book to help identify opportunities in your data related to content types, language usage, content ideas, and more.

Conduct an Audit to Determine Existing Content Areas in Both Your Primary Online and Offline Assets and Also in Both Owned and Shared Spaces It is imperative that you audit your existing content to understand where there are gaps, and where there might be opportunities to bring new content online. This data can be utilized for high-level strategic guidance, or you can delve deeper into specific SWOT analysis. Auditing your content helps you focus and prioritize in the right new areas and not duplicate any previous efforts. The next chapter will delve deeper into these areas.

Perform Competitive Research Competitive research is also critical to understanding the real-time publishing space. Use a refined keyword list to see how competitors are doing in order to catch up or to identify a potential opportunity that a competitor may be missing.

Identify Types of Content to Be Targeted (Videos, Images, News, Text, and So On) In the research stage, it is also important to determine what types of content your audience prefers to utilize and consume. In some businesses, the target audience may prefer news updates and videos. In another, they may prefer text-based articles and FAQs. In others, they may prefer all of the above. You won't know until you ask, and making assumptions could blindside your content strategy from the get-go. The following chapter will discuss more on content types and where they should reside.

Plan to Develop Containers for the Asset Types That Will Be Promoted (HTML, Feeds, Website Architecture, and So On) Although for some it may go without saying, if you proceed with a particular type of asset, then you will need to allocate a place for it on your own digital assets and also in third-party networks. When building out websites or other digital assets, be sure to enable a spot for multiple asset types for both immediate and future needs.

Develop a Strategic Plan for Content Distribution Delivery platforms are a critical aspect of spreading digital content, and getting this part right is the difference between success, failure, or just not getting as much as you could have otherwise.

Create an Editorial Plan and Publishing Calendar As the depth and themes of a robust publishing strategy are planned, having an editorial plan and publishing calendar will help keep your content production and dissemination focused and also help you achieve a level of consistency with your audience.

Program for Maintenance and "Keeping It Fresh" Beyond ramping up a team and becoming fluid in publishing and conversation, plan to constantly revisit your strategy. Set aside time to brainstorm new ideas for content, freshen up existing content assets and address many other aspects of maintaining a real-time publishing platform.

Developing Agility in Content Publishing

Publishing in a world where information and conversation propagate in real-time is not something most businesses are accustomed to. Marketers typically spend time planning and ramping up for a *campaign* that has a defined beginning and end. While the practice of real-time publishing may have a beginning, it is an ongoing effort that does not have any defined end and is refined and perfected throughout the process. In other words, it takes a lot of planning and forethought to begin publishing and executing effectively in a real-time environment, but the rest is an ongoing process of engagement, not a finite one. Consideration must be given to a wide variety of questions that are common to all digital marketers but must be answered subjectively for your own business goals and objectives.

- Where will you be present?
- How will you monitor conversations?
- Who is writing content?
- Who is conversing directly with your audience?
- What types of content are being written?
- Is my content optimized well enough for search engines?
- Is my network big enough to distribute content to a wider audience?
- How does each piece of content map to various stages of the conversion funnel?

- How will my organization address this?
- How do I develop my voice through content?
- Can I trust people in my company to act on behalf of my business?

All of these questions must be answered, and planning must be done well ahead of time before you begin to achieve a level of fluidity in your real-time content and conversation flow. It is worth stating again: it takes a lot of planning to be a real-time publisher in the search and social world of "right now." You may be thinking that this approach goes against the grain in the way many companies are traditionally set up to protect their brand or the way your business is set up for brand protection and reactive response, and you are right. Real-time publishing means taking a proactive approach, and you may find that the biggest opponent of developing a real-time publishing platform is most often the business or company itself.

Developing Your Platform Strategy

Your "platform strategy" is essentially the main areas you plan to engage and publish. Developing your platform strategy is the process of assessing and identifying networks for publishing and where you plan to be present in real-time, including your own websites and blogs. This mix of networks and owned assets will form the base of your real-time publishing platform, outline the key areas for building up earned network attention, and be the place where you fundamentally converse and publish. Beyond an engagement and conversational strategy, it involves using market research, online listening tools, and analytics, among other elements. Although this book can't directly choose your networks for you, much of the rest of this text will show you the methods and networks that will form the nucleus of your platform strategy, as well as how to find out where your relevant conversations exist and what type of content your audience seeks.

It is also important to be aware of the transient conversations that exist in networks outside your core attention areas like Twitter or Facebook. Being active and alive online means going out and looking for questions and conversations wherever they may exist, studying the written and unwritten rules of those communities, and getting involved in those conversations when appropriate. In other words, while you might not be involved in some of these networks every day, they can still be addressed in a helpful and useful way, and the sum of these conversations may be bigger than some of the networks by themselves. The point is not to get too hyper-focused on one area or network. Some of the tools mentioned in the next chapter will be useful in identifying these conversations.

Finding relevant networks for the foundation of your real-time platform is a combination of using automated tools and also what Dallas marketer Jim Gilbert likes to call the "best tool of all—your brain." Tools can help you find new questions and conversations as they happen, but more often than not, you already know exactly where the key networks are *because you already use them* or they are well known in your business community. While an airline marketer may be well aware that there is a lot of discussion about their general area of business on Twitter, they also know that the FlyerTalk.com discussion forum is a key network to be responsive and helpful toward. Travel marketers might even find that there are many transient conversations to be addressed on Craigslist and City-Data forums, as well as answer sites like Yahoo! Answers, and Answers.com. And of course, if they are using that golden combination of a good tool set and a good brain, a good real-time marketer will know that a question or conversation could pop up at any time from a new or unknown network, and a real-time frame of mind will help them to respond in a timely manner.

In addition to assessing which networks and content platforms are best suited for your own platform, the actual real-time needs of each network must be addressed. In other words, how "real-time" is each network, and what level of attention and monitoring is required? Some busy networks like Twitter or Facebook may require full attention and participation, while others may require partial monitoring and participation only when needed. For example, if you are operating a blog, you would want to pay close attention to comments on your posts in order to acknowledge that person as soon as possible, help answer any questions, and retain them as a regular visitor. If you are an active participant in a forum discussion, you should also be very quick to respond to other comments, at the risk of losing out on the conversation at large.

Questions for Choosing a Network As Part of Your Platform

Similar to the beginning approach for establishing your high-level content strategy, there are many strategic questions to ask when choosing the best areas to engage, participate, converse, and publish when it comes to choosing social networks and other elements of your real-time platform. It is also important to inform this part of your strategy from your research and analyze and distill it into actionable tasks to develop your publishing platform. When considering the mix of social networks, forums, blogs, wikis, answer sites, and other real-time publishing platforms, ask yourself the following questions:

- Who interacts in this network that you are considering?
- Is it a broad or niche audience, or both?
- Do you or your known customers ever mention this network or that it ever influenced them in any way?
- How do you determine which people in the group are influencers?
- What proportion of the potential audience is passive or nonparticipatory but still observes the network interactions?
- What are the key concerns of this audience?
- Are they asking direct questions about your business or company?

- Are they asking general questions about areas in which you are an expert on or can provide a high level of expertise?
- What networks do your best customers use, and why?
- What types of assets does your target audience use, and is there a special sharing network for that type of asset (for example, YouTube for video, SlideShare for PowerPoint presentations, and so on)?
- When you type your brand or core generic keywords into a social network or website, do a lot of results come up? Is there a lot of conversation going on about your company in that network?
- Are there any smaller social networks or discussion forums that should be considered as part of your platform?
- How does your platform balance out in terms of owned assets (a hosted blog or forum) vs. "unowned" assets (like your Facebook or Twitter presence)?

To the last point, I am a firm advocate of basing your publishing platform on your own hosted assets, such as a blog, website, or other type of content platform where you own the domain that the content originates from. The reason for this is simple: as you publish content and act in networks, you are building up real-time credibility in both a search and social sense. Ultimately, there is a conversation that exists outside of your controlled spaces in social networks and other off-site areas, but maintaining a parallel conversation on your assets allows you more control of some of the conversation, in the sense that your assets will have an owned audience, owned search equity, and owned bookmark and traffic equity.

Identifying Niche Real-Time Communities

In addition to the large and common networks previously listed, it is also imperative that you seek out smaller networks, forums, blogs, and answer sites where discussion may be occurring about your company or about the general conversations about your industry, products, or services. You may very well find that the combination of all of the smaller conversations (think of them as the "long-tail networks") may be bigger and have a greater impact than the sum of activity on three or four of the largest networks like Facebook, Twitter, and LinkedIn.

The best ways to find your smaller relevant networks include the following:

Perform a Keyword Search in Google Discussions Over the Past Six Months for a Head Term in Your Industry Think *travel* or *hotels*, or get even more detailed by adding *city+travel* or *city+hotels*. The top results will return the most active forums and discussion site for those particular themes. Answer sites like Yahoo! Answers and WikiAnswers are also included in this Google vertical search engine.

Perform a Keyword Search in Google Blog Search Google Blog Search is a great way to find fresh and active blogs that have content and discussion most relevant to the theme you are seeking. Keep an eye on these blogs, add them to your RSS reader, and consider getting involved and commenting on posts as it makes sense to your strategy.

Review the Blog Rolls and Link Lists of Popular Blogs and Discussion Sites If you find one or two good blogs and discover that they also share link lists of other blogs they read, use their lists as a guide to find other relevant blog or discussion sites. You may find that many like-themed bloggers also frequently comment on other similar blogs, and you may want to consider this for your own strategy as well.

Perform a Keyword Search in Google News News is a critical area to address in a real-time marketing and publishing scenario, so it is also critical to be aware of the sites that specialize in your theme. Add these sites to your blog or RSS feed reader, depending on how active they are. To find top sites for news, simply enter your main keywords into Google News and review the top sites that appear often or that may have the most commenting activity.

Ask Your Customer and Audience Targets Which Social Networks and Discussion Sites They Use and Like the Most What's one the quickest ways to find out small niche sites where conversations are occurring in real-time? Just ask your customers in a survey, questionnaire, or live conversation. You will get an idea very quickly where people go.

Ask Your Co-workers, Employees, and Colleagues Which Social Networks and Sites They Use the Most for Industry Chatter or for a Particular Purpose The people in your business who use the Internet actively will provide priceless data on where to find a good conversation or two.

Review Your Analytics Data for Top-Referring Social Sites Digging into your analytics data can help you find all kinds of news sites related to your respective area of business, big and small. Look for single articles or discussions from forums or blogs that may be driving traffic to your site, and evaluate those sites individually to determine whether they fit your overall strategy. You may be surprised to find new areas of conversation where audiences are already talking about you.

Be resourceful, and ask around in order to find those sites that might not be so obvious at first. Again, you may find that the sum of many smaller networks is greater than the whole of Twitter, Facebook, and LinkedIn combined, particularly as it relates to your business. By taking a more detailed view, you may also find many other new opportunities that your competitors are missing.

Also remember that this type of research may be only as good as the keyword list you are using. It helps to inform your own internal keyword list using the same market-research process outlined previously in this chapter. If you make major assumptions in your keyword lists, you could make major mistakes in the selection of your primary networks.

A Sample Platform Model for Real-Time Publishing

Figure 3.1 displays a generic social publishing platform, represented by a sampling of social-media sites and three separate rings. The inside circle or ring represents your owned media assets that you will publish to and that you will also interact on. The second or middle ring features some of the top-tier social media sites that allow for various types of digital asset publishing and sharing. While your own publishing platform may or may not include these specific networks or sites, they represent areas where a marketer might place a key focus on publishing and real-time interaction. As you develop your own platform, theoretically any one of these sites could reside in the middle ring. On the outside ring, a list of sites involving "transient" conversations is displayed, as are other social spaces where intermittent conversation or participation is required or desired. These sites might include comments on newspaper websites, answer sites like Yahoo! Answers or Ask.com, other relevant blogs that may not be a major priority, sites with product or business reviews like Amazon.com or Yelp, or even Usenet, among many other places where conversations occur. This model is not intended to represent your own real-time platform but rather to show different levels of potential engagement and content development at a very high level. As you begin to select the networks that you will be publishing to, use a similar model and gradually fill in the spaces one by one. Your middle ring may have 3 or 30 circles, depending on the size of your strategy. Your outside rings may have 5 or 500 places to watch where conversations may occur. Even new sites may spring into the third ring as you continuously monitor conversations. There is no set number, because every strategy is subjective and requires specific analysis. But you won't know for sure until you perform your market research and dig deep into the social keyword space of your target audiences.

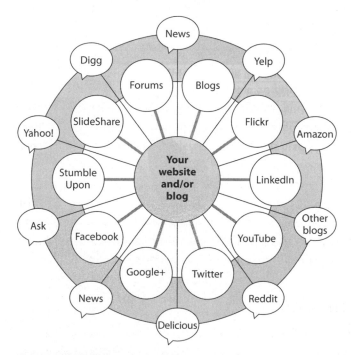

Figure 3.1 This model for real-time publishing revolves around your owned assets, such as a blog or website.

Figure 3.2 is an example of a real-time publishing platform for a hotel marketer. Similar to the previous example, the hotel marketer's website and proprietary blog resides in the inner circle. On the second ring, the hotel marketer has determined seven primary areas in which they will actively publish and engage in real time: the Virtual Tourist forum for conversations, Flickr to publish travel images related to the destinations they serve, LinkedIn to appeal to business travelers and recruit new talent, YouTube to provide a video channel featuring cool things to do around their hotels, Twitter to converse in real-time and also monitor customer feedback, Facebook to engage with new and returning customers, and the Lonely Planet forum to help answer questions and provide insight on their areas of expertise.

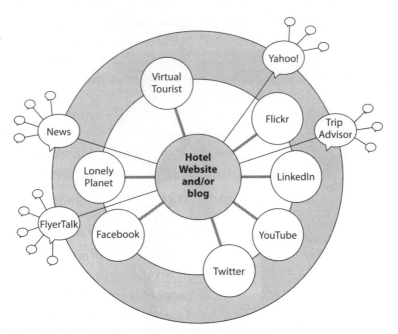

Figure 3.2 A sample publishing platform for a fictional hotel marketer

Also in this fictional hotel marketer's example in Figure 3.2, there is a variety of different networks in the outside ring. In the upper-right bubble on the outer ring, this marketer is finding a large number of unanswered travel- and hotel-related questions in Yahoo! Answers and other Q&A-related sites. The marketer has determined that answer sites should be a regular part of their outreach network, though not quite as involved as the primary publishing networks like Twitter and Facebook. Beyond Yahoo! Answers, they have also included Ask.com and Answers.com.

TripAdvisor is also on the fictional hotel marketer's radar for answering questions and responding to feedback about their properties. The marketer places particular importance in this network because TripAdvisor has heavy site traffic and is often the first results found for high-ranking travel searches in Bing, Yahoo!, and Google. Other sites that include travel reviews are also stemmed from the TripAdvisor conversation bubble and include Google Places among other sites. Rounding out the outside ring are FlyerTalk and other hotel-related forums, the comments section on the travel section of the *New York Times* website, and the other travel columns of other major online news sites.

Developing Your Community-Outreach and -Engagement Strategy

Developing your community- and audience-outreach strategy may very well be one of the toughest things you do in real-time marketing. It takes a lot of planning, careful practice, and development of your business voice and style. You will find yourself getting comfortable with network interaction and training others to do so. You may also want to seek outside help from an agency or consultant. Again, this is an iterative process of constantly developing a relationship with your audience (either passive or engaged), building up a network, identifying new opportunities, and publishing within your defined objectives. One of my clients once put it another way: *you are never done.* Community outreach is not a campaign-oriented initiative. It is an ongoing conversation between your company and your audience.

Although later chapters will cover community management in more detail, here are some key considerations as you begin to assemble your real-time marketing strategy and plan:

Resource Commitment Be prepared to allocate plenty of time with your real-time-engagement staff. It is not realistic to expect community managers to juggle multiple tasks and also respond live online at all times. As you determine the size of the opportunity, you will begin to see the amount of dedication involved, both on human-resources and budgetary levels.

Thought-Leadership Drivers While you may have multiple thought leaders, it is also important to keep your messages consistent while still allowing for the flexibility of natural language and conversation. Work toward consistency of your messaging across all networks.

Internal Technical Capabilities and Execution If you haven't already done so, start to get a handle on the technical capabilities of your organization. This will help you determine how much technical implementation will be done in-house, outside your company, or both.

Development of Outside Resources and Tools As it will be presented in later chapters, you should consider both free and paid tools for real-time marketing. Start becoming familiar with the basics now in order to understand them more subjectively later.

Setting an Audit, Research, Strategy, and Execution Timeline While real-time marketing is an ongoing process, ramping up is not. Set dates, times, and other expectations for completion, or else it will never happen.

Establishing Key Events in This Process Use this book to help define the key events and milestones in the planning and execution process. Not all of the items described here may apply to your situation, so isolate the ones that do, and set firm expectations and times for an outcome.

Some Final Thoughts About Real-Time-Strategy Development

This chapter has covered many aspects of getting started with a real-time marketing and publishing and strategy. I hope you are starting to absorb a lot of the moving parts and envisioning them as one bigger picture. To recap, here are some high-level elements of real-time content marketing strategy that you should be ready to take to the next level:

- Outlining the basic plan for your big-picture strategy
- Determining your business purpose for being active in real-time
- Rethinking your approach to user experience in real-time
- Getting into an "in-the-moment" frame of mind
- Being as consistent as possible with your online engagement and content efforts
- Setting realistic and attainable goals
- Understanding your potential return on investment for real-time marketing
- Planning to integrate your search and social teams, if they currently exist
- Being ready to address the tough questions about going real-time with your marketing strategy
- Formulating your strategy through research, content, platform, and outreach
- Becoming agile in your online execution
- Choosing your social spaces and content-publishing spaces
- Empowering your networks
- Determining your authentic voices
- Knowing how to structure your team using internal and external resources

Now that you have the high-level strategic aspects covered, let's get deeper into planning and execution, starting with the next chapter—on content-planning and strategy.

Market Research and Content Types

4

Developing a real-time marketing and publishing strategy requires more than just creating and deploying content, and in this chapter and the one that follows, I will cover the key elements and considerations for your content strategy. The Internet is like a living focus group. As a marketer, the key to understanding your audience better is to simply know where to look online, and how to both qualify and quantify the data you find. There is no need to sample audiences, or even guess at what your audience is thinking, as many of the tools and databases shown in this chapter are a raw reflection of the behaviors and tastes of their users. This chapter will show you where to look, and how to think about the data to turn into actionable insights. Also refer back to Chapter 3 for more tools to help you with your ongoing market-research strategy.

Chapter Contents
Market-research approach
Market-research tools
Keyword, social, and demographic research tools
Digital asset types

Keyword and Market Research

Much of this chapter focuses on the topic of market research, which will be used to help you define your audience and your content strategy altogether. The previous chapters discussed the importance of building personas and conducting surveys and, in some cases, focus groups, but here I will outline some of the key free and paid tools that will help you learn more about your target audience, what types of content to use, and what language your audience uses.

Keyword research can be considered *market research* in that a keyword is a vote for interest around a particular topic, theme, or other desire to seek and connect with relevant information. Social marketers should keep in mind that keyword research is not just for search, though, in the sense that you are just trying to get people to find you.

 Note: For social and real-time marketers, *keyword research also helps you find and seek out your audience* in order to connect to people at a greater level.

Keyword research and knowledge of online marketing tools should be considered a *mandatory skill* for any sophisticated search or social-media marketer. This chapter focuses more on how "search and social" marketers can use tools to help solve a variety of problems encountered regularly in content strategy and assessment.

Keyword Research and the Living Language of Your Audience

As you go through the various tools and research processes, keep in mind that search and social research is a living and breathing process. You will very likely be spending much more time on your up-front research the first time around. The language of your audience changes and does not remain fully static, so this initial research will help inform your content strategy, as well as provide you with a solid basis for future research to build upon. Keyword research and other types of research should be ongoing processes used by a wide variety of roles on your search and social teams, not only to seek new opportunities for content but also to validate existing ideas.

I discuss market research in many places throughout this book for one reason in particular: you should not base your entire content marketing strategy on your own assumptions about audience. You as a person and marketer are biased to a certain degree, whether a little bit or a lot. As a business owner and marketer, you are different in some ways from your target audience, no matter how you try to identify with them. You may be like them in more ways than not, but there are still differences. Making assumptions could be the difference between finding an entirely new market and revenue stream and not. On top of this, don't assume that the language of your audience does not iterate and change.

In your research, make certain you start with the right seed language. Seed language is the basic list of keywords that may stem off to areas of much greater theme detail. Pull this seed language from your internal stakeholders; from your surveys, analytics, past successful paid search campaigns, past marketing intelligence and efforts; and from your own experience. Think about the obvious terms, but seek out semantic meanings as well. Seed terms may be one word or multiple phrases. Sometimes it takes only one seed word to accomplish a huge difference in your business. Just *one word*. Take the time to get this part right. You may be surprised at what you find and where it takes your strategy.

Keyword, Social, and Demographic Research Tools

This section provides an overview of a variety of online marketing tools that are helpful in identifying your audience, the key places they hang out, the language they use online, and the demand for and gap in content that will help drive your real-time content strategy. Again, there are other methods of obtaining market data, such as conducting surveys, developing personas, and conducting primary research. However, here I will focus on the search and social tools that should be familiar to the search and social marketer. Within this mix, both free and paid tools are included, along with their basic function and a direct URL.

Trellian Keyword Discovery Trellian Keyword Discovery is a longtime favorite tool of search marketers; it sources data from more than 200 search engines worldwide. Like many other keyword tools, use this data directionally to reveal a potential level of interest for content. Free and paid versions are available, and Keyword Discovery has data for organic vs. paid search click-throughs at the keyword level, among many other features. See www.keyworddiscovery.com.

Google Keyword Tool This tool shows directional keyword data for searches in Google. Because it is sourced from actual query volume in the world's largest search engine, consider the Google Keyword Tool as a primary resource in every keyword-research project. Though the data is taken from the source, think of the data as being directional in that the numbers reported by Google are normalized and often skew much higher than the actual data marketers see in their own paid search campaigns and direct natural referrals. Also note that this tool will skew lower for terms and phrases with less search demand, in many cases showing zero searches for terms that may actually be producing traffic in analytics reports. Whether or not the data skews high, this is still a key tool to help you determine the relative search frequency and volume to expect in this engine. Figure 4.1 shows the results for the keyword *Lamborghini*, with estimated worldwide search volume along with many other stemmed and similar phrases. See https://adwords.google.com/select/KeywordToolExternal.

Figure 4.1 Google Keyword Tool example: Lamborghini

Google Traffic Estimator This is another useful keyword tool provided by Google, but rather than show you the estimated searches, it shows how much traffic you can expect based on your relative search media budget. Google Traffic Estimator URL is https://adwords.google.com/o/TrafficEstimator.

SEMrush This tool shows how your key competitors are targeting their content strategy and also reveals content gaps that they may not be capitalizing upon. If you have a search- or social-savvy competitor who has done a lot of their own research, using SEMrush is an opportunity to discover new content for testing or to start developing. Reports feature a site's number of rankings, estimated traffic volume, specific page rankings, and more. Keep in mind that you can receive traffic only if you have at least one page of matching optimized content, so this data will quickly reveal where your site stands in comparison to your competitors or similarly themed sites. See www.semrush.com.

Spyfu Spyfu is a "keyword spy" tool and shows where your competitors may be buying their keyword visibility in paid search. Reviewing your competitor's priorities in keyword media spend toward a particular keyword phrase or theme may indicate that these terms are profitable for your competitor. Exercise caution, because as paid-search expert Kevin Lee frequently says, aggressive bidding is an indicator of either "great intelligence or great ignorance." When reviewing your competitor's terms in paid search, be smart and test first before going "all in" on your own content strategy. Spyfu also provides insight into natural search data. See www.spyfu.com.

WordStream This tool claims to have a database of more than 1 trillion unique words and phrases and features keyword suggestions, grouping tools, and a "niche finder" that identifies keywords by profitability. It also offers a long-tail keyphrase database for competitive or advanced content marketers. See www.wordstream.com.

Wordtracker Wordtracker is another keyword tool used by many Internet marketing veterans. Wordtracker offers a nice balance to viewing data in other tools and helps validate and keep your other keyword data in check. See www.wordtracker.com.

Microsoft Advertising Intelligence Excel Plug-In This is one of my favorite tools, particularly because it leverages actual search data from the Bing search engine, operates directly in Excel, and is also free. By downloading the Microsoft Advertising Intelligence plug-in for Excel and entering your adCenter user and password into Excel, you can import keyword data directly into a spreadsheet for sorting and gaining keyword ideas. Considering that this tool pulls data directly from Bing, it is one of the most reliable tools for determining and projecting traffic and searches in that engine. Ad Intelligence reveals "similar" and "associated" keywords and also displays spiking and trending terms by recency, up to the last day, week, or month. It will also display demographics mapped to keyword data. Figure 4.2 shows the Ad Intelligence tab in Excel, as well as a travel-related keyword report. See http://advertising.microsoft.com/small-business/adcenter-downloads/microsoft-advertising-intelligence.

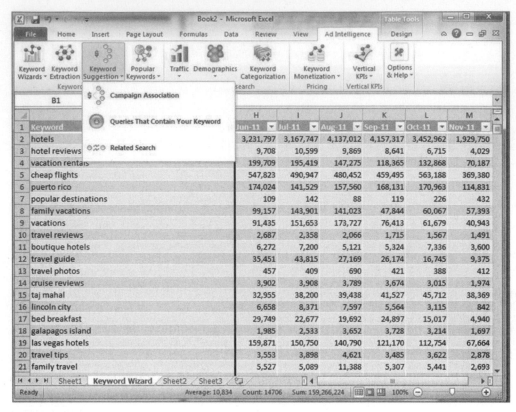

Figure 4.2 The Microsoft Advertising Intelligence plug-in for Excel

Google Insights for Search (Beta) Insights for Search is a highly valuable tool for revealing search and topical trend interest over time, as well as comparing topics or categorical interest. Insights for Search shows real-time data in its "rising searches" column and can also be embedded as an RSS feed into your iGoogle personalized page. In addition, you can view geographical and regional search interest, which is very helpful for local-ized or geographically based content strategies. Figure 4.3 shows a sample Insights for Search page comparing the worldwide search popularity for the words *apples*, *oranges*, and *bananas*. Just like the Keyword Tool, Google normalizes its data in Insights for Search, and this data can be viewed directionally, not as an exact representation of what you should expect in your marketing efforts. See www.google.com/insights/search/.

DoubleClick Ad Planner by Google This is an excellent free tool for finding your audience and finding out who visits a particular website in terms of age, education, gender, simi-lar sites visited, and interest, among other factors. This tool can be used to find the sites where your audience like to hang out and interact, and combined with your own detailed content analysis of these same sites, it can provide key direction in the types

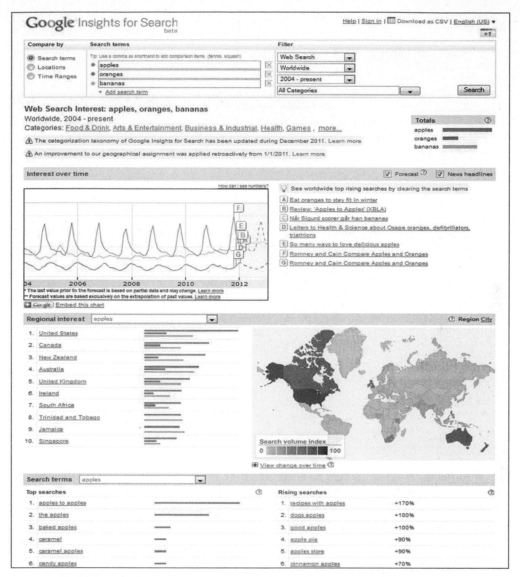

Figure 4.3 The Google Insights for Search report comparing worldwide interest for apples vs. oranges vs. bananas

of content your audience desires. Featured in Figure 4.4 is a site report for musical-instrument manufacturer Fender, showing audience statistics and similar sites visited. Overall, this is a very handy report for aligning site visitors with your own defined targets. In this example, several of the top similar sites shown are social networks dedicated to musical gear and discussion, providing great directional information for you to potentially add to your community-outreach and publishing strategy. See www.google.com/adplanner.

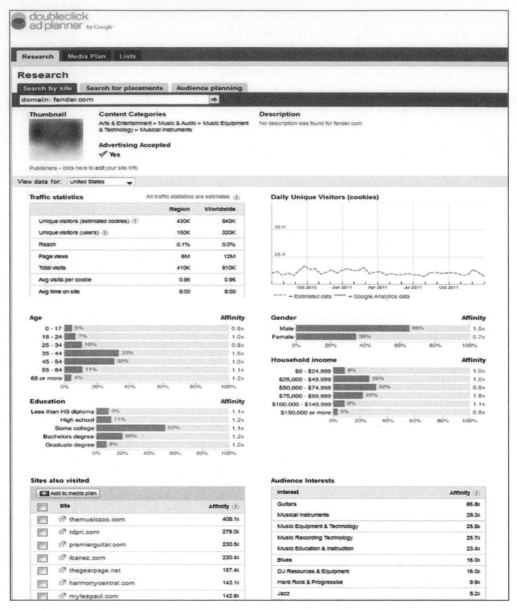

Figure 4.4 Demographic report on DoubleClick Ad Planner for musical-instrument manufacturer Fender

Google Suggest This keyword-research tool pops right up in the search box as you type and can be used in a variety of ways to help inform market-research strategy or individual keyword-targeting efforts. Google Suggest is a quick way to see stemmed phrases from a single word or phrase and can give hints about the topic areas that are top-of-mind for like-minded searchers. Google Suggest runs in near real-time, so spiking queries can be included in the suggestion stream. There is also a handy tool called

Übersuggest, which allows you to pull stemmed phrases from Google Suggest to add to a sublist and then copy into a text file. Overall, this is a great "social" way to get keyword suggestions from the greater search crowd in order to help inform your long-term community outreach and real-time content strategies. See www.google.com and http://ubersuggest.org.

Bing and Yahoo! keyword suggestions Similar to the Google Suggest tool, these queries skew toward the Bing or Yahoo! search audiences. Use them to help gain different ideas or validate other findings and market-research data. See www.yahoo.com and www.bing.com.

YouTube keyword suggestions If you are planning on creating a content channel on YouTube and looking for compelling ideas that video watchers are searching for, then look no further than the search box of YouTube to provide answers and ideas. Some searches in YouTube's keyword suggestion dropdown may lean toward an existing video, so you will have to think critically when determining which keywords point toward an existing asset and which ones are more generic and thematic. See www.youtube.com.

Scribe This tool was developed by the smart folks over at Copyblogger to help copywriters get quick keyword suggestions for their writing efforts and to ensure that their keywords are in the right place. It is a great way to assess your existing content and also pull in data from multiple sources at one time. Figure 4.5 shows a Scribe report for the term *seo software* and scores the document on a number of factors, including demographics, PPC value, social signals, and more. See www.scribeseo.com.

Figure 4.5 The Scribe report for seo software

Wordle This tool provides an elegant way to analyze site or page data at the keyword level and shows what keyword themes are being used on your own site or on a competitor's site. If you are bored with staring at spreadsheets, then Wordle is an instant cure, and its visual styling makes the weighting on keyword language plain for all to understand. You can either paste text into the tool or enter an RSS-feed URL to view your word cloud. Figure 4.6 shows a word cloud for the Great Finds blog at iCrossing.com and reveals that most of the keyword conversation weight revolves around *Facebook* and *social*, among many other terms. See `www.wordle.net`.

Figure 4.6 Wordle provides beautiful keyword displays that emphasize keyword weight within a blog feed or other supplied text.

How to Apply Keyword Research to Social Strategy

With all of these great tools for conducting keyword search, it is important to consider how you can use them in the social sense, not merely in the SEO and content senses. Remember, search engines do a lot of the heavy lifting needed to identify obscure networks. Using the right language and keywords is imperative for social marketers, in addition to search marketers. With this in mind, here are some ideas for using the previously described tools and keyword research to increase your opportunities in social and better serve your audience in social networks through conversation and content:

• Use target keywords to search for similar or hot conversations in Google+, Twitter, Facebook, or LinkedIn, using the search feature of each site.

- Use keywords to find relevant social networks in various search engines, particularly by entering keywords into Google Discussion search.

- Use keyword research to identify blogs or other content with an active readership or commenting community, in a variety of vertical blog search engines like Technorati or even Google Blog search.

- Use keywords and phrases as triggers in Google Alerts, news sites, or press-release services to get breaking news and conversations by keyword as things happen.

- Use research to change the way you speak to your audience by using more of *their language*, not the language that your business wants people to use.

- Use targeted keywords to better describe social content in the anchor text of links.

- Use keyword language to describe and name your social spaces on the Web, rather than using bland or nondescriptive language that your audience wouldn't know to search for.

- Use keyword research to help label the architecture and categories of your blog or website.

- Use keywords to better define the topic and focus of your posts on blogs or in social networks.

To the last point, your blog should be optimized at the page and the site level for the content you create. Chapter 6 will cover SEO copywriting style in more detail.

Keyword and Conversation Buzz Tools for Content and Search

As you begin to create content for a sharper edge of recency, you will discover there are many different tools that can help quickly assess conversation buzz at the keyword level in order to both jump into the conversation and create buzzworthy content. In the interest of performing market research more fluidly and "on the fly," here are some additional excellent tools you can use to better understand what people are searching for and what content they are consuming right now:

Google Trends Trends is a very useful tool in comparing popular topics and seasonal spikes in order to predict content that will soon be searched in real-time. Because this data comes from the source of the dominant search engine for most of the world, it should be monitored on a regular basis. Google Trends does not provide quantitative data but rather shows qualitative trends that can be useful when compared and benchmarked against other data. Figure 4.7 illustrates a Trends search for *tax preparation*, a seasonal keyword phrase that spikes in the first quarter of every year in the United States, without fail. Anticipating seasonal keywords and producing "evergreen" content that produces traffic from year to year will prepare you for the real-time search and social spikes to come and also enable you to benefit from these spikes every year (or at whatever frequency your seasonal keyword traffic occurs). See www.google.com/trends/.

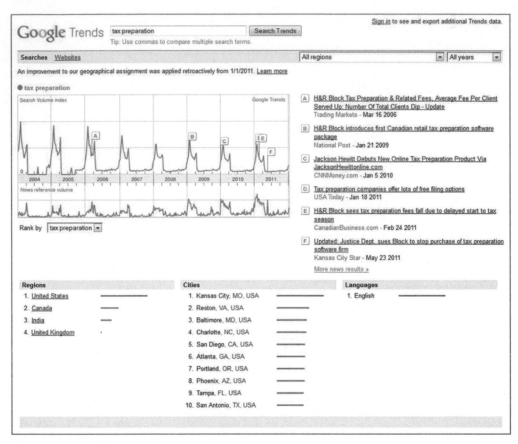

Figure 4.7 Google Trends

Google Hot Searches Google Hot Searches is an extension of Google Trends, and just as you may have guessed, it focuses on the last 24 hours of the hottest trending searches in Google Web and News search. If you study these queries for some time, you will see that this area of search often mirrors current conversations and status updates in social networks like Twitter, Google+, LinkedIn, and Facebook, as well as various discussion forums. Hot Trends offers a great way to quickly identify spiking content and is an essential read for any marketers working with news sites, entertainment sites, or social networks. Google Hot Searches is also available as an RSS feed, allowing you to push your results into your favorite feed reader to monitor real-time multiple feeds at the same time. Figure 4.8 shows a Hot Trends list for July 10, 2012, that features spiking search interest around entertainer Frank Ocean and athlete Hope Solo. See www.google.com/trends/hottrends.

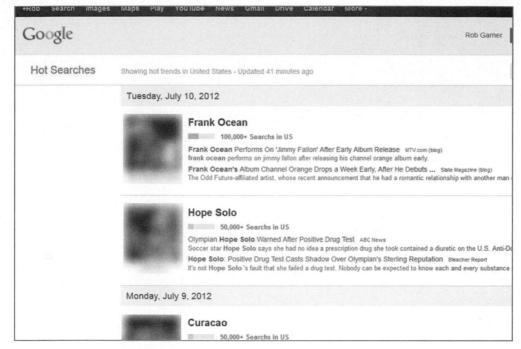

Figure 4.8 Google Hot Searches

Twitter Trending Topics on Home, Discover, and Search pages One of the kings of real-time buzz, Twitter Trends can help you identify all the memes, news, and trends as they happen. It also offers segmentation by geographic location. If you have a localized social presence, you should set your location parameters accordingly. But be careful, because Trends is sometimes the target of hackers who push up meaningless hash tags into the trending stream just for kicks. Monitoring Twitter Search at the keyword level is one of the best methods for monitoring real-time discussion. In fact, as I was writing Chapter 1 of this book, a rare earthquake occurred in my location of Dallas, Texas. Because I was sitting at my computer when it occurred, I quickly searched Twitter and discovered that other people had tweeted about it, before I even felt it myself. See www.twitter.com.

Google Alerts The Google Alerts email and RSS alert system is one of the oldest forms of real-time search. When you set your alert trigger to As-It-Happens, Google will send you a result *almost immediately as it is crawled and indexed*. When using advanced keyword operators, alerts can be very handy in identifying breaking news and content around a particular topic and for competitive research. For busier queries, set your email subscription to once a day or once a week, or view RSS feeds in real-time using iGoogle or other feed readers. Figure 4.9 shows the Google Alerts setup interface set to feed new results As-It-Happens. See www.google.com/alerts.

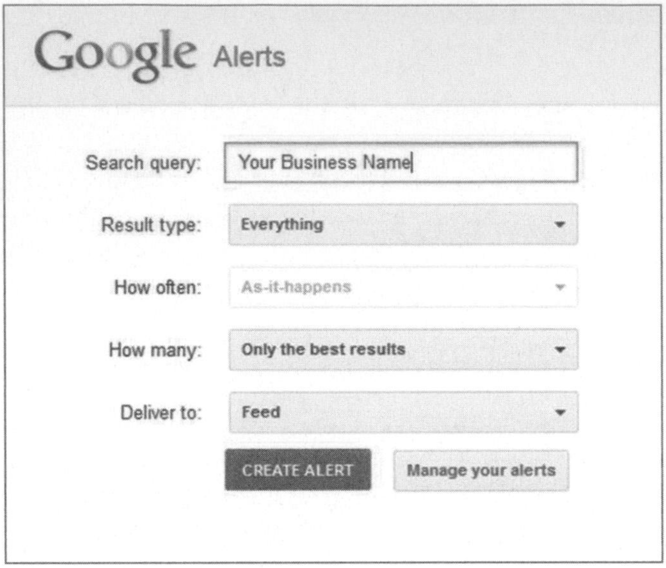

Figure 4.9 Google Alerts

Google+ Real-Time Search Google's Real-Time Search offering is in many ways the ultimate search and social combination and is detailed in Chapter 2, "Understanding Search and Social." Though it started as a segmented form of web search and once had its own stand-alone URL, it is now the search function within Google+. It continues to expand with the evolution of Google+ as part of the technology behind Search Plus Your World.

Google News This news source can help you gauge the popularity of a given topic at the keyword level. Bigger stories will have more content sources, whereas less buzzworthy or newsworthy topics may have few results, if any. See http://news.google.com.

Bing's Twitter and Facebook Search Bing is currently the only major search engine directly tapped into both Twitter and Facebook data and provides an excellent social search engine at www.bing.com/social. View current keyword, search trends and hash tags over the last hour, last day, or last week for Twitter, Facebook, or both.

eBay Pulse eBay Pulse is a section in a real-time popularity report with a sales and retail skew and provides data on most-popular searches, as well as most-watched items. This is incredibly useful data for retailers or retail content providers. See http://pulse.ebay.com.

Think with Google Real-Time Insights Finder This site is provided by Google as a dashboard for multiple real-time insights using Google tools. This site has lots of handy stats, insights, research, and other data related to the real-time Web. See www.thinkwithgoogle.com/insights/tools.

Questions for Your Audience Assessment

The tools addressed in this chapter will help you answer many of the questions about your audience. Turning data into actionable strategies requires both your amazing creative and analytical brain and your business knowledge. Using the preparations listed in Chapter 3, "Ramping Up for a Real-Time Content Marketing Strategy," along with reviewing your analysis using the tools in this chapter, you should answer the following questions to synthesize your data into a clear picture and definition of the audience you intend to target, from both a content perspective and a social perspective:

- How does your audience search, and what keywords do they use? (Hint: use the Google AdPlanner Tool to identify your audience, and review the top keywords for natural search in SEMRush.)

- Do their questions get answered in social networks on a regular basis, or do they often go unanswered? Are the people giving the answers knowledgeable, or are they partially or wholly misinformed? Why or why not? (Hint: use targeted keywords and search forums, discussion sites, comments in blogs, review sites, and answers sites to see whether all questions are being answered authoritatively and helpfully.)

- Which websites does your audience use on a regular basis? Which sites may be considered similar, from a topical and demographic basis?

- What are the common questions from your audience throughout the content-consumption and decision-making processes?

- How do you currently address these needs through participation and content-inventory? How would you change your strategy based on the new findings?

- What do the demographic tools tell you about the audiences who visit your competitors' websites? Do these audiences match your targets?

- Are you choosing the right competitors to match up against in your site assessment? Why or why not?

- Does your business cater to a particular age group or across multiple generations?

- How does your audience divide up in terms of being content consumers, sharers, participators, or creators? How do you plan to engage each type of user, and will you do so on-site, off-site, or both? (Also see Chapter 13, "Social Media Management," and Forrester's definition of social-media behaviors for deeper definitions of audience classification.)

These are just a few of the key questions to be asking about your audience, and you should also be thinking up your own questions that are more subjective to your business space. Be creative, and poke as many holes in your assumptions and theories as possible. Doing so will allow you to find new streams of traffic and build up your networks, which ultimately leads to meeting your stated business goals.

Types of Digital Assets

In developing your overall content strategy, it is important to fully understand a variety of content types. In the next few pages, I will describe some of the basic digital asset types to consider for your content strategy. It is important to evaluate each of the types of content that your audience might consume, share, converse about, or create, and not to be dismissive of all of the potential options. Some of the asset types described here have their own dedicated social networks, with sharing and community built around presentations, images, and videos, among others. All digital asset types can be optimized, just like a web page can be optimized. Please note that some of these assets will be described at greater length later in the book.

Text Text-based content will be a foundation of your content strategy, no matter what vertical your business is in. Text-based assets run the gamut of short conversations in status updates to long or short informational articles, and they are the crux of many other asset types listed in this section. Many of the search and keyword trigger systems will read and interpret your text assets literally, so be cognizant of what you write, how you label it, and where you put it. Having a mastery of the written word will be the most critical role in your asset strategy, even if you specialize in images, video, or other nontext assets in your strategy.

Infographics Infographics have a long history in publishing and provide engaging content in an image-based "one-stop shop." Making useful and unique infographics attracts direct traffic, social sharing, and valuable backlinks that help push up your visibility in search engines. Like other image assets, infographics should be properly labeled in the image metadata and also fed out via RSS to allow embedding and commentary on third-party websites. Many creators also put their infographics into a Creative Commons license, which allows them to be repurposed freely around the Internet and in other mediums, as long as certain provisions of the license are observed (more about Creative Commons later in the book). Figure 4.10 shows an iCrossing infographic that displays the key findings in a major study of millions of search-query referrals, showing the top natural click-through rates by ranking position.

Video When the topic of the "world's biggest search engines" comes up, most people don't stop to consider that YouTube is a world leader in search, second only to Google Web Search in terms of sheer query volume. As you progress with your market-research strategy, you will likely find that your targeted audience prefers to consume online video in some fashion, and therefore video should become a primary part of your real-time publishing strategy. Creating video goes well beyond YouTube, however, and you will need to pay attention to the details of production, optimization, engagement, and the general management of an online video channel, both on your site and on third-party video networks. Having a presence on YouTube will help your video-asset visibility in Google search, and a video XML site map should also be included if your assets are hosted in owned spaces. Video optimization and platform considerations will be discussed at greater length in Chapter 11, "Video and Images."

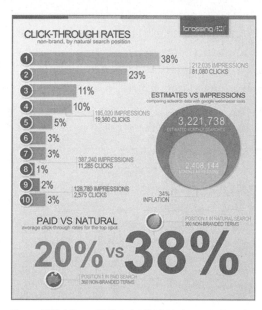

Figure 4.10 Infographic that visually displays a research study on SERP referral data

Images Digital photographs and other image assets can provide an amazing amount of value to your business in the amount of direct search traffic and social sharing it may attract and the volume of search traffic it may trigger from image-based search engines. Images can be optimized in the filename, alt text attributes, titles, descriptions, and other metadata, and the pages in which they may be embedded. There are also entire image-based social media sites like Flickr, which are dedicated entirely to image files and the sharing and community built around these assets. Many savvy search marketers report that Google Images refers a dominant share of all of their search traffic. More information will be provided in a later chapter about the deeper optimization aspects of images. Overall, businesses should consider different ways to use images in their marketing efforts, because the potential opportunities are tremendous. Evaluating image content and audience usage of image engines ia a fundamental part of your content audit and market research.

Applications When you consider developing an application as a primary part of your content-publishing strategy, think about what your users need and what currently does not exist in the marketplace. An application can be developed for a website, within a social network, or for a mobile device. All of these scenarios have their own search and social deployment considerations.

Databases If you have a useful database, getting it in online and optimized for search makes it a useful tool for your audience and can help build out the breadth of the unique pages on your website at the domain level. When promoting large databases, focus on using unique content, but avoid explosively growing your site by 100 times overnight. When deploying any large number of pages on your site, work with an experienced SEO to determine how to effectively deploy this content, based on the volume of pages you will be creating. Figure 4.11 shows information specialist Melissa Data and the wide number of search-database applications it offers for free to its users.

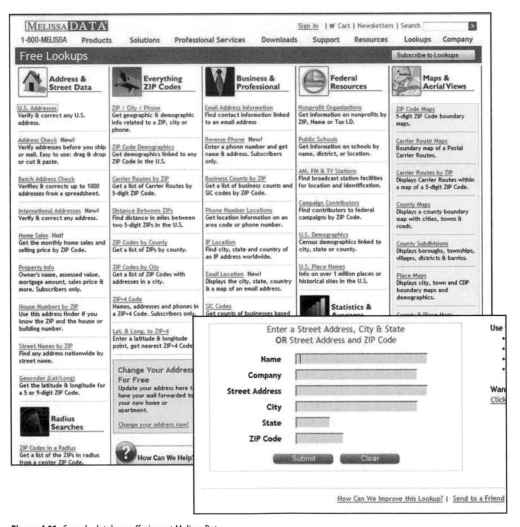

Figure 4.11 Sample database offerings at Melissa Data

PDFs and Document Files Just like any other web page, Portable Document Format (PDF) files and other text-based files such as Microsoft Word are fully crawlable and retrievable by search engines. Your content strategy may involve putting factual or recorded documents or white papers online. For search, it is recommended that a text version of a PDF, not image-based text docs, be used.

Microsoft PowerPoint If you are a business-to-business (B2B) marketer or often present at conferences, you may find that Microsoft PowerPoint slide shows can help convey your messaging. If so, then a channel for presentations just might be what your audience is looking for. Because PowerPoint files have a textual layer, search engines can grab these files and retrieve them in standard web search. Using the right keywords in your slide titles and body text can help your files get found by a wider audience. There is also an entire social network dedicated to PowerPoint presentations, called SlideShare (acquired in 2012 by LinkedIn), and it also features PDFs and text documents. One other great aspect of SlideShare is that it creates an RSS feed of your presentations, which can be embedded into outside feed readers and third-party blogs. Even LinkedIn has a SlideShare plug-in to pull your presentation directly into your personal profiles. Figure 4.12 features a screen capture of my own presentation and white paper channel on SlideShare, with a document viewer, statistics, and more features.

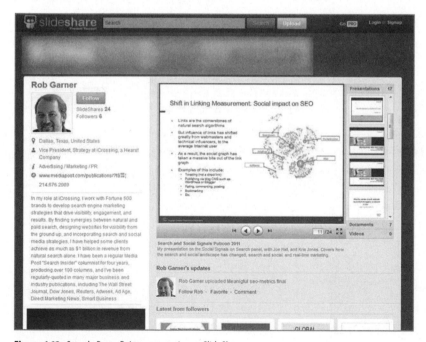

Figure 4.12 Sample PowerPoint presentation on SlideShare

Live and Recorded Webinars Beyond producing static PowerPoint slide presentations, offering them as recorded webinars is a great way to elicit feedback from your audience and also get the most out of your presentation efforts. WebEx and GoToMeeting are two of the biggest providers of live and recorded webinars. Note that most of these services require a fee or subscription plan.

Audio The importance of sound files can be very subjective depending on the type of business you run. If you are in music production, the sound file will likely be one of the most critical asset types, so optimization, channel selection, promotion, distribution, and markup will all be critical. Your use of audio can range from producing a live podcast to adding sound files and recordings to blog posts or providing an audio file of a presentation, conversation, music, or interview.

Press Releases I have listed press releases as an asset type, mainly because they can be composed of various types of digital assets bundled and distributed across a press wire, and run passively in syndicated channels. Just like a text document or web page, the press release should be optimized with all key elements, including the title, headings, page body, reverse keyword and category triggers, and anchor text. Many press-release services also allow video and image attachments, so the entire bundle should be optimized before it is sent. Press-release optimization will be discussed in more detail in Chapter 8.

Email Email is the original "social" asset and distribution method. Your content can be deployed directly to your existing customers and audiences via direct automated messages, personalized messages, opt-in distribution lists, and opt-in mail lists, among other ways. Email is very much a real-time asset, and when properly enabled, it can respond automatically to specific needs based upon permission settings (think about order tracking or other types of status updates), and it is a key method to communicate in a personal way in one-to-one and one-to-many manners. When you consider that emails have historically been forwarded or shared within networks of networks, then email fits the primary definition of what is considered social in modern marketing terms.

Really Simple Syndication (RSS) RSS and XML feeds are like a reverse website-publishing process. Rather than pulling in people to view your pages, data, and information, these feeds push data, links, and other information outside of your domain, into an interface providing additional functionality or usability features. Enabling RSS is critical to getting your fresh content found in both search and social spaces. When deployed by recency factors—in other words, the newest result first—it also makes RSS one of the most real-time of the assets in this entire list. Almost all of the assets described in this section can be deployed via RSS and are a critical link between your audience, your networks, and your search visibility.

That wraps up the market-research and asset-type discussion for this chapter. As mentioned throughout the chapter, much of this content will be described in more detail in later chapters, focusing on how to optimize these assets individually. The next chapter will specifically focus more on creating engaging content for these asset types, as well as how to combine multiple types to create compelling, shareable, and linkable content.

Content Strategy: Auditing, Assessment, and Planning

5

This chapter will focus on planning for actual content strategy and development, examining real-time publishing in more depth, and performing basic content audits and competitive assessments. It will also address considerations for editorial and publishing planning and how to think about content marketing in a different way. Some of the additional concepts include thinking critically about content, going with a big content strategy, and how to apply a keyword approach to finding content and conversations in social spaces.

Chapter Contents

Creating a content-auditing and -assessment approach

Planning the roles on your content team

Creating an editorial plan and publishing calendar

Creating a style guide

How to Think About Strategy, Planning, and Assessment

As you read this section, keep in mind that the process of building a cohesive content plan and strategy requires a number of resources. In addition to reading this book, be sure to read content blogs on this topic to stay continuously informed of changes as well as other books and periodicals. Joe Pulizzi and the Content Marketing Institute publish a print magazine on this topic, and Arnie Kuenn has also published a book that is complementary to this one (*Accelerate!*). Other key blogs to monitor include Copyblogger, ClickZ, Mashable, Search Engine Watch, and Search Engine Land. WebmasterWorld is also a popular forum for discussion. Also check out the appendix in this book for additional resources.

Getting into the details of a search and social publishing strategy can be overwhelming at first to even the most experienced online marketers. It is, therefore, important to begin your strategic planning with some high-level thinking; specifically, you'll want to know what you are doing, learn how to think the way that most successful search and social marketers think, and teach yourself to be nimble and adaptive to the overall process. Being adaptive begins with the understanding that you must think critically and be a creative problem solver to be successful in real-time marketing.

Be Creative, Think Critically, and Learn to Solve Problems

While this chapter focuses on the tools, planning, auditing, and other preparations for producing real-time content and dialogue, the source of much of your ongoing research should result from your own, or your team's, creative and critical thinking. In short, all the tools in the world can't replace human analysis for translating what your data really means to your strategy. No book can solve every problem for your business, but applying these lessons in the right way can *help you help yourself* and your business.

Tools and data sources should inspire ideas that will further your own testing and execution. Knowing your tools well will cultivate more creativity in your efforts. There will be times when you or your team members are absolutely exhausted from seeing the same old data, and I challenge you to constantly strive to compare your data in different lights and apply it to your strategy in a different way. Maybe last month you viewed the top-referring keywords, so this month, look at the bottom of the barrel and ask where this traffic is coming from. Are there any new insights? Are there any unique ideas for new content? Are there any ways to group these terms into a unifying theme? Why or why not?

This book will provide the seed for some of your ideas, but ideally it should spark some of the creativity and critical thinking that is necessary to execute a real-time strategy. Brainstorm, bounce ideas between you and your teams, and exchange ideas with like-minded audiences in social networks. Ask "why?" Remain creative and encourage ideas, and your content will never stagnate.

Think Big: Approach Content Strategy Like a Forest, Not a Weed

One thing you can bank on in any engaging content strategy is that quality content wins for the long term. As a real-time marketer and publisher, there is a greater ongoing challenge to create and distribute a *higher quantity* of *higher-quality* content. When you begin to take the view of marketing strategy as media publishing, your focus shifts toward becoming an engaging authority at the *site level*, like a hub, as opposed to just producing individual pages. In addition to building volume at the site level, you are working toward credibility in the eyes of your audience. The bottom line is this: if you are planning to succeed with your online publishing strategy, you need to play big on both quality and quantity. You need to look at the big-picture opportunity, and you need to embrace what makes the best sense for your business. Thinking "strategically" about content means considering what the opportunity is and not getting off-track by concerning yourself with 1, 10, or 100 pages of content when the real opportunity is about getting your site to 10,000, 100,000, or *1 million* or more pieces of unique content. Remember, *content* means many different things, such as databases, status updates, articles, user-generated content, and more, so don't get overwhelmed by seemingly insurmountable numbers. These larger numbers are attainable for small proprietors to enterprise businesses, but you must be smart in the way your content strategy is approached.

Search provides many great lessons about ramping up and building out a robust real-time digital publishing strategy. In search-engine optimization, content must be scaled in a way that enables a search engine to recognize a site as being a substantive resource, and trust is calculated at both the page and domain levels. When developing a new content strategy, I analyze the top competitors' sites for many different keyword sets. In doing so, I have consistently found that the top sites for the broadest groups of themed keyword lists (both head and long-tail lists, and any mix thereof) have the following characteristics in common at varying levels:

- They are most often well-written and well-edited.
- They have significant word counts at both the page level and the site level.
- Highly visible sites provide substantial content that backs up the theme of the site, as it relates to the respective keyword set.
- Their site content is generally engaging and good enough that people would want to link and share it without being asked.
- Each site has a large number of high-quality unique pages within the domain.

Table 5.1 shows a chart of the most popular domains ranked in order of visible top-10 rankings for a (truncated) list of 225 highly searched travel and hotel-based keyword phrases. The top sites not only meet the aforementioned characteristics but also include themed sites (for example: Expedia) and sites outside the core theme (for example, Wikipedia).

Domains	Total Page Rankings in Google, Yahoo!, and Bing for kw set
www.expedia.com	127
www.fivestaralliance.com	118
www.tripadvisor.com	107
travel.yahoo.com	94
www.orbitz.com	51
www.hotels.com	32
en.wikipedia.com	29
www.allstays.com	24
www.hotelrooms.com	21
www.allstays.com	18

The bottom line is that digital-content strategy is better served by "going big" than by tending to a smaller garden of 100 to 500 pages or a few videos, apps, or images. It takes a lot of work to prepare a large-sized content strategy, but doing the following will help you devise a meaningful foundation:

- Conduct a full audit of the content on your site (and off-site on social networks) to understand what you already have.

- Identify duplicate content areas, both on- and off-site, and query the various engines to learn how many unique pages they have indexed for your site at the domain level (use the query operator *site:domain.com* in both Bing and Google to find your unique pages).

- Conduct a full content gap analysis to see where content is lacking for your target term set at the keyword level. You must have at least one page of themed and targeted content for each ranking you want to achieve. Competitive terms may require even more supporting content.

- Review any offline archives to determine opportunities for expanding your digital-content depth by placing this content online.

- Ensure that you are building out thematically, with a sound architecture.

- As you prepare to scale up, continue to follow your strategic and tactical plans, but consider changes or new ideas along the way.

Thinking big with your content approach not only increases visibility in natural search results but also provides a large bank of content to refer to in social media. I will discuss audience-management strategies for sharing your existing content inventory in networks in Chapter 13, "Social Media Management."

Understanding Keyword Demand

Keyword demand (also commonly referred to as *keyword research*) simply means looking deeper and more strategically at keyword metrics in order to determine how many people are searching for a particular theme and how much content competition exists in that respective keyword space. As the phrase implies, for every keyword or phrase, there is an expectation or demand for content. So, for example, a search for the keyword phrase and theme of *digital camera reviews* is very popular, and many sites have this content available. Real-time content marketers can capitalize on keyword demand for newer and fresher terms, where there is little content available to match a particular term (think of a newly released digital camera model and how a well-thought-out article can catapult your content into the mainstream conversation). Overall, a solid strategic content plan takes keyword demand and research into primary consideration, in addition to measuring a marketer's existing content supply (or gaps in content) for the targeted keyword sets.

Natural search practitioners have long touted the opportunities for marketers to become publishers, mainly because of their exposure to keyword research and the knowledge that there must be at least one page of content to even get in the search-ranking game. Fundamentally, a search query is a request for content, and many queries go unanswered through the content shown in results. One of the great marketing opportunities of keyword demand is to find areas where there is little to no competition from other publishers and to analyze your own content strategy to determine where the gaps between your targeted keyword set exist.

One company that capitalized on keyword demand in a big way is Demand Media, led by its CEO and longtime digital visionary Richard Rosenblatt (also of MySpace). He realized that there were massive quantities of keyword searches across a wide spectrum that lacked substantive content matches to meet the intentions of the searchers, and he proceeded to create a content network that met these specific needs. Soon, Demand Media content from eHow and many other sites began ranking highly for search queries. His networks became popular through natural search and social promotion, eventually ranking in the top 500 networks on the entire Internet. No matter how big or small their content strategies, astute marketers would be well served by following Rosenblatt's example of looking for unmet keyword opportunities for their own businesses.

Understanding Conversational Demand

Conversational demand is a complementary form of keyword demand, but it requires different tools and research to extract the variety of content types that your audiences are seeking. Simply put, conversational demand is any conversation in a network that may present a question, a problem, a desire for dialogue, or a suggestion, and it requires a live real-time response or acknowledgment from a marketer. Identifying conversations presents marketers with the opportunity to be useful, engage with an audience, show thought leadership, integrate feedback into products and services, or simply solve a problem. This process is similar to search-engine seeking and finding, except the expectation in social networks is that a proactive human will be able to provide an answer to a query. Furthermore, it is about taking the relevancy process directly to the audience, wherever they may be. In essence, a question asked in social spaces is parallel to a keyword being entered in a search box. A real-time marketer must seek out these questions using search techniques, but provide a human response.

Ultimately, any unanswered question in social is still an unanswered query, even in the search sense. As a proactive search and social marketer, the process is just as much about *seeking out the question* as it is to *providing answers, feedback, and engagement* in a relevant way. The comparison between conversation demand and the early history of search engines is incredibly similar. By addressing conversation demand for both brand and generic themes, an opportunity exists to engage with these social-network participants in a sincere way.

Conversational demand is a new concept for identifying social activity and requires an analyst with interpretive skills. Here are several questions to consider when utilizing a conversation-demand approach to help guide your active participation in social networks:

- What is your audience looking for, and what specific keywords and language do they use?
- Where do they seek this information and conversation?
- How do they communicate (do they prefer blogs, forums, Twitter, and so on)?
- What type of digital assets does your audience prefer to consume?
- Will you be ready to communicate properly when a key conversation arises?
- Will you be ready to communicate in a way that fits your overall voice?
- Do you have an FAQ that answers the most common questions about your business?

Determining and assessing conversational demand is much more complex than assessing keyword demand through tools such as the Google Traffic Estimator or Keyword Tool. Social conversation demand can be assessed in a single social network or a variety of social networks. The main methods are the same, though effective tools and smart brains are required. Your company's answer to assessing conversational demand might exist on LinkedIn, Facebook, Google Discussions, comments on blogs, smaller or lesser-known social networks, or any combination of these.

Search expertise can make your social efforts become much more effective. Conversations occur all across the Internet and other networks, and as I have discussed about the innovation of real-time search in previous chapters, a robust algorithm is necessary to surface all of this information in a useful way. It also takes keen keyword-research search skills to identify these conversations in order to know how to locate social conversations in a search engine or other online monitoring services (even third-party tools such as HootSuite and Radian6 have characteristics similar to many search-based research tools).

While search optimizers and marketers are accustomed to prioritizing their own keyword lists around the most searched and popular terms in their respective areas of search, conversational demand–seekers must utilize an entirely different set of keywords and modifiers. For example, the priority keywords for an online electronics retailer might include *digital cameras*, *LCD TVs*, and *laptop computers*. These terms have high popularity, a segment of intention that includes a desire to purchase, and massive targeted traffic opportunities coming from search engines alone.

When this same retailer begins to seek the conversational demand in social networks, an entirely new set of words should be used to complement the popular terms. These words and phrases provide a critical connection to the retailer's audience and include the following:

- *what should I*
- *where do I*
- *how many*
- *I am considering*
- *looking for*
- *what is the*

When used in the context of electronics retail and combined with other priority terms, there is a massive launching point for this retailer to seek active engagement in social networks and around the Internet. Figure 5.1 shows some questions that might be used for an electronics-retail engagement strategy, captured from Google Suggest.

Figure 5.1 Google Suggest reveals a goldmine of social keyword research for the term *laptop*.

Figure 5.2 shows how to take these new queries and search Google Discussions to find key ways to begin engaging in social communities. Notice that there are 1,150,000 resulting pages for the query within the prior 30-day period. Although these are not all exact matches, they are still a good indicator that this is a popular and fresh topic area. There is also an opportunity for an electronics-retail expert to be very helpful toward a wide variety of communities, in the same way they might answer this question in person at the store.

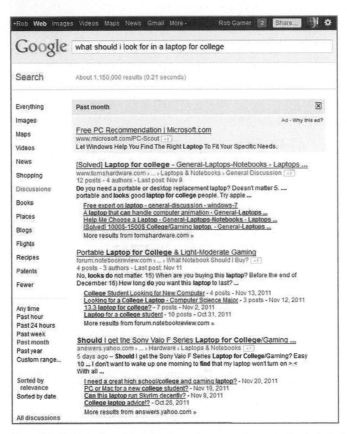

Figure 5.2 Searching for social conversation and engagement opportunities for *laptop* in Google Discussions

Overall, these are just a few suggested conversational modifiers. As you apply modifiers to your standard priority keyword set, use tools like the Google Keyword Tool, Google Suggest, and Yahoo! suggestion dropdown box to discover new keywords that will lead you to current conversations across the Internet.

A Factual Content Approach to Conversational Demand

There are a few major obstacles that can hinder effectively measuring and acting upon keyword demand, and this becomes even truer for conversation demand. When a marketer goes out to measure the space for either brand or generic keyword terms (or brand and generic conversations), there is a broad commonality that breaks into two key areas: the factual, and the more PR-based and sensitive questions about the brand.

Often the show-stopper for any marketing work that includes the word *social* is the perception that a marketer is "encroaching" in any areas that might otherwise fall into the domain of public relations, crisis management, legal, or brand management. This is a problem that is reflective of large businesses, in that they often consider any-thing labeled "social" as being owned by a certain group within the business. The busi-nesses that think this way have not come to terms with the fact that *social is something that runs through all parts of a business*. Therefore, it is important to avoid viewing search, social, or real-time as a channel or campaign or as a small department that should be sheltered from the rest of your organization. This is an important point to acknowledge as you are ramping up, because marketers who want to engage effectively are often completely locked out of the process because of the incorrect perception that they are moving in on someone else's territory. This is the not the fault of the market-ers, who are simply doing their jobs; to the contrary, it is a problem that will come back to bite at the organization's overall marketing efforts. In consideration of these perceptions, there is another way of looking at social engagement and conversational demand that should be appealing to both marketers and other stakeholders within an organization who interact socially.

In assessing conversation demand, marketers who focus on the *factual for their primary content strategy* will have more than enough to address for a long period to come. This does not mean that sensitive issues will be avoided or should not be dealt with, but it provides a simple framework for marketers to work within social spaces.

Both keywords and conversations can be divided into either the factual or the PR/crisis–related. Within this purview, the duties of the real-time marketer and real-time communications professional are clearly divided in a useful and meaningful way. Extending this concept into conversation demand, a marketing team has more freedom to address the factual happenings around their brand in various networks, addressing them in a live setting and directing network users to the proper factual content.

Dealing with the factual means utilizing the existing vetted information on your website and affords the engaged real-time content marketer with the ability to answer questions outside of the website. As organizations grow their extended networks in a variety of ways, the marketer can be the first line in helping identify crises or sensitive situations that a business might otherwise have missed entirely.

For example, if you conduct an audit of various conversations around the Internet about your company, you may find that people are asking about a well-known facet of your history or value proposition that is already available on your website. Converse with them, answer them directly as best as possible, and direct them to the appropriate area or page on your site. If a person inquires about a new store location, help them out by answering their question, create that page for future inquiries, and point them to another site if more information is needed. You can answer questions and create content about the facts of your business and generic conversation space all day long. In every vertical space, the conversation opportunity is so massive that you may not be able to address it all for many years.

By addressing factual conversational demand in a sincere and meaningful way, there is more than enough potential dialogue to engage with an audience who already wants to talk to *you* in real-time.

Targeting Unpredictable Real-Time Search Queries

At the 2007 Supernova conference, Google's VP of engineering, Udi Manber, made a startling revelation. Of the searches conducted on Google on any given day, 20 to 25 percent *had never been searched before* (www.readwriteweb.com/archives/udi_manber_search_is_a_hard_problem.php). That's right: 20 to 25 percent of all queries were entirely new in terms of either syntax, typographic variation, or emerging topic, and they had never been entered into a Google search box before. Google has since updated this statistic from 20 to 25 percent to 15 percent at its real-time marketing research site (www.thinkwithgoogle.com), but this is still a massive segment of their daily searches.

This tidbit of information has immense implications for cutting-edge search and social marketers who want to take their visibility to the next level:

- First, with this high volume of previously unknown searches, there is no possible way any marketer or researcher can predict all or even part of these queries or predict or dictate the language of their audience and customers in any timely manner.

- Second, it proves that the keyword language of your audience is iterative and ever-changing, just like language and linguistics. Don't harbor any illusions that keyword-research efforts are "one and done." In fact, this statistic proves quite the opposite. Researching and refreshing your data on a daily or real-time basis will prove itself beneficial in a real-time publishing strategy or in any search and social strategy.

- Third, in lieu of some sort of future mind-reading keyword and thought-prediction device, the next best thing to capitalize on real-time language development is to enable real-time user-generated content communities and collaboration. By doing so, new keyword topics are created and indexed in search in real-time and also consumed by social audiences. Humans are the keepers of the living process of language development, and they create links and pages at the inception of these new words. Unfortunately, there is no mind-reading tool, and you can't guess what your audience is thinking at such a scale.

While you are creating and participating in much of your own content, there is another, bigger opportunity that lies ahead for you to capture real-time conversations and search traffic by enabling real-time communities. Stay tuned, because this topic is covered in greater depth in Chapter 8, "Blogs, Google News, and Press Releases."

Content Auditing, Strategy, and Assessment

At this point you will likely have an idea of the direction you may be headed with your content strategy. But first you need to balance your initial approach with a thorough assessment of where your content strategy truly stands in its currents state. The following sections will not only help you on your way to producing a viable real-time content strategy, but also prevent major obstacles that can greatly inhibit your success down the road.

Performing a Content Audit

While the SEO aspects of a site audit run very deep and are often a full-time responsibility in themselves for your SEO team, there is a short recipe that real-time and social-media marketers can use to determine how well their content resonates in both search engines and their social audiences. As you begin a content assessment for your site, you are essentially looking for two things:

- What you have
- What you don't have

I outlined a number of tools in the previous chapter to analyze your audience, to understand how they consume content, and to inform your content strategy. It is important to ensure that you have a direction when using different tools. Here are some primary questions to consider when using tools to inform your content strategy and to find out where your site stands in its current state:

- How many *unique* pages reside within your domain or domains?
- How many pages within your site match a given phrase or set of phrases?
- How much of your site's content is duplicated or repurposed in other parts of your site or on other sites outside of your domain?
- How well does your content inventory match up to your targeted keyword lists? Does your content support your keywords in the literal sense, at the page and site theme levels?
- Is your site optimized for search engines and also optimized for social networks (shareable, portable, keyword-friendly, researched, and so on)?
- How fresh is your content, and how often do you publish?
- How many backlinks does your site have at the domain level?

- When checking your analytics and log files, do you notice any distinct patterns of declining or increasing traffic? Why or why not?
- Does your site push content out via RSS and XML feeds?

Each of these questions will have different subjective answers, depending on the outcome of your testing and diagnostics. If you don't know the answer, ask a search-optimization consultant, join a search-optimization forum or network, or hire an agency or in-house team that can solve these issues for you. In addition to the previous questions, also consider the following when assessing the current state of your own content approach:

- Do you have any content that is not being utilized online?
- How does your existing content resolve problems for your audience, as directly observed in your market research?
- Are there any opportunities to assist your audience through content?
- Are you solving problems for your users through content outside of your website in networks?
- Are all of your content creators and stakeholders aware of the basic processes of how content is produced and disseminated in search and social networks?
- Are there any organizational issues that prevent your content from being produced or approved in a timely manner? If so, how can this be resolved?
- Which content platforms are you currently using, and what new types may be needed?
- Does your content-management system create any technical obstacles for search visibility?

Content Assessment

Continuing deeper into content assessment will require more site reviews not just for your own properties but also for your competitors. If you are just getting started, you should first focus your analysis only on direct and indirect competitors. When using the previously mentioned content tools to analyze your site, here are some other key actions you should be addressing for important areas of your content strategy:

Identify Your Domain Name (or Multiple Domains) This may seem to be a no-brainer step, but it is a very important one in understanding the full scope of content visibility in both search and social networks. Make sure you have identified all unique domains (Domain1.com, Domain2.com) as well as all subdomains (Sub.domain1.com, Sub2.domain1.com) in your content network.

Define Your Key Competitors—Both Direct and Indirect In both the search and social spaces, you will have direct business competitors and indirect competitors that may be clamoring for the same shelf space you are. Look for the sites that have high visibility in search or are highly participatory in networks, because these will be the entities that have set the bar that you will need to reach in your own efforts. Your direct competitors are the known businesses that you commonly come up against, and indirect competitors may not be in the same business as you, but they have competing content (such as, for example, eHow or Wikipedia).

Analyze Strengths and Weaknesses As you continue to synthesize all of your findings, take sharp notes about what your best assets are and what your weakest assets are. It will be very clear from these observations what needs to be improved either a little or a lot.

Identify Areas of Opportunity and Where Your Strategic Gaps Lie Both market research and competitive analysis should provide you with more than enough ideas on how to improve or build up your content strategy. Look closely at the gaps in keyword language, audiences, network visibility, and content types in order to find new areas to build upon.

Determine Dominant Keywords and Themes Which keyword themes do you tend to emphasize that your competitors don't? Which themes do your competitors use that you don't? Which themes from your paid search programs drive your business goals, and where do gaps exist between your paid keyword lexicon and your natural lexicon? Remember that success in keyword research can lie in identifying just *one single seed-word theme* that you may not already be using, along with all of the stemmed phrases that go along with it.

Measure and Compare Traffic How much traffic are you getting compared to your direct and indirect competitors? What traffic types convert to your desired goals? Does the theme of your content strategy mirror the theme of your top-performing placements in various forms of paid media? Why or why not? Sources for analyzing traffic include comScore, Hitwise, and Google Ad Planner. Their data is not exact but can be used directionally.

Locate Networks and Websites in Which Your Audience Is Active and Participatory In what social networks are you and your competitors most present? What gaps exist in the networks you participate in vs. the competition? Are you able to mobilize and get active in a particular social network or website? Why or why not? How well do you execute when compared to your competition? Have you performed enough research to really know the whole story of your competitors, or are you relying on just scant knowledge or a little bit of data and analysis?

Determine Demographics What are the demographics of the sites you compete against or participate in, and do they match your targets? Why or why not?

Identify Unique Pages in Google How do your domains stack up against various competitors, aggregators, similarly themed social networks, and other similarly themed blogs? Does your site have only a fraction of the unique pages of your highest-volume competitor? Why? What would it take to scale to 5, 25, 50, or even 150 percent of the unique page content of your greatest competitor?

Quantify and Qualify Backlinks How many backlinks does your site have, and would a search engine be able to trust your site in real-time based on the quality and quantity of the links alone? How does your link profile compare to your direct and indirect competitors? How much work and time would it take to get a backlink profile similar to that of your competitors'? Should you take a traditional link-building approach, a social link-building approach, or both?

Assess Site-Level Keyword Visibility How does your site stack up against the competition in terms of your most coveted keyword and phrase set? Do the major search engines see your site as an authority in your keyword space, or are you presented only sporadically in the results for your target keywords? Do you see a lot of aggregators or direct competitors in this site profile? (See "Think Big: Approach Content Strategy Like a Forest, Not a Weed" earlier in this chapter.)

Assess the Freshness of Content in Search and Social Would you consider your site to have a "fresh" presence in search engines and live promotion in social networks? When was the last time you published a new page or blog post? Was it today, last week, last month, or last year? Are there any obstacles preventing you from publishing on a regular basis? Why or why not? Are you running RSS feeds for content? Are you including schema or RDFa markup in your website code? (See Chapter 10, "Technical Considerations and Implementation," for more information.) Are your social media managers regularly publishing new links to your friends and followers in major networks?

Creating a Visual Site Map for Your Content Inventory

Visual information-architecture content site maps (*not* the XML or page-based site map that search crawlers and searchers use to find your site's content) are very helpful in seeing the big picture for what you already have on your website. Information architects use visual site maps to show the overall structure of a website, along with potential paths for the user experience.

In an example ecommerce site scenario, the visual site map looks like a pyramid, which trickles down to the top category levels, then to the product-type levels, and then to the more granular item levels. A simple representation can be created for a large site and can go into even greater detail. I recommend you create a visual site map (even it takes simply jotting down a diagram with pencil and paper) for your existing content to provide a literal picture of what you already have. From there you can then outline the direction from a content-development perspective.

When to Spend More Time Finding Out What You Already Have

While many marketers focus on what they don't have in their content-marketing programs, many others should focus more on what they do have in their content audit. At iCrossing, we often find that our clients have been producing content online for many years, with many different divisions of an organization contributing on a regular basis while not fully knowing what the others are producing. In one recent content-architecture project, iCrossing's VP of content strategy, Dr. Karen Pate, and her team analyzed a client site that contained more than 1 million unique pages, and they created a *visual architectural sitemap of the entire site*. This was by no means a small undertaking, and Dr. Pate and team managed to break down this massive website into its unique themes and keywords in a way that the client's entire organization could understand.

If this organization's employees had proceeded with a robust real-time content strategy without knowing the depth of what they had in their content inventory, they very well may have ended up duplicating results and entire content themes in other parts of the site. By conducting a deep audit of their content, they were able to focus on new areas and topics and address gaps where they lacked content. The content audit also helped the company's audience managers gain a better understanding of their own content inventory to inform the company's community-management strategy.

Auditing Your Domain for Unique Optimized Pages

When considering the context of the depth of your site, it is important early on to get a handle on how many unique pages it contains. One of the best ways to audit the number of unique (nonduplicated) pages is to let the search engines do it for you. Every major search engine will show you the number of unique pages it believes is within your website, based on the number of pages it has crawled, subtracted by the number of duplicate pages it believes it has found. I typically use Google for this type of exercise, because it has historically been the best search engine at removing duplicate content from its list of unique pages on your website. To find out the number of unique pages in your website or your competitors' sites, simply type the following query into the Google search box, substituting your desired URL for *domain*:

Site:*domain*.com

The query will show the number of unique pages for all content within the domain (pages that are not behind a secured server or login), including subdomains. Also note that Google Webmaster Tools will show this number for your own sites. The following query can also be used to find unique pages behind subdomains:

Site:www.*domain*.com
Site:*subdomain.domain*.com

Figure 5.3 shows what the Google results will look like in a query for the domain bankrate.com, including all subdomains.

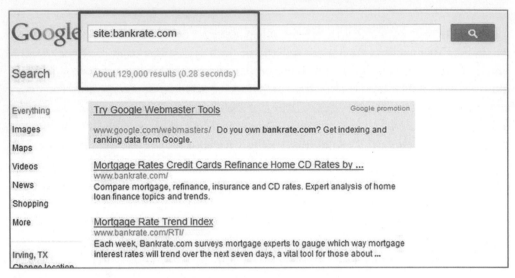

Figure 5.3 Unique page count query in Google for the domain bankrate.com

This domain query reveals that there are approximately 129,000 unique pages on the domain www.bankrate.com, making it a formidable presence in the financial keyword space based on the sheer number of unique pages alone. If you are planning on a new content play that captures search share in the financial-services area, get ready to produce content on a major level if you really want to compete with the big sites (or just set your expectations accordingly).

If you see that you have only 100 unique pages or fewer, it is probably safe to assume that your site is not a major player in any search or user-generated content space. If you discover that you have 10,000 unique pages online, more work may be needed to find out what you already have in terms of content inventory. With this knowledge, you can build on your existing themes, remove content, or find gaps in your themes that will become the focus of your future tactics and strategies.

Be sure to perform the same type of analysis for your own sites and for your competitors. You will quickly gain a strategic perspective of where you stand in terms of the scale of your future efforts and goals.

How to Find Out Whether Your Site Has a Page Optimized for a Particular Keyword

One very quick way to determine whether your site is optimized for a particular keyword phrase is to see whether the search engines are finding any relevancy on your website for a given term or phrase. Again, I use Google for this exercise, because it will deduplicate any potential problem content and show the highest-ranked pages on a domain for a given keyword or phrase. To determine how many pages rank (if any at all), use the following query in Google:

```
Site:yourdomain.com intitle:"keyword phrase here"
```

The point of this exercise is that if you come up with zero pages indexed in Google without a keyword match in the title element, then you basically have no horses in the race from a content perspective. The title element of a page is still considered one of the most powerful factors in how search engines rank pages. I recommend using quotations around your exact keyword phrases in order to return results that show competitive pages. Figure 5.4 shows an example of a domain and *intitle* operator query in Google, searching for the number of unique optimized pages found for the phrase *"Portland travel guide"*.

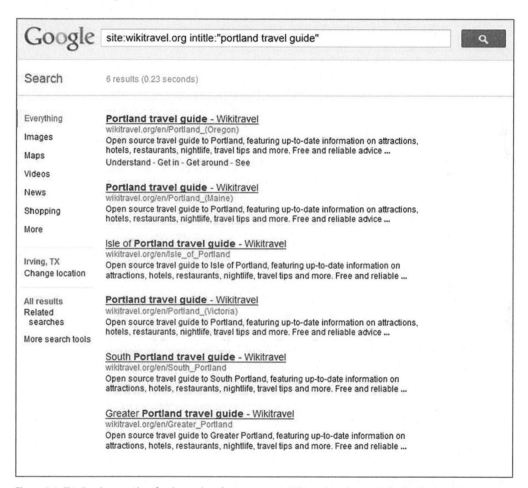

Figure 5.4 This Google query identifies the number of unique pages on Wikitravel.org that match the "Portland travel guide" phrase in the title element.

Notice that Google has returned six unique pages within the site Wikitravel. org that are optimized for the *"Portland travel guide"* phrase, with the page it believes is the most relevant from the site listed first. If any pages from Wikitravel show up at all in the natural results, it will be the first result shown here. This tells you that the existence of optimized content means that Wikitravel has some competitive content pages in the search game, supported by multiple pages. If Wikitravel.org is not ranking for this phrase, the strategy should not necessarily revolve around creating more pages but rather around reinforcing linking and sharing tactics around these pages. If other sites contain substantially more content with this exact phrase, such as an entire travel guide dedicated solely to Portland travel, Wikitravel.org might want to reconsider bolstering the unique content pages a bit.

Again, if Google or Bing shows that you do not have any pages for a given keyword or phrase, *you are not even in the game for visibility at the keyword or phrase level*. This should provide a clear signal that basic content is needed at the keyword level if you want to rank for the phrase at all.

The SEO Problem with Duplicate, or Repurposed, Content

Duplicate content can become a serious problem for your website or blog's visibility in search engines. Much of the discussion about the negative aspects of duplicate content in search revolve around whether your site pages "disappear," your pages are "ignored," or your site is "penalized," but all of these terms are simply a matter of semantics. The major search engines deduplicate content because it allows for more variety in your search results, discourages spammers from trying to stack the search results, and eliminates the less-than-useful experience of seeing a list of the same pages in your search results. There are many legitimate reasons for utilizing duplicate content either on your own domain or across multiple domains, but you will need to take some precautions to protect the search health of your owned assets.

I caution all of my clients to reduce the level of duplicate content within a site as much as possible, if not deduplicate it altogether. If an engine determines that a certain percentage of a site's content is duplicated on other sources, it may flag the site as not being an original content provider or conclude that a given threshold of the site's content is just a rehash of content that could be obtained somewhere else on the Web. Most of the time, having a single-digit percentage of duplicated content is not an issue with search engines, but if that percentage gets to 40 percent, 50 percent, or higher, you could be looking at a serious visibility problem that is difficult to correct. As Google's Matt Cutts likes to say, a site perceived to be spammy or too diluted may "catch a cold" and never quite do as well as it could have otherwise.

Content can be duplicated in four basic ways:

Exact Duplicates of Pages *Within the Same Domain* This is defined as an exact copy of an existing page (usually the page body text at minimum, and exclusive of navigation and files) but hosted at a separate URL. This approach is sometimes taken by the marketer or webmaster to provide content within separate directories, without any intention of spamming the search engines. The existence of two or more versions of the same page means that search engines will choose one and omit or ignore all other versions.

Exact Duplicates of Pages *on Separate Domains* This is a common problem for large companies with unique domains for varying brands or companies with a presence in different countries, with each domain having its own unique country code. If an exact site is replicated on Domain.com and also Domain.co.uk, then the engine will ultimately choose which site to show in its results. Press releases are also common forms of duplicate content across different domains, and the engines have gotten good at ignoring these duplicates rather than penalizing a site.

Exact Duplication of Snippets of Content from Page to Page *Within the Same Domain* This begins to address the ratio of duplicated content at the *page level*. If you repurpose product descriptions on multiple pages, that is OK, as long as it doesn't make up the majority of the page's content. But if a page is 70 percent duplicated from another page and only the intro paragraph has changed, this may create a page-level duplicate content issue for the search engine, and again, the page might be ignored or not perform as well as if it were entirely unique. If you have this duplicate-snippet issue with a large number of pages within your site, then the problem extends beyond the page and will negatively impact your search-engine visibility at the site level. Remember, it is not the fact that you have duplicated snippets but rather the percentage of the page that is duplicated vs. unique content.

Exact Duplication of Snippets of Content from Page to Page *on Separate Domains* This is similar to the previous example on the same domain, except it is produced across multiple domains.

The bottom line is that you do not want your site or blog to appear to search engines watered down with duplicate content. Search engines work very hard to fight the constant onslaught of spam, and one measure of basic relevance is determined by the amount of duplicate content contained within a website. Unfortunately, many legitimate websites have been negatively impacted by the mismanagement of their duplicated content, even though they had legitimate usability reasons for duplicating that content.

Blocking Duplicate Content in Search Engines

There are many viable and non-spammy reasons to utilize duplicated and repurposed content, so using established SEO principles can help you extend the life of your content and search visibility. Work with your IT department or SEO specialist to implement these methods and develop a plan for identifying and cleaning up duplicate content on your website:

Use the `noindex`, `nofollow` Meta Tag If you have a duplicate page of content that is necessary for the user experience, you can place a meta tag at the page level that will instruct the search engines not to index or follow links on the page. Place the following code in the `<HEAD>` element of your page code to prevent search engines from indexing your duplicate page:

```
<meta name="robots" content="noindex,nofollow">
```

Robots.txt `Robots.txt` is a text file that is located on the root of your domain server, and it instructs search engines about what parts of a site you do not want them to crawl (major search crawlers will copy your entire site if no `Robots.txt` file exists). `Robots.txt` will not allow you to block snippets of text, but you can block individual pages or entire sections of duplicate content if it exists.

301 Permanent Redirect Redirected URLs can often cause search engines to think that there are multiple duplicate pages in a website, when in fact there is only one web page but multiple unique points of entry. In short, this can become a tremendous mess for search crawlers if not properly maintained. A 301 status permanent redirect tells the search engine that a page has moved permanently, and the search engine should discard the old page information and apply it to the new one. This is similar to when someone moves and they get a new phone number; the phone company tells people calling the old number to call you at the new one.

Canonical Tag The canonical tag is a line of code that is also added to the `<HEAD>` element of a web page; it provides instructions to the search engines on the definitive URL they should crawl and applies link attributes of all other redirected URLs. Read more about the canonical tag at www.mattcutts.com/blog/canonical-link-tag/.

Apply Variation to Titles If you have a lot of pages with similar keywords or page titles and with a minimal amount of unique text, I encourage the practice of writing title elements to be as unique as possible. Major emphasis is placed on the `<TITLE>` element by search engines, and if titles are too similar, they could dilute your overall page value. This advice would also apply to `<H>` page-heading titles as well (ex. `<H1>`, `<H2>`, etc.), whenever possible.

Other Considerations for Content Strategy and Planning

This section of the chapter covers other important considerations for content strategy. These areas include creating a style guide, creating a publishing plan, developing a publishing calendar, and defining the various roles in content production and strategy.

Defining Roles in Content Production and Strategy

As you begin to develop your strategy and execution, you will inevitably be enlisting various team members, consultants, or agencies to help in the effort. Keep in mind that you may need to play a number of roles as you carry out some of the lessons in this book, depending on the size and scale of your strategy. Also be realistic in considering how much work you can take on and in what areas you will need to get some additional leadership or resources. Right now you are the key strategist for your content approach, so here are some different roles you will need to consider as you begin to scale up and execute:

Chief Editor or Strategist This role focuses on setting the overall content strategy and agenda, guiding market research, and thinking critically about how to synthesize insights into an actionable plan for content. Depending on the size of your organization, this hat may be worn by one or more people.

Content Creators Content creators take on a variety of roles and depend upon the asset types you choose to pursue for your audience. The fundamental creator is the writer, because the written word will be required for labeling, conversation, descriptions, optimization, or otherwise communicating in search and networks to reach your audience. Other types of creators may include videographers, photographers, audience managers, and application developers, among others.

Administrators Depending on the volume of content you are dealing with, an administrator helps keep content on time, has a strong handle on various types of publishing interfaces and content-management systems, and has technical knowledge for moving assets and installing new features.

Digital Asset Optimizers No matter what content types you are producing, every piece should be optimized for its highest potential in both search and social networks. Your optimizer could be an individual role that makes recommendations and ensures quality prior to publication, or it could be an added role for content creators or administrators. Either way, optimization basics should be clearly understood and practiced by all roles on your team.

IT/Technologists If your content plan depends on any advanced website applications, functions, or databases, you will likely need an information-technology professional to implement or translate your vision into reality. Identify resources you may need to tap for technical implementation and bring them in at the right time.

Freelancers Because your needs will vary for the aforementioned roles, pulling in a freelancer, consultant, or agency resource can help you achieve all the functions needed for a successful publishing strategy. As you determine your content direction, begin thinking about your potential resources for addressing the different needs listed throughout this chapter.

Other Stakeholders Legal departments, public relations, and other parts of your organization may have a key stake in the content of your company for a variety of reasons, so it is important that you pull them into the process when warranted. Put them directly on the team if necessary, and work closely with them to educate them on your marketing strategy.

Allowing for skill diversity in these roles will help your strategy and execution in a number of ways. Understanding keyword strategy, reviewing networks, brainstorming, providing timely training and insight to other team members, and social listening are all useful and necessary skills to cultivate within your team or with your consultants and agencies.

Also ensure that your teams have a strategy or goal in mind for targeting long-tail, midtail, and head keyword terms in content, search, and networks. You may try to attack one or all of these, but awareness of this element is a key first step to addressing it.

Creating Your Editorial Plan and Publishing Calendar

Once you have audited and assessed your own content and your competitor's content and also analyzed and synthesized your market research, you should begin to create an editorial plan and publishing calendar. An editorial plan and publishing calendar will help provide a production framework for your content and lend focus to your ongoing efforts.

Considering that this book is focused on real-time and active publishing, most marketers will need to start their publishing plan on a weekly basis, publishing at least several times per week and also setting a plan for monitoring and participating in social networks.

As another primary consideration, you should include a plan for building up a content bank or content inventory that addresses many of the keyword themes you find in your market research. Your content bank should help your overall number of unique pages rise to the level of your indirect and direct competitors or greater and should address many of the common themes and problems that your target audience may encounter. Again, the definition of *content* includes a wide variety of asset types, so there are many ways of achieving deeper breadth of unique pages than just producing text articles.

Your calendar should outline the following:

- Asset types to be published
- Location of where you plan to publish (your blog, videos on YouTube, and so on)
- Social networks that you will be participating in, and frequency of participation
- Planning for execution and research for in-the-moment content topics

Figure 5.5 shows a sample spreadsheet with rows and columns labeled for your publishing calendar.

Producing a publishing calendar is useful whether you are an individual business owner or manage a team of content creators. It provides focus and planning in your development efforts and removes the pressure of constantly developing content on the fly. You should plan on maintaining a calendar for at least one month in advance of your content timeline.

As you create and execute on your calendar, you may also discover that your actual day-to-day activities may not be totally reflected in your plan. As this book has stated many times, real-time marketing and publishing is an iterative process that never ends. It is acceptable (and recommended) to edit your calendar to reflect the actualities of your day-to-day content production and social interaction.

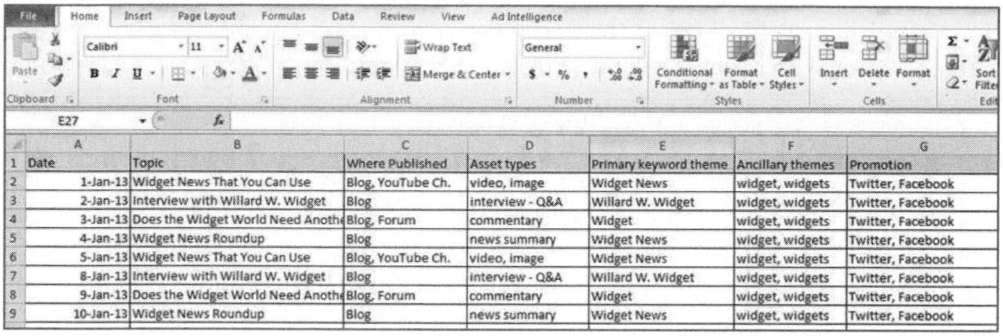

	A	B	C	D	E	F	G
1	Date	Topic	Where Published	Asset types	Primary keyword theme	Ancillary themes	Promotion
2	1-Jan-13	Widget News That You Can Use	Blog, YouTube Ch.	video, image	Widget News	widget, widgets	Twitter, Facebook
3	2-Jan-13	Interview with Willard W. Widget	Blog	interview - Q&A	Willard W. Widget	widget, widgets	Twitter, Facebook
4	3-Jan-13	Does the Widget World Need Anoth	Blog, Forum	commentary	Widget	widget, widgets	Twitter, Facebook
5	4-Jan-13	Widget News Roundup	Blog	news summary	Widget News	widget, widgets	Twitter, Facebook
6	5-Jan-13	Widget News That You Can Use	Blog, YouTube Ch.	video, image	Widget News	widget, widgets	Twitter, Facebook
7	8-Jan-13	Interview with Willard W. Widget	Blog	interview - Q&A	Willard W. Widget	widget, widgets	Twitter, Facebook
8	9-Jan-13	Does the Widget World Need Anoth	Blog, Forum	commentary	Widget	widget, widgets	Twitter, Facebook
9	10-Jan-13	Widget News Roundup	Blog	news summary	Widget News	widget, widgets	Twitter, Facebook

Figure 5.5 A sample publishing calendar in Excel

Creating a Style Guide

As mentioned in Chapter 3, "Ramping Up for a Real-Time Content Marketing Strategy," it is important to remain as consistent as possible. One of the ways to maintain consistency is by creating a style guide. A style guide for copywriting and presenting your brand is very useful for enabling your content creators to maintain a level voice, without being constraining. Within this guide you should outline the following, because it relates to the way you want your company to be promoted online:

- Trademarks
- Tone and voice (how you want your customers to be addressed)
- Style and grammar

Engaging outside of your owned spaces can be more casual, and it will also require your audience and community managers to include the voice of your audience whenever relevant. A style guide should be just that when acting in real-time search and social spaces: a guide. Remember that your business is a combination of what you say about yourself and what others say about you. Trying to control your language too strictly in networks could cause some unwanted backlash down the road.

This ends the chapter discussion on content planning and strategy. Remember that you will need to stay nimble and creative for your long-term strategy, and you will always need to think critically. While content will continue to be addressed throughout the remainder of this book, the next chapter is devoted entirely to engaging content ideas, along with a quick guide to writing search engine–friendly copy, which will be highly useful whether you are writing for search engines, social networks, or both.

Creating Effective and Engaging Content

Content is the connective element that runs through every concept described in this book. Overall, this chapter is designed to provide more tactical ideas for you to begin creating content. At the end of the chapter, you will have a breadth of ideas, types, and tactics to choose from. Don't get too far ahead in developing content just yet, though, because I will be addressing where you are going to publish it in later chapters, and this concept will have some bearing on the content types you choose.

Use this chapter to help frame your overall strategy, but also revisit it periodically to get new ideas for future content strategies, as well as to inform your actual hands-on copywriting and digital asset–optimization activities.

6

Chapter Contents
Specific content types
Brainstorming
Optimizing headlines for search and social
A concise guide to SEO copywriting and optimizing digital assets

Engaging Content Idea Types

Before assessing the content ideas and types you will be creating, first reconsider the strategic elements that were discussed in previous chapters. Keep your audience in mind as you go with a particular idea. Have other competitors created a similar asset? Did it work for them? Will a particular content idea seem out of place or unusual in your business landscape?

These ideas do not have to be articles, web pages, or blog posts. Databases, infographics, and videos can also be used to help execute the following ideas. You can also use multiple asset types to accomplish the same goal. Consider how your audience consumes content, and use each asset type accordingly.

Also work to match the right topic with the right content type. Later in the chapter, I will provide source ideas on identifying hot topics. Overall, there must be a synergy between the content type and the individual idea. Here are some of the main content types to begin optimizing and disseminating content across your various content platforms:

FAQs If there is any one particular content idea or type that should be considered mandatory for any business, product, or service on the Internet, it is the "frequently asked questions" section of your site, otherwise known as the FAQ. FAQs represent exactly what the name suggests—the most commonly asked questions about your business or service. Creating a thorough FAQ on your website provides the answers that your core audience most commonly seeks. It also offers your audience and social-media managers a basis for answering and referring to questions outside of a website and into social networks. Content for FAQs should come from your customer-service department (if you have one), from frequently asked questions on answer sites and forums, and from common-sense questions about your products or services. The development of your FAQ is an iterative process, and the more often you interact with your audience, the more awareness you will have around their common questions. Remember that FAQs are not only for social outreach but also for search, because many people will enter their common questions about your business into a search box.

Curated Link Lists Link lists are as old as the commercial Internet itself, and they represent the ascension of many great web properties like Yahoo! and Google. Creating valuable link lists can attract many readers to your owned assets through social sharing and search. Consider a regular content program for subjects in your themed area, such as "top blogs," "top news posts today," a "complete resource list," "funniest," or "most useful." You can also categorize a particular area of the Web that you may find to be lacking structure and create value for people who are interested in the core subject or theme.

Tips If your goal is to show thought leadership or demonstrate commanding knowledge in a particular area of expertise, offer tips and helpful advice using various asset types, such as text, apps, video, images, and so on. Helpful tip lists are good share bait, and they provide traffic and social conversation consideration for your business and brand.

Stories or Anecdotes A potential unique content offering might be sharing your own business experience. Relating experiences or examples to your audience, within the context of a current topic or business problem, may promote the development of a deeper relationship with your audience. Consider relating a business experience in a blog post and share on a major social network or discuss in a live presentation or webinar.

An Outline of the Basics or Advanced Elements of a Particular Topic Online conversations can move quickly away from their original context, especially as the buzz increases. A quick overview of the basics or an outline of key issues around a topic may be beneficial to your new and existing audience. If you see a complex business topic increasing in interest on Twitter, you may find that the best way to earn your way into the content conversation may be to summarize the events or circumstances leading up to a particular story, issue, or situation.

"Complete" Lists A "complete" list is similar to a link list but is distinguished as being more exhaustive and comprehensively researched. "Complete" lists might contain as many as 50 unique items or more, with detailed information, images, and commentary for each item, while reinforcing each one within the context of the article title. Complete lists might fall along the lines of "best of" lists, "top ranked" lists, or some other context of viewing an entire scope of a particular topic or theme. These types of lists typically help attract social sharing but will also link back to the unique article. Figure 6.1 shows an article on Smashing Magazine, a well-known blog for providing useful long-form content lists to online content publishers.

Reviews Consider providing regular reviews or commentary on products, services, or even business strategies within your relative area of concentration. Use text, video, audio, or a variety of combinations of asset types. You might even want to use reviews as an entire community strategy by enabling customized community tools and applications for your audience to weigh in on particular areas of interest.

How-to Articles How-to articles are a staple of the Internet, and this content type even has its own dedicated sites, like eHow and wikiHow. How-to articles can be social, in the sense that people may contribute to the conversation via wikis or comments, and "how-to"–related searches represent a major segment of search-query volume. Whether you create your how-to and step-by-step articles in text, images, video, or other asset types, consider how this content idea applies to a wide range of businesses, including shopping, finance, travel, home, and living, among many other topic and service areas.

Figure 6.1 A "complete" post on Smashing Magazine, a great resource for web designers and bloggers

Interviews Providing insightful Q&As with interesting people or thought leaders in your business area is a great way to attract a like-minded audience. Interviews can include many asset types, including video, audio, text, and images.

Recommendations Providing recommendations on particular products, services, or resources is a great way to illustrate your knowledge of a particular topic by relaying helpful choices to your audience. It also puts a more positive spin on the review process, without being negative or creating any ill will with your audience.

Quizzes Putting together a quiz for your audience is a fun way to earn their attention and help test the knowledge of your audience on a particular topic of interest. Quizzes help your audience to grow in their knowledge and reveal potential content ideas for your own strategy.

Polls and Surveys Polls and surveys are a great way to gauge what your audience is thinking and get a pulse on your market-research efforts. There are many free and paid survey applications that you can use with your blog or on a social network.

Contests and Giveaways If you give away something of keen interest to your key audience, you will likely receive a lot of attention in return. Use your entries as a way to offer additional content-opt-in opportunities or to simply ask them to connect with you directly in social networks (examples: "Please follow us on Twitter" or "Like us on Facebook"). Keep in mind that your giveaway should be relevant to your end goals, or else you will attract a nonrelevant audience that will not contribute to your ultimate business goals.

Live Video Use Ustream, Google Hangouts, or other live video services to broadcast content and create a live discussion format with your audience. For instance, Dallas radio talk show-host Richard Hunter broadcasts with real-time video on his Ustream channel (see Figure 6.2) as people follow and chat along with him.

Case Studies Creating a real-world business case is another excellent way to attract a like-minded business or consumer audience in both earned and social spaces. Good case studies can take on a life of their own and often get shared around the Web.

Research and Statistical Data If you have any data or statistics that provide unique insights into a business or consumer problem, then research is one content idea that could catapult your website and social presence into the mainstream social conversation. Think about the unique data that you may be collecting in some form, or think of a potential research study you would like to conduct. You can show your results as simple charts or graphs or in more complex ways, such as a searchable database or application that produces customized charts and reports.

Figure 6.2 The Ustream channel for radio talk-show host Richard Hunter

Scoops or Exclusive Announcements Consider contacting the press-relations departments of the major players in your business space (you might want to consider noncompetitive companies for this type of content), and ask whether they have any new products or services that you could cover for your blog or other publishing site. If you have a relationship with the provider, they might even offer you information under embargo, which means they give you information prior to a public announcement, as long as you wait to publish the information. This delay in publishing usually provides plenty of time to create quality content and also get the scoop on other bloggers or news content providers in your space. Being first with a great story can be a tremendous advantage as content breaks out in real-time.

Q&As from People within Your Network Answering questions and offering expert advice should be a fundamental part of your content strategy. Answer questions that you may find on third-party networks, or create a blog post with three to five common questions you receive and answer them for your audience. Also remember to add your answers to your site FAQ.

Images and Image Channels Photos and images are great digital assets to post on a regular basis, as they are captured. Photos are common regular content features on a wide range of blogs and suitable for many types of businesses. You can showcase entire galleries or photo channels on Flickr or SmugMug or create your own galleries on your blog or website (find more information about blog plug-ins in Chapter 8, "Blogs, Google News, and Press Releases"). If you want to engage your audience directly, shoot an industry or consumer event and tell your subjects where to find you online. You will likely find that audiences are almost always captivated by content about themselves.

Bios and "Get to Know You" Features Whether you have a small or large organization, consider a content feature that routinely spotlights different people on your team or within your company. Add a picture and publish a Q&A.

Community and Current-Event Coverage Covering community events is a great way to capture topical and real-time search interest around an event. It also provides your audience with a window into an important event that they may not be able to attend but would still like to know more about while it happens.

Live Blogging and Live Tweeting If you are attending a business conference or other consumer conference or event, consider blogging live from the event. Give a factual recap of what is being said in real-time, or offer your own side commentary. It is very common now for people to monitor social streams by hashtag or keyword during these types of events. Injecting your content into the conversation is a great way to gain real-time attention in a meaningful way while the event is happening.

"Things to Do" If you are in an area that you know well, offer recommendations for local attractions, restaurants, and other helpful localized tips. If a sizable amount of your audience is from out of town and attending an event in your area, show a little bit of hospitality and provide useful content that they won't forget.

Posts About Other Posts When I write a column for MediaPost, I will often include an additional post on my company blog or personal blog. This way, I can tell the regular audience in one channel about my MediaPost column and also offer different bits of information to supplement the topic. Sometimes I will also write a quick blog post about a press mention or citation with additional background and commentary.

Commentary and Editorial In establishing yourself as a conversation leader, it is important to communicate your opinions on the main issues and topics that are critical to your industry and business or to the needs of your audience. This commentary can come in the form of a blog post, social conversation and status updates, or research and longer white papers, among many other forms. If you have an opinion and you know you are right, don't be shy; share it with your network. Be ready to elaborate on your position and to follow up with comments from your audience or network.

Thought Leadership A good piece of insight is one of the best ways to establish yourself and your business as a thought leader in both the content space and your business space. Thought leadership may take on the form of a book, live speaking, webinars, PowerPoint slides, white papers, or a blog. It doesn't happen overnight, and you will need to be diligent, consistent, and focused in your efforts.

Glossaries Providing a glossary, or dictionary of terms related to your area of business, is a great way to provide informative content that can be referenced in social spaces when needed, and to appear in search-engine results. Consider putting all of your glossary terms on a single page, or create unique pages for each term for expanded definitions.

Downloadable Assets Offering up an application, screensavers, plug-ins, ebook, and other productivity enhancements is another great way to solve a problem for your audience and create a shareable event. Useful assets can travel quickly via shared networks and gain a lot of exposure for your business.

Five Quick Ideas for Topic Brainstorming

Now that I have established a number of ideas for content types, you need a topic or theme that will captivate and engage your audience. I highly recommend flipping back and forth between this chapter and Chapter 4, "Market Research and Content Types," to apply methods of synthesizing data into actual topics. Use these tips as a starting point for creativity, take careful notes on your ideas, and begin mapping your ideas together into an actionable content strategy and editorial plan.

Use a Keyword-Research Tool Using one or more of the keyword-research tools listed in Chapter 4 is a quick way to gauge the relative search and social popularity of a particular subject at the keyword level. Choosing topics at the keyword level also helps provide you and your content creators with a thematic focus to build upon, either at the page level or for a whole section of pages or assets.

Use a Real-Time Research Tool If you recall the discussion of velocity in Chapter 1, "Real-Time Publishing and Marketing," you know that good real-time keyword research tools will reveal trending and popular topics. If you are fast enough to produce and distribute content while the topic is still hot, then real-time keyword research will provide you with more than enough ideas to choose from on a daily basis. See "Keyword and Conversation Buzz Tools for Content and Search" in Chapter 4 for more buzz-keyword inspiration.

Monitor Twitter, Facebook, Google+, or Other Status-Update Networks for Hot Topics In addition to the real-time tools mentioned earlier, monitoring the status updates of your networks is one of the best ways to find out what people are talking about right now. If you need more than 140 characters to communicate additional thoughts on a topic, it might be just enough to warrant an expanded blog post or forum discussion.

Use Your Brain (or Team of Brains) Have brainstorming sessions and editorial-calendar meetings with your team to drum up new ideas for topics, and do this on a regular basis. While tools can be helpful, it takes a good brain to synthesize your data into captivating content. Be creative, be engaging, and plan topic ideas and themes for weeks and months ahead of time.

Read Your Analytics Files to Find Out What People Want from Your Site If you have an existing website, you might be surprised to find that many of the people who come to your site already have an expectation of what they want from your content. Reviewing analytics reports will reveal the most popular term referrals and reflect much of the content that is currently on your site. As you determine the most popular terms that your site attracts, also determine the stemmed topics or related themes that would appeal to this audience, and keep them coming back for more.

Ambient Truth: In Search and Social, the Headline Is the Message

Every day in the world of real-time publishing, both great and terrible articles alike live or die by the quality of their asset title or headline. In just a short line of text, content creators have the opportunity to relay the gist of their message and utility and to include all relevant triggers that might encourage a click or an "open." As content creators, we have *just one line of text* to include a keyword or phrase that might match a search keyword or to engage an individual or audience who will make a final judgment on the quality or truth of the content piece right on the spot.

Many usability studies have shown that Internet users generally scan headlines, link lists, or status updates. When some articles or assets are ranked highly for a particular keyword or widely shared in social networks, they are often subliminally taken as fact without even critically assessing or reading the document.

Consider the story of United Airlines. In September 2008, a long-outdated news story (with an ambiguous date stamp) about United's six-year-old bankruptcy (United was in fact *not bankrupt in 2008* and was well past its 2002 troubles) was recrawled by Google and subsequently posted in Google News current headlines.

Without carefully reading the date of the story, a financial advisory site picked up the old headline, and a link was posted to Bloomberg News, where it was perceived by readers as a fresh story. Subsequently, a massive stock sell-off ensued, taking a 76 percent chomp out of United's share price before trading stopped. United began to regain share value when people actually started to read the story, but it ended up losing nearly 11 percent in its overall market cap for the day. Many of the investors who sold at the bottom lost big bucks. Remember, this sell-off was based on an unchecked headline. It could have been easily verified by anyone who bothered to read this story and check the sources beyond the headline. Read more about the story at www.nytimes.com/2008/09/09/business/09air.html.

Writing titles (as well as thinking critically as a reader, searcher, and social-media user) is a serious matter as far as your audience is concerned, and the success of your digital asset-sharing depends on it. Here are some of the key things for you to consider as you write engaging headlines for all of your digital marketing assets:

Write an Engaging Heading That Readers Will Quickly Understand How would you describe your article or digital asset in 7 to 10 words? Be clear and succinct, and cover at least one of the captivating ideas or features of your digital asset.

Accurately Describe What the Reader Should Expect to See Make your title relevant, because your audience does not like to be tricked. On the flipside, they will appreciate the truthfulness in consistency between the title and actual content. The same goes for search engines—don't try to stuff irrelevant keywords into your title, because engines' algorithms can detect this type inconsistency and ignore your content altogether.

Reveal an Outcome of the Article or a Provocative Question That the Article Might Answer What thoughts or conclusion would you like your reader or consumer to walk away with after clicking through to read or view your content? Entice your audience by asking a question or providing the answer in the title, and be sure that your content lives up to your title. Sample titles that exhibit this consideration include "How a Graffiti Artist Earned $200 Million on the Facebook IPO" and "Is Google Making Us Stupid?"

Use a Relevant Keyword or Keyword Phrase in the Title Keywords are connections to people who use social networks. A good keyword in the title that reflects the literal theme of the article or asset will ultimately determine whether it ranks in search and social. If you are writing a 10,000-word review of the best hotels in New York City, it would be beneficial to include the relevant phrase "New York City Hotels" somewhere in the title to reinforce the main theme for your audience and for search engines. Not all articles have an exact keyword fit, though most should. If you do not place a keyword in this highly competitive spot, don't expect to automatically rank in search, because search engines still apply heavy weight to this page element.

Quick-Start SEO Copywriting Guide for Social Marketers

This section will focus on providing a basic search engine optimization (SEO) copywriting and asset-labeling guide for various types of web content. While search engines do not provide set guidelines for elements such as title-element character counts or word counts, I have provided suggestions in order to get the best general results in search engines and social networks. Every website and asset has a different competitive set, so you should benchmark some of these attributes of your successful direct and indirect competitors to obtain a more subjective assessment of your keyword space (namely, word counts and how well your competitors are optimized).

It is also important that SEO-friendly copywriting is an art more than science. So when you see estimates for character counts, word counts, etc., they are based on what has generally been known to work for a wide number of rankings and pages, and sites. No set of general copywriting guidelines are applicable to every subjective situation, so you will need to analyze your competition, address the nuances of your content and keyword space, and adjust accordingly. There is no set guide provided by search engines regarding specific elements, as it would give away their algorithms. Again, just keep in mind that this is a directional guide, and you should experiment with your copywriting approach and find the sweet spot that works for you.

This guide can be used to describe and mark up various types of digital assets to make them search and social-friendly. Generally speaking, optimization for titles of web pages works the same as titles for images, videos, and other assets. Practice these guidelines with your own blog posts and web pages, and track the results in search engines until you gain a greater command of search engine–friendly copywriting style. Before I outline the individual high-level SEO elements, here are some general recommendations for search engine and keyword–friendly copywriting for various asset types across the Internet:

- Focus your page themes on only one to three keywords or phrases per page. Be consistent when applying these keywords and phrases throughout the remaining elements of the page (an example of keyword page-theme consistency will be discussed at the conclusion of this chapter). Other parts of the page that require consistency include the page title element, first sentence of the first paragraph of body text, meta description, anchor text attribute of links, and alt text attributes of images.

- Include variations and secondary keyword concepts as they relate to the context of your page or digital asset (for example, for an article on digital cameras, reinforce with ancillary phrases like "digital camera lenses" and "digital camera cases" whenever appropriate and relevant and whenever it flows).

- Write content starting at a minimum of 150 words for pages that you want to remain in the search results for longer periods of time. This helps search engines distinguish longer-form pages from more-ephemeral pages, such as short 140-character status update pages on Twitter. Pages with shorter word counts tend to be generally treated with less long-term visibility than longer pages with good external link and social signals applied.

- Review your existing pages and assets to determine whether they are targeted too broadly. For example, the term *travel* is very broad and competitive, but *holiday travel to New York City* is much more targeted and will have less competition, meaning a greater chance for your page to rank highly for a relevant phrase.

- Avoid inundating your titles with keywords, because this may appear to be "keyword-stuffing" to a search engine and look unnatural to a human reader.

- Ensure that your metadata (descriptions, keywords tags, and so on), title elements, main headings, and alt text attributes are specific to your page theme, and not written broadly to your site theme.

The Title Element

Since the beginnings of search engines, the title element (in HTML, <TITLE>) has been one of the most heavily weighted on-page SEO factors. Though the title is technically hidden in the code of the site, it can be viewed in the browser and is usually the first text a searcher sees in a search engine. The title element is technically not metadata, as it is often mistakenly referred to, and is visible outside of the page code layer. Here are the basic recommended practices for creating effective titles for a variety of digital assets:

- Create a unique title for every page of unique content, accurately describing that page's content.

- Include your most targeted and desired keyword or keyword phrase somewhere within the title, preferably toward the beginning of the title.

- Use a call to action to help entice click-throughs, if it is relevant to your page content or desired actions.

- Avoid keyword-stuffing (gratuitously inserting keywords into the title), because it is a turnoff to your audience and to search engines.

- Ensure a readable title length of 70 characters or less (including spaces).

- Create title copy that reads just as well with people as it does with search engines.

- Avoid using words that are irrelevant to the digital asset you are describing.

These are *recommendations* for creating effective titles for both people and search engines; however, emphasis on including a keyword in your title is the most important tip of all (*this can make or break your visibility in search and social networks*). Keep it as natural as possible, without obsessing that every page fits the previous criteria. If you can make a large proportion of your content fit the criteria, you are generally in a good place. Also, be aware that your titles are the first impression that a potential search or social user may see of your content outside of your website. Keep the appearance consistent with how you would prefer it to be viewed. Figure 6.3 shows a highlighted example of a title element for an Amazon.com product and how it appears in a browser.

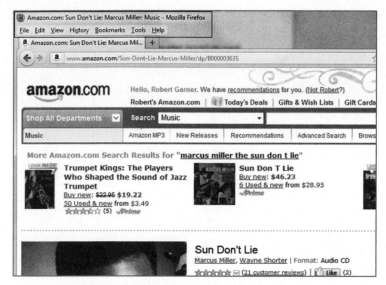

Figure 6.3 The product listing on Amazon.com for Marcus Miller's CD The Sun Don't Lie. Notice how the title element carries exactly into the readable display title in the browser.

This is how the title element pictured in Figure 6.3 appears in the code:

```
<title>Amazon.com: Sun Don&#39;t Lie: Marcus Miller: Music</title>
```

While Figure 6.3 shows how a title element appears in a browser, Figure 6.4 shows how that same title element appears in a Bing search result.

The Meta Description

The meta description tag delivers messaging about a digital asset to search-engine users, though it carries no weight in how search engines rank these assets. This description is embedded into the head of your HTML code and is not visible on the actual page when viewed in a browser. When written with the right keywords in the right places, search engines will trigger the meta description in the search results pages when it matches a keyword used by a searcher. Also note that social networks will pull this description into a share on Facebook, LinkedIn, and Google+. Remember that while the meta description is not weighted toward any particular keyword in the search results, your descriptions will often be the first impression of your website and social digital assets in various search engines and social spaces. It doesn't always trigger, but it still puts a small amount of control back into the hands of the content creator. Consider the following when creating meta descriptions for your content:

- Write a unique meta description for every individual nonduplicated page of content.

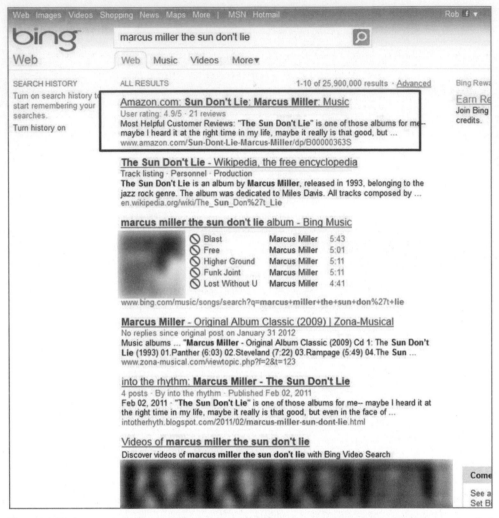

Figure 6.4 The Amazon.com product-listing title as it appears in Bing search results. Notice again how the title element carries into the search results and often directly mirrors the keywords that are used in the search query.

- Include relevant keywords related to the core theme of the page or digital asset so that search engines will trigger a meta description, as opposed to pulling a random snippet of text from somewhere on the page.

- Describe your page in two or three sentences. This should be sufficient to ensure that targeted keywords are reinforced in the meta description for each page. The first two sentences of well-written page copy are often easily modified for use as your meta description tag.

- Limit your meta description tag length to 100 to 200 characters in length, including spaces. Though the engines do not have set guidelines for meta description length, this limit is a fair number to shoot for and also prevents "wordy" writers from creating a dissertation in this tag.

Here are two HTML code examples of meta descriptions that appear for the Google search results of *travel to Peru*:

Lonely Planet: `<meta name="description" content="Peru tourism and travel information including facts, maps, history, culture, transport and weather in Peru. Find popular places to visit in Peru - Lonely Planet" />`

Wikitravel: `<meta name="description" content="Open source travel guide to Peru, featuring up-to-date information on attractions, hotels, restaurants, nightlife, travel tips and more. Free and reliable advice written by Wikitravellers from around the globe." />`

Figure 6.5 shows an example of how these two descriptions are triggered in the viewable search results in Google for the phrase *travel to Peru*.

Figure 6.5 Google search results page for the phrase *travel to Peru*. Because the meta description for both of the highlighted sites includes the targeted keywords in the meta description, the search engine has chosen to display this text on the results page.

The Meta Keywords Tag

The meta keywords tag no longer has any influence in Google or Bing, and there is some indication that Bing may use it as signal for spam if the tag is implemented improperly. But many seasoned search marketers will still often create this tag to provide focus for their page-level keyword strategies. Prioritizing meta keywords tags can also be useful to search and social marketers in other areas of on-page tagging, like a blog, Delicious, YouTube, or other network that utilizes on-page descriptive keywords for various digital assets. Even if you omit the meta keywords tag on your page, prioritizing your main keywords will help provide keyword focus for your content assets as a writer and creator. Here are the main recommended practices for writing and prioritizing effective meta keywords tags:

- Separate keywords and keyword phrases with a comma.
- Use four keywords or phrases, at most.
- Avoid using broad keywords by keeping your keywords and phrases very specific to the exact theme of the content on the page.
- Utilize keywords and keyword phrases that reinforce the main theme of the page.
- Place the most important keyword or keyword phrase at the beginning of the tag.
- Avoid keyword-stuffing in the meta keywords tag—it does not help your pages at all.

The HTML Heading Element and Body Copy

The HTML heading tag (different from the *title element*) is the visible on-page title, and in addition to describing the context, it provides literal keyword focus for search engines and search-engine users. There have been disagreements between search engine optimizers (SEOs) about the effectiveness of the HTML heading elements (HTML tags include <H1>, <H2>, <H3>, and so on) on search results over the years, with some SEOs seeing actual lift and others seeing no lift at all. It is fair to say that Google has been "on and off" about giving weight to this aspect of the page over the last 10 years. My experience is that it is a helpful tag to search engines and audiences, as well as visually impaired persons using text-to-voice programs like JAWS, so I generally recommend its use.

Your <H1> heading title is often used to name a file or is pushed into a social network, and in effect, having keywords in this area can make or break the keyword visibility of your page. The most weighted page-heading element is the <H1> tag, but semantic influence is also applied to subheadings (<H2>, <H3>, and so on). The heading element (<H1>) is still generally considered by most optimizers to be one of the most important on-page SEO elements, next to the title element. In many content-management systems, this title will also automatically become your title element. For more information on properly creating page headings, visit the W3C article entitled "The global structure of an HTML document" at www.w3.org/TR/html401/struct/global.html#h-7.5.5.

In addition to the heading element, there are various aspects of the body copy that a marketer with an SEO frame of mind can use to increase the overall keyword weight of the page. Here are the recommended practices for writing effective page-heading elements and body copy:

- Use your main keyword or descriptive keyword title in the <H1> element and page title. Only one H1 should be used per page.

- Use relevant keywords and keyword phrases in the body of the first paragraph, and in the first sentence if possible.

- Use relevant keywords and key phrases in the subsequent page subheadings (<H2>, <H3>, and so on), and describe subheadings accurately.

- Modify popular single keywords to match frequently searched phrases (for example, modify *toys* to *birthday toys* or *Christmas toys*), but only when it matches the exact context of your content.

- Keep the page length at 150 words or greater for longer-form text articles and blog posts in order to compete with other competitive pages in the keyword space. This will also help distinguish your pages from shorter ephemeral pages that do not typically do well in search for the long term. This word count is not a set number but rather serves as a rule of thumb. I recommend you review the page weight and word counts, of your top competitors that rank in both Google and Bing to establish your own subjective word-count minimum. For example, pages in the travel vertical are very competitive and may have higher word counts, in the 800- to 1,000-word range. In this scenario, a 150-word page isn't going to cut it, unless it is compensated with highly powerful links and social signals.

- Keep in mind that past tense, present tense, singular, and plural versions of a keyword all contribute to increased visibility for the targeted keyword term or phrase. Reinforce your page theme with variations of your core keyword or phrase to maintain a natural-language approach, and send a stronger keyword signal to search engines (for example, *bass fishing*, *bass*, and *bass fish* all reinforce the same concept and theme).

- Pay attention to spelling, grammar, and the reading level of your document. The search engines look at these factors to determine the value of a document, and Google even goes so far as to allow searchers to sort content by reading level.

- For longer-form articles, consider breaking up, or "chunking," your text for ease of scannability and readability. Writing for the Web is not the same as writing for print, so make sure your content is easily readable.

Internal-Link Naming

Internal links (links that point other pages within the same domain) are an important factor in how search engines rank your website and social-media content. Whether you are coding links in HTML or using a built-in content management or data-entry system, using the right keywords to describe your links for both people and search engines is critical. Here is an example of link anchor text in an HTML-encoded link taken from the SEMPO website; it describes another web page within sempo.org as "Webinars":

```
<a href=" http://www.sempo.org/?page=webinars">Webinars</a>
```

Again, in this example, Webinars (capitalized) is the anchor text. Figure 6.6 shows how that same HTML link looks in a web browser. Notice that the underlined anchor text is a signal used by search engines to understand how you describe your own pages on your website, in your own language. Using accurately descriptive keywords in the anchor text increases your search visibility for similar or exact matched terms. It is not a guarantee that you will rank, but it does contribute to the myriad other factors that engines use to rank sites and other digital assets.

Figure 6.6 SEMPO uses internal anchor text links all throughout the SEMPO site to improve search-engine relevancy and help users navigate content more intuitively.

Now that you have a basic understanding of how they work, here are some recommended practices for creating internal site links and anchor text:

- Use relevant keywords in the anchor text of the link that accurately describe and reinforce the keywords of the page being linked to.

- Activate the text keywords used in the body of your pages into internal keyword links pointing to another relevant article or page within your site, similar to the SEMPO example in Figure 6.6.

- Use text links whenever possible, and avoid using images as text.

- Include keywords in the alt text exactly as the image is rendered, if you choose to use images as text (more in the next section, "Alt Text Attributes").

- Do not gratuitously stuff keywords into your anchor text.

Alt Text Attributes

Alt text attributes of images help users who are visually impaired and users who choose to view web pages with images turned off in their browser. Search engines also use alt text attributes to help identify relevant keywords to accurately describe the image. As you browse web pages on your own, you can view anchor text by turning off images or hovering over an image with your cursor (the text that appears on mouseover of an image is the alt text). Here are the recommended practices for creating alt text attributes for images:

- Always accurately describe the image; remember that alt text is for both search engines and visually impaired users.

- Include alt text attributes for all images, except for images intended for formatting (bullets, line breaks, and so on).

- Keep accessibility and visually impaired users in mind when writing your alt text for images (or any other elements mentioned in this guide, for that matter). Visually impaired web users rely on special browsers to read text using speech output methods, and stuffed keyword text can create a terrible experience for these users. You can find more information on web accessibility at www.w3.org/WAI/intro/accessibility.php.

- If an image contains text, then the alt text should reflect this text exactly as it is rendered or very closely described.

- If you need a maximum word count for describing pictures or scenes, 6 to 10 words should be sufficient.

It is generally a good practice to reinforce the alt text keyword in the file name or URL path of the image.

Maintaining Keyword Consistency at the Page Level for SEO

Now that you have learned about some of the basics of SEO-based copywriting, let's consider the consistency of a theme through the page. In addition to putting your keywords in the right places, being consistent with your page or asset theme is critical. As you look at more pages from an SEO point of view, you will start to notice that a good portion of the most highly visible pages have consistency of a single keyword or keyword phrase throughout the aforementioned aspects of a page. For example, let's review the web page for the philosopher and sociologist Manuel Castells on Wikipedia. Wikipedia is a well-optimized site, in addition to its breadth of content, and it serves as an overall example for good on-page optimization, no matter what page you are viewing. The keyword theme of the sample page is *Manuel Castells*. Figure 6.7 shows various elements highlighted to illustrate the consistency of the phrase throughout different key areas of the page.

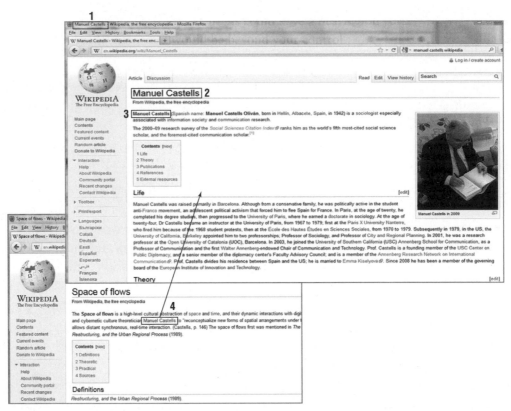

Figure 6.7 A view and analysis showing the consistency of the key phrase *Manuel Castells* through four key areas of the page and inbound anchor text links from other pages.

1. The main keyword theme is emphasized in the title element.

2. The on-page title contains the main keyword.

3. The target keyword phrase is emphasized in the first paragraph.

4. The breakout screen cap for the "Space of Flows" page features a link with the anchor text *Manuel Castells*, which points to the Manuel Castells page on Wikipedia. By including this anchor text in the link, the keyword *Manuel Castells* is reinforced for both the user and the search engine.

There is an easy method to see how a search engine views the textual layer of a web page, and I recommend you use it to assess the on-page optimization of your own web pages in Google and the social-media sites that you commonly use. When you enter a search result in Google, hover over the arrow next to the result with your cursor, and a pop-out window of the page will appear. Click the link just above the image that says "Cached" in the anchor text, as shown in Figure 6.8. Google will show you the HTML cached version of the page with a separate browser heading above the cached copy, as shown in Figure 6.9.

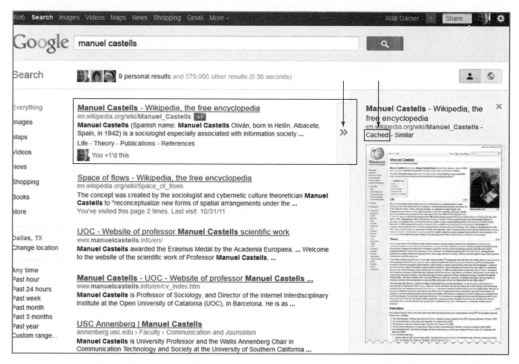

Figure 6.8 How to find the Google cached page for each search result. Click the arrow to reveal a side pop-out window on the search page.

Click the Text-Only Version link. This link will take you to a stripped-down textual skeleton of the page, as Google sees it in the code markup, shown in Figure 6.10.

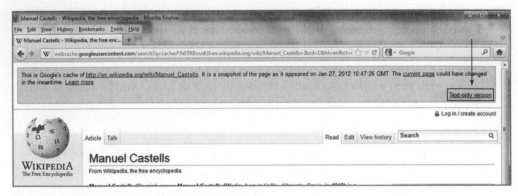

Figure 6.9 The link to the text-only version of the cached page for a search result

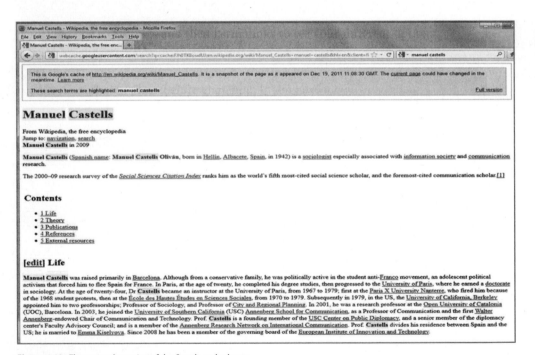

Figure 6.10 The text-only version of the Google cached page

Notice that this page highlights the keyword theme through the page, in addition to revealing the consistency of a keyword throughout the page. It also shows the semantic markup of the headings or, in other words, the headings and text that have a larger font size. No matter how much fluff or code you may view on a particular website, this is one version of how search engines strip pages down to their barest textual elements in order to determine on-page themes and to get a literal meaning of what the page is about.

By now I have covered many aspects of the landscape, strategy, and content for developing a real-time publishing strategy. As mentioned at this beginning, I would recommend that you refer to this chapter periodically for new content ideas, and also as a guide to digital asset optimization. In the next chapter you will venture into the deep space of social networks on the Internet to view the most popular social-network platforms.

Social-Network Platforms

Now that you have the basic elements of content strategy, market research, and content development simmering in your brain, it is time to start thinking about your primary social platform for distributing great content to your audience. Recall Figure 3.1 in Chapter 3, "Ramping Up for a Real-Time Content Marketing Strategy"; it illustrated a middle ring of key social-media sites that will be critical to your real-time publishing platform. This chapter will focus on four of the largest social-media sites for content sharing, audience engagement, and content distribution. They are Google+, Twitter, LinkedIn, and Facebook, and they will become part of the middle ring for your own publishing strategy.

7

Chapter Contents
Why you should engage in the top-tier social networks
How to start developing a social publishing platform
How to optimize your social presence for search
How to build up your networks
How to understand the combined search and social nuances of each network

Though this chapter focuses on the larger networks, it is worth noting that smaller networks (forums or answer sites, for example) can be extremely important to your social strategy. For many businesses, these niche networks may even be more important to your strategy than the larger networks, because there is often a higher concentration of like-minded people, at least as they relate to your specific business. I also strongly believe that increasing the specificity of a social network is a key element of social relevancy and that you will continue to see a trend of networks getting smaller and more niche in the future, rather than trying to be the biggest.

How to Think About "Search and Social" for the Major Networks

The topic of top-tier social platforms is a big one in the context of the overall picture for Internet marketing, and I do not intend for this chapter to be the "be all, end all" for your social network-targeting strategy. There are many great books that address each of these networks individually, and some of these books are listed in the appendix for additional reading. This chapter will focus on recognizing the interdependent "search and social" aspects of each network, gaining real-time trust with these networks, and optimizing your search presence both for external search engines and for visibility within your network.

If you have already begun engaging in one or more of the top-tier networks, you can use this chapter as a guide to optimize your existing presence and examine the other top-tier networks that you may not already be using. This chapter will serve as a well-rounded guide for the search and social elements of major networks, but it should also serve as the beginning to understanding the greater nuances and engagement aspects of each one.

Why Top-Tier Networks Are Fundamental to Your Publishing Platform

In addition to being a primary launch point for content and conversation in your audience-engagement strategy, there are many other great reasons to make Google+, Twitter, Facebook, or LinkedIn part of your primary strategy for publishing content. Here are some of the principal reasons for engaging in these major networks:

They Have the Biggest Built-in Audiences The four networks listed here cast a wide net to reach your audience and cover a large percentage of all Internet users.

Your Audience Is Already There Whether you sell rocket fuel, food, or fishing gear, your targeted audience is likely using one or more of the networks covered in this chapter, either directly for business or for other uses. Your job is to determine how they interact, where they interact, how they consume information, and how they find information in networks.

They Are Primary Distribution Points for Content Across the Entire Web For both search and social, these four networks are among the top places where information and content travels first across the Web in real-time. If the current state of the Internet can be described as a digital organism, then these social networks might be considered its main arteries for distribution.

They Resonate Directly with Search-Engine Results As social signals have become more important than ever for ranking content, these top networks are well known to send the social signals that the engines look for.

Again, the top four networks covered in this chapter should serve as a launching point for your real-time publishing platform. Remember that there are other social networks to consider for your primary distribution strategy, both popular and more nuanced to your business.

The Basic Interdependencies between Social Engagement and Search Visibility

In many ways, the merging disciplines of search and social are still emerging and being defined. Understanding the interdependencies between search and social will help you attain the most from these top social networks, but also help your search presence. As you go through the following sections to establish or optimize your existing social spaces, here are a few considerations that apply to all four major networks:

Building Up Your Networks Is an SEO Tactic Simply put, the larger the size of your network, the faster your content can travel across the Web to spread the signals that search engines look for. Spend time cultivating your networks in a meaningful way, and good search visibility will follow in a multitude of ways that will be described later in this chapter.

"Engagement" Is Both a Strategy and a Tactic Focus on engaging your audience in a human way, and build up the quality and quantity of your network of friends, followers, and circles. While the size and quality of your networks are important to search, make search a secondary purpose for engaging in social media, and the search results will follow.

Social Interaction Is a New Form of Publishing Whether you *like* or *retweet* or *friend* or *follow*, you and your company leave behind an online trail of pages, links, and connections everywhere you go. All of these interactions can be considered a new form of publishing in the sense that this trail is a reflection of your identity, where you have been, and where you are going. Your interactions are used by both search engines and social networks to better inform their products and services and to improve how people connect and find information in a relevant way.

Social Platforms Are Constantly Evolving Remember that social networks are constantly changing to add new features and updates to, ideally, improve your networking experience. While this chapter includes what is known today about the search and social aspects of each, always look at new updates in terms of how it impacts the "search and social" experience.

Natural-Language Keywords and Content Connect You Directly with Your Audience A human touch is required to converse and share in networks, but also remember that connections are rooted in content and by keyword association. The words you choose may be the difference between engaging with someone in your audience and missing a connection entirely by omission. In many ways, your command of keyword research is directly related to how well you will engage in social channels, and expert search and social marketers should have an expert command of this skill set. In social spaces and in search, natural language (and by extension keyword language) evolves in real-time.

Think Like a Search Engine When Engaging in Social Social networks are starting to think like search engines, and search engines are starting to think like social networks. Turn this thinking around to your own advantage when engaging in social by applying the search concepts described in previous chapters to the network experience. Remember that keywords are connections to people, that people in your networks are links, and you can always be *relevant* to create better social experiences. Read Chapter 13, "Social Media Management," for more information.

Work to Achieve Rising Velocity in Social, with Spikes in Clicks, Searches, and Sharing Remember the term *velocity* as you engage and publish in networks. Velocity in search and social means the speed of spiking keyword search, spiking shared assets, and spiking click-throughs for a digital asset. It culminates in increased visibility for that asset in a speedier timeframe through search and social channels.

Share, Comment, Engage, Converse, and Do It All Again As discussed in previous chapters, sharing and engaging are core tactics for success in social channels, so do them often and in a relevant way across each of these networks.

While this chapter focuses on the search aspects of social spaces, it is important to remember that some of these signals may be in flux, and others are constantly changing. New features may have come and gone by the time this book is printed, and the different elements covered may have also changed. As these new features change, continue to consider the potential implication of the change from both the search and social levels. Also see Chapter 12, "More Considerations for Real-Time Content Marketing, Search, and Social," for a table showing the various social signals picked up by Bing and Google.

Increasing Velocity for Publishing in Networks

In earlier chapters, I discussed the concept of velocity as it relates to real-time interaction, real-time search, and real-time publishing. While the search engines and social networks offer no specific marketing prescription about the velocity aspects of their algorithms, it is worth noting the top three elements of content velocity and distribution in real-time publishing:

Keyword-Interest Velocity Both search engines and social networks track the velocity of keyword-search interest in the form of trends. Fast-rising keyword interest in search engines triggers freshness filters that spread content beyond social search channels. Fast-rising conversations in social networks like Twitter bubble up in the form of trending topics. Keyword velocity is often based on an event, such as a reaction to news or an announcement. Marketers generally should be less concerned with creating search interest, and more concerned with monitoring it closely and reacting quickly to spiking interest by creating content and conversation.

Sharing Velocity Google and Bing have both publicly stated on multiple occasions that they view tweets and other status updates that contain a URL "differently." This means that this information is seen as sort of a real-time networked link, and the velocity at which it is shared (or retweeted, in the case of Twitter) determines the actual velocity. Marketers should focus on knowing what topics are rising or hot and share and create information accordingly to capture increased visibility.

Click-Rate Velocity Google in particular is known to time-stamp clicks to track velocity, and it is likely that other social networks and engines are tracking click-rate velocity as well. By tracking the rate of clicks to a URL over time (seconds, minutes, hours, and so on), the velocity rate of clicks through the URL can be tracked to become an indicator of its rising popularity. Once a piece of content is released into the social wilds, the click rate will be used to determine the popularity of that content.

When you get the perfect storm of all three velocity events happening at once, content can ascend to becoming visible in a way that can described only as a new form of digital mass media.

In a real-time marketing and publishing environment, publishers that do well have repeated success with all three aspects of velocity. There are four basic characteristics of successful real-time publishers:

They Live in the Language and Sharing Trends of Their Audience Cutting-edge publishers use keyword tools, monitor the buzz of their competition, and constantly work to interpret what their audience is saying in networks. They understand that natural audience language is a living concept and the only way to stay ahead is to understand the history of the language of their target audience and that it is constantly evolving. Furthermore, they live and publish in the language of their audience, so many of their publishing strategies come about intuitively and serendipitously.

They Publish Fluidly and Quickly Upon understanding or anticipating what the audience may be thinking, publishing in real-time requires a speedy response to getting content live. In many cases, you may have only seconds or minutes to get a major scoop or ride the wave of a trending conversation.

They Have Broad and/or Relevant Networks in Which to Disseminate Their Content While this chapter is largely about the combined "search and social" aspects of the top-tier social networks, it also about considering the buildup of your network reach as an SEO and content-visibility tactic. Successful digital publishers produce great content that is informed by the ongoing and spiking interests of their audience, but they also have networks (friends, followers, connections, circles, influencers, and so on) of like-minded audiences in which to disseminate their content. Use this chapter to determine which networks you want to use (one or all), and get busy building up your networks in a meaningful and sustainable way.

They Publish a Lot, and They Don't Expect Every Publishing Attempt to Be a Home Run Successful real-time publishers don't fret over every single digital asset and wonder why it isn't trending on the home page of Twitter. Instead, they create a lot of good content, knowing that some of it will stick from time to time. It is a self-reinforcing principle in the sense that gradual publishing will attract new users and readers over time. As one of my clients once stated, you can forget about obsessing about your first 25 blog posts or your first 50 videos on YouTube, because you don't have an audience yet, and no one is watching.

The Big-Four Social Networks

Over the remaining sections of this chapter, I will cover four of the largest social networks: Google+, Twitter, Facebook, and LinkedIn. There is a plethora of information written about these networks, both in print and on the Web, but in this section I will focus on the combined "search and social" aspects of each one. You will learn about how to extend your visibility by building up your networks, how to optimize your profiles for maximum visibility, and how to get the most out of your social efforts by applying time-tested search-optimization principles. So, without further delay, let's get started with the "new big kid" on the social block, Google+.

The Quick Search and Social Guide to Google+

When Google introduced its own social network, Google+, in late June 2011, it was the beginning of what the company views as a long-term play into the world of search and social combined. Similar to the way Google leveraged Twitter as its own human social layer for Google's Real-Time Search product in December 2009, Google+ has since become a key social layer for the Search Plus Your World search service in Google+. Google+ is still in its infancy, and new features and tweaks are rolled out on a weekly basis as of this writing. As described previously, it is important to "think like a search engine" in Google+, because you will constantly be challenged as a user and marketer to navigate and understand changes as they occur.

In many ways, Google+ is like an SEO gift for first movers into the network. Many companies and businesses are slow to embrace Google+ as a social network, and the result is that the early adopters are getting the lion's share of the search visibility. Google+ wants new users to join up, and the lack of visibility of other companies provides priority visibility to current participants in new socially personalized results. As more companies get online, this visibility may become crowded out, but clearly this is an advantage to the first participants to get there and establish a presence.

The bottom line is that Google+ is Google's own proprietary human social lens that serves as a social network and informs real-time search, personalized search, and even web search. In many ways, it is the epitome of "search and social" together, and if you value your own SEO results, then Google+ is one of the primary methods of generating the social signals that Google uses for its search results.

Getting Started

Getting started with Google+ is as easy as signing up for Gmail (www.gmail.com) and then creating a Google+ account at https://plus.google.com. Once you are in, there are many features to explore and consider for your search and social presence. This section will focus on the aspects that have the most direct impact for optimizing your profile, and it will elaborate on the combined search and social effects of using various elements of the Google+ network.

It is also very important to read Google's full guidelines before getting involved in this network. You can read the terms here: www.google.com/intl/en/+/policy/pagesterm.html. Because Google+ is changing on a weekly basis, many of the items covered in this section reflect only the mainstay elements that have been around since its inception or are elements that I believe are important to "search and social."

A Basic Algorithmic View of Google+ Compared to Traditional Website SEO

In July 2009, I wrote a column for MediaPost entitled "What an Algorithmic Approach to Twitter's Social-Search Layer Might Look Like" (www.mediapost.com/publications/article/109358/) to illustrate how search engines could evaluate authority, influence, and relevancy in a social network. As many SEOs try to better understand how traditional search principles can apply to people in networks, I re-created a comparison from that article for this chapter to illustrate the SEO view to Google+ (and later in the chapter, Twitter). Using the same methods as that column, here is a comparison of how Google might view the connections, relationships, and content in Google+ in order to evaluate them for greater visibility and social relevancy in Google+ search:

Algorithmic SEO view of websites	Algorithmic view of Google+
Domain authority (root level and sitewide; example: Domain.com)	User ID (tertiary domain; example: plus.google.com/userid)
Duplicate content	+1'd and shared content
Freshness of content	Freshness of interactions and activity
Incoming links	People who have circled you, +1s, or shares
Outgoing and internal site links	People you have circled or have +1'd or shared content with
Keyword anchor text	Text used to describe circles, both incoming and outgoing
Link quality and authority	Authority of people and companies you are connected to, both incoming and outgoing

Algorithmic SEO view of websites	Algorithmic view of Google+
Bad link neighborhoods	Shady circles (containing spam or otherwise irrelevant to you and your business)
Theme and topic of site	Predominant themes and topics of your network connections, shares, comments, and so on
Ratio of incoming vs. outgoing links	Ratio of circled people to the number of people you have been circled by

Social Connections in Google+

It is important to note from the outset that Google+ relies on many other factors outside of your Google+ network to personalize your search and social experience. In addition to your Google+ Circles, the Google+ help page (`http://support.google.com/websearch/bin/answer.py?hl=en&answer=1067707`) states that the social connections can influence visibility or other elements of your social experience. These connections include people in your Gmail chat list, people in your Google contacts, people you're following on Google Reader, and people who are publicly connected to you in other networks, such as Twitter.

In addition to social connections, Google has also bundled its privacy policy to cover all of its 60+ properties. So, theoretically, your video-watching patterns on YouTube could impact how your results are shown in Google web search. Any behavior that is observed on any other property within the Google network can spread over to inform other Google services. Before starting your Google presence, read all of Google's terms of service to ensure that you are comfortable with its requirements for both your personal presence and your business presence.

The +1 Feature

The +1 feature arrived in Google just prior to the launch of Google+ and is core to the search and social experience in Google+ and other Google properties. In traditional SEO terms, a +1 is somewhat like a link or a vote toward a particular web page, digital asset, or comment on Google+, and it is visible to others in your network but also publicly shown on your profile. In the Webmaster FAQ (`http://support.google.com/webmasters/bin/answer.py?hl=en&answer=1140194`), Google states that +1s from people in your network can be a "useful signal" to help determine the relevance of a search query.

As with any other potential ranking signal, Google is always testing and weighing the effect of these signals on its overall results. At this writing, +1s are having the most impact on results seen by *people who have circled you*. Just as links and tweets with URLs also impact the search results, you should monitor the progress of how Google views +1s on the main web-earch results over time. Google also allows you to see the impact of +1s when connected in Webmaster Central, including areas it defines as "search impact," "activity," and "audience."

As a result of +1s for content, Google may apply annotations to the search results of people in your network. Figure 7.1 shows a +1 annotation with a user's icon next to the result. Also shown is an example of the +1 button, which is appended at the end of the URL.

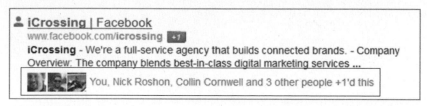

Figure 7.1 Sample Google search result with +1 social annotations. The +1 button is in the upper-right corner.

When logged into a Google account, Google+ users will see the +1 annotations of people in their circles on web-search results. As Google alludes to in the FAQ previously quoted, the elements of social relevancy—that is, the known recommendations from people within a network—help people identify results that are more useful to them or that may better satisfy their search intent.

Historically, going for #1 in the natural results has always been a core goal for search engine-optimizers, but with increased personalization and network presence, your lower-ranked web pages can now trump a #1 ranking with a simple thumbs-up from an influencer in your network. Remember, social relevancy is about quality and authority, so the influence that your little icon has in your search results is directly proportional to how highly the people in your network value your opinion or contribution to the social community. Cultivate and curate quality, and your relevancy will increase in search as well.

There have also been claims that +1'd content receives a generally higher click-through rate than nonannotated results. A study by SEO Effect suggests that there is a 20 percent increase in click-through rate for friends in your network who see an annotated result (www.seoeffect.com/images/the%20seo%20effect%20google%20%2B1%20 button%20experiment.pdf).

+1s are somewhat like Twitter's version of the tweet or Facebook's version of the like. +1'ing content is as simple as clicking the +1 button on the content you are reading, the content shared in Google+, or the content in the Google search results. As mentioned in earlier chapters, aggregate +1s also help a URL attain the status of a "networked link" and should be a mandatory element of your search and social strategy. Here are some basic tips and considerations for +1s:

+1 Only the Pages You Would Want People in Your Network to See One of the "gifts" I mentioned earlier is that +1'ing a particular page is like an external link or vote for that page. It is visible between you and the person in your network. It is only as relevant to the others in your network *as they believe you are relevant.* In other words, if you consistently

+1 relevant and thematic content that others find useful, then your +1s will carry a higher mark of authority with those users. In simple terms, +1s are a mark of your own personal credibility with other people in your network, and your +1s are only as "good" as you are "credible." This is a fundamental mark of user engagement. Do not spam, and always monitor the terms of service—both the written terms of service and the implied "unwritten" terms of service espoused by Google's Matt Cutts and other Google insiders. Don't go overboard with your +1s. Do what is right for the people and users in your network as a guide, and monitor any changes in Google's policies and recommended practices for +1s. Also note that your +1s default to public view.

+1s on the Search Engine Results Page Will Capture the Context of the Search Phrase Used   Remember that when you +1 a result in Google search, Google captures the query you used to find that result and adds the context of that keyword to your annotation. SEOs might observe that this attribution of keyword phrases is similar to the way search engines apply the context of anchor text to a link.

Add +1 and Sharing Buttons to Your Own Content, Including the Home Page, Individual Pages, and Category Pages   Your digital assets can be +1'd at the site and page levels and directly from your own pages using Google+ graphic buttons. Using a Google+ button makes it easier for users to share your content with their networks to provide higher visibility for your pages within Google+. See the following links for more information about how to set up +1s and Google+ sharing for your own content: www.google.com/webmasters/+1/button/ and www.google.com/+/business/promote.html. One other note—before implementing +1s on your own digital assets, see the last point in this list, about +1s and Robots.txt.

+1 Comments of People in Your Circles Only When You Really Like the Content or Believe It Could Be Useful to Others in Your Network   Remember that +1s are a reflection of your own credibility and social relevancy, so only +1 the content that you would want to have your name and picture tied directly to. If you focus on spending more time engaging in your Google+ network, then the volume of +1 engagement comes naturally. If you stop and think "I've got only 20 minutes to +1 everything I can find," then you may be doing it for the wrong reasons.

Connect Your Website to Your Google+ Page with a Google Badge   A Google Badge is a way to connect your website directly to your Google profile, and in its FAQ, Google "strongly recommends" that webmasters make this connection. Google also recommends it as an "enhanced version of the +1 button." In effect, it creates a sort of handshake between your main web asset and your Google+ presence and verifies your web presence with Google as a publisher. Read more about Google Badges at https://developers.google.com/+/plugins/badge/config.

Don't Buy +1s, or Use Any Commercial Influence   Buying +1s is akin to buying links, and Google doesn't like it when users and webmasters buy links. In short, don't do it. Google will catch on, and you can't buy credibility in Google+ anyway. You have to earn it and work for it by being present and by participating. If Google follows its practices in

Google+ in the way it approaches buying links in natural search, then the potential penalty may be an outright ban from the search index, Google+, or both.

Don't +1 Anything Perceived as a "Bad Neighborhood" or Spam In link development, there is a common SEO description of spammy link networks as being part of a "bad neighborhood." A "bad link neighborhood" is a place that you don't want to your own site links to be found, lest the search engines start to align your own site with a bad link profile and relegate your search visibility to the junk pile. The same goes for your +1 profile. Align your business with quality publishers that are authoritative and within your realm of influence, and you too will be identified as part of that theme.

+1s Override `Robots.txt` `Robots.txt` is a text file that sits on your root domain server and tells search engines and other agents which pages you would like them to crawl for the index. Crawlers do not have to obey this directive, but the major engines will. Google has stated that it perceives pages that host +1 buttons or scripts on a page as a "public action" or, in other words, pages that a webmaster wants Google to crawl. When placing +1 buttons or scripts on your pages, ensure that you are not making any of your private pages public, because the +1 overrides your `Robots.txt` directives to otherwise ignore the page. (See `http://support.google.com/webmasters/bin/answer.py?hl=en&answer=1140194`.)

Also note that when a URL is shared, the text shown is pulled from the *title element* and the *meta description* tag of the web page. These two elements were detailed in Chapter 6, "Creating Effective and Engaging Content." Google's use of the meta description tag underscores the need to create great meta description tags for all pages that you want users to check out, based on the idea that your description tag is like a welcome mat, even though it does not provide a direct keyword impact on search results. In Figure 7.2, the share display for the example page pulls in a clean title and description to show to the user.

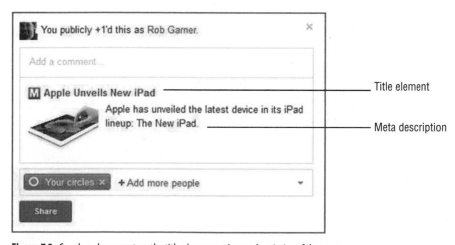

Figure 7.2 Google+ shares capture the title element and meta description of the asset.

Circles

Your company presence becomes more prominent within the SERPs of those who have circled you, and there is tremendous first-mover advantage for participating now, just as many webmasters who have sites dating back to 1998 to 1999 are still doing well in natural search today. Creating and segmenting your network streams for personal and business profiles is a primary feature of Google+, so here are some of the key considerations for managing your network of circles:

Build Up Your Network of Circles Building up your network of circled people (and being circled) can be considered a method of increasing your visibility in Google+ search, particularly for those within your network. Circling will help introduce you to others within your business area or theme and will often attract reciprocating circles back to you. I recommend you do not go wild or overboard with circling, because your network is only as useful as the people you have circled in it. Curate lists of people you would like to connect with by association, that you would like to read on a regular basis, or with whom you share an interest.

Circle People Who Are Relevant to You Remember that being relevant is as much a social principle as it is a search principle. Stay focused on your goals for participation in the network and create themes of circled people and companies that you would like to be aligned with. The great thing about Google+ Circles is that it allows you to segment multiple interests. This allows you to put all of your sales- and marketing-geek friends in one circle, and a segment of your other geeky friends in another.

Invite People via Email If you have a Gmail account, Google+ will take your email list and find other people in your contact list who are already Google+ members; it provides an easy process for circling and inviting those people to join Google+. Take advantage of this feature to get your network started quickly. You can also add your Google+ account link in your email signature lines of any email client and promote your Google+ account just as you would a LinkedIn, Twitter, or Facebook profile.

Circle Those Who Align Descriptively with the Main Keyword Theme of Your Business Use the Google+ search functionality to find others in Google+ who may share a common and relevant interest with the network you are trying to build. At this point, it helps to leverage your keyword research and tools described in previous chapters to find highly relevant companies and individuals to circle and connect with. This is another prime example of how keywords are connections to people.

Don't Always Expect Everyone to Circle You Back Just because you circle someone does not mean they have to circle you back. Circle them because you want to read their content or because their profile fits one of your reasons for using Google+ with your business.

You Don't Have to Circle Everyone Who Circles You As previously described, it is not mandatory to reciprocate with a circle. Circle them back to form a stronger connection or if there is some other reason that you think they are a sustainable and worthy connection.

Label Your Circles Appropriately, Using Searchable Keyword Language When Applicable The way you label your circles is similar to the link anchor text principles described in Chapter 6, "Creating Effective and Engaging Content." In SEO terms, by circling someone, you are effectively linking to them internally, and by writing a keyword description, you are creating anchor text for that link. Labeling your circle is a potential way that Google can apply a label or keyword tag to groups of people in your network as you see them and think about them in your own language.

Segment Who Should See Your Post in Circles, by Group Remember that when you label someone or a company, this view can become public, depending on your settings. Switch to full public view, or hide them by adjusting your account settings. See `www.google.com/+/ business/share.html`.

Use Circles to Send Out or Filter Relevant Messages The good news with Google+ is that the world does not have to be one big fishbowl, and you can send out relevant messages to people and companies based on similar interests. So, save your sales and marketing quips for the people in your marketing-geek circle, and save your tech quips for your tech-geek circle.

Optimizing Your Personal Page

Like Twitter profile pages, Google+ profile pages are the hub of activity and content for its users, and many are ranking in the top results for primary brand terms and personal names in Google search. In addition, Google+ profile pages are appearing in drop-down menus for Google Suggest and are also being given prominent placement in the right column of the Google main web search, for both users who are logged in and those who are logged out. Like on other social-media sites, you are often given very little that is "optimizable," but considering Google's direct connection between its social and search services, it is important to pay as much attention as possible to optimizing the profile page. Here are the basic considerations for optimizing your primary Google+ personal profile:

Complete as Much of the Profile as Possible Google will apply a percentage grade to show how much of your personal profile is complete. From a search perspective, a complete profile offers you more opportunities to become visible in search and to show others in Google+ how you are relevant to their network.

Use Keywords Use keywords in your profiles whenever reasonable and relevant. It is important to note that you should apply your own keyword research established in previous chapters to optimizing your profile. A keyword is not just a word or phrase for search engines; it is a connection to your like-minded audience, which consists of real people.

Add Photos While the overall design of Google+ profile templates is sparse and simple, the one area you have for visual appeal is in your photos. Google+ tiles multiple photos at the top of your profile, so this is your opportunity to make a great visual first impression. Use images that best illustrate who you are and what your main interests are. Be sure to read Google's complete terms of service and fine print in image licensing for Google+ uploaded photos before setting up any galleries (`www.google.com/intl/en/+/policy/pagesterm.html`).

Enhance Your Description ("Bragging Rights") Your "bragging rights" are the credentials or traits you tout in the basic area that you get to describe yourself. If you put on your search hat, choose common keywords that describe who you are and can also be used by others to describe who they are. While this can help you become found in search, it can also help you connect socially with others using a common keyword-trigger language. Take advantage of the full length of your description in terms of overall word count, if possible.

Link to Twitter, Facebook, and Other Social Media Profiles Google+ offers you the option to link to social profiles in both Twitter and Facebook, among other major networks. In the past, Google used Twitter links in other Google profile pages to create your social-circle results. While Google+ now relies on its own social layer to inform social search, it is possible and likely that your other crawlable connections could be blended in with social search in the future, as noted in the Google+ FAQ excerpt described earlier in this chapter.

Add Location for Georelevancy Adding your geographic location makes your presence more relevant to local discussions and local search. If your business or company focuses on a particular region of city, then be sure to complete this section.

Optimizing Your Brand or Product Page

Brand and product pages are currently very sparse in Google+, and the search and social benefits are in the sweat equity that you put into them (see Figure 7.3 for an example of the brand page for the Ford Motor Company). In addition to the optimizations previously discussed for personal pages, consider these other elements for optimizing your brand pages.

Add Photos and Images, and Tag Them Properly Ensure that you have a full photo gallery of relevant images, and describe them properly. Other people who circled you or your business can also upload photos to their profiles, and these photos may appear in your image gallery. Google+ also allows you to tag the photos to add keyword and textual descriptions—take advantage of this feature, because keyword tagging is a standard principle of SEO. You can also add readable captions to your photos. Be sure to read Google's complete terms of service and fine print in image licensing for Google+ uploaded photos before setting up any galleries.

Place Your Page in the Proper Category Remember to describe your business or product pages as accurately as possible, based on the options provided. This increases your social relevancy and tells Google how you ultimately see the theme of your business at a high level.

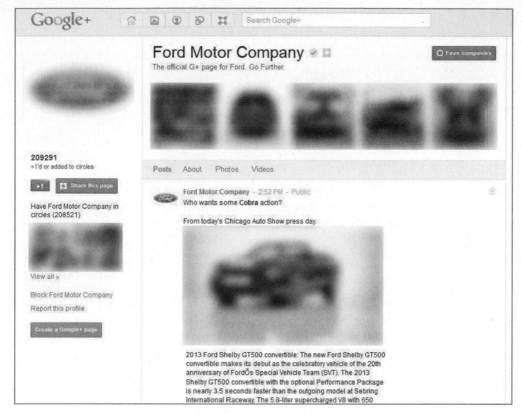

Figure 7.3 Google+ brand page for the Ford Motor Company

Follow People Back Once They Have Circled You   Currently business pages can circle individuals only if those individuals have first initiated a circle around your business. If people are interested enough in your business, complete the handshake to enable two-way communication by circling them back.

Encourage Others to Circle You on Your Website and from Other Social Spaces   Just as you would promote your Facebook or Twitter presence, add Google+ to the mix and ask people to circle you. Put your account ID in clickable links wherever you may have a web presence, and put in a call to action to get new people to circle you. You can also add a Google Badge to help make a direct connection between your digital assets and your Google+ brand page. Remember that the more your network grows in Google+, the greater footprint you will have in Google search (personalized and social search).

Confirming Ownership of Your Website in Google+

Just as in traditional SEO, anything you can do to increase trust with Google will help your search and social visibility. Google recommends that you add a Google Badge and establish your owned brand presence as a publisher. In addition to adding a Google Badge, there are two ways to confirm ownership of your site with Google:

- Create a `rel="publisher"` link from the main page of your website to your Google+ page. The link code follows:

  ```
  <a rel="publisher" href="https://plus.google.com/
  YourGoogle+AcctURLHere">Find us on Google+</a>
  ```

- If you don't want to put the link on your public-facing page, you can include the following code in the head section of your main page:

  ```
  <link rel="publisher" href="https://plus.google.com/[yourpageID]" />
  ```

Read more about connecting your website as a publisher at `http://support` `.google.com/webmasters/bin/answer.py?hl=en&answer=1708844&topic=1634166&ctx=topic`.

The `rel=author` markup is another great feature that integrates your Google+ account information and will be discussed at greater length inChapter 10, "Technical Considerations and Implementation."

Google+ Local

In May 2012, Google announced that it was transitioning place pages into Google+ and renaming them to Google+ Local. The result is a more consistent look and feel with other Google+ pages, giving the business owner greater control of the listing. Also included in this update are the addition of Zagat reviews and new tabs that include additional information about a business. Google+ Local pages will also be indexed in Google search, so it is important to ensure that you have completed as much of the information for the listing as possible. The biggest news in this latest iteration of Google local services is that the business owner has more control through social participation and updating of the listing. Prior to this update, business owners had little to no control at all of their local listings, which often resulted in having outdated or incorrect data or having their listing hijacked by a competing business or spammer. Visit `www.google.com/+/learnmore/local/` for more information.

The Quick Search and Social Guide to Twitter

The rise of Twitter has brought about a revolution in status-based networks, in terms of both the speed at which information travels in social networks and how it can inform search engines at the bleeding edge of recency, as described in Chapter 2, "Understanding Search and Social." While search engineers don't give out the secret sauce of their algorithms, they have increasingly been discussing the impact of social status updates on web-search results. The bottom line is that Twitter can't be ignored by digital-content publishers as a source for setting off a chain of content sharing. Real-time publishers should have a live presence and be aware of the search implications of their actions in Twitter, and in this section you will learn how to optimize your Twitter presence by utilizing search principles.

Twitter has been at the center of many key real-time search-engine innovations over the past three to four years. Small start-up and now Walmart-owned OneRiot developed a search engine (before Google and Bing) that took the velocity and volume of rising retweets and turned it into a direct signal and ranking factor (results showed the highest number of retweeted URLs first). Bing and Google later tapped into the Twitter social layer to inform their own real-time search services in December 2009. Google has since replaced the Twitter stream of data with its own proprietary Google+, though Bing notably continues to have an exclusive license to use real-time Twitter data to inform its Bing search results.

Nofollow Links in Twitter and What It Means to Search

One common question SEOs have about Twitter is whether links "count" toward their link profiles in search algorithms. Twitter, along with many other major social-media sites, implement the "nofollow" attribute to their links, which is an instruction or request that search engines not follow those links. The reason for nofollow is that on many social sites consisting mainly of user-generated content, links were being used to game search engines, and as a result, websites of all sizes were having to clean up and police spam on a massive level. The nofollow link attribute is only a request, and the engines may disregard them if they find the links to be useful in some way. So, although nofollow generally discourages spam, the engines still reserve judgment on whether to apply link values at their own discretion.

Twitter data is a classic example where the search engines have provided solid evidence that it has ignored the nofollow attribute and has counted those links toward search visibility within one or more of its search services. As mentioned in Chapter 6, engines started treating tweets that contained links "differently" and therefore at some level consider it as a direct or indirect signal.

So, this action raises a question: do nofollow links count toward search results? Again, the answer lies in thinking like a search engine. Yes, they want to discourage spam as much as possible, but using tweets and status updates in the right way can provide a useful signal toward search results. It is my belief, and the belief among many leading search experts, that Twitter and other status-based networks do provide some link benefits, with, of course, many other quantitative and qualitative considerations. The same goes for any other site that implements nofollow—you have to think about how the information is used and how either direct or indirect link benefits can come about before engaging or dismissing that particular social network as part of your content-dissemination and link-development strategy.

A Basic Algorithmic View of Twitter Compared to Traditional Website SEO

As an extension of the algorithmic example provided for Google in this chapter, here is a similar algorithmic comparison of Twitter, as I described it in an original article for MediaPost in July 2009. Bing has since confirmed that they do take a similar algorithmic view of Twitter data to help inform search results.

Algorithmic SEO view of websites	Algorithmic view of Twitter
Domain authority	Twitter user ID
Duplicate content (ignored, sign of lower quality)	Retweets (compressed as a network link signal, more valuable when grouped)
Freshness of content	Freshness of interactions and activity
Incoming links	Followers
Outgoing links	Accounts you follow
Link quality and authority	Authority or people and companies that follow you
Bad link neighborhoods	Tweets or accounts with links to spammy sites; following spam accounts
Theme and topic of site	Predominant themes and topics of your account, people in your network, and tweets
Ratio of incoming vs. outgoing links	Ratio of accounts you follow to the quantity and quality of accounts that follow you

Since this column was written, Bing has confirmed in public interviews and at conferences that it views Twitter and other forms of social-network data and connections in this manner. For more information on how Bing treats Twitter data in its search results, read about Bing search and social engineer Paul Yiu in Chapter 2.

Optimization for Tweets

The way you optimize your tweets can determine how visible your content becomes in both Google and Bing search, and how well the search engines can process your Twitter social signals. When you consider the implications of status updates on search results as they have been described by search engineers in previous chapters, it becomes quickly apparent that there is a lot going on inside a short "140 characters or less" tweet. The search-optimization implications of tweets vary from individual tweets ranking in search to accumulated links from tweets to and the dissemination of your content that may lead to other citations or links, and so on. It is also important to remember that you may be optimizing tweets for web search, for internal Twitter search, or for both. The following are some considerations for optimizing tweets for higher visibility in both web search and internal Twitter search. Figure 7.4 shows a short breakdown of the core elements of a tweet.

Establish the Primary Value Provided to Your Followers Remember to answer the question of "why?" before you send a single tweet. Know your purpose for sharing information, who is in your network, who you are trying to attract, and who you are trying to convert as a customer. If your purpose is broad, consider creating multiple accounts or testing with one specific theme to start.

Include a Keyword in Your Tweet When Relevant This is not the first time or last time you will encounter the following statement in this book: keywords (and hash tags) are connections to people in both search and social networks. Know and learn the keyword language that your audience uses to communicate directly to them in tweets but also leave a keyword trail so that others outside your network can find it using tools like TweetDeck, HootSuite, and other search services. Also remember that the language and keywords you use often help establish a consistent theme for both your social profile and how you might appear in search results.

Include a Direct Link to Your Content When Relevant If you have a direct link to content on your owned digital assets, then tweet out a link when it is relevant. Search engines and networks have stated publicly that they treat indexed tweets with a link "differently" than text-only tweets. This generally means that they are crawling these links to determine whether they can be used as search signals. Although this is an emerging area of SEO, I generally believe, as do many other leading SEOs, that tweets are being counted as links, particularly in the Bing search-engine algorithm.

Write Tweets That Will Entice Your Audience to Respond, Click, or Retweet Encourage participation by including a call to action or request for a retweet if needed. Don't be salesy, though, and instead focus on being clear in your requests. Also, don't get frustrated if your requests go unanswered from time to time.

Figure 7.4 Breakdown of the core elements of a tweet

Retweet the Tweets That You Like, and Use an @reply to Let the Other Person or Company Know That You Are Reading and Sharing Them Retweeting is a two-way street, because you should also retweet for others in your network (or from Twitter search) without them asking you to and without reciprocation. Remember the "give and you get" principle and that the more you give to your community, the more you will get back, however directly or indirectly. Precede a public message to another user by including their handle in the tweet, preceded by an @. The example would appear as @exampleusername.

Favorite the Tweets That You Want to Come Back To A "favorite" tweet is essentially a bookmark for a tweet, but it also automatically sends a direct message to the original tweet poster. It has long been reported that search engines have gone so far as to crawl browser bookmarks for use as a possible link citation source. While there is no definitive information that bookmarks have any impact on internal Twitter search or at Bing, I wouldn't be surprised if they found a good use for this type of data. This is certainly not a recommendation to go crazy with favorites, but just know that they are a useful tool that can help you organize tweets and send a signal to other users that you are reading and appreciating their content and conversation.

Promote Your Own Content Links Only When It Makes Sense to Your Audience of Followers Simply put, don't annoy your users. If they expect a rapid flow of automated link tweets, that's fine, but most casual Twitter users will unfollow if you tweet too rapidly or too much. Think of it this way: if you and everyone following you were all in the same room, what would you say to them and how would you say it? Would you yell, or would you be conversational, with a little bit of give and take? Would you shout, or would you be polite? The same rules for the offline world can apply to Twitter.

Keep Your Tweets Fresh and Up-to-Date, but Don't Overdo It Twitter is all about *right now*, or more cutting-edge frames of recency (see Chapter 2 for more information on recency as a social and search tactic). The bottom line is that Twitter is a fresh human indicator for informing on what is happening in social spaces and what is happening within a recent timeframe. Being active and participatory is a primary factor in a healthy Twitter presence, but don't overdo it. If you tweet every five seconds, it could annoy your followers and result in a higher drop-off rate.

Use Hashtags to Get Your Tweet into Wider Conversations Hashtags are like a meta keyword or keyword phrase for a larger public conversation visible to all users of Twitter using the "discover" search box. A single tweet could potentially be seen by a mass audience if it is engaging enough and is connected to a greater conversation through keywords. A hashtag is preceded by the pound sign (#), but it is not required to monitor the conversation in search. Twitter users still use the hashtag to apply context to tweets, and it is a primary part of the Twitter vernacular. Be careful, however, not to overuse hashtags, and focus on use when you are contributing to the larger conversation.

Tweet Out Images One way to stand out from the crowd on Twitter is to tweet out images that will be of the most interest to your audience. Considering that many activity streams are predominantly composed of text, posting a photo or image is a great way to increase engagement and sharing.

Study Popular Trending Topics and Real-Time Keywords, and Jump into the Conversation When Relevant to Your Business Use the Twitter search engine (Twitter "discover" button) to find conversations that are hot or relevant to your area of expertise. TweetDeck (www.tweetdeck.com) is also an excellent tool for monitoring multiple Twitter keyword streams and will allow you to jump into the conversation as needed.

Keep It Short Enough So It Can Be Retweeted Monitor your character counts to ensure that there is enough room for someone to retweet your tweets. Generally, it is a good practice to leave at least 15 to 20 characters available in order to encourage retweets.

Every Tweet Creates Its Own Optimized Web Page Though these pages often have a very ephemeral shelf life, individual tweets beget a unique web page that is picked up in both Bing and Google search. Because the text depth of these pages is extremely low (remember, less than 140 characters), the effect is these pages are often extremely weak in web search and fall out of Twitter search after one to two weeks. Unless they are highly cited on other authoritative websites outside of Twitter, they rarely hit page 1 of search results, unless it is for an extremely unique phrase with little to no competition.

Optimizing Your Profile Page

Pay close attention to how you optimize your Twitter profile page, because the method in which it is set up can have a great impact on how it becomes visible in web search and in Twitter's internal search engine. Active profile pages resonate very strongly in both Bing and Google search, and it is not uncommon to see a profile rank highly for the user's personal name, company name, or account name, especially if the account is active and follows sustainable practices for social relevancy and SEO. Figure 7.5 shows an example of the MediaPost Twitter profile page, and Figure 7.6 features an example of the account-settings page. There are not too many areas to optimize a Twitter profile page, but you will get the most out of what you have to work with by considering and implementing the following tips.

Pick an Account Name That Accurately Reflects Who You Are or What Your Business Does Remember that this name will represent you and your business. Consider how easy it is to say your account name to someone in an elevator pitch and how close or exact it is to your real name or business. Many people perform keyword searches for exact names or company names, plus *twitter*, while they are searching for your Twitter account. Make it easy for them to find you.

Custom background   Image icon   Page title   Account name

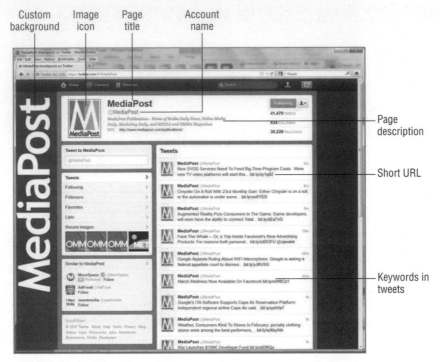

Page description

Short URL

Keywords in tweets

Figure 7.5 Twitter profile-page elements

Provide a Secondary Identifier in the Account Name Field Put your name or company in the page title field, and note that it can be the same as your handle or different. This secondary identifier will be placed in the title element of the Twitter page, so the name and keywords used here carry a lot of weight in the search engines.

Describe Who You Are, and Use the Right Keywords You have only a few characters to describe who you are, what you do, and what your followers can expect. Choose your words carefully, because like the description of a web page, this is essentially the welcome mat for your profile from other doors within Twitter and outside of Twitter, like Google or Bing search.

Add Your Geographic Location A geographic citation in your profile can weight your relevancy in Twitter search toward others in your area or toward tweets related to your geographic location.

Add a Photo Similar to Google+, fill out your profile as completely as possible and include a photo. A photo helps a potential follower or reader better orient to what your account may offer, sends another signal of trust to your potential audience, and offers you an opportunity to provide some consistency between your profiles on multiple social sites.

Add a Link Your links are nofollowed, but still take the opportunity to link back to the most relevant areas of your owned web presence in the "website" box. Avoid using a URL shortener in this area, and use your full direct URL.

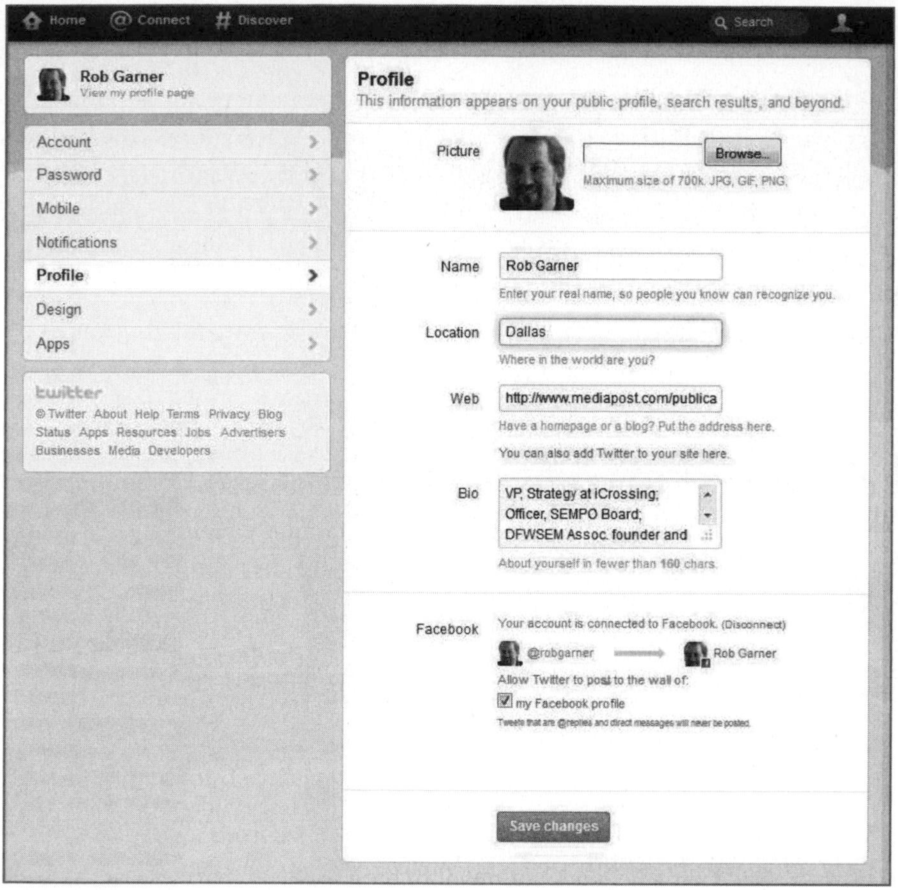

Figure 7.6 My profile account-settings page

Building Followers

I've mentioned many times in this book how building up your networks can be considered an SEO tactic. In this case, building up your followers can help benefit your Bing search results, because it pulls directly from the Twitter "fire hose" to inform its real-time search engine, and Bing has noted in interviews that Twitter is having an increasing influence on its algorithms.

This chapter is designed to highlight some of the search and social synergies of social networks, so please take note that *increased network reach* helps spread social signals that search engines look for and applies to all networks mentioned in this chapter. I am not going to go into the details of "how to earn followers," because there are already many great books in print that accomplish this at much greater length, but I do have some helpful tips and considerations to get you started. Here is a short checklist for building Twitter followers and engaging in Twitter as a network:

Be Present, in Real-Time Since Twitter is all about content streaming in real-time, simply being present and communicative can help you build followers. Respond to those who tweet something interesting, share an interesting URL, pass along news that your followers should know, and reply accordingly. Showing that you are active will make people more interested in following you, because those who haven't tweeted in a while are less appealing to follow.

Run Twitter RSS Feeds into Owned Assets One of the best ways to show you are active on Twitter is to run feeds from Twitter into your own website content pages. Showing recent content from Twitter and other status networks also gives your site more of a real-time pulse and encourages engagement from your website users, when they might have not otherwise engaged. Twitter no longer offers direct RSS feeds, but a number of third-party applications provide this service.

Promote Your Account Name This is just Marketing 101. Just like a telephone number or physical address, promote your Twitter handle in press releases, product packaging, service forms and receipts, print, radio, direct mail, and TV. You can also promote it in any other digital space, like in an email, on web pages, and on other social profiles. Put your handle in your email signature and bylines as well.

Add "Follow Me" Calls to Action and Links from Posts and Other Content As you promote your handle, it doesn't hurt to give a little nudge and tell your audience what you would like for them to do.

Employ "Follow Me" Buttons For the visually minded, a simple Twitter button from your content is an instant cue for them to follow you.

Engage with Others Again, it is imperative to be present and engage with people who follow you, people you follow, or people you want to follow. Converse naturally with your followers, and don't force it; look for new like-minded people and companies in Twitter search.

Write a Blog Post on Why People Should Follow You As a digital publisher, create a blog post or web page describing your purpose for being active on Twitter. If you can't think of any reasons, then you need to go back to the drawing board and determine your purpose for engaging in social networks as a whole (see "Answering the Question 'Why?'" in Chapter 3).

Avoid Auto-DM Responders with Canned Messaging—Be Personal A lot of people, including myself, find canned autoresponding and thank-you services on Twitter to be very annoying, but a personal thank-you response is almost always appreciated.

Don't Flood Your Followers' Streams with a Long Succession of Tweets If you want to keep those followers, remember the concept of social relevancy. Your followers may want to get sporadic bits of information from you, but may find it a turn-off to see a long succession of your tweets hogging up their Twitter stream. Use common sense and treat your followers how you would like to be treated.

If you are running a larger business or manage a larger social team, then I recommend establishing a more detailed voice and engagement strategy for Twitter, which will be outlined in Chapter 12. Also review the appendix for a long list of Twitter tools and services, both free and paid.

The Quick Search and Social Guide to Facebook

Facebook is the largest social network on the Internet, and optimizing your presence can help extend visibility both internally in Facebook search and streams and in Bing web search—and even Google search to a degree. This section will help you optimize your presence for both internal search and web search.

Currently, both Bing and Google index Facebook pages. Bing has a direct line into Facebook data through an exclusive partnership and leverages likes and shared links as a direct signal in Bing search. Similarly to Google+, Bing shows your Facebook connections in Bing web-search results and has alternated between showing a quantified number of likes and including Facebook icons of friends who liked a similar result.

EdgeRank Optimization

EdgeRank is Facebook's proprietary algorithm that determines how visible content and interactions will become within the Facebook data stream. In a way, it is very similar to standard search optimization principles applied to content within the Facebook network. The impact of not optimizing your Facebook content and interactions is that they might not even be seen. Like Google and Bing, Facebook is very protective of giving away the "secret sauce" of the algorithms, but it has revealed some of the basic elements at several Facebook developer and marketing conferences. Here are the three key elements of EdgeRank that determine content placement:

Affinity Score This is a score that evaluates the relationships between you and your connections. More-frequent connections and conversations between users can reveal a higher level of engagement and weight your posts and content higher toward that person's feed. Essentially, the more you engage with people in your network (comments, likes, recommendations, posts, and so on), the more visibility you gain with those connections.

Type of Content At a very basic level, a like may be less weighted than a comment, and longer content posts and images may also have an emphasized weight in the feed.

Recency As mentioned in Chapter 2, one key element of social relevancy is the concept of *recency*, in the sense that the freshest content tends to gain an advantage toward visibility in the stream. In fact, recency may be the single most important factor in Facebook optimization. The implication is that there is a need to be present and participatory in order to gain the most return. Conversely, it is fair to say that Facebook content does not have as long of a shelf life.

Like other networks mentioned in this chapter, much of the SEO value of Facebook is in how you set your profile, the keywords you choose, how much you participate and publish, and the size of your network. At a very high level, consider the following basic elements of optimizing your Facebook presence for both external search and internal visibility in the EdgeRank algorithm:

Update Often and in Real-Time Search engines are constantly looking for fresh signals and content to inform the search results. Being active keeps your account alive and sends a pulse to the engines.

Emphasize Your Brand and Company Keywords The most relevant keywords are about you and your business. Don't go into Facebook with the idea of dominating for a category killer keyword like digital cameras or books—it is not going to happen. Staying true to who you really are as a business and person will reflect positively in the search results.

Use Images Appropriately Use images and photos as a content strategy. One of the biggest segments of sharing in Facebook is around images. Remember to review Facebook's policy on uploading photos to help set your approach for a Facebook image strategy.

Build in External Links to Your Facebook Pages from Outside the Facebook Domain Both Google and Bing look at external links pointing into Facebook pages (all links outside of the primary Facebook.com domain). Ensure that you are linking to your page from other social-media accounts, your website and blogs, and other marketing collateral.

Use Keywords in Your Description When Appropriate and Relevant Although you should focus on your brand and name keywords, also utilize generic descriptors of your business.

Use Relevant Keywords in Your Status Updates Remember that status updates are also a form of publishing, so use the right keywords to trigger the internal Facebook function, but only when relevant and appropriate. Don't stuff keywords into your status updates or use keywords gratuitously. It is annoying to your audience, and you want to keep them in your network.

Enable Like, Recommend, and Share Buttons on All of Your Relevant Assets, Including Blogs and Website Pages *Liking*, or recommending, content or links is a fundamental aspect of Facebook. Be sure to add Facebook Like buttons directly on your own website and content pages. Posting status updates that generate activity in the form of likes and comments also helps increase your visibility across the Facebook network and sends search signals to help extend visibility in Bing search results.

GraphRank Optimization

GraphRank is Facebook's algorithm for applications, and determines how application interactions will appear in a news feed. Like the EdgeRank algorithm, GraphRank will weight interaction and engagement as a factor for how application data will be emphasized within a stream. GraphRank can be thought of as a more personalized view of your application stream in a news feed (or the data that appears in your stream), based on relationships and interactions within your networks and the related networks of people in your list of friends and connections.

Also importantly, GraphRank looks at recency as a major factor. Simply put, being participatory and present is amajor factor of GraphRank visibility.

The Quick Search and Social Guide to LinkedIn

I have been a user of LinkedIn since 2003, and it has long been my personal favorite business network. LinkedIn came around even before the popular use of the term *social* arose in 2004 to 2005 and was one of the first mainstream business networks (as opposed to "social" networks). There is a variety of ways that individuals and companies can use LinkedIn to build their businesses:

Individual Profiles Your personal profile is one of the key opportunities to optimize your presence in LinkedIn. This will be discussed in detail later in the chapter.

Business Profiles As a business, you can create a separate page that allows a different way to interact with others in the network. Business profile pages are indexed by the major search engines and will often rank highly for your exact business name when developed properly.

Groups LinkedIn groups can be set up for companies, business associations, discipline development, or other types of business networking. Well-tended group profile pages often rank prominently for primary and ancillary keywords in search engines.

Discussions Discussions and Q&As occur within groups and appear within internal LinkedIn search functionality. Participating in discussions is a great way to increase your visibility within LinkedIn to like-minded groups of people.

Email Lists and Updates One of the other great things about LinkedIn is that a substantial part of the group network subscribes to LinkedIn email status updates. If people did not see your discussion or comment when you first posted it, that content can still become visible in LinkedIn through pushed email lists. Participate in group discussions, and LinkedIn will do the rest.

What *Business* Does Your Business Have in a *Social* Network?

When I give talks about social media to both clients and conferences, I often ask the following question to answer why businesses would want to engage in social-media marketing: what *business* does your *business* have in a *social* network?

This is a tough question for many marketers to answer for many major social-media sites, but I rarely find a case where LinkedIn is not applicable for business-to-business marketing, recruitment, and thought-leadership development, among other areas. LinkedIn is all about business. In this section, I will focus on increasing your visibility by optimizing your profile and business pages and provide some tips on building your network to achieve greater visibility. In addition, I will be talking with LinkedIn expert Viveka von Rosen about some other key considerations for optimizing your LinkedIn presence.

I recommend using the LinkedIn InMaps tool as you start building your presence or using it to assess your existing LinkedIn influence and network development (http://inmaps.linkedinlabs.com/). InMaps is a data-visualization tool that uses colored maps to show the connections in your network. If you are new to LinkedIn, run a map on your account profile as a benchmark for later use and comparison. If you have been in LinkedIn for some time or have already established connections, you can run an InMap to see where you currently stand. Carefully analyze your groups and hubs of your networks to determine the depth and reach of your network, along with the particular themes of your network.

Figure 7.7 shows a LinkedIn InMap for my network. I spent time analyzing these connections and their relationships (you can hover over connections to see the people in the network), and I used labels to group them. The spheres of influence naturally occurred with groups from current and past jobs I worked, the search industry, the social-media industry, the overall Internet industry, and the domain industry, among a few others. It is no surprise that these are the areas I work in, and the people I network with reflect these interests—flocks of birds of several feathers, if you will.

A network is useful and relevant to you only if it is cultivated carefully. My strategy early on was to focus on influencers, people I had actually met, and people I worked with. I have nearly a thousand connections over about nine years of participation. This may seem like a lot of people to some and not a lot to others with many thousands of connections. But the people in my network are relevant to my business and reflective of where I've been and where I want to go. The bottom line is that when I have content related to these industries, it goes on LinkedIn. I know they read it, and I know they are often up-to-date on what I've been doing, because they tell me so when I see them in person, across all of the places that I travel.

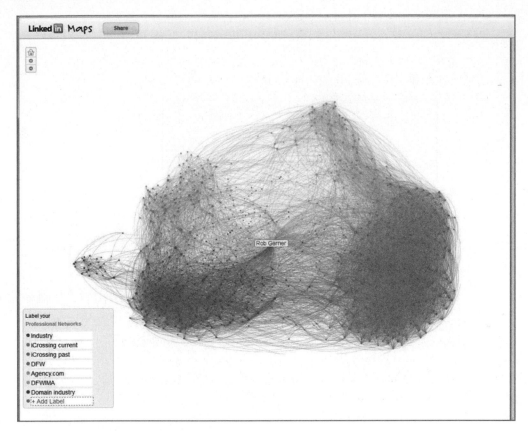

Figure 7.7 InMap data visualization of the author's LinkedIn network

Optimizing Your Personal Page on LinkedIn

In many ways, the opportunities to "optimize" your LinkedIn profile and pages are limited. Much of the optimization occurs through building your network, publishing content to the network, and sharing content within the network. Here are some basic elements of optimizing your presence on LinkedIn:

- Create a 100-percent-complete profile page.
- Run your blog feeds into your profile page.
- Take advantage of the SlideShare plug-in to pull your presentations directly into your profile.
- Add associations to a number of relevant groups.

Viveka von Rosen: Keywords, Keywords, Keywords

I asked Viveka von Rosen about her own recommendations for LinkedIn optimization. Viveka is the author of *LinkedIn Marketing: An Hour a Day,* also by Sybex, and says that paying attention to keywords—in keyword research and placement—is among the most critical aspects of LinkedIn optimization, both for internal LinkedIn search and for search engines. Here is what she says:

> *First of all, you need to know what keywords to use to optimize your profile. Create a specific list of keywords by which you want to be found. They should describe*

- You
- Your company
- Your product
- Your service
- Your industry
- Your client's industry

> *These keywords do not need to be sophisticated, but they do need to be clear. If someone were doing a keyword search for you on Google, what would they be typing in? Think verb, noun, acronym, synonym, skills, and tools (accounting, accountant, CPA, certified public accountant, bookkeeping, QuickBooks, Peachtree). Keep these keywords by your computer at all times, and use them often in your social-media efforts.*

In addition to keyword selection and categorization, placing those keywords in the right spot is of critical importance for being found. Viveka recommends emphasizing the following areas for optimization:

> *Your LinkedIn Professional Headline field gives you 120 characters to really describe who you are and what you do. While this field is not heavily weighted in the LinkedIn search analytic, it is seen in almost every LinkedIn transaction: from a simple search to messaging to answering questions to participating in your group discussions. Your professional headline is part of the snapshot seen across LinkedIn that includes your photo, headline, location, and industry. So, spend a little time to make your professional headline pop.*

> *The Title fields in your past and present experience section are probably the most important search fields on LinkedIn. Most people underutilize these sections, only adding their official titles. However, you have 100 characters to really describe what you did for the company. Let's face it: how many of you only do what your job title states? Probably no one reading this book. We all bring many skills and talents to our jobs, and this is a place to highlight them.*

Networked Link Effects of Sharing Content in LinkedIn

The "networked link" effect I mentioned in Chapter 2 also occurs on LinkedIn in the news section. Every day the most engaging and shared content makes it to the front page of LinkedIn and is pushed out to LinkedIn users. In addition to building your network in LinkedIn, make the best use of it by updating your profile status with your latest relevant content. A rising story can increase your visibility within your network and attract new like-minded audience to you content hubs. Figure 7.8 features an example of LinkedIn networked links, with the number of aggregate network shares placed in the bottom-right corner of each story preview. The inset shows an example of the people who shared the link within LinkedIn.

Figure 7.8 Capture of LinkedIn Internet-category headlines. Notice that the top shared (networked) links gain the highest visibility.

So far, I have covered the landscape, strategic considerations, research, planning, and content development. With this chapter, I have covered the major social networks that you will publish your content to, along with the basic search-optimization principles for each network. In the next chapter, you will dig deeper into publishing on your own blog assets, and I will cover news and press-release optimization for extending your visibility.

Search and social publishing is not just for the big networks, and arguably the biggest opportunities for you as a marketer lie in embracing smaller, more relevant social networks. In this sense, the term *social relevancy* still applies. In other words, biggest isn't always best for your business, but the smaller and most relevant social networks are better for your business. I will cover some of the aspects of niche networks in later chapters and in the appendix.

Blogs, Google News, and Press Releases

In this chapter and following ones, you will take a closer look at some of the common vehicles and channels for real-time publishing and also learn about the search and social nuances of each. While the major social networks presented in the previous chapter are a major hub of all online activity, they are still only one part of a bigger picture for real-time content production and participation across your publishing platform. You will also dig deeper into WordPress, the leading open-source blog platform, and learn how to best optimize this content-management system for better SEO performance, without compromising your content or your audience.

8

Chapter Contents

Blog optimization for search and social media to enable your own
real-time content production as an owned asset

Search and social news, Google News, and determining whether a
real-time news strategy is right for your business

Digital press-release optimization for both search and social spaces

Blogs

Blogs are like real-time content management systems for the Web. They are designed for fluid content production, push-and-pull distribution of content (with the dual design of both a website and an RSS feed), and social interaction. Many blog systems are created to be fundamentally search engine–friendly. In this section, I will cover the real-time, search, and social elements of running your own blog, as well as blogger outreach. Search-optimization considerations and basics for the WordPress blog platform are interspersed throughout this section, while all other recommendations apply to both WordPress and other blog platforms.

The Real-Time Elements of Blogs

A well-maintained blog, in terms of both SEO and timely content production, is one of the most effective ways to capitalize on the high-speed publishing benefits of real-time marketing in a search and social world. Overall, blog content management systems are highly conducive to publishing in real-time. They allow content creators, social-media managers, and other digital-asset producers a medium to quickly create and distribute content in a way that often parallels real-time conversations occurring in social networks. In short, the combination of a hot blog and a wide group of followers and friends in networks is one of the quickest ways to get published and distributed instantaneously. With this in mind, here are some of the core elements that make blogs "real-time" and alive:

- Like any other page that goes back to the beginnings of the Internet, blogs are available worldwide to your audience, crossing all geospatial boundaries from the moment you hit the "publish" button.

- RSS feeds push out blog content in real-time directly to readers and content-consumers as it is published.

- Through comment systems, additional conversation and feedback occur immediately as the content is being consumed.

- Blog posts and articles can be shared in real-time via links, likes, retweets, +1s, and LinkedIn shares, among others types of shares.

- Frequency and timeliness of blog posts and news updates indicate to both a person and a search engine that the blog has a live presence, is relevant to the moment, and is fresh.

- Posts appear in reverse chronological order (freshest post first), so readers know exactly how active you are when they hit your front page or receive your feed.

- Live feeds can be pulled into the top and side navigation to provide other real-time and up-to-the second views of content and activity in other social spaces.

- A well-maintained and trusted blog can go from published post to live in Google search results in as little as one minute.

Overall, blogs serve as a method of delivering your messages quickly and in real-time to your audience. Whether you are providing fast news, sporadic updates, full-length articles, or instant updates to your audience, a blog should be a fundamental owned hub in every real-time content marketing strategy.

The Interdependent Search and Social Elements of Blogs

When you decide to publish a blog, it is important to note that its success depends on key factors related to social-network distribution and search engines. To build an ongoing flow of new readers, your blog will need to become highly visible in search engines and attract your direct audience by reflecting the keyword language they use. Language is critical, and as in preceding chapters, creating content that reflects the natural language used by your audience is a fundamental element of real-time marketing. This language is reflected in how you write and optimize the content, in the natural language you use, and in how you interpret the evolving keyword landscape. In addition, your blog must be engaging and timely enough that people will want to read it on a regular, if not daily, basis. With these thoughts in mind, here are some of the key aspects of blogs that illustrate their primary "search and social" nature:

- Content that is written both for people and for search engines has a longer shelf life than content that emphasizes only the former or the latter.

- Search engines have suggested that RSS feeds provide a signal toward search visibility. Google even uses FeedBurner (`http://feedburner.com`) as a signal to gauge blog feed popularity.

- Blog content management systems have made it incredibly easy for the average person to create a website, in that they have "democratized" the Web and search visibility, at least in terms of making it less technical.

- Optimized blogs attract search traffic from like-minded audiences, who may in turn become regular readers of content, participators (commenters), and even creators (guest bloggers).

- The number of legitimate comments on a blog across many posts can be considered an indicator of popularity to search engines and also a potential social signal.

- The social community that has built up around WordPress has created excellent free plug-ins to increase the visibility of your posts, using standard SEO practices.

- The WordPress information-architecture system makes it easy for a search engine to crawl through and determine hierarchical content structure, from top to bottom.

- A highly shared blog post in social networks can generate substantial traffic and buzz in the short term and more authoritative links and search authority in the long term.

- Many of the top blog content management systems are inherently search-friendly, particularly WordPress and Blogger.

- Comments add a consistent element of freshness to content, which search engines look for.

- Comment systems also allow for comment-sharing and feedback, and encourage community around content.

When taking on a blog strategy for centralized content distribution, remember that approaching it with search and social in mind will help extend the reach and response of your content by leaps and bounds. The following sections will help you understand the search and social basics of blogs to get more out of your efforts, for the short term and long term.

Blog Basics for Search and Social

There are several considerations for setting up a social and search blog so that you can get going with your real-time content production. Decisions made in the beginning around URL design, duplicate content, duplicate URL structures (canonicalization), blog-platform selection, spam management, and content management will all have an impact on how well your blog performs, from both search and social perspectives. With these considerations in mind, let's start by reviewing some of the key elements of setting up your blogging platform.

Of course, your theme and choice of topic focus are central and strategic and should be informed by the research and assessment outlined in previous chapters. By now you should have a good idea of who your audience is, where they currently congregate, the type of content they like to consume, and any gaps in content demand that your blog will be able to seize upon and capture. Your blog will be a combination of these elements and will be able to incorporate various assets types, mixed with some of the previously mentioned content ideas. In short, there are very few limitations to the types of ideas and assets that can be published in a blog.

Setting Up a Blog

There are several key technical considerations for starting your own blog, including web-host selection, domain choice, blogging platform, and setup. Blogger (www.blogger.com) is a popular blogging platform that is owned by Google, and a well-maintained blog on this platform will perform well socially and in Google, though Google claims to be unbiased in how it displays varying platforms in search, even its own. For this section, I will focus on how to set up a WordPress blog. WordPress was chosen for this example because it is the most popular open-source blog platform in the world, and it is maintained by a community dedicated to keeping it up-to-date, search-friendly, and stocked with useful plug-ins and tools.

There are two basic types of WordPress blogs. The first is the hosted version on WordPress.com, in which bloggers can choose a subdomain and host their presence at `http://mydomain.wordpress.com`. One of the main benefits is that WordPress keeps the blog code maintained so you don't have to worry about it. One of the downsides is that technically you will not own or control the domain, because it is hosted on the proprietary WordPress.com URL. So, if you ever decide to move your blog, you can take your content with you as an XML export, but you may lose all of your valuable link and SEO equity and have to effectively earn your way back in. WordPress.com also offers a Premium Features service for a fee that allows you to use your own domain, allowing you to retain more control of your web presence. Learn more at `http://en.wordpress.com/products/`.

I believe in owning your own primary content assets, and producing a blog on your own domain is one way to accomplish this. Some webhosting providers have automatic installers for WordPress (look for web hosts with CPanel and a package of autoinstalled open-source software) and can go live with a basic site in minutes once the domain is configured properly to your web-hosting-name servers. Another option is to have your IT administrator install on your web host the latest version of WordPress, which can be found at `http://wordpress.org/download/`. WordPress even provides a full guide for the "famous" five-minute installation, which can be found at `http://codex.wordpress.org/Installing_WordPress`. When researching webhosting providers, ask them about security from spammers and whether they offer an automatic installer for WordPress.

Choosing Your Domain for Installation

Choosing the right domain for your WordPress blog installation can be tricky, depending on what you want to achieve. You have basically three different options for a blog hosted on your own proprietary URL.

- Entirely new domain: ExampleBlog.com
- Subdomain of your existing website: Blog.yourdomain.com
- Tertiary domain (subfolder or subdirectory) of existing website: Yourdomain.com/Blog

For ExampleBlog.com, this would be a new site (unless the domain has some prior SEO and web-hosting history), and it would have to earn its way into the search results by building trusted links, social signals, content development, and so on.

For the subdomain example, some of the search history of the primary domain is inherited and may have some initial trust with search engines, more so than a new domain. You will still have to work to gain authority on a subdomain, even though it may inherit some positive search equity.

Finally, a tertiary domain at the directory level may also inherit some search equity, especially if it is linked from the primary domain. Remember that search engine trust is critical when you are publishing in real-time, and gaining search equity can provide a slight head start in some cases, depending on how well your current domain is performing in the search engines. Generally speaking, hosting your blog on a sub-folder is suitable, unless your site is based entirely on the blog, and then you would feature it on the root URL without a subdirectory (on the home page).

Managing Spam

If you are running a blog, managing spam is one unfortunate aspect of the job. When you run a popular system like WordPress, spam is automated by scripts and is already looking to attack your blog, so you will need to be ready to protect it for yourself, for your readers and community, and for its own SEO hygiene.

Search engines consider how much spam and illicit content may be contained on a blog to determine whether it can be trusted for inclusion in search results in real-time. Therefore, it should be a high priority to keep your blog protected and spam-free. Here are some of the common ways to prevent spam from taking over your blog:

Always Keep Your Blog Software Updated to the Most Recent Version WordPress is constantly updated, and having the latest version will deter people and scripts that are attempting to exploit holes in earlier versions of the code. As with other key WordPress updates, you can update your version directly from the admin panel whenever a new version is available.

Always Keep Your Plug-ins Updated to the Latest Version Outdated plug-ins can sometimes be exploited as a back door for spammers, so ensure that your plug-ins are up-to-date and secure. WordPress also allows you to update your plug-ins directly from the admin interface in the Plugins section and will alert you whenever a new update is available.

Look for a Trustworthy and Frequently Updated Theme Good themes not only make your blog appealing but are also well-coded and updated periodically to plug holes in any code that allow a back door for hackers or spam. When seeking out any theme, consider the aesthetics, but also research what precautions the designer has taken to keep the theme secure. WordPress allows you to update your themes directly from the admin interface in the Plugins section whenever a new update is available. iThemes and StudioPress are both good sources for WordPress themes.

Choose a Secure Hosting Provider Web-host selection for your blog is also important, so take time choosing the right host for your blog. Before selecting a host, ask the host about its track record for uptime and how well other WordPress blogs perform on its server.

Enable the Akismet Plug-in for WordPress Akismet is a plug-in that helps filter out automated spam and keeps a good chunk of spam off your blog without moderation. Get the plug-in, sign up for your key, and let it go to work for you.

Consider Using Additional Security Plug-ins Several other plug-ins will also help secure your blog and keep spam at bay. WP Security Scan (`http://wordpress.org/extend/plugins/wp-security-scan/`) looks for vulnerabilities and back doors that may be exposing your blog to harm.

Use a Secure Password and Login Name Adding a secure password can prevent a hacker from guessing your login. As a general rule, use eight or more characters, at least one number, a mix of uppercase and lowercase letters, and punctuation. By all means, do not use your login name for your password. Also, avoid using *admin* as your login, because it is one of the most commonly guessed login names.

Remember, keeping your blog clean from spam is both a "search thing" and a "social thing." Little to no spam means that your users know you are taking care of your house, and search engines know that it is clean enough to include in their indexes within a shorter frame of recency.

Managing Duplicate Content in WordPress

A duplicate-content issue can occur with your blog when a search engine is able to crawl and index pages with exact or highly similar content on different URLs. While search engines say there is no "penalty" for duplicate content, the fact is that the amount of duplicate content within your domain—as perceived by a search engine—can have an impact on whether your site becomes highly visible or is watered down or ignored by search engines altogether. The good news is that there are a few good plug-ins for addressing this issue, particularly the All in One SEO Pack plug-in for WordPress.

When using the All in One SEO Pack plug-in, make sure the Canonical URLs box is checked so that pages with multiple URLs assigned to them will be correctly assigned to search engines (see Figure 8.1). Search engines can create duplicate content when multiple URLs are used, so setting canonical URLs helps tell the search engines "which is the real page" they should index, which URLs they should apply link value to, and which ones to ignore.

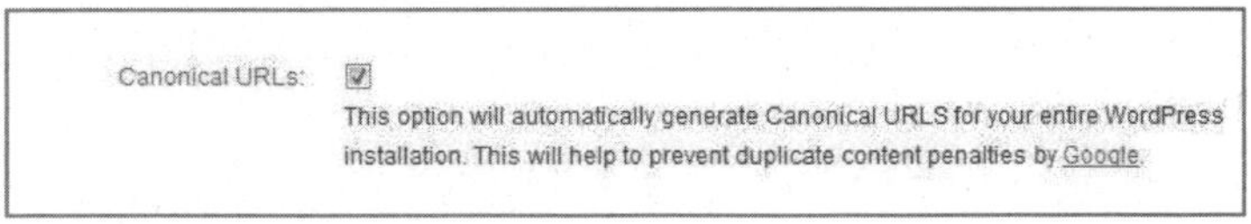

Canonical URLs: ☑
This option will automatically generate Canonical URLS for your entire WordPress installation. This will help to prevent duplicate content penalties by Google.

Figure 8.1 Setting Canonical URLs in the All in One SEO Pack plug-in for WordPress

The most common duplicate issue for WordPress blogs involves similar content in the Categories, Archives, and Tags sections. These pages may overlap altogether or contain snippets to previously replicated content across your site. Using the noindex box on the settings page of the All in One SEO Pack plug-in, you can choose to block these sections from search-engine crawlers in order to create a stronger signal to the other unique content in your site. The Tags category is particularly important to block, because this section contains ephemeral content for search engines. Figure 8.2 shows the noindex panel in the WordPress admin panel for the All in One SEO Pack plug-in.

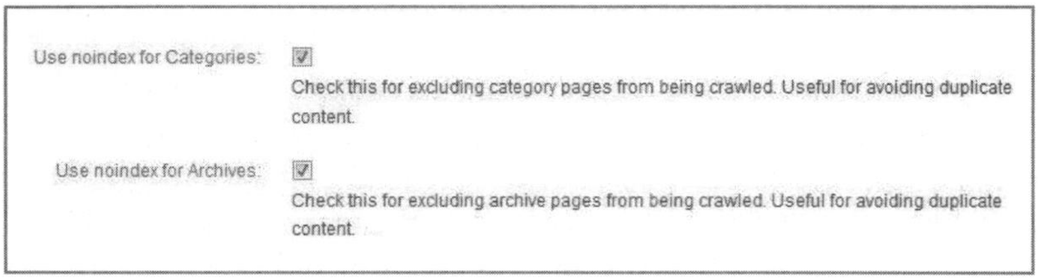

Figure 8.2 Noindex settings in the All in One SEO Pack plug-in for WordPress

Managing Comments in Real-Time

As a blog producer, comments are both your best friend and your worst enemy. They help define the character of your blog based on the people who comment and the thoughtfulness of the posts, and it happens in real-time. On the one hand, comments foster community and shared conversation around your content from a social perspective and can be seen as a positive signal by search engines, in terms of quality, quantity, and recency. On the other hand, they also attract people and rogue scripts that have no intention of engaging in your great conversation. They instead want to gain the attention of your readers by interrupting the conversation with irrelevant information, and they also attempt to drive search crawlers to their links. Malicious commenters do so in both a human fashion and an automated one.

Comments must be policed and edited, just as you would edit your own content articles or assets on your blog, and it should be done in real-time, or as expediently as possible. There is currently a great crisis in the way many major sites manage comments, and it is nothing short of the Wild West in some places, such as YouTube and some major new publications. Comments on these sites are often chaotic, ugly, and revealing of the darker side of human nature. By ignoring the comment-editing process, these publishers allow negative comments to define the character of their network or their publication online. Real-time Internet publishing is not about letting anyone say *anything*, at any time, and is not the way I recommend running a company, brand, or online publication. The Web already has enough negative sentiment, and there is a great demand for communities that actually pay editorial attention to comments and community management. Ultimately, the way you manage your comments will reflect in your search visibility and your social audience, so it will serve you well to run a tight ship in this area.

Good editors filter out the spam, trolls, and comments that are irrelevant to the conversation at hand. Good editors also foster reasonable debate and help de-escalate conflicts. They also determine when a comment is out of line, detracting from the conversation, and when it should be removed. A lot of blog editors are hesitant to edit any comments, but the fact is that your audience actually appreciates this type of attention to detail. Establishing the trust and authority of comments and site members also contributes to the trust factor of comments to both humans and algorithms. *The New York Times* (`http://nytimes.com`) is a great example of a publication making comments more relevant, as is the Huffington Post (`www.huffingtonpost.com`). These sites have created ways to push up popular comments, and also sort them by recency factors.

Commenting systems are getting better, with popularity lists and real names leading the way. Simply encouraging your community to use their real names will cut out much of the muck, because the negative posters generally do so only under the mask of account-name anonymity. In effect, using a real name keeps the conversation honest and respectful. On the other hand, it can also keep people from saying what is on their minds, so it is up to you to determine the balance that is best for your blog.

Managing Comments for SEO

Now that I have covered some of the pluses and minuses of commenting on blogs, here are some tips on how to manage comments, both for your audience and for search engines. Remember that the less spam you have on your blog, the more a search engine can trust your blog in real-time search results.

Set Links to Nofollow To discourage spammers from trying to game your blog for link value, I recommend setting comment links to nofollow or disallowing links in comments altogether. As mentioned previously, nofollow is a message asking search engines not to count the link for search relevancy, though using nofollow is entirely at the discretion of the search engine (in other words, if they think it will value relevancy, they may use it anyway). Setting your comment links to nofollow won't entirely discourage spammers, but it will help a lot.

Disable Comments Altogether In some cases, you may choose to not allow any comments at all. No comments, no spam or troll problem, but it does decrease engagement. WordPress will allow you to prohibit comments at the post or site level.

Hold Comments for Moderation One of the best ways to prevent spam is to review the comments coming in to your administration queue and approving only the legitimate and relevant comments, while sending spam to the trash can. You can take this a step further by allowing comments only from approved blog members and holding them in the queue until approved. Holding comments means that you need to be highly engaged with your blog, because you may lose your audience if comments are held up for any length of time.

The All in One SEO Pack Plug-in for WordPress

While there are many different SEO-related plug-in tools to help you with your blog performance, many bloggers like to use the All in One SEO Pack for its variety of key tools and also general ease of use. This plug-in was one of the first to provide a number of key SEO tools for WordPress bloggers and offers a variety of uses for bloggers who care about search engines as an additional way to extend their message and attract a new audience. In this section, I will highlight some of the key features of this free plug-in, why each feature is important, and how to use it. The following sections are highlighted in the Options Configuration panel of the All in One SEO Pack Plug-in:

Customize Your Homepage Title and Meta Data   This section of entry fields will allow you to override the title element and meta description for the home page. Your home page should have some of the greatest SEO strength, so choose your keywords and keyword phrases wisely in this area. A meta keywords tag is also available, but as discussed in the copywriting guide of Chapter 5, "Content Strategy: Auditing, Assessment, and Planning," this tag no longer has any search value.

Tag Title Format   This series of boxes allows you to format how you want the page titles to appear in various settings. Generally speaking, keeping the key unique page title or keywords toward the beginning of the title is recommended. If you have a short company name, you may also consider putting your company name at the beginning of the format. Do not enter exact keywords or phrases in these entry boxes. These are dynamic calls and pull in the data based on the name, as shown in Figure 8.3.

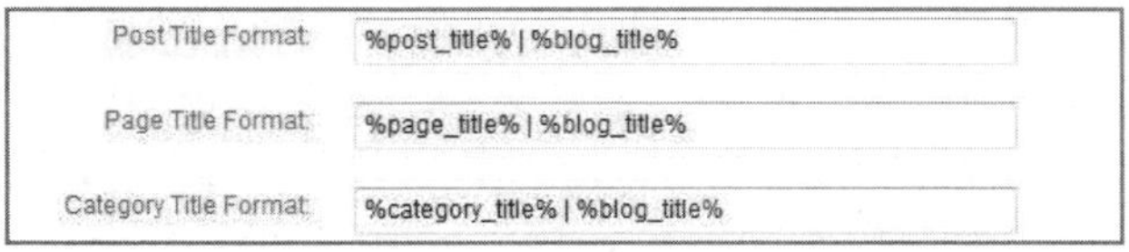

Post Title Format:	%post_title% | %blog_title%
Page Title Format:	%page_title% | %blog_title%
Category Title Format:	%category_title% | %blog_title%

Figure 8.3   Dynamic title-element settings in the All in One SEO Pack plug-in for WordPress

Autogenerate Descriptions   This will create automated meta descriptions for each of your post pages, though it can be overridden at the page level.

As mentioned, you also have the option of overriding title and meta descriptions at the page level. With this plug-in installed, each of your pages will have entry boxes, as they appear in Figure 8.4.

To get the All in One SEO Pack and other WordPress plug-ins, simply go to the Plugin page on your blog (*yourdomain*.com/wp-admin/plugins.php), click Add New in the upper-left corner of the page body, and search for *all in one SEO*. Once you find the plug-in, click Install Now and then Activate Plugin on the download success page, and you're done. Or visit WordPress and download it directly at http://wordpress.org/extend/plugins/all-in-one-seo-pack/.

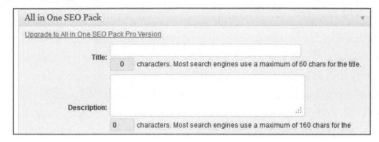

Figure 8.4 The page-level title and meta-description override in the All in One SEO Pack

WordPress SEO Plug-in by Joost de Valk

Another excellent free SEO plug-in utilized by many bloggers is WordPress SEO, produced by Joost de Valk and Yoast (http://yoast.com). This tool set has many of the features of the All in One SEO Pack plug-in but goes a few steps further. In this section, I will cover some of the other unique parts of the tool and how you can use it. The following are among the differentiating features:

XML Sitemaps With this plug-in, your XML sitemap generator is included. Check the box, and grab the sitemap URL for submission in your Google Webmaster Central account and Bing Webmaster Central account (covered more in Chapter 10, "Technical Considerations and Implementation"). While engines can typically crawl your blog quickly, it is also a good SEO practice to enable the XML sitemap feature.

Indexation de Valk previously provided this feature as a separate plug-in, and it is a must-have for managing search crawlers, duplicate content, and canonicalization within your blog. It offers extremely robust features for controlling how search engines see your content and how you can effectively manage and prevent duplicate-content issues.

Webmaster Tools Account Verification Quickly verify your site with Google and Bing with an FTP client by placing your account-verification codes in this administration panel.

Permalink Settings Here you can strip from URLs unnecessary naming conventions such as category or set sitewide canonical URL settings when hosting on a secure server (HTTPs vs. HTTP).

Breadcrumb Settings A taxonomically based URL structure can provide additional keyword-based anchor text throughout your site, and an additional system for a search engine to analyze your site's information architecture. WordPress SEO contains a system to easily configure breadcrumbs throughout your site.

Edit .htaccess and robots.txt Files WordPress SEO also allows admin access to these two key system files without having to constantly upload them to the server via File Transfer Protocol (FTP).

Download the plug-in in your Plugin Admin panel in WordPress (*yourdomain.com*/wp-admin/plugins.php), or visit http://wordpress.org/extend/plugins/wordpress-seo/.

Blogger Outreach

Blogger outreach has long been considered one of the fundamental "search and social" things a marketer can do. This is because it involves a blog and authentic and personal outreach to the blogger, which is technically the "social" side of outreach. The search benefit for you is in second-tier search-engine visibility, exposure to that blog's audience, and in some cases a link from that blog. With these tactics in mind, here are some key considerations and tips for blogger outreach:

- Identify influential blogs by reviewing blog rolls, using search engines (such as Google Blog search and Technorati), and looking for social-media influencers with established blogs.

- Before approaching a blogger, know their blog and their perspective by reading the blog, and know what type of content they publish.

- Get to know the person on social media first, such as on Twitter, Google+, LinkedIn, or Facebook.

- If possible, get to know or meet the blogger in person prior to outreach.

- Determine whether they accept guest bloggers or requests for coverage before you ask them.

- Determine whether they have previously published or linked to other blogs or websites or whether they have hosted any other guest bloggers.

- Offer a blogger an exclusive news story or research.

- Be laser-targeted and relevant, and ensure that your content and theme are direct matches to the blog you are reaching out to; otherwise, your outreach may just turn out to be pure annoyance.

- Build relationships that last for the long term, and make blog influencers part of your own network.

Blogger outreach is a two-way street, so if you are going to ask someone to consider helping out your own blog, put yourself in their shoes and determine whether helping other blogs in the same way is right for your blog. Generally speaking, being receptive to other bloggers and content creators spreads goodwill (remember "The First Rule of Reciprocation: You Give, and You Get" from Chapter 1, "Real-Time Publishing and Marketing") and helps you (and your blog) to become regarded as a good social citizen interested in helping others, and not just yourself. As also mentioned in the first chapter of this book, a solid search and social strategy requires you to enable the spirit of your audience. A blog is a great vehicle for you to accomplish this. Here are some of the key benefits for covering other bloggers, accepting tips for stories, and letting outside bloggers guest-blog:

- It creates another source of content for your blog.

- It provides expanded viewpoints for your audience.

- It provides an outlet for your readers, some of whom may aspire to create content.

- It fosters goodwill with other content providers by offering a separate network for them to distribute content.

- It creates new pages that will rank in search engines and pull search traffic right back to your blog.

Blogger outreach is an excellent method of gaining second-tier SERP visibility, as well as authoritative backlinks to your own content. And of course, there is all of the additional exposure that a third-party blog can provide to a greater audience outside of your own. Starting now with an outreach program can provide publishing contacts that you may use for years to come.

How to Analyze a Blog for Search Effectiveness and Link-Request Targeting

As you look for targets for blogger outreach or to seek out quality links, you should pay attention to how well a target blog is optimized and viewed by search engines. In search, you are often defined algorithmically by association. One of the key steps to being seen as a trusted source is to be linked to other trusted and authoritative sources.

One of the key ways to do this is to simply perform multiple searches in Google or Bing and determine which sources come up most frequently. Also, use the tools mentioned in Chapter 4, "Market Research and Content Types," for assessing sites and the audiences who frequent those sites, including Google Insights and DoubleClick Ad Planner by Google. Look for the sites that are most frequently included in other blog rolls or cited in the posts that you read the most. Also, perform a content assessment your blog targets, in the same way you would perform one for your own site, as detailed in Chapter 5.

Roles and Responsibilities of a Blog Editor or Administrator

If you are going to be an active and participatory real-time publisher, then you should consider admin resources that have a substantial amount of time to maintain and develop your blog. This admin may be you as an individual, or if you are running a business, you may want to bring in additional help. A blog serves as a real-time owned hub for your content strategy, and the amount that you get back is directly proportional to what you put in and how persistent you are in maintaining it for depth and quality (remember the lessons about content from previous chapters). With these considerations in mind, there is always something to do on a blog, and it requires stewardship, development, strategy, and a lot of sweat equity. Here are some of the key duties of a blog-editor and admin role (the duties can be met by a single editor or multiple admins-depending upon the size of your initiative):

- Creates and executes content strategies

- Establishes blogging policy

- Establishes editorial calendar and frequency of content posts
- Establishes additional staffing requirements and content production
- Provides training to stakeholders and other blog contributors
- For larger businesses, acts as an extension and/or liaison to communications and PR departments
- Synthesizes market research and data into actionable content strategies
- Manages and administrates content from contributors
- Posts new content (video, images, articles, commentary, and so on)
- Writes regular posts on relevant current events and news stories related to your main category topics
- Interacts and comments on other related blogs

Recap of Additional Considerations for Blogging with Search and Social in Mind

There are many different considerations for setting up and maintaining a blog, but as I previously mentioned, this section focuses more on the search and social elements of blogging. With some of the main considerations for key plug-ins, duplicate content, strategy, roles and responsibilities, comments, and spam in mind, here are some additional tips for getting the most out of your blog by leveraging the combined elements of search and social:

- Optimize your posts for search and social spaces.
- Pull in multiple assets to your blog posts (images, video, etc.).
- Create unique post topics and ideas.
- Set a "search and social–friendly" URL structure.
- Promote your content in social-networks and email subscriptions.
- Enable sharing and social-network links.
- Remember that trusted blogs get indexed in near real-time.
- Use multiple authors and writers for your blog.
- Determine whether to place nofollow directives on comments and other links.

Content Velocity: Throwing Snowballs to Start an Avalanche in Search and Social

Every day in nature, avalanches both big and small occur and are never seen by humans. They happen in areas that are unreachable and so remote that they are not even missed. In the world of real-time publishing, avalanches of traffic, shares, links, and social signals, both large and small in scope, also occur every day, but they can have a highly beneficial impact on publishing efforts. These opportunities for massive attention are largely being missed, at least in the participatory publishing sense, and marketers need only open their eyes to see them.

Avalanches of traffic and link-sharing start as a blip and increase with great velocity until they take over an entire conversation and become a focal point of discussion in networks, in conversations big and small. As a conversation becomes bigger, the ability to extend your voice is directly proportional to your ability to act and publish with agility. Content velocity reaches a crescendo with spiking keyword searches, spiking shares, spiking conversation, and the spiking desire for this new audience to consume more content on the topic at hand.

A search and social avalanche can be beneficial to your overall content-marketing scheme in terms of driving eyeballs, engagement, traffic, long-term links, and social signals toward search, but only astute marketers capture this type of attention. These marketers must monitor real-time keyword trends, have large networks in key social spaces, and be highly fluid in publishing to achieve this kind of velocity. Even capturing a series of smaller rolling drifts can help your search and social presence, especially when the process is repeated consistently over long periods of time.

The good news is that your blog, combined with close trend monitoring in real-time keyword tools and social spaces, is one of the best ways to accomplish this. In effect, each blog post created in real-time and based on a trending topic is like throwing a snowball to start an avalanche of traffic and links.

I have spoken about this phenomenon at a number of conferences and client strategy sessions over the last several years and have even used this technique in my MediaPost column over this time. In one case, a timely post I wrote about a spiking news story on Google's rising dominance in its share of overall search market went from the column to becoming shared in volume all over Twitter. It then hit the front page of Digg, and I watched and analyzed in real-time as the traffic, comments, and velocity of shares went through the roof. Popularity lists and streams in certain networks triggered the cascading dissemination effect of networks to networks, or many-to-many. In this scenario, content takes on an active and passive distribution life of its own (*passive* by pushing through triggers and syndication; *active* by social sharing and viral resonance). The long-term effects of that avalanche provided thousands of backlinks to MediaPost and a nice traffic surge. The good news is that this is something that business blogs big and small can also replicate, using the information outlined in this book.

Planned Real-Time Publishing

While my MediaPost example involves topic for spiking interest within a 12-hour timeframe, the real opportunities exist for developing content in real-time or preparing for predictable seasonal real-time queries. During the 2012 Super Bowl, one company prepared content to coincide with spiking search and social interest around half-time performers and compiled best- and -worst lists and published them on their blog. Their result was worldwide attention on Twitter as a "Top Retweet," which resulted in high content visibility for one of the most popular searches of the year.

Unplanned Real-Time Publishing

While the previous example allowed for content ramp-up based on seasonal and anticipated real-time queries, it is the aspect of the unpredictable real-time query avalanche that presents some of the greatest opportunities. Bloggers who are able to best take advantage of this concept are ready to publish in an agile manner, are monitoring conversation and trends in their respective keyword space in real-time, and have a sizeable network to turn that snowball into an avalanche of shares, links, and traffic back to their blog assets.

I have talked about a lot of different tools in this book, but in this element, your brain is your best tool. Just as Google and Bing need a human social layer to inform their algorithms in real-time, you need to be present in the real-time conversation to know and process what is happening. While tools do a lot to help us out, there is currently no real-time tool that can match the mind of a knowledgeable and authentic human content producer in real-time.

You Have to Throw a Lot of Snowballs to Start an Avalanche

In 2011 I spoke with an attendee at a marketing conference who got caught up in a major positive news story related to one of their services. For unknown reasons, an interesting phenomenon that happens every year in this person's business had become a major news story, and his blog was an indirect but authoritative source of the news. He had already created content around this trending topic, and he tweeted a link out to his followers, waiting for the rush of traffic. But because of a few mistakes he missed the avalanche of traffic, links, and social signals that should have come his way. He missed using the natural keyword language that social audiences had assigned to the topic in real-time. In effect, people were searching in Google and Twitter for this story by a completely different name, and his content simply did not match the query according to those two engines. He also did not have a big enough network to get the snowball rolling. A wider distribution network with the right keyword would have helped him own the story.

This marketer's biggest issue of all was that he had not thrown enough snowballs. One time won't cut it. In short, you have to throw a lot of snowballs over a long period of time to capture this kind of traffic, links, and social signals. Consistently publishing to a real-time audience shows people that you are present and participating in the conversation. It shows search engines that you provide fresh content, that social promotion is creating fresh signals that search engines like to see, and that you are an authoritative source for your theme—a source that can be trusted to provide quality content in the search results, in short, without a worry that you are trying to push spam into the index.

It is fair to say that a lot of the high-velocity content-sharing going on is around news and entertainment categories. But remember the statistic that Google provided in 2007 that between 20 to 25 percent of queries searched every day are new and have never been seen before. Granted, many of these queries may include typos and variations of existing themes and terms. But the bottom line is that the natural language of your audience is constantly evolving in real-time, and knowing your audience means knowing how they think, how they converse, and what language they use to find new information. Getting traffic doesn't have to be a mass-media exercise every time. To the contrary, a balanced, present, persistent, and steady approach will get your blog where it needs to be.

News

The way we receive and consume the news has been forever revolutionized by search, social, and real-time dissemination. Greg Jarboe (see his interview later in this chapter) has stated that news is so fast-paced in today's synaptic publishing environment that it takes more than a webmaster to run it—it takes a *newsmaster*. Even in the editorial rooms of traditional newspapers, print magazines, and TV news programs, search and social have made a primary mark. Newscasters on major networks like CNN read directly from breaking Twitter streams on live broadcasts. In newspaper editorial rooms, the editor calls on the SEO guy to find out what news is trending and what is of most interest to their audience on any given day.

Real-time news also takes on a different dimension when it is crowd-sourced, as is the case with Wikipedia. At almost any point of a major breaking news story, a corresponding Wikipedia news page or topic may be edited in real-time, as it happens. Sources are cited, and facts are separated from rumors. In the end, the Wikipedia Edit tab provides one of the best records of a breaking news story, with the facts, missteps, corrections, and conclusions all in one chronicle. To see for yourself, go to Google News to find a breaking news story right now, and then search for that topic in Wikipedia. You will often find that the Wikipedia story is completely up-to-date and as comprehensive as any story listed by a news aggregator.

This section will explore some of the search and social elements of news and whether creating a news source is right for your business. In addition, you will look closely at optimization for Google News.

The Real-Time Elements of News

News and its various distribution channels are one of the most "real-time" publishing channels on the Internet. In the digital realm, new stories start with a person reporting the news or observing events, whether it is in a status update on Twitter, a blog post, or a news story on a major media outlet. Depending on the urgency of the news, passive network distribution may occur, with subscribed RSS feeds being updated, triggered email alerts going out, or popularity streams pushing a story to the top of the fold. On the flip side, active network distribution complements the passive, with people sharing news in their networks based on the level of individual interest or importance. Both passive and active distribution feed each other. In real-time channels, an editor or producer at a news desk doesn't determine what the lead story is that day but rather the concept of increasing velocity and interest does, as it is measured in real-time with a search and social lens. With this in mind, here are some of the core elements of news that make it "real-time":

- It disseminates at lightning-fast speeds in social networks.
- When breaking news travels across social networks, keyword searches around the news topic spike as well.
- A news provider or publisher must take great care with the search authority and trust of a website in order to be trusted enough by the search engines to allow content to flow in real-time.
- A newsroom mind-set toward news content prepares the publisher to be fluid enough for search and social distribution.
- Comments on news stories also happen at a greater velocity and therefore require more participation from the writer or editor to direct conversation, maintain the context of comments, delete anything that is spammy or off-topic, or otherwise be present as a live editor.

The Interdependent Search and Social Elements of Online News

As previously mentioned, news distribution and dissemination is widely determined by many long-known search and social factors. Here are some of the key elements of digital news distribution and channels:

- When breaking news hits, search engines seek out fresh content to meet the spiking search interest of a given news topic.
- Real-time shared news can attract an avalanche of links and social signals that can create search benefits for a long time to come.
- Real-time shared news can create a large number of optimized pages that create second-tier SERP visibility.
- In the tradition of SEO-based keyword research, understanding the linguistics and natural keyword language of news publishing is critical in order to connect news content to audiences in both search and social channels, in real-time.

- When breaking news hits, the velocity of people sharing and discussing content also spikes. This provides great opportunities for real-time content creators who are acting in-the-moment to capture spiking traffic, conversation, pages, and links.
- XML feeds and sitemaps are critical to real-time news delivery, just as search engines utilize feeds for traditional web search and product search.
- A news story can have "long-tail appeal," or, in other words, be highly relevant to a smaller audience, with laser targeting to relevant audiences.
- The authority and influence of both the *site* hosting content and the *sharer* are considered to determine influence.

Search engines and social networks also determine the velocity of sharing to identify hot trends within short periods of time. News is one of the most popular universal placements to go to the top of primetime web-search results in Google when "query deserves freshness" (QDF) parameters are triggered. The speed of news-sharing is tracked at the keyword level by both search engines and social networks. Personalization is a fundamental element of the search and social experience, and online news sites and aggregators are increasingly using social signals and a person's own network as a way to filter relevant news stories.

Determining Whether News Should Be Part of Your Real-Time Content Strategy

Embarking on a news-publishing strategy is not necessarily for every business. But if you find that there is limited coverage in the topics of your business that interest your audience or that interest you, you may have identified a potential opportunity. You may also find that you have a different editorial point of view in the way certain news is covered and that you can provide value to your audience.

You don't have to take the "news source" route to be a provider of news, though. Posting up-to-date information about current events and topics keeps your blog and website fresh and appealing, and provides a reason for your audience to check out your content on a regular basis. Post news, post links to other news, and add your own commentary about current news stories. This is one of the simplest methods of staying in the real-time conversation on the Internet at large, though your news source may still not qualify for Google News (and that's okay).

The Problem with Social Personalization of News

With the increased emphasis of social signals by the major search engines, a new phenomenon has emerged in the way we consume the news, particularly based on social signals, personal interests, popularity, and people in our network. With personalization, a person's own biases provide a filter to the news the see. Theoretically, if all the news a person consumes is entertainment-related, they may be up-to-date on what Lady Gaga ate for lunch but not know who won the U.S. presidential election of 2012.

I first wrote about some of my own concerns about personalization of search results in June 2007 and August 2008 for MediaPost Search Insider. Personalization was heating up, as Google started to allow more subjective influence on the search results. At the time, this was a huge shift for Google from relying on objective results (everyone sees the same number-one result around the world), to focusing on subjective results (everyone sees their own personal bias in the results). But the shift to personalization was still in line with Google's goal of developing artificial intelligence to better serve the user's needs.

Prior bias that once consisted of only small elements such as location and search behavior has now extended to Google News as well. In addition to seeing the stories that Google deems to be important, you will now also prominently see results that people in your circles have +1ed or shared. In other words, people in your network are having an editorial impact on the news you see. In this sense, your news stream is only as relevant as the people in your network, so it is important to develop a network that is socially relevant to you.

Of course, not all of our friends and co-workers are experts in global politics, so it also helpful and informative to turn it off some times and listen to the experts. As I stated in that column, I don't always want to know what I think should be number one—I want to know what you (the engine) thinks should be number one. And I want to be able to turn it off and on as a filter. Google+ has a little toggle for your own stream to turn your friends' posts up or down in terms of visibility, and it will be great when the engines and major networks realize that objective editorial is just as important as subjective biases.

In the meantime, this exemplifies another opportunity for you and your business to gain reach throughout the news product in Google. And it doesn't stop with News. As I wrote in Chapter 7, "Social-Network Platforms," Google+ is a long-term project for Google, and it has stated that we will begin to see more and more application of your circles and Google+ network reaching out to many more of its products and services. You can let your imagination run wild, but the bottom line is that increasing your network size will increase your visibility throughout Google's various services and properties as time goes by. If you already have your networks established, then it will be a boon for your business with each new rollout. But as a user, it is important to still think critically about the information you consume and also build a meaningful and relevant network.

Google News Optimization

If your site and content qualify as legitimate news sources on either a broad or a niche level, then optimizing for Google News should be a core part of your online news strategy. There are many different considerations for optimization, on both human and technical levels.

First you need to make sure your site is a trusted source of news by your audience and that anyone manually reviewing your site would immediately find your site to be credible and authoritative. In addition to the technical aspects of managing Google News, Google reviews sites to ensure that sites meet the basic quality and criteria that it has established for news sources in its FAQ. In other words, all the SEO and content in the world won't help you if a human editor does not agree that your site is worthy of inclusion. With this in mind, your editorial strategy, usability, layout, creative, publishing frequency, and many other areas take a high place in the "optimization" of your site or blog for Google News. And there are no guarantees that Google will include your site in News.

Crawling, Indexing, Clustering, Grouping, and Ranking in Google News

Google goes through a five-step process for gathering and ranking stories for Google News: crawling, indexing, clustering, grouping, and ranking. Fundamentally, Google News seeks content that is fresh and recent, original, well-written, and geographically relevant, among other factors.

News is crawled by Google's main web crawler, Googlebot (crawler Googlebot-News was retired in August 2011). Google also crawls news sources and determines the prominence of page placement of the stories to determine how they may rank in Google News. Similar to the standard web-search algorithm, Google also applies an authority score to news sources. Stories are clustered and grouped based on their similarity and are ultimately ranked based on velocity of the topic.

Beyond the basic SEO and news feed-optimization tactics that follow, some of the best things you can do to achieve placement in Google News are to be present, to publish actively, and to provide a lot of fresh news content that also receives plenty of social signals.

Google+ Rel=Author and Rel=Standout Impact on Google News

As with many other aspects of Google+, people in a network of Google Circles are having a major impact on the way the news is viewed by others in their network. When you log into your Google account and go to http://news.google.com, you will now see stories from people in your Google+ network who have shared or +1ed news-source content. The `rel=author` attribute is also allowing news writers with a Google+ account to have their profiles show up alongside major news stories, from the front page of Google News on down to more detailed keyword searches. In Figure 8.5, you can see an annotation to a front-page Google News story that includes a link to the Google+ profile of SlashGear writer Chris Burns.

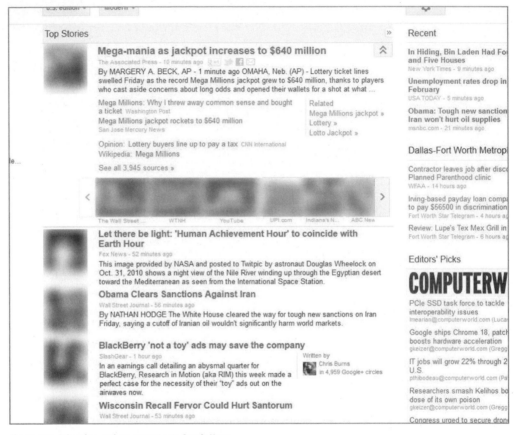

Figure 8.5 A Google+ author annotation in Google News

The implication here again is that building up your network will increase your visibility and influence within that network of news readers, and implementing the `rel=author` markup for your news story will give you heightened visibility in the network. Authorship may also likely become a ranking feature for content, including real-time content, in future iterations of the Google search algorithm. You'll find more on setting up the `rel=author` attribute for your own news-publishing efforts in Chapter 10.

Google also offers publishers an additional tag to allow specific content to be featured, or "stand out." This enables your content potentially to be shown with a "featured" label on the front page of Google News and relevant sections. Google requests that news organizations use the standout attribute no more than seven times per week. Citing stories more than seven times a week could cause Google to ignore your standout attributes in the future, or at least weaken them as a signal. Read more at http://googlenewsblog.blogspot.com/2011/09/recognizing-publishers-standout-content.html and http://support.google.com/news/publisher/bin/answer.py?hl=en&answer=191283.

Google News Optimization Considerations

On the technical side, you must consider a few things, in addition to following Google's detailed guidelines for inclusion (http://support.google.com/news/publisher/bin/news_pub/bin/answer.py?hl=en&answer=40787). If you are not technically inclined, then you will need to have someone in your IT department (or consultant or agency) create a specialized News XML sitemap, specifically for Google News. URLs must also meet a requirement to include three digits that are not date-specific in the URL. Special considerations are also given to optimizing images and video for Google News placement. Image and video opportunities should not be overlooked, because these two areas of news have a potential to drive massive volumes of traffic directly to your site or to your YouTube video channel.

Again, your IT resource should read the specifications carefully for creating a Google News feed, but here are some other key considerations for optimization, as you consider whether to become a news provider or begin to optimize your existing news channels:

Create a News Sitemap Remember that a news sitemap is different from other XML sitemaps and should be configured for Google News. News sitemaps follow the sitemap protocol (www.sitemaps.org/protocol.html), and additional tags are required. Sitemaps can include URLs only for the prior two days of updates, must have fewer than 1,000 URLs, and should be uploaded to the highest-level directory that houses the news sections of your site. Read more at http://support.google.com/news/publisher/bin/answer.py?hl=en&answer=74288.

Optimize As If a Google News Administrator Is Reading Your News Google News uses human editors to review news sites to confirm their legitimacy as a news source, so consider how your news site would look to a Google News editor. It could mean the difference between being accepted into Google News and not at all.

Optimize Your URL Structure Google News requires that at least three numerical digits different from a date are included in the URL structure. Read more at http://support.google.com/news/publisher/bin/answer.py?hl=en&answer=2481391, and also review the URL structure of existing news-story URLs at http://news.google.com.

Avoid Rich Internet Applications (RIAs) for Publishing News Flash, JavaScript, frames, and other rich Internet applications are not crawlable by Google News bots. Keep your page delivery flat and simple so that the Googlebot can easily get your content.

Optimize Images While this book covers image optimization in great detail in Chapter 11, "Video and Images," Google has very specific recommendations for optimizing images for Google News. These recommendations include using standard image formats and extensions (JPEG, .TIF), creating larger image sizes (minimum 60×60 pixels is recommended), placing images near the article title, and also providing well-written captions for images. Read the full Google News image-optimization FAQ when approaching this area (http://support.google.com/news/publisher/bin/answer.py?hl=en&answer=13369), because optimized images in Google News can become a huge traffic rush for your site.

Optimize Video for Google News Google has a specific set of guidelines and considerations for segmenting out video for inclusion in Google News. It fundamentally requests that news videos included in a specific YouTube channel be original and unique, production quality be clear and in focus, and some amount of context be provided in your video assets in descriptions, titles, and metadata. Read the full Google News video-optimization FAQ at http://support.google.com/news/publisher/bin/answer.py?hl=en&answer=93985.

These are just a few considerations for optimizing and submitting your site to Google News, and you and your technical resources should read the entire Google News FAQ before proceeding. Overall, news is one of the most popular content-consuming activities on the Internet, and becoming a source of the news could help you reap much of this traffic and exposure for your online publication, in real-time.

Press Releases

Distributing press releases is just one element of public relations, and in the Internet age, a new approach to distribution and development is required. In this section, you will learn the following:

- How to think about the real-time, search, and social elements of writing a press release
- How to optimize a press release
- How to write an engaging press release that resonates in both search and social networks
- Additional tips from two top PR pros

So, let's kick off this section with an overview of the real-time, search, and social elements of writing and distributing press releases.

The Real-Time Elements of Press Releases

When you send out a press release with big news or important information about your business, you work is not done. If the news resonates, then people will comment, share, republish, and have questions. If your press releases are effective, you will start a beehive of activity around your release, and it happens in real-time. All along the way, this beehive of activity sets off a chain of links and pages that search engines will also look to for signals. Ultimately, the amount of attention you get is directly proportional to how well-optimized and buzzworthy your press release is from a human and algorithmic standpoint. Here are some of the other real-time aspects of digital press releases:

- Press releases go out live to networks in real-time.
- Press releases are pushed out via RSS feeds in real-time.
- Major press-release services will tweet or share press-release links automatically to their subscribed networks in real-time.
- Senders should be present and participatory upon release, at least for the initial monitoring phase.

The Search and Social Elements of Press Releases

In many ways, the success of your press release is dependent on how well it is optimized for various search and social features. It's important to be ready for real-time distribution of your release, and a missed keyword or share could be a missed connection with your audience. When considering digital press-release production and distribution, the following characteristics become more important to the consumption in search and social channels:

- Just like any other web page, a press release must be optimized both for keyword visibility and for appeal to people.
- Releases can be triggered at the keyword level, via email, via alerts, and through RSS feeds.
- A well-written press release can rank for noncompetitive or low-competition terms in a relatively short period of time. Sometimes multiple pages can rank for the same term.
- Press releases can sometimes provide backlink value to your hosted content, from relevant links placed within the release.
- Press releases can be shared easily via links, or even tweeted, liked, or +1ed directly from the newswire service or source.
- Good press releases for interesting news get picked up by bloggers or other news outlets covering news in real-time. This leads to additional links and pages that may appear in search results as a second-tier search result, as well as any other social sharing and discussion from the news pickup.

- As mentioned in an earlier chapter, a well-written headline is imperative for a release to track in both search and social to make it newsworthy.

Press Release-Optimization Basics

Now that you understand some of the key search and social elements of press releases, it is worthwhile to take a quick look at some basic considerations for digital press-release optimization. Here are some of the key reasons that you should optimize releases and also pay attention to the constantly changing landscape as it relates to press-release distribution:

- Online newswires such as PRWeb, PR Newswire, and Business Wire have become a direct source for content and act as press release search engines.
- Universal search and freshness parameters means greater inclusion of news-based content in the algorithmic search-engine results pages, and that news releases hold greater importance as naturally optimized assets. This does not imply that press releases get you directly in news placement. Releases alone do not, but press-release pickup by news outlets can.
- There is a substantial audience of journalists, bloggers, and end readers who rely on keyword-triggered alert systems to find news and press-release content, so keyword-research skills are imperative.
- Press releases push out automatically into some social services and also RSS-based subscription services. Social and search consumption is the new "pickup," and the process of getting it there is automated and triggered.
- News-based keyword research in the form of trending topics and trend search is making it easier to relate directly to an audience at the keyword level.

Many of these are not new concepts, but they're as important as ever with the evolution of real-time publishing tactics.

Tips for Press-Release Optimization

Remember the quick SEO copywriting guide in Chapter 6, "Creating Effective and Engaging Content"? A process for search engine–friendly copywriting was outlined, along with specific examples of how to best lay out the elements and maintain a consistency of your keyword themes to build a strong page for search engines. As you go through this section, it is important to think about press releases as being similar to any other web page you would optimize. A press release entered into a content-management system will have the same fields and similar HTML markup. With the copywriting guide in mind, here are some of the key tips for writing optimized press releases in order to extend their visibility using established search engine-optimization search tactics:

In the Title Headline, Include Popular Keywords and Phrases That Correspond with the Major Theme of the Release Of all on-page attributes, the title element is the single heaviest-weighted aspect in the way that engines determine search ranking. Press releases are no different. Choose your keywords carefully, because in most cases a release will not rank for a competitive keyword or phrase unless it is emphasized in the title.

Include Popular Keyword Phrases in the Release Summary or the Secondary Release Heading The secondary heading summary can also be a place to incorporate other valuable ancillary keywords and phrases that support your overall theme.

Reinforce the Major Keyword Theme in the Body of the Release Once again, what works for optimizing web pages goes for press releases as well. Include your title keyword theme in the first paragraph to reinforce the overall theme of the release.

Include the Company URL in the First Paragraph, After the Company Name The engines put more emphasis on a link in the first paragraph or sentence of a page, so include the URL in that spot in each release. Also, many news aggregators will scrape and post the first paragraph, or first few sentences, and this allows you an additional opportunity to capture a link.

Use Relevant Keywords to Describe Your Business at the End of the Press Release Adding your generic keyword phrase or category to describe the nature of your business not only serves to describe and introduce what your company does, but also gives the engines a little bit of keyword context to go by. Ensure that a generic and relevant description of your business is in the boilerplate.

Use Relevant Links in the Body of the Release When Appropriate The major press-release services will allow the use of links in the body of the release. Use keyword-based anchor text for links when it makes sense, and don't gratuitously insert links that might put off your readers.

Add Relevant Ancillary Keywords to Trigger the Release via Keyword-Alert Services Remember that keywords and keyword phrases placed anywhere in the document can trigger a release alert via Google Alerts, Yahoo! Alerts, online newswires, or any other keyword-based notification system. Use relevant trigger keywords all throughout the release to extend the distribution in these various channels, but only when it is relevant and within the context of your release.

Use Keyword Research to Reach Your Target Keywords are connections to people. Just as search engine marketers regularly research keywords and phrases for SEM campaigns, understanding how journalists or bloggers think at the query level can put your release directly in their inboxes, without having to make an additional phone call or send an email. Utilizing the terminology that searchers use to find information ultimately increases your chances of being found.

Distribute Your Press-Release URL to Your Own Networks A solid network of connections who are receptive to news about your business can act as a sort of earned or organic newswire of its own. As I have written many times in this book, building up your network reach is an optimization and distribution tactic, and it is earned by participation and engaging content. Get started building up your networks today in order to have a solid base in the next one to three years. Include consumers of your content and also influencers who share and create content on their own.

Place a Copy of Your Release on Your Own Blog or Website If your release is newsworthy enough to warrant a press release, then in most cases it should also be worthy-enough content for your owned digital assets. While placement may be subjective, especially in the case of addressing any critical situations, your website and blog are fundamentally places for all news about your company and business.

Add Multiple Digital Assets to the Release Most major newswires will allow the addition of images and even video clips to a release. Take advantage of this by adding relevant info as it fits the context of your release.

Educate Your PR team on Press-Release Optimization If you're not the person who is responsible for writing your company's press releases, talk to your team or PR resource. Using best practices for writing releases to attract journalists' attention generally helps with overall visibility in search and social spaces. Start by having them read this chapter, along with other parts of this book.

Add a Stock-Ticker Symbol, If Appropriate This will increase pickup on financial outlets and also distribute the release to people who are monitoring news keywords based on the ticker symbol.

An Interview with Greg Jarboe, of SEO-PR

I have been very fortunate to know and work with some of the top digital public-relations professionals in the online marketing business for many years now, through iCrossing, industry work, and speaking. Digital PR requires a mind for traditional PR strategy, adapted to the new digital landscape. I first heard Greg Jarboe speak at a search conference more than 10 years ago, and he has consistently proven to be one of the leading thinkers in digitally focused public-relations strategies. I've since had the pleasure of copresenting with him at various search conferences across the United States. Jarboe is the president and cofounder of SEO-PR and pioneered what is now known as the *SEO press release*. He proved that SEO and analytics not only could extend the visibility of your release, but also could show a return on investment. Essentially, Jarboe helped bring the public-relations world of old into the new world of digital distribution, with search and social at the core.

An Interview with Greg Jarboe, of SEO-PR *(Continued)*

Jarboe also teaches online PR in the Rutgers mini-MBA program and is the online PR faculty chair at Market Motive. He is profiled in *Online Marketing Heroes* by Michael Miller (Wiley, 2008). I asked Greg about some of the key considerations for optimizing press releases and about helping PR professionals to become more digitally literate.

While many of the basic rules of digital press-release optimization have been established for years now, it seems that many PR professionals are just now becoming aware of them. Why do you believe this is so?

As Columbus discovered, training the crews of the *Niña*, *Pinta*, and *Santa Maria* how to sail west was relatively straightforward. The real challenge was convincing King Ferdinand and Queen Isabella that the ships wouldn't fall off the edge of the world. News search engines represent a shift in the PR paradigm. That explains why so few PR people have started exploring this new world.

What do you consider to be the first step in press-release optimization?

Identifying your target audiences and developing a segmentation strategy. This requires a redefinition of public relations that is significantly broader than media relations. When users search for a term or phrase in Google News or Yahoo! News, they often find press releases as well as articles in the results. This means that PR people can use news search engines to pitch their news stories directly to the public as well as the press. This puts "the public" back into public relations.

What is the next step in the process, and are there any tools that you recommend that will aid this step?

Conducting keyword research and finding two to three relevant search terms. Among the free keyword-suggestion tools that you can use are Google Insights for Search and Yahoo! News Search Assist. The first one lets you compare search volume patterns across specific regions, categories, timeframes, and Google properties, while the second provides near real-time suggestions in Yahoo! News Search.

Are there any other considerations that marketers and PR professionals should take with regard to press-release optimization?

Making sure that your press release actually includes the search terms you've identified. The news search engine algorithms scan the title, the headline, and at least the first hundred words or so of news articles and press releases. So, the best way to ensure your SEO press release appears for particular searches is to include the most relevant search terms in your headline, subhead, and lead paragraph.

Which press–release distribution service should you use? Should multiple services be used?

Google News currently crawls more than 25,000 news sources, including dozens that distribute press releases. Yahoo! News enables users to search more than 7,000 news sources, including Business Wire, GlobeNewswire, Marketwire, PR Newswire, and PRWeb. Neither of these news search engines is able to manually add press releases that are sent to them. So, you need to use one of these press release–distribution services.

(Continues)

An Interview with Greg Jarboe, of SEO-PR *(Continued)*

What final steps should be taken in press-release optimization?

Adding hyperlinks to help people find interesting, related content on your website. This enables PR people to use web analytics to measure what matters. This includes

Increasing website traffic: SEO-PR helped *The Christian Science Monitor* drive 450,000 unique visitors to "Hostage: The Jill Carroll Story" in the first 24 hours.

Generating leads online: SEO-PR helped *Parents* magazine generate 129,155 entries to its cover-photo contest.

Producing online sales: By adding analytics tracking, SEO-PR helped Southwest Airlines link $2.5 million in ticket sales to SEO press releases.

Measuring marketing ROI: SEO-PR helped the Rutgers Center for Management Development get an 8.6 return on marketing investment.

As Jarboe says, optimization represents a shift in the PR paradigm. Clearly the press release that was once just a sheet of paper or two can now have a network of its own. Nevertheless, it is a new world that you will want to start exploring in order to reap all of the benefits from search and social.

An Interview with Sarah Skerik, PR Newswire

In addition to speaking with Greg Jarboe, I also wanted to gain some current insight about the state of search and social factors on press releases directly from one of the wire services. Sarah Skerik, VP of social media at PR Newswire, was kind enough to answer a few questions to give you the press-release wire's point of view on the impact of search and social on press-release consumption.

What are the three key social factors that help increase the visibility of a press release?

The three social factors most likely to increase the visibility of a press release (or any other content a brand distributes, for that matter) are, in my opinion, the following:

The brand's social graph: Cultivating an audience via social networks and building what Adam Lavelle of iCrossing calls a truly "connected brand" is instrumental in achieving visibility today. An engaged audience can help amplify the message by sharing it with their own networks. Simply blasting messages out on Twitter isn't enough.

Smart writing and formatting: Press releases need be interesting, and they need to be written and formatted to encourage sharing. Short, punchy headlines are ideal for search engines and Twitterers. Highlighting facts and submessages with paragraph subheads and bullet points makes it easier for readers to find interesting tidbits to share with their followers. Embedded social-sharing buttons encourage people to easily spread the message by making it easy for them to like, +1, and share the content with their followers.

(Continues)

An Interview with Sarah Skerik, PR Newswire *(Continued)*

Inclusion of visuals in the message: We looked at the analytics around one month's worth of press releases (more than 20,000) and found that press releases that included multimedia generated better overall results and were more widely and frequently shared on social networks than plain-text stories. (Details: `http://blog.prnewswire.com/2011/05/02/` `multimedia-content-drives-better-press-release-results/`.)

What impact are social signals having on your press-release visibility and sharing in PR Newswire?

Press releases are shared with staggering frequency on Twitter, Facebook, LinkedIn, and, increasingly, Pinterest. Search engines notice when social noise is refined into a signal, and the underlying message (in this case, a press release) will get better visibility as a result. As a result of social sharing, we're seeing significant referring traffic coming to press releases and other content directly from social networks, indicating that social audiences respect press releases as a credible source of information from the brand, and one that is worth sharing.

This ends another chapter on some of the common vehicles for real-time content distribution. In the next chapter, you will learn about other real-time content-management systems and communities, including forums, wikis, and answer sites.

Developing and Engaging in Real-Time Communities

In this chapter, I will cover some of the most important—and often most overlooked—social networks, including discussion forums, answer sites, and wikis. Though they don't get as much publicity as Twitter, Facebook, or LinkedIn, the wide variety of discussion forums, answer sites, and wikis are worthy of search and social publishing considerations for almost any business.

9

Chapter Contents

Why forums, answer sites, and wikis are real-time social networks
Considerations for starting your own forum or wiki community
How to engage in forums and answer sites
The reciprocating search and social elements of forums, answer sites, and wikis

Introduction to Real-Time Communities

Engaging in these areas as either a site owner or a participant requires community and audience management, and knowing the written and unwritten rules of each social space that you plan to engage in. Also common to forums, answer sites, and wikis is that they are "always-on," and it is important to be present and alive in your publishing efforts in order to get the most out of these channels. While the key real-time and search and social elements are outlined individually for these three content types, all three have the following in common:

- They provide second-tier search visibility.
- They are resources for living keyword research and development.
- They provide resources for user-generated content development.
- Their content-management platforms are designed for real-time management.
- Each platform is a real-world example of the search and social reciprocation rule described in Chapter 1, "Real-Time Publishing and Marketing.".
- Trusted platforms are crawled and indexed rapidly by search engines.

You may already be engaging in one or more of these types of publishing, and if so, this chapter can also help increase the reach and opportunities of what you are already doing.

To get the most out the following sections, be clear in how your business goals translate to these publishing platforms. Also, determine how you will strike a balance between achieving business goals and providing a meaningful community experience that doesn't make your audience feel like they are being sold to.

Search and Social Reciprocation in Real-Time Communities

If you want to see the conflux of many different search and social elements online, just visit a popular discussion forum, wiki, or answer site. There is an interesting dynamic that occurs in terms of how search and social reciprocate to help grow these entities in an almost organic and synaptic way. These sites, whether attached to a bigger publishing entity or operating as stand-alone entities, generate content that gets picked up in search engines. The natural language of the audience enables it to achieve high velocity, in the sense that the content is available in real-time and as a collective stream of consciousness in the keyword and content sense.

The search and social synergies of real-time communities are very simple. When user-generated content is created in the social scenario, it is then crawled by search engines, and this traffic from engines drives more like-minded visitors back to the originating sites. Remember how the first chapter described how to speak in the voice of your audience? User-generated content helps accomplish this for you by simply allowing your audience to converse naturally or by engaging in a third-party site for conversation and content contribution. This is one of the key benefits of direct search visibility or second-tier search visibility through engagement.

When search-engine traffic comes back to real-time content communities, another interesting thing happens. A segment of the audience referred by search engines becomes posters and content generators themselves. Remember in the first chapter when I wrote about how you need to think more deeply about search traffic, because there are real people behind those keywords? Those real search people become members of social networks, content producers, and content consumers. In effect, those searchers become part of the community and generate more content. This cycle continues to churn as long as the community remains active and alive.

Real-time communities are also great examples of the "you give, and you get" principles. Running/engaging in these platforms takes a tremendous amount of hard work and patience and can take years to develop. The payoff is that you gain increased visibility in both the community and the search results that pick up this content. *Visibility* can be defined as search visibility, but more importantly, it translates to heightened awareness of you or your business as a key contributor or expert in a particular social space. This expertise can be local or worldwide—it just depends on the theme and social area you choose to pursue.

It takes a lot of time and hard work to accomplish building a robust real-time community or building up a network in a real-time community. As a very wise person once said, the *first best time* to plant a tree was 30 years ago; the *second best time* is right now. If you haven't already started building or engaging in real-time user-generated content communities, then *right now* may be the best time to start.

Forums

Discussion forums are one of the original "social" elements of the Web. They have long been the place where people of like-minded interests hang out, chat, argue, and share content, among many other activities. They are also curated and created by people, they attract lots of search traffic, and many people form lifelong bonds there.

I could write a whole book on how forums have affected me in my personal and professional life. As an online marketer, they have been part of my daily routine for many years as a reader, as a participant, and even as a forum administrator. When we had our first baby, my wife joined a forum where all of the moms were expecting in the same month and year. Nine years later, this community continues to be part of our lives, and these moms have helped each other out and shared their experiences throughout their children's entire lives. Their level of engagement ranges from the typical day-to-day aspects of motherhood to sometimes life-threatening emergencies. To my wife and this group of moms, their board isn't just a forum or social network—it's a support network.

Some forum communities take their act offline. Brett Tabke's WebmasterWorld discussion forum has evolved into one of largest physical Internet-marketing conferences in the United States, and it started right on an Internet forum in the late 1990s. Today, the Pubcon conference in Las Vegas is attended by thousands of people every year and is one of the world's leading conferences on the topics of search and social. Forum and conference owner Brett Tabke will provide some additional insight on marketing as a forum publisher and/or participant later in this chapter.

The Real-Time Elements of Forums

Running a forum and being an active participant requires an always-on mind-set and the fluid ability to react. A good forum can take years to develop and becomes more of a real-time platform as it matures. With this in mind, here are some of the key real-time elements of developed online discussion forums:

- Forums require active real-time participation by both the administrator and forum members.

- A major segment of forum content is produced in real-time and is user-generated.

- When trusted by search crawlers, forum content can be retrievable by search engines in minutes or seconds after it is published.

- RSS feeds push content beyond the forum itself in real-time and into social channels, aggregators, and feed readers.

- Forum content is often based on real-time news and other discussion that concerns topical themes, particularly news stories, buzz, and entertainment.

- Popular forums attract a steady base of users, and a crowd is almost always present.

- Similar to a blog, forum and discussion content is presented in reverse chronological order, and the freshness of content is indicative of the level of real-time participation.

Popular forum systems also share real-time data, such as the number of users online, newest posts, newest members, identities of current members online, number of views, and ratings of threads. A lot of this type of data is made public by default in form of a CMS like vBulletin and phpBB and gives the site a live and real-time feel.

The Interdependent Search and Social Elements of Forums

As mentioned at the beginning of this section, forums are one of best examples of search and social interdependency in action, and there are tens of thousands of them online right now. With this in mind, here are some of the key reciprocating elements of discussion forums:

- Forum content is based on the collective and subjective language of the community and creates unpredictable keyword-friendly content for search engines that requires no research.

- Forum content is segmented into one of Google's social search engines, Google Discussions, which is also part of the main Google web-search engine.

- Popular forums naturally attract links at the domain level and at the page level, so the link profile is somewhat proportional to the interest level of the content.

- Standard forum-software programs such as vBulletin and PHPBB are search engine–friendly and have many different SEO plug-ins available to further optimize your site and extend your reach.

- Links from signatures, profile pages, and discussion threads can provide link equity back to your assets, provided that they are "dofollow" links.

- Interacting on third-party forums will help you gain second-tier SERP visibility by leveraging the good SEO visibility of those sites.

- Forums are excellent sources for keyword research, particularly for studying the living and evolving language of the forum's audience.

- A question asked on a forum is similar to a query entered in a search engine—except on a forum, a human answers the query.

- If someone has a question on a forum, then it is likely that many more people are asking the same question in search engines, and the forum provides answers both to its users and to similar search queries when indexed properly.

- Forum content enables less-technical users to create search engine–friendly pages and links on third-party sites that rank well in search.

- Forum content is self-reinforcing, in the sense that if the content is good and popular enough, then search engines will return a substantial amount of relevant traffic.

Also note that quantitative metrics such as the number of replies, page word count, views, and thread length can increase search visibility. This is not always the case for low-competition keywords in search engines, but it does become more important as the keywords and phrases increase in popularity and competition.

Is a Forum Right for Your Business?

Hosting and developing a new forum take a lot of work and patience. Some businesses may be better off engaging in established forums, while others may benefit from the "grow your own" approach. Before jumping in and setting up your own forum, considering the following for your analysis and review:

Assess Your Audience Does your audience use forums, or do they prefer to consume content in other ways? Before developing, poll people in your existing social networks to determine whether this is something they would be interested in.

Perform Content Gap Analysis When performing a content gap analysis, review your own site against your target keyword set. Does your content represent a wide range of keywords? Could you use a boost from user-generated content? Also, look at your competitors using the tools in Chapter 4, "Market Research and Content Types," and determine what you believe your competition might be getting.

Determine Competition Your competitors are both direct and indirect and even internal. When reviewing the keyword space, are there currently any other discussion forums serving the same theme or topic? If so, what are their strengths, and how would your forum be different? Would you be happy being the second, third, fourth, or fifth largest forum? You may find that there is little to no competition, and a great opportunity may exist to capture that keyword and social space. Also, use Google Discussion search to identify existing forums for your target theme and keyword set.

Determine Your Resources for Managing a Forum Forum development is a long-term proposition. Your first year will be spent building and developing an audience. There are costs in terms of time, manpower, maintenance, and hosting. Do you have the time to manage a forum yourself, or do you currently have other capable resources who can take this on? Will you need to hire a resource, consultant, or agency?

Determine Your Business Reason for Starting a Forum As previously outlined in Chapter 3, "Ramping Up for a Real-Time Content Marketing Strategy," you need to know why you are engaging in forums or why you should build your own. What is the business reason for creating a forum? How will it benefit your business? Will your audience and customer base benefit from a forum in any way?

It is also a good idea to join a forum and participate to better understand the user experience. Reply to other posts, write and submit posts, and engage with other forum members to gain a good understanding of the forum experience before you jump in.

Selecting a Forum Package and Host

Many different forum packages are available, but I will focus on only two of them in this section to help get you started. One other option is to code your own, as Brett Tabke did, but he did this at a time when reliable forum packages were not available. At this point, you are probably better off not reinventing the wheel, either vBulletin or phpBB will provide you with the foundation you need.

Many different forum packages have robust features and years of development and testing behind them. The good companies and communities that produce forum software are constantly developing their next version, working out any bugs or newly discovered exploits, and generally working to keep these systems at top performance. In the case of popular forums like vBulletin and PHPBB, many users are already accustomed to the standard forum interface, so there is less to worry about in terms of basic usability, and it will allow you more time to focus on community and content. Again, there are many great companies producing forum software, but these two are among the most popular.

vBulletin

vBulletin (www.vbulletin.com) is the most popular fee-based forum software. It has robust support within its own forum, and there are many coders who are very familiar with fixing, maintaining, and installing this software. This company routinely maintains its codebase and is constantly on top of security issues and quick to follow up with patches. There are also many diverse setups and plug-ins for use with vBulletin, and it is easy to customize with themes, as well as customize the forum layout and administration. vBulletin also listens closely to the needs of its own forum members and responds and adapts to the needs of the contemporary webmaster. For a paid forum option, vBulletin can't be beat and is used by thousands of webmasters and businesses worldwide. Figure 9.1 shows the vBulletin support forum, which displays an example of its basic interface and functionality.

Figure 9.1 The standard vBulletin interface

vBulletin also has a number of SEO plug-ins available to better optimize your forum. Google in particular is good about recognizing the vBulletin forum structure and will index most active communities for the Google Discussion vertical in fairly short order.

PHPBB

PHPBB (www.phpbb.com/community/) is the most popular open-source forum and is free to download and use. There is also a robust community that is built around PHPBB, and it is frequently updated to include new features. It is fundamentally search engine–friendly out of the box, and there also many different methods to customize it. Like other popular forum software, PHPBB is the target of malicious scripts that will try to autoregister accounts and post illicit content and links. It is imperative that a good web-host is utilized and that the software is always upgraded to the most current versions. Figure 9.2 shows the PHPBB forum for G&L Guitars' GuitarsbyLeo.com site, with a customized theme.

Figure 9.2 A customized PHPBB forum, by G&L Guitars

SEO Elements of Setting Up a Forum

There are many aspects of optimizing your forum, but some of the key opportunities involve category and site naming, and managing duplicate content. Both PHPBB and vBulletin are fundamentally crawlable and indexable and have taken care of many of the optimization aspects of page layout, internal linking, and threading of keyword consistency at the page level.

The other great thing about forum content is that it is created by the community, so you don't always know what you are going to get from a keyword standpoint, but it reflects the unpredictable natural language of your audience and will often attract a ton of new traffic, depending on the search popularity of the topics.

Category naming offers one key opportunity for setting the tone of your forum both for people and for search engines. After you have determined the theme of your forum, perform keyword research to determine the popularity of terms related to the theme. Also, perform an audit for similar forums, and look for their strengths and weaknesses. Are these forums dominant in one keyword area? Are they deficient in another area, and can you capitalize on this in the keyword sense? Categories are important because they also provide literal keyword theme influence on the higher-level pages and help direct the tone of the sublevel content. Overall, think carefully about your keywords when setting up the forum, and provide keywords and detail in the descriptions of the forum categories, for both search engines and your audience.

Duplicate content is sometimes an issue with forums. Printer-friendly pages in vBulletin can create multiple versions of the same unique content, as can the posting of duplicate content or snippets of content by your community. Manage this carefully, and use the SEO plug-ins offered by each forum to block out printer-friendly duplicate content. Setting content to "archive" can also create duplicate issues for search-engine optimization, so strongly consider blocking search crawlers from this content.

Managing Forum Spam

Like managing a blog, spam is one annoying aspect of running a forum that you will have to get used to and manage very carefully. Your key areas of observation involve the monitoring of automated spam targeted at your forum and the monitoring of your human users to make sure they are not using more-subtle forms of spam. Managing spam carefully helps ensure a better social experience for your audience and more trust from search engines so that your content can appear in real-time search functions.

One of the downsides of using popular forum software is that there are many scripts and bots trained to seek out your forum in order to autoregister and post malicious or deceptive content. Much if this spam can be remedied by requiring a registration to post or comment and also having a moderator or admin approve all new accounts to look for signals of spammers. Typical signals of autoregistered accounts include gibberish in the username, nonsensical usernames in the registering email address, unusual patterns in email addresses from different country-code top-level domains where you lack any in-language content for that country's official language, mass email-provider addresses as opposed to verifiable domains or ISPs, and IP addresses. If you are running a larger forum and decide to preapprove registrations, make it as quick as possible so you don't have to keep your real users waiting.

The other type of spam is more human-based and sometimes harder to detect. It may be in the form of someone shilling for their own product, an overly salesy tone while trying to sound objective, dropping links in every post, or posting irrelevant content that is designed only to promote themselves and their business. Be considerate when first approaching these users, because they may be unaware of the rules. Once they learn the rules, they can become some of your best forum members. The way you publicly deal with user spam will directly set and reflect the tone of your audience over time.

The bottom line is that spam is an ongoing fight, and you should utilize all the tools offered to you by the forum software, including plug-ins, CAPTCHAs, and moderation, to get the job done. Managing spam is not an option—it is a necessary requirement of keeping the place safe for search engines so they can trust your content at the finer windows of recency, and for your regular users so they know that spam will not be tolerated.

Engaging on Other Forums

You don't have to set up and administrate your own forum to use a forum. Becoming a member and participant of a popular forum community is a great way to become better informed, to learn, to share, and to spread goodwill through content and contribution. Here are a few tips for getting started with forum participation:

Observe and Obey the *Written* Rules Long before you place your first post or reply, it is important that you read the expressed rules of the forum. These are often posted on sign-up and are often specifically written by the site owner or admin. Also, read the "pinned" or "sticky note" topics at the top of each individual forum category before engaging. In some ways, the written rules become *de facto* law of the forum, so abide carefully to be a good member, and avoid ruffling up any of the regular members. Most forums have an expressed policy against self-promotion, sales, and advertising.

Observe and Obey the *Unwritten* Rules Study first before posting. Read and observe who the top posters are, see how they converse, and interpret the general tone of the forum. Is it nice, helpful, rude, or very sensitive to salesy-ness? If so, these are the things that may not be in the rule book but can still determine your success or failure in engaging in a particular forum.

Be Helpful Stick to what you know when helping out others, but continue to learn and grow. Be helpful by answering questions for other forum members or pointing them to previous threads or FAQs that might answer the question. You may even provide original articles, research, or anecdotes to start a conversation and demonstrate expertise.

Avoid Trolls and Flame Baiters There is always someone trying to either overtly or subtly pick a fight on popular forums, so the best advice is to avoid this type of conflict. Nothing good ever really comes from responding to a troll, so it is best to leave it alone and let a moderator deal with it, or ignore trolling altogether.

Do Not Spam If you want to produce a sustainable marketing strategy, this should go without saying, but it is always worth repeating. Robust content communities and forums hate spammers, and you do not want to be the object of a community tar-and-feathering. This is common sense for most people, but it is worth restating, or else your fellow forum members will have the tar barrel all nice and warmed up for you.

Contribute Remember the "give and get" principle. The more you give to the community, the more you will get back. Contribute articles, expert advice, commentary, and whatever else your community allows to show you are active and participatory. As Copyblogger's Brian Clark stated at a DFWSEM/Social Media Club of Dallas speaking engagement in April 2012, "If you feel like you are giving too much, then you are on the right track."

Speak in the Language of the Community Jumping into a forum and spouting off prefabbed snippets of legalese is not going to cut it in forum communities. You have to speak to your audience in their own language, and you have to be fluid enough to do so in real-time. This means being authentic, being honest with the community, and even being ready to address and concede some of the faults of your business at times. Remember that your business is both a combination of what you say it is and what other people say it is. When engaging in other communities, you are fully engaging in a conversation about what other people say your business is.

Many businesses use forums for customer-relationship management (CRM). These companies monitor keywords and conversations across one or more discussion sites and respond directly to forum users in a thread or by private message (PM). In earlier chapters, I discussed how to take the experience to the user in real-time, and the businesses that engage in forums are walking that walk and talking that talk. It is not always easy, and sometimes these individuals take some flack. What is important is that in many cases they are sincerely and authentically engaging in the conversations that are happening—good or bad—and they are not letting all of the conversations control them.

These are some examples of large companies engaging in online forums for CRM:

- Hilton
- Bank of America
- Google
- American Airlines

Thousands of others use forum engagement as a way to generate business or just help out the community. These include many medium to small businesses, real-estate agents, home service providers, product manufacturers, and more. Figure 9.3 shows a post from "GoogleGuy" on the WebmasterWorld forum, which just so happens to be Matt Cutts from Google. Cutts began using WebmasterWorld as a channel for outreach in 2001.

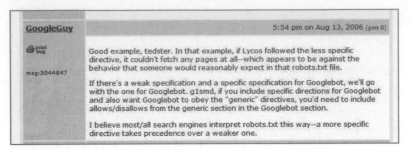

GoogleGuy   5:54 pm on Aug 13, 2006 (gmt 0)

print
img

msg:3044847

Good example, tedster. In that example, if Lycos followed the less specific
directive, it couldn't fetch any pages at all--which appears to be against the
behavior that someone would reasonably expect in that robots.txt file.

If there's a weak specification and a specific specification for Googlebot, we'll go
with the one for Googlebot. g1smd, if you include specific directions for Googlebot
and also want Googlebot to obey the "generic" directives, you'd need to include
allows/disallows from the generic section in the Googlebot section.

I believe most/all search engines interpret robots.txt this way--a more specific
directive takes precedence over a weaker one.

Figure 9.3 A WebmasterWorld forum post by Google engineer Matt Cutts, also known as GoogleGuy

Interview with Brett Tabke

When I stop to think about the Internet marketers who should truly be considered pioneers in the field, one name that always comes to my mind is Brett Tabke, developer of the WebmasterWorld forum and Pubcon conferences. When I moved from independent consulting to work on the client side for a medium-sized business in the early aughts, I spent quite a bit of time on WebmasterWorld, trading out findings with other online marketers and soaking up thousands of pages of threads. Tabke has been coding and working online since 1983 and essentially helped take the common bulletin board service (BBS) to a new level, more in the form of a content-management system rather than a simple threaded list of messages. Common forum features such as the private message (PM) system were first developed by Tabke, and his articles on WebmasterWorld helped many marketers and developers reach their business goals. In this sidebar, Brett discusses some of the key considerations of forum engagement and management.

What reciprocating effects do you see occurring between search and social content?

I see search as a branding effort. As we all know, branding is difficult to measure (for example, what is the value of *Coke*?). However, when you combine branding and social, I think they form a special mix. We use search as a branding effort purely. That exposure is invaluable. I think if search has done anything for us, it has been exposure and branding. That branding later has turned into influence, which ultimately fuels the bottom line.

What are some of the challenges of managing a community forum in real-time?

It is easier today than it ever has been in the past. For the first 10 years, we had trouble with expectations. People just felt they should be able to post anything at any time. If you dared edit them for cause, they came unglued. Then came the Facebook and Twitter "real name" revolution that gave the web user "identity." That left the rabble-rousers and problem children out in the cold. The marginal troublemaker just evaporated as everyone realized they were responsible online for their words.

The other major change has been the growth of the Internet around the world. No longer do those people need to look at dot-coms for their information or support. They can get the necessary support on a local TLD [top level domain]-level site. That means that on forums and community sites, there are not the wild expectations and actions that go with cross-border citizen interaction.

Interview with Brett Tabke *(Continued)*

Those two major changes over the last 10 years have meant that the users have all sorta "fallen in line." Everyone knows what to expect and how to behave in public. The number of problem messages we have in a day has fallen steadily over the last 10 years. It is down to less than .001 percent of all messages posted now.

How do you think community members have benefited from participating at WebmasterWorld, and how can readers of this book apply this advice across a wide variety of different forum types?

Getting quality answers to common questions is not always easy. There is huge value in trusted Q&A. Facebook isn't set up to do quality Q&A, Twitter is unintelligible in 140 characters, and LinkedIn groups are a wasteland of promotional SPAM. WebmasterWorld provides spirited discussions in the general SE [search engine] forums. Here, you will see a slow consensus build. Panda [Google algorithm update] absolutely baffled a lot of SEO writers around the Web. Many of them ended up in the huge update threads discussing what was going on. After a couple of weeks, it became clear that WebmasterWorld members had figured out what was going on with links and that it marginally had anything to do with content.

Then over in the code forums, I can't count the number of times I have had a technical question that no one else could answer. There have been many times I have put a query into Google and ended up right back at WebmasterWorld for the answer. The classic example is one where I have ended up back at WebmasterWorld for the answer in a thread that I started a dozen years ago on a similar question.

What search and social advice would you give to marketers and business owners who are considering starting their own discussion forum?

Make sure you have good goals before you start. If any of your goals include the word *content* or *SEO* in them, then I'd reconsider. Good forums are not going to produce either—good forums are about learning, education, and support.

What advice would you give to marketers who just want to participate in discussion forums?

Be non-promotional and jump in. There are tidbits of high-quality info buried in so many threads around the Web. Once you dive in, you can start to uncover many of them.

You coded your own forum, but which forum software would you use if you were starting a new forum today—vBulletin or PHPBB?

vBulletin for sure. The number of features in the latest versions is outstanding. I have a few sites now that we replaced WordPress with the VB "article" setup on the front page—and they are running better than ever.

Answer Marketing

Answer sites are like human-driven search engines and fill a basic content and social need. Instead of entering a query or question in a search box and waiting for search results, a person writes a question and creates a new web page and then solicits answers from the community. The people who answer the questions are the collective engine that provides the results, and the relevancy is often scored by the community reading and soliciting the answers. In addition to the human search elements, answer sites also do double-duty and provide second-tier search-results visibility.

Answer sites offer a great opportunity for businesses to share their expertise with a ready-made audience. As described in previous chapters, businesses can "take the experience to the user" by finding and answering questions and helping them solve problems. When people post a question, they are often anxiously waiting for an answer, so timeliness and fluidity are imperative to success in this channel. To accomplish this, real-time monitoring and good keyword research are critical.

"Answer marketing" is not about spamming; it is about being useful to a community, in a way that fits within that community. As you will see in the later interview with Gil Reich, answer sites even encourage business and product experts of all types to participate by answering questions about their area of expertise.

The Real-Time Elements of Answer Marketing

From a distance, it may seem that answer sites are passive libraries of knowledge and information. The reality is that popular answer sites are more like beehives of real-time activity. With this in mind, here are some of the key real-time aspects of answer marketing:

- Answer-site content goes live in minutes or seconds and is prominently displayed to large answer communities.

- New open questions appear every few seconds, minutes, or hours.

- Answer sites are based on software that acts as a real-time content-management system for questions and answers.

- Well-indexed answer sites can go live to search results in minutes.

- When search engines do not have the right results, answer sites are often the first place many Internet users go to when they have a question about a real-time topic of interest.

Also be aware that people who post questions often have a real-time need and want the question answered as quickly as possible, without having to wait hours or days. Sharpen your real-time marketing strategy by monitoring questions in real-time and responding as quickly as possible.

The Interdependent Search and Social Elements of Answer Marketing

Like forums, answer sites are great examples of search and social synergy in action. Here are some of the common search and social crossover points:

- Answer sites consist of user-generated content that increases with search and social reciprocation.

- Answer content utilizes the living language of the user, and answer sites provide optimized content for keywords and phrases that marketers could not reasonably predict.

- Answer sites are an excellent venue for marketers to provide nonsales content to achieve second-tier SERP visibility.

- Good keyword research is required for audience managers to find and seek out new and relevant questions.

- A question asked on an answer site is similar to a query entered in a search engine—except on an answer site, a human answers the query.

- If someone has a question on an answer site, then it is likely that people are asking the same query in search engines.

- Established answer sites can index in Google in less than five minutes from the time they are published, and little bit longer for Bing.

- Good answers may get liked, retweeted, and shared, which in turn feeds social signals to search engines.

- Answer sites are excellent sources for keyword research, particularly for studying the natural language of their audience.

Answer sites also offer an easy-to-use content-management system, which enables less-technical users to create search engine–friendly pages and links on third-party sites that rank well in search.

Be an Expert, or Just Be a Good Researcher

If you are going to start an answer-marketing campaign, then it is important to be an expert and focus on what you know. Answer questions authoritatively, and focus on helping solve an issue for people. You can also enlist other experts in your company as the social authority. Researching answers for people is also helpful, so a simple Google or Bing search can help people find what they are looking for.

You may be an expert on a product or service, on your area or region, or on a particular technical topic. You may even be a researcher or content steward and direct people to the answer they are looking for, like a librarian. The bottom line is that when people have a question, there is usually a more complex problem they are trying to resolve, and there are multiple ways to help them out.

Overview of Selected Answer Sites

There are many excellent answer sites on the Internet, but I have chosen some of the top sites for this overview. When starting an answer-marketing engagement strategy, make sure that these sites are on the top of your list for consideration of your answer-marketing platform:

Yahoo! Answers One of the top answer sites, Yahoo! Answers (http://answers.yahoo.com/) has a robust community, with questions ranging over a wide variety of topics and categories. Yahoo! Answers offers RSS feeds at the keyword level, making it easy for you to set up a monitoring platform in your favorite feed reader (see Figure 9.4 later in this chapter for an example of feed monitoring in Netvibes). Yahoo! Answers indexes quickly in the major search engines and can have a long life in the search results depending on how many answers are received and rated. Overall, this is a top-tier answer site that should be a primary consideration in almost every answer-marketing outreach strategy.

LinkedIn Answers LinkedIn Answers (www.linkedin.com/answers/) is a top Q&A site for businesses and features a wide range of topics. This site is also well indexed in Google and Bing, and most questions generally get crawled and indexed in a day or less. LinkedIn Answers also offers RSS feeds at the category level sorted by recency, or newest question first, making it easy to monitor a multiple-question stream in a feed reader. You can also achieve additional visibility as in expert when your answer is cited as "best" by the person who asks the question, and your profile gets extended visibility for both your own network and all of LinkedIn Answers, depending on the number of expert answers provided.

Answers Answers (www.answers.com) is one of the mainstay answer sites, having been originally founded in 1999 as GuruNet. Answers is well indexed, optimized for search engine-visibility, and provides RSS feeds for monitoring new questions at the keyword, category, and user levels. Answers are edited in a wiki-style format. Users are offered a profile page, with attribution given to the last user to edit the page.

Quora Quora (www.quora.com) is one of the newest social answer sites on the block and integrates your Facebook network for increased participation. Quora is also optimized for search engines, and questions get picked up and retrieved with relative speed in the major search engines. Quora shows lists of unanswered questions, as well as topic experts at the keyword level.

Ask Ask (www.ask.com) started as a question-based search engine and is now a hybrid search engine and expert answer site.

These are among the top answer sites on the Internet; there are many other great answer sites to discover beyond this list. Check out this full list of answer sites at Wikipedia for more information: http://en.wikipedia.org/wiki/List_of_question-and-answer_websites.

Use Answer Sites for Content Ideas and Keyword Research

Answer sites are also like a focus group, in the sense that you get to see what is on the mind of the community in real-time. Answer sites can be helpful in finding new ideas for your own blog content or an extended article addressing the problem in a way that the answer site will not allow. Identify the problem, and determine how to use the idea to develop images, videos, text articles, and infographics, among many of the other types of content listed in Chapter 4 and in Chapter 5, "Content Strategy: Auditing, Assessment, and Planning."

Answer sites are also a great source for keyword and linguistic research. By studying questions and answers carefully, you may stumble upon one or more words that will have an impact on your approach to content. Test these new words and phrases in one of the keyword tools from Chapter 4, and try to find new stemmed keyword lists. You may be very surprised at what you find, and it can shape how you speak to your audience and how you approach your overall content strategy.

General Tips for Answer-Marketing Management

In addition to choosing the right answer sites as the basis for engagement and outreach strategy, there are many considerations for getting started with an answer-marketing strategy. Here are some of the top tips to help get you started:

Choose the Right Networks You may find that some answer sites may skew more toward your target keyword set than others. Other sites may be more business- or entertainment-focused. Research the networks that have the most relevant questions and audience, and use these networks as your main focus.

Choose Your Topical Areas of Engagement The previous answer sites cover a wide range of themes and topics, so you will have to create a keyword and category focus for your efforts. You may be well versed on a wide variety of topics, but it is still a good practice to have a thematic foundation for how you are going to approach your keyword research, monitoring, and answer strategy.

Register Consistent Login and Account Names When Answering Questions Across Multiple Sites When answering questions across a variety of sites, maintain a consistent identity by registering similar or exact account names if available. This will help reinforce your company or personal identity across multiple channels.

Use RSS Feeds for Monitoring in a Feed Reader Some answer sites offer RSS feeds for monitoring questions. Sort your feeds by recency for latest open questions (newest question first), and pull in multiple feeds into a single feed reader like Netvibes. Yahoo! Answers offers RSS feeds at the keyword level, and LinkedIn offers them at the category level. Figure 9.4 shows my LinkedIn RSS feed set up on Netvibes, showing open questions sorted by recency.

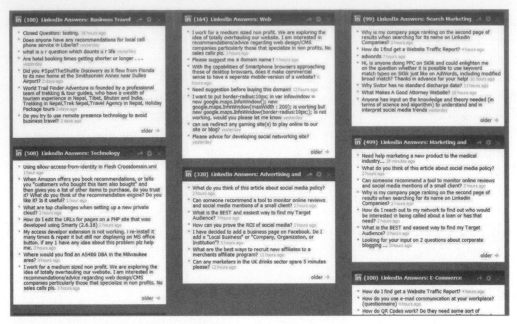

Figure 9.4 Monitor answer-site RSS feeds with Netvibes.

Read the Entire Question Before Answering Some people elaborate on their questions a bit deeper beyond the main title, and it is here that the real question is asked. Don't just read the title and bolded part of the question—read the whole question and provide a thoughtful answer.

Fill Out Your Profile Pages The amount of profile detail varies from site to site, so take advantage of all the real information given to you in the area. Profile pages may rank well in search engines and be used by people in the answer network to learn more about you or your company. Remember to use your targeted keywords for your profile pages as well.

Use Links When They Can Help Your Answers, But Remember That They Are Nofollowed Provide the answer to the user's question first, and provide a link if it helps with additional infor-mation. Links in answer sites won't provide any link juice from search engines because they are nofollowed. But they can provide traffic back to your site. In other cases, someone researching for other content may see your link and give attribution in a "dofollow" link on their own content. Remember—answer the user's question directly first, and only provide a link if it directly applies to the question. Do not gratuitously link in every answer. Also remember that some answer sites frown upon adding links in the answers, so respect each set of rules accordingly.

Use a Robust Keyword List to Find Questions Interacting on social sites is not just about pulling in visitors; it's also about using search techniques to find your audience. Use a well-researched keyword list to expand the reach of your relevant audience.

Use the Right Keywords When Answering Questions and Only When It Is Relevant to the Answer Don't stuff your answers with keywords. Use natural language and voice, and use keywords only when it is appropriate for the question.

Always Be on the Lookout for New Terms Remember that search and social language is constantly evolving, and answer sites are a great place to find out what is on people's minds at any given time. Look for new queues that may lead to new topics and new content or keyword opportunities. Leverage this research in your paid, natural, content, and social initiatives.

Monitor Your Brand and Company Keywords In addition to generic keywords, monitor your keywords for brand or company-related terms and phrases. These types of conversations are usually a high priority for monitoring and engagement.

Don't Spam It should go without saying, but if you are thinking about doing it, don't. It can get you banned from a site, and spamming just isn't a sustainable strategy if you plan to be around a social space for any length of time.

Create Your Own FAQ for Commonly Asked Questions Many questions on answer sites are asked repeatedly, and as a parallel, many other people are searching for the same answer in search engines. Create your own FAQ, but use these links only to provide supplemental information after you have directly answered the person's question first.

Use Google Discussion Search to Monitor "Transient" Questions Across a Wide Variety of Internet Sites In addition to monitoring primary answer sites, use feeds and discussion search to monitor questions that occur on other sites. "Transient" questions exist sporadically in fragmented areas of the Web, rather than being concentrated on a small group of large answer sites or social networks. These questions might occur as a "one-off" in Craigslist forums, on an obscure but relevant blog, or in a forum. You may answer on these sites just one time, but remember that you are trying to help people address a particular problem as it relates to your area of business or directly concerning you company. By doing so, you are taking the experience to your audience.

Interview with Gil Reich

I first co-presented on a real-time search panel with Gil Reich at the SMX Toronto conference in March 2010. Gil served as a longtime executive at Answers and currently publishes the Managing Greatness blog at http://managinggreatness.com. In this interview he talks about some of the nuances of answer marketing in a world of search and social media.

What search and social benefits does the marketer receive from an answer-marketing initiative?

The most direct benefit is that you're connecting with potential customers who are looking for the service you provide. I actually benefitted from this a few weeks ago when a friend of mine was on Quora, noticed somebody asking for a service that I provide, and she recommended me. I didn't even realize she had done this until I was doing keyword research for this client and one of the top results for a phrase I was investigating was this Quora conversation that apparently led to the engagement.

(Continues)

So, connecting with the individual who actually submitted the question is the most direct benefit, but the bigger benefits usually come from the voyeurs, subsequent visitors to the page where you left your answer. Some of that is people navigating that Q&A site, and most of it is Googlers who see your answer in the Google SERPs.

If your business is ad revenue on your website, then you need to get people to your website. But if your business is selling some product or service and your website is just a channel to get your message across, then Q&A sites may be a great additional channel for spreading your message. Many of these Q&A sites rank very well in Google, and you may have a better chance getting Googlers to see your message by putting it on a Q&A site's page than by just focusing on your own site's pages.

Additionally, you're improving your site's rankings and relevance by having pages on Q&A sites that discuss your brand and link to your site, assuming you're doing it in a way that the community appreciates.

The Q&A sites are social networks themselves, and they can help you with the other social networks. They're great places to build relationships with people who are probably also active on other social networks. So, a relationship that starts on Quora can quickly travel to Twitter, Facebook, Google+, and LinkedIn.

How active and "real-time" does a marketer have to be to successfully participate in answer marketing?

Depends on the site. Answers, for example, is mostly geared toward permanence; that is, they're trying to build the world's greatest question-and-answer database. Most pages are always open for editing, and most of their traffic comes from search engines long after the original discussion is over. So, you can head to a site like that and interact with all of their old questions for which you have good information to contribute and get a lot of the benefits of answer marketing.

Most of the other sites are more real-time-oriented, and you want to be in the conversation as it's happening. Yahoo! Answers even closes most of its questions after a few days, so if you're too late on a question, you're too late.

How can a marketer establish himself or herself as an expert?

Most sites have a profile page you can fill in. That's where you should establish your expertise. Also, where you can, link to the other pages (LinkedIn, etc.) where you're already showing your expertise.

Quora does a good job giving you a field to establish what bio snippet should be displayed above your answer, so definitely take advantage of that.

On other sites, if you can establish your expertise without sounding like an arrogant jerk, do that. If you're getting your message out, you need to identify yourself for reasonable disclosure, and that may cover the expertise issue as well. For example, "I'm the marketing director at Company X" may be an appropriate intro that establishes expertise, provides context and disclosure, and pushes your brand.

Interview with Gil Reich *(Continued)*

How many answers does it take to establish oneself as an expert in a social-answer community?

You can do it in one answer. It's not really about quantity. Give good answers to the right questions.

Is it OK to post links in answer sites?

Depends on the site. Answers provides a separate "Add a related link" feature for this. Most of the other sites let you put a link inside the content. But do so only if the link is a legitimate part of the answer. For example, if somebody asks "What product do you recommend...," you can mention and link to your own product, with full disclosure, with extra credit if you also mention and link to your competitors' products. Rand Fishkin of SEOmoz does a great job with this. He'll find people asking for SEO tools and say, "We have great tools for this, and here are some other interesting tools." This is a great way to establish credibility and expertise, and I bet he gets more clicks on his own tools because he's forthcoming about the competition.

Another way your link could legitimately be part of an answer is when you give at least a few sentences with a brief answer and then a link to a content page with a more complete answer.

It's generally bad form to just put a link to your site if that link isn't integral to your answer. That said, each answer site has its own norms, so look to see what everybody else is doing on the site and how the community is responding to it.

Wikis

In this section, you will learn about the steps for starting your own wiki. A wiki is a content-management platform that allows for communities of editors and writers to create and edit content in real-time. They are fundamentally "search and social" in the sense that common platforms are search engine–friendly and are created socially by communities. If you identify a unique opportunity or gap in your content space or theme, a wiki may be a good way to leverage an audience to help build content for the benefit of your customers, business targets, or people who are interested in learning about a particular topic. This chapter covers the following elements of starting a wiki community:

- Determining whether a wiki is the right platform for your business
- Key considerations for running a wiki
- Dos and don'ts of running a wiki and engaging in wikis

The benefits you receive from producing a useful wiki are generally in the form of goodwill and appreciation from content editors and consumers of that content. It is acceptable for some business-owned wikis to mention their name, though many choose to keep a low profile and keep the focus on the content. Other benefits include helping to establish yourself as an authority on a topic by contributing and editing articles and providing the wiki platform.

You can use a wiki in many ways. Many companies that offer a technical product or service use wikis to allow their customers to collaborate and share findings and knowledge. Others use wikis as an intranet for internal use only. Starting a wiki is not for every business, but if you determined a particular knowledge gap online that could be addressed by a community wiki, then you may have found your opportunity.

The Real-Time Elements of Wikis

If you have ever read a Wikipedia story on a breaking-news topic, then you already know that these articles are almost living records of events unfolding in real-time. Wikis are always-on and can be edited at any given moment. Here are some of the key real-time elements of wikis:

- With popular wikis like Wikipedia, topics and content are created in real-time, often as a topic is occurring.
- When trusted by search crawlers, wiki content can be indexed in search engines in minutes or seconds after it is published.
- With many wikis, changes and edits to content go live to public view as they are created.

The Interdependent Search and Social Elements of Wikis

Wikis also share many characteristics of search and social reciprocation. Here are some of the main crossover points:

- Standard MediaWiki software, as well as many other wiki software suites, are generally search engine–friendly (but verify before using any wiki software).
- All content is user-generated, created socially by communities, and picked up and disseminated in search engines.
- A good wiki can become trusted as an information source by both people and search engines, and in time much of the content may become highly visible in search results.
- Though links in wikis are most often set to nofollow, many content creators use wikis to research new website links and create "dofollow" links to these sites in their own content.
- If there are enough people interested in a topic to create a wiki, then there is most often a mirrored and parallel keyword interest in search engines.

Establishing a Theme and Community

If you have performed an audit for either a blog or a forum, then you should have a good idea about which themes and topics your business will typically play in. Just as with those other content platforms, be sure that there is a gap and need for the type of wiki community you want to create. Wikipedia has a wide range of topics, but it doesn't cover every topic in the universe. Consider the technical aspects of your business, profiles on people or businesses in a particular vertical, or other types of information where a knowledge base is helpful or required.

When starting a wiki community, it can be very helpful to leverage an existing network or community to pitch in and create or edit content. Your network might consist of people in your company, people you are connected with in social networks, email lists, or other business organizations or affiliations. You might even want to test the waters first by polling your network to see whether you have any volunteers to step forward and help with your idea or whether they think the wiki you are proposing is filling a particular need. Starting off with a base of users will be very helpful in getting your wiki off to the right start.

MediaWiki Software

MediaWiki is free open-source software developed by the Wikimedia Foundation, and it is the wiki muscle behind major sites like Wikipedia and Wiktionary, among many others. While there are many different wiki content-management systems available for free or fee, MediaWiki is one of the most robust and well-maintained systems available to wiki publishers. The software offers more than 700 different settings and 1,800 plug-ins developed by the wiki community. Read more about installation and other features at `http://en.wikipedia.org/wiki/MediaWiki`.

Managing Spam

Wikis that are instantly open for edits and changes are also highly susceptible to spam. Wikipedia runs in real-time but is generally able to manage spam because of the high volume of human editors. Though wikis have real-time capabilities, you should consider having a trusted editor approve any changes before posting to prevent spam. Also, use spam-protection plug-ins recommended by your wiki-software provider, and use a reliable web host.

Examples of Business-Themed Wikis

There are many different examples of business and community wikis around the Web. Some businesses use wikis to create user-based documentation for their products or service, while others provide knowledge bases for their audience to edit. Here are some examples of various companies and publishing entities using wikis to crowd-source information in real-time, while simultaneously soaking up the benefits of search and social:

- `www.dealipedia.com`
- `www.flyerguide.com`
- `http://wiki.fool.com`

A full list of sites using MediaWiki is available at www.mediawiki.org/wiki/Sites_using_MediaWiki/en. Figure 9.5 shows the wiki page for the term *compound interest* on Foolsaurus, the wiki thesaurus provided by the Motley Fool.

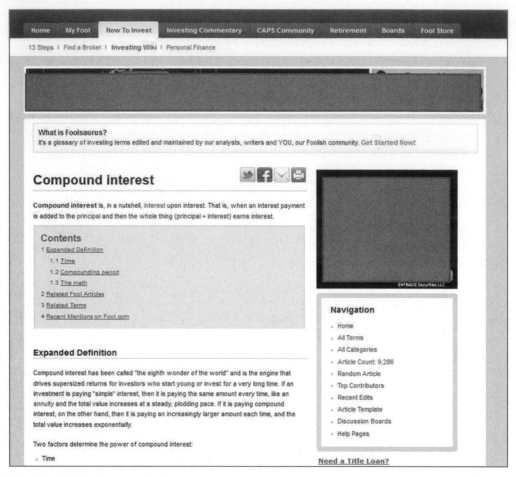

Figure 9.5 Motley Fool's Foolsaurus wiki

A Few Other Considerations for Wikis

You will need to be aware of a few basic considerations when operating or editing wikis. There is a general spirit of wiki communities that focuses on the group, rather than self-promotion. Do not use wikis to promote your own business (by adding links to articles, creating articles about yourself or company, and so forth). It goes against the community and spirit of content creation in wiki spaces, violates most wiki terms of service and agreements, and will likely get you banned from a site or deter others from contributing if you are the owner. Use wiki sites to help develop objective content and to help build the content for the community that uses it. Do create new articles relevant to your theme. Do create a style guide and set of community rules. Do encourage others to edit and create content.

I hope that you have gained a new sense for forums, answer sites, and wikis as real-time content platforms and as excellent hubs for search and social reciprocation. While other popularly hyped social networks like Twitter and Facebook are basic parts of any social strategy, many marketers have overlooked the search and social benefits of the platforms outlined in this chapter. You may find that while everyone else is focused on the big networks, there may be an even bigger opportunity for you to start one of these communities while no one else is looking.

Technical Considerations and Implementation

10

In this chapter, you will learn about some of the technical aspects of managing a search and social presence in real-time. These elements represent how your content will show up in search, how your content will travel in networks, how to keep your sites clean for search engines, and how to increase the distribution of your content through social channels. In addition, you will learn why these elements are important for your search and social presence and how they help your real-time presence online.

Chapter Contents

Setting Up a Short-URL Service

Shortened-URL redirects have become a basic utility in social-networking channels and Internet marketing as a whole. A short-URL service is used to share links in status networks such as Twitter, Google+, LinkedIn, and Facebook. Short URLs are succinct and cleaner and allow for more commenting space, particularly in Twitter, which allows only 140 characters. Longer URLs can take up significant sharing space, so short URLs have been widely accepted by users and publishers as a method of making it easier for people to share and comment on content in real-time spaces.

When choosing a short-URL service based on a third-party domain, there are many features to consider in order to maintain the search equity, user trust, and measurability of your efforts. Here are some key issues you should be aware of when choosing and utilizing a short-URL service on a third-party domain:

Be Ready to Relinquish Control of at Least Some of Your Traffic via Third-Party URL Services Third-party services like Bitly effectively control all social traffic and search links to your site. If the service goes down permanently, then this could have a bearing on your future traffic referrals and link equity and would be beyond your control.

Use a Shortener That Utilizes 301 Redirects For the purpose of attributing and passing through backlinks to your final landing page, a 301 redirect should be in place. This tells the search engines about the final destination URL and where search credit should be applied. In many cases where 301s are absent, the short URL gets the backlink credit, because the accrued links have been applied to that domain, not yours. Both Bitly and the Google URL shortener use 301 redirects and are search-friendly in this sense. Test your URL shortener using a proxy reader that shows HTML headers.

Remember That Services Utilizing a CCTLD Put Full Faith in the Stability of That Country Code Many services are based on somewhat obscure country-code top-level domains (CCTLDs) because of their catchiness, but their political stability and web policies might be worth checking into if you plan on utilizing or setting up a service on this TLD. At least one CCTLD has been retired (.um), though reportedly it was for lack of use. Here are a few sample common CCTLDs used for short-URL services, and the countries they represent: .ly, Libya; .im, Isle of Man; .am, Armenia; .gd, Grenada; and .ma, Morocco. Bitly managed to maintain service in Libya (.ly) during the period of uprising and political instability in 2011.

Choose a Short URL That People in Your Network Can Trust to Click When I click a shortened-URL service, I don't click it because I trust the URL itself; I click it because I trust the user who posted it. There is a growing number of people who are hesitant to click a URL from a source that is not well-known or trusted by them. However, a short URL on a trusted domain, say apple.com or goo.gl, would be less of an issue with regular users of those sites. Trust can be built with an existing domain, on a new domain, or even with a service that crawls URLs and roots out spam and malicious applications.

Remember That the Shortening Service Used Gets the Domain Branding Impression Traffic is one thing, but impressions throughout social sharing networks are also worth mentioning here. Even if a user doesn't click, they still view the domain. That's part of the reason why bitly.com is one of the most recognized domains in the world. You can get in on this action by creating your own short URL on your own domain, which I will demonstrate later in this section.

Determine Whether Your Short-URL Service Has an Expiration Date Before going with a particular service, ensure that your URLs do not expire, especially if you have a relatively long shelf life for your content. This will help search engines apply the proper link citation and will help users who may be clicking an old link.

Some services have ceased operation altogether, without notice, leaving all social traffic and link benefits hanging for the site owner. Potential reasons why services may shut down range from not being able to support the cost of running a service to just not wanting to maintain it any longer. In the end, these services are free, and users should have no expectation that they will be run indefinitely or that uptime is guaranteed.

If any one of these snags applies to a URL service that you are using, here is how it can impact your search program and social-traffic flow:

- Links are not properly applied in all search engines.
- Backlinks may disappear altogether.
- Long-term social and web traffic will disappear.
- If trust is lost in a service because of spamming, it could diminish the likelihood of some users clicking through or linking to your final destination site.
- Branding impressions are lost.

Third-Party URL-Shortening Services

Many good shortened-URL services observe SEO best practices for redirection. One of the most popular now is Bitly (www.bitly.com), and it also does a good job of weeding out spam, providing metrics, and combining multiple short URLs pointing to a single page.

The Google URL shortener (http://goo.gl) is also a handy short-URL service, and it provides Google with more direct data about URLs shared throughout various status networks. This can enable it to better trust and rank content. If you are going with a third-party service with search and social strategy in mind, then the Google URL shortener is one of the top services to consider.

Short-URL services won't be going away anytime soon for sending links to other sites, and the concept of utilizing a short URL is effective in helping links travel quickly through networks. Give serious consideration to your URL strategy if you are thinking long-term for both search and social.

How to Set Up a Vanity URL Shortener on Your Own Domain

One way to avoid the hassle of the previously mentioned SEO and traffic issues of third-party services is to set up a URL service on your own registered domain. Retaining control of some search benefits and social traffic is as easy as controlling your own domain name, though obviously not all traffic can be controlled, because a person sharing a link in a network can go with the short-URL service of their choice. But the benefit of passing the first link on your domain to your followers and friends can do a lot toward pulling traffic and link credit to your proprietary site, especially as your network reach grows larger and larger. Marketers who plan on engaging heavily in social media and networks for disseminating information should seriously consider this option.

Solutions for setting up a service on your own domain vary. You can use your existing domain name if it is short enough (generally seven characters or less), or you can register an entirely new name specifically for a shortener. One alternative is to go with a short naming convention off the root domain for redirection. If you use WordPress, you can use are plug-ins that allow for manual creation of shortened URLs, or you could use the default numbering convention based on the domain root. To set your URL length in WordPress, go to Settings and then Permalinks to see your different options. Remember that changing your URL setting will change every URL for your existing content and could impact your search rankings in the short or long term. If so, make sure you have a redirection plan in place before changing. If you have a new blog, then you can adjust your URL length accordingly, but keep in mind that this short convention can come at the cost of not having keywords in the URL, and such keywords have been long touted by SEOs to help improve search rankings and visibility. WordPress is now offering a new option that allows you to use the shortened-URL convention as a shorty service, while maintaining your original, longer, descriptive link convention in place.

There are also different services available to create your own custom URL shortener on your own domain. Bitly's custom URL solution, called Bitly Enterprise (http://bitlyenterprise.com). While the cost of entry for a Bitly Enterprise is considered steep by many small and medium-sized businesses, it is a one-stop shop for larger businesses.

A second option for creating a custom URL is called YOURLS (www.yourls.org). This is one of the early URL-shortening services to offer custom short URLs configured on your own domain. It features private or public creation of custom URLs, traffic reports, and an Ajax interface. There is also a WordPress plug-in available for YOURLS at http://yourls.org/#Plugin. YOURLS requires a server with mod_rewrite enabled, a minimum version of PHP 4.3 or later, and MySQL 4.1 or later. YOURLS is free.

Schema.org: Integrating Rich Snippets

Enhanced natural listings in major search engines have been around for many years now with Google's "one box" and the development of universal search. Now the search engines have teamed up to endorse a standard for enhanced search listing and semantic markup called *schemas*, conveniently located at www.schema.org. Schema.org is not a programming language but rather a set of definitions for portable data markup that allow you to apply more context and semantic meaning to your own fragments of data. Overall, Schema.org is a method of semantically parsing specific pieces of data on a web page and making it portable to other applications. Search engines currently use this data for enhanced search listings, called *rich snippets*. Enhanced rich snippets are currently visible for a wide range of data types and will be detailed more in this section.

Schema.org is the latest iteration of what the engines had previously endorsed as *microformats*, another type of listing enhancement for search results. One other type of attribute recognized by search engines is Resource Description Framework in Attributes (RDFa). While all three are recognized by Google and Bing to help enhance your listings in search results, this section will focus mainly on Schema.org but will also include some of the search and social benefits of implementing RDFa. Microformats are still recognized by search engines, but the engines have shifted focus to developing the Schema.org standard moving forward.

Schema.org is in its very early stages, though adoption by web publishers continues to increase. While search engines are not fully implementing every schema directly into some type of modified listing, they say they are still developing uses, and searchers and webmasters should expect to see new applications of Schema.org over time. Search is only one application, and the story around Schema.org may get more interesting as social networks learn how to better leverage this data. As it relates to this book, implementing schemas is another way to help your direct or indirect audience solve issues in search, and also enables some social data directly in the search results. Remember, search is about real people, with real problems they are trying to solve.

In its current form, rich snippets and Schema.org provide additional data to a searcher directly while they are searching, and this data brings out your listing off the search results page in a variety of ways to increase click-through rates and brand impressions. There is certainly a first-mover advantage for those publishers implementing schema vocabulary, but there is also a risk that your website could get drowned out in the visibility race by ignoring it altogether.

Rich Snippet Types and Examples

Let's take a look at some examples of enhanced search listings using rich snippets directly in the search results to illustrate how you can use Schema.org, RDFa, and microformats to enhance your own search visibility.

Recipes Recipe data can be broken down using the recipe schema, and Google offers a variety of methods of searching this data. You can see in Figure 10.1 that this schema allows for a photo, time to prepare, and social reviews on the actual search listing. In the left column, a searcher can sort recipes by ingredient and cook time. If recipes are a big part of your content strategy, then it is worth noting that only the publishers that provide the Schema.org data for ingredients and cooking time will appear on search results using that filter, making Schema.org a very important consideration for organic search visibility.

Figure 10.1 Recipes have a robust, rich snippet display in Google Web Search.

Ratings, Reviews, and Quantifiable Social Data Ratings and review counts were one of the first forms of rich snippet data to appear in the search results. Because ratings are often the result of a community vote toward a particular subject, this is a prime example of social data crossing over to the search experience. While the total number of ratings is not always a factor in search visibility, the top results are often those with a significant number of rayings. The quantity of reviews on a site is also shown on Google results (Figure 10.2) and provides the searcher with an idea of how much social pulse is occurring on a site, before clicking through.

> Riu **Florida Beach** (Miami **Beach, FL**) - **Hotel Reviews** - TripAdvisor
> www.tripadvisor.com/Hotel_Review-g34439-d217386-Reviews-Riu_...
> ★★★★☆ Rating: 3.5 - 718 reviews - Price range: $168 - $392
> Riu **Florida Beach**, Miami **Beach**: See 718 traveler **reviews**, 283 candid photos, and
> great deals for Riu **Florida Beach**, ranked #85 of 203 hotels in Miami **Beach** ...
> + Show map of 3101 Collins Avenue, Miami Beach, FL 33140

Figure 10.2 Rich snippets show the searchers a variety of social data, right on the search results page.

Events Data around events and "things to do" is one of the most popular search categories and one of the most popular social-network subjects. The event schema allows for event specification and applies an element of recency to date listings, optimizing them for query deserves freshness (QDF) in Google, as described in Chapter 2, "Understanding Search and Social." Overall, date-based schemas can make your content much more relevant in real-time and with other time-based search filters (see Figure 10.3).

Price Ranges Price ranges are a common breakout data point on review sites, guides, and directories. In Figure 10.4, you can see how a restaurant price range is shown in Google search results. Figure 10.5 shows a Bing listing for the same Yelp page. Notice how the result display differs using the same data and also how Bing uses additional data in the right flyout display.

Dallas Concerts - Eventful
eventful.com/dallas/events/categories/music
Jul 14 - Gexa Energy Pavilion. Reach 157000 people in **Dallas**-Ft. Worth, TX ...

Fri, Apr 6	Shinedown with Avalanche Tour ... - House of Blues - Dallas
Tue, May 1	Florence and the Machine - The Palladium Ballroom / The Loft
Fri, May 4	Uncle Kracker - Billy Bob's Texas

Figure 10.3 If you publish event data, then you should be using schemas to get expanded visibility in search results.

Wo Hop Restaurant - Chinatown - **New York**, NY
www.yelp.com › Restaurants › Chinese
★★★★★ 367 reviews - Price range: $
367 Reviews of **Wo Hop** Restaurant "Went here on a late night. I don't care what people say but this reminds me to good Americanized Cantonese that I grew up ...

Figure 10.4 Rich snippet display in Google for Wo Hop in Chinatown, New York City

Figure 10.5 Rich snippet display in Bing for Wo Hop in Chinatown, New York City

While the context and applied meaning data on your own website pages may be clear, adding Schema.org or RDFa allows for your data to retain that context and port the data outside of your website into a variety of applications and networks. Some of the schema types and definitions available include the following:

- Articles
- Blogs
- Maps
- Audio
- Images
- Video
- Events

- Recipes
- Job listings
- Geographical features
- Reviews
- Ratings
- Comments
- Organizations
- People
- Places
- Products

There are also schemas for various types of HTML markup, including menus, breadcrumbs, and so on. Many of these attributes break into more detailed descriptions, so for a full list of schema types that apply to your publishing theme, visit `http://schema .org/docs/full.html`. Table 10.1 shows the deep level of sample detail for a local business with multiple schemas, as quoted directly from Schema.org (source: `http://schema.org/ LocalBusiness`).

▶ **Table 10.1** Properties, expected data types, and descriptions for a local business, from `http://schema.org/LocalBusiness`

Property	Expected data type	Description
properties from "Thing"		
description	Text	A short description of the item.
image	URL	URL of an image of the item.
name	Text	The name of the item.
url	URL	URL of the item.
Properties from "Place"		
address	PostalAddress	Physical address of the item.
aggregateRating	AggregateRating	The overall rating, based on a collection of reviews or ratings of the item.
containedIn	Place	The basic containment relation between places.
event	Event	Upcoming or past event associated with this place or organization.
events	Event	Upcoming or past events associated with this place or organization (legacy spelling; see singular form, event).
faxNumber	Text	The fax number.
geo	GeoCoordinates or GeoShape	The geocoordinates of the place.
interactionCount	Text	A count of a specific user interactions with this item— for example, 20 UserLikes, 5 UserComments, or 300 UserDownloads. The user interaction type should be one of the subtypes of UserInteraction.

Property	Expected data type	Description
map	URL	A URL to a map of the place.
maps	URL	A URL to a map of the place (legacy spelling; see singular form, map).
photo	Photograph or ImageObject	A photograph of this place.
photos	Photograph or ImageObject	Photographs of this place (legacy spelling; see singular form, photo).
review	Review	A review of the item.
reviews	Review	Review of the item (legacy spelling; see singular form, review).
telephone	Text	The telephone number.
Properties from "Organization"		
contactPoint	ContactPoint	A contact point for a person or organization.
contactPoints	ContactPoint	A contact point for a person or organization (legacy spelling; see singular form, contactPoint).
Email	Text	Email address.
Employee	Person	Someone working for this organization.
Employees	Person	People working for this organization (legacy spelling; see singular form, employee).
Founder	Person	A person who founded this organization.
Founders	Person	A person who founded this organization (legacy spelling; see singular form, founder).
foundingDate	Date	The date that this organization was founded.
Location	Place or PostalAddress	The location of the event or organization.
Member	Person or Organization	A member of this organization.
Members	Person or Organization	A member of this organization (legacy spelling; see singular form, member).
Properties from "LocalBusiness"		
branchOf	Organization	The larger organization that this local business is a branch of, if any.
currenciesAccepted	Text	The currency accepted (in ISO 4217 currency format).
openingHours	Duration	The opening hours for a business.
paymentAccepted	Text	Cash, credit card, etc.
priceRange	Text	The price range of the business, for example $$$.

Notice that there are four different schemas rolled into the LocalBusiness schema: "Thing," "Place," "Organization," and "LocalBusiness." The left column shows the actual properties defined in your data, and the middle column shows the expected data type, such as text, a name, an event, or a place. The right column provides a description of the purpose for the property and in what cases it should be used to develop the semantic meanings of your data.

Optimizing for Rich Snippets and the Semantic Web

Rich snippets are very useful for enhancing your search results and also allowing your page data and information to become more portable. By creating microdata (Schema.org) or RDFa attributes, you add another dimension of semantic meaning to your content, which allows it to be further applied in a variety of contextual applications outside of your owned web presence.

The general quick answer to the question of "whether to optimize" is that *most publishers should be using Schema.org or RDFa* if they want to expand their visibility in search engines and also make their content more portable. If you have databases or pages of any of the aforementioned categories, then Schema.org should be a serious consideration. Schema.org also goes much deeper with its list definitions, so be sure to visit http://schema.org/docs/full.html to determine whether there is already an attribute labeled for your type of content. If not, keep checking back, because this is still a relative new standard, and more definitions are continuously being added.

Also, note that if you have previously employed RDFa or microformats, the engines will still recognize this markup, but they are promoting the Schema.org and microdata format moving forward.

Top Considerations for Implementing Semantic Attributes

When assessing whether Schema.org is right for your platform, consider the following tips and ideas:

Remember That Not All Modified SERP Formats Are Rich Snippets Based on Schema.org, RDFa, or Microformats Google in particular is very good at identifying data structure and replicating this in the SERPs. Common examples of rich markup in SERPs that do not use microformats, Schema.org, or RDFa include sports scores and forums. Figure 10.6 shows a real-time search example where rich snippets appear based on the code structure of the site. In this case, the publisher is using software by vBulletin.

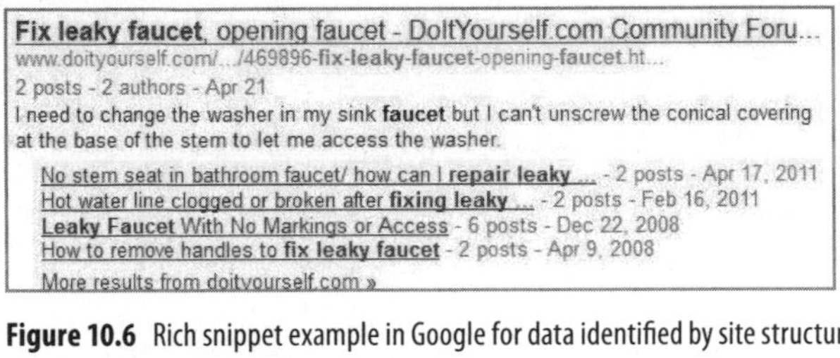

Figure 10.6 Rich snippet example in Google for data identified by site structure

Determine Whether Your Competitors Are Using Schema.org or RDFa In many competitive areas such as reviews, recipes, and events, implementing Schema.org or RDFa will most likely be a "must-do" if you want to stay competitive in search-engine visibility. Check the search results for your key head and long-tail terms to assess the state of rich snippets in your keyword space.

Note That Search Engines Are Placing More Emphasis on Schema.org, but RDFa Is Used by Both Engines and Facebook Find the right balance for your goals between search and social before determining which format to implement. If your strategy is to gain the highest visibility for both search and Facebook, then RDFa should be strongly considered; otherwise, Schema.org will take care of rich snippets in the major search engines.

Keep in Mind That One of the Biggest Benefits of Schemas and Microdata Will Be Expanded Results in SERPs Expanded visibility in search has a huge impact on results, in terms of heightening click-through rates and expanding your SERP real estate. It also creates greater enticement for click-throughs, even if you are in positions 2 through 9.

Also Note That Rich Snippets Are Not Guaranteed for Every Result Expect to see sporadic appearance of your rich snippets, and expect to see engines and social networks experiment with semantic data for many years to come.

You can also test your snippets and roll out your updates slowly before implementing them throughout all of your site code. This will ensure the stability of your site and allow you to address any bugs before applying the code to your entire site structure. Google provides an excellent testing tool for rich snippets at `www.google.com/webmasters/tools/richsnippets`. As of August 2012, Google is also providing a new view in Google Webmaster Tools called the Structured Data Dashboard that shows how the appearance of rich snippets is impacting the search performance of your web assets.

Sample Schema.org and Microdata for a Person

Schema.org provides vocabulary definitions for a wide variety of data types, so visit Schema.org for the definitions that apply directly to your content and data. One of the most "search and social" examples of microdata is for a person, so I have chosen the following example source to better illustrate this type of semantic markup. This example shows a "before and after" example of how the markup should be written to fit this schema:

Example 1

Original HTML:

```
1. John Smith
2. <img src="johnsmith.jpg" />
3.
4. Lead Researcher
```

```
5. 12345 Market Research Plaza

6. St. 456

7. Buffalo, Wyoming 82834

8. (555) 123-4567

9. <a href="mailto:j.smith@xyz--123.org">j.smith@xyz--123.org</a>

10.

11. John's personal web site:

12. <a href="www.john--smith.com">john--smith.com</a>

13.

14. Research assistants:

15. <a href="www.xyz--123.org/assistants/matthewconnor.html">Matthew Connor</a>

16. <a href="www.xyz--123.org/assistants/clairebailey.html">Claire Bailey</a>
```

With Schema.org Microdata:

```
1. <div itemscope itemtype="http://schema.org/Person">

2.   <span itemprop="name">John Smith</span>

3. <img src="johnsmith.jpg" itemprop="image" />

4.

5.   <span itemprop="jobTitle">Lead Researcher</span>

6.   <div itemprop="address" itemscope itemtype="http://schema.org/PostalAddress">

7.    <span itemprop="streetAddress">

8.     12345 Market Research Plaza

9.    St. 456

10.  </span>

11.  <span itemprop="addressLocality">Buffalo</span>,

12.   <span itemprop="addressRegion">WY</span>

13.  <span itemprop="postalCode">82834</span>

14.  </div>

15.  <span itemprop="telephone">(555) 123-4567</span>

16.  <a href="mailto: j.smith@xyz--123.org" itemprop="email">

17.   j.smith@xyz--123.org</a>

18.

19.   John's personal web site:

20.  <a href="www.john--smith.com" itemprop="url">john--smith.com</a>

21.

22.   Research assistants:

23.  <a href=" www.xyz--123.org/assistants/matthewconnor.html"

24.  itemprop="colleague">Matthew Connor</a>

25.  <a href=" www.xyz--123.org/assistants/clairebailey.html"

26.  itemprop="colleague">Claire Bailey</a>

27. </div>
```

Notice in the "Microdata" section of the example how the properties are added to help define extended context of bits of information on the page. Line 1 contains a direct link reference to the schema vocabulary (`http://schema.org/Person`). In line 2, you can see an example of how a property is defined for a name, rather than just simply including a name in the body of the page as text. On line 6, there is additional schema vocabulary referenced for a postal address at the URL `http://schema.org/PostalAddress`. Even the telephone, email address, and URL in lines 15, 16, and 20, respectively, are given their own properties. Also notice that the research assistant links in lines 22 to 26 have an additional item, "colleague," to apply a personal relationship context to the link.

Remember that this is just one sample of a schema for a person, so be sure to visit Schema.org for a detailed list of definitions that apply specifically to your area of business or publishing theme.

Raven offers a quick and easy way to create schema markup for your data with a tool it descriptively calls Schema Creator (`http://www.schema-creator.org`). Just plug in data for a Person, Product, Event, Organization, Movie, Book, or Publication, and Schema Creator will provide the schema code output for you to add to your web pages. Raven Tools has also introduced a similar free schema creation plugin for WordPress, which can be found at `http://wordpress.org/extend/plugins/schema-creator/`.

The RDFa specification gets much deeper than schema, so check out `www.w3.org/TR/xhtml-rdfa-primer/` for more information if you plan on implementing RDFa.

Author Rank and the *rel=author* Attribute

Content creators have an excellent new option for receiving expanded visibility in Google search results. The `rel=author` attribute establishes a trusted handshake between your articles and your authors with Google. Once a connection is made between Google and your content, your Google+ profile icon will appear next to your articles in Google search results. As mentioned in Chapter 8, "Blogs, Google News, and Press Releases," publishers who already appear in Google News will also receive additional visibility for articles that appear there. Google has stated repeatedly that Google+ will expand to inform more and more products and services, so don't be surprised if this attribute moves into the other services as well. In an interview with Eric Enge, published on April 11, 2012 (`www.stonetemple.com/relauthor-defined-with-googles-sagar-kamdar/`), Google's Sagar Kamdar noted `rel=author` is designed to help authors get set up easily and better connect with fans of their work.

The implications for this attribute are tremendous from a publishing perspective. If you have a backlog of articles, you can gain additional search authority and visibility by enabling the `rel=author` attribute. Enhanced visibility in an author universal search placement means that you can generally have higher click-through rates for your search listing, no matter what position it is in. Figure 10.7 shows a Google search result-listing for two of my previous columns for MediaPost. Notice the expanded Google+ profile picture inserted into the left of the listing, with additional results for associated content in the Rob Garner link, followed by a link to more articles written by me in the More by Rob Garner link.

Figure 10.7 Sample of a Google search result with authorship markup

Author Rank and the Author Graph

This attribute has also spawned the concept of *author rank*, which theoretically can begin to inform rankings based on SEO-like attributes for authors, such as authority of sites an author has previously published upon, the link graph of the sites published upon, the link relationship between sites published, the theme and topic of previous published articles, and so on. As you read in Chapter 8, Google News checks for the page position of articles and news stories on a site to determine prominence at a given period of time. This measurement could provide even further evidence of the prominence of certain authors, within the context of the publication that they write for.

Author rank does a fantastic job of separating the good stuff from the nameless spam and rewards authors of quality content in the process with an enhanced search listing and deeper search access to an author's content across many different sites.

Establishing Author Information in Google+ Using Links

One method that Google+ uses to create a handshake between your profile and your content sites is to link to them from your Google+ profile page. To get started connecting your pages in Google for author rank, you will need to first get a Google+ profile page if you haven't already done so. In your profile, click Edit, and you will see an area of the page that says Contributor To (see Figure 10.8). Place a link here to the bio pages of the publications that you write for. This will allow Google to get a sense of your identity on the other site and make a connection between the articles within that site.

Figure 10.8 The Contributor To section of a Google+ profile

Once you have linked to your publications in the Contributor To section of your profile page, you must also create a link back from your profile pages on the third-party sites. If you contribute to your own sites, this will be easier to complete because you have more control to add this link yourself or have someone in your company do it for you. If you are publishing on sites that you do not own, you will need to have an administrator place these links back to your profile.

The link on the publishing site must include the `rel=author` attribute and link back to your profile on Google+. Your profile link should look like this:

```
<a href="https://plus.google.com/2222221111112?rel=author">Google</a>
```

In your link, replace the 2222221111112 with your own Google+ ID. Be patient, because it may take up to several weeks to start appearing in the search results. You can also use the Google rich snippet tool to test your authorship markup, but remember that proper implementation does not guarantee that your markup will appear in the search results.

Establishing Authorship with a Verified Email Address

A second method of verifying your connection between a website and Google is with a verified email address. This email address should contain the domain of the site that you publish on and that was submitted in the box on the following URL: `https://plus.google.com/authorship`. Once your email address has been authenticated, Google will add your address to the Work section of your profile. You can then edit your profile to make it private or adjust the settings of who should see your contact info.

Make sure that all of your articles contain a byline with a brief description of who you are and that each article you wrote is preceded with "by." Google looks for snippets of text that contain the phrase "by+Author+Name" as a signal to reinforce authorship.

Establishing Authorship Using WordPress Plug-ins

There is a variety of different WordPress plug-ins to help you quickly establish `rel=author` for your individual authors or blogs with multiple authors. Here are two examples of plug-ins to help get you going:

Authorsure This plug-in works for both single-author and multiauthor WordPress blogs. See http://wordpress.org/extend/plugins/authorsure/.

Google Authorship for Multiple Authors This tool is designed mainly for blogs with multiple authors, and its creator states that it needs to be customized in order to work for single-author blogs. See http://wordpress.org/extend/plugins/google-authorship-for-multiple-writers/.

Adding Social-Network Sharing Buttons to Digital-Content Assets

Share buttons and network buttons are basic add-ons to any content that you want to travel easily throughout social networks. If you want to make it easy to "strike while the iron is hot" and encourage your audience to share or network with you at the moment they are consuming your content, then adding social sharing buttons to your content is a must-do. There are two basic types of social buttons for your own content:

Share Buttons These buttons appear on your content at the site and page levels and make it easy for content consumers to share, like, +1, tweet, pin, or stumble your content to other networks, without having to leave your site. Share buttons can also provide the number of shares you have on a particular network and give your readers an indication of the participation level on your site, in real-time. Figure 10.9 shows some common share buttons on an iCrossing blog post at http://greatfinds.icrossing.com.

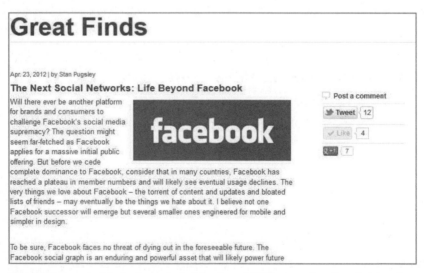

Figure 10.9 Example of sharing buttons in the right column of this blog post at http://greatfinds.icrossing.com

Network Buttons These buttons are different from sharing buttons, in that they ask your content consumers to follow you, friend you, circle you, subscribe to you, or connect with you in a social network. Overall, they help increase the size of your networks over time and expand your footprint and reach when disseminating content into these networks. I write about "building your networks" throughout this book as a method of increasing your reach. Using this type of button on your content is one of the best ways to help grow your network over time. Figure 10.10 shows a sample of network buttons on Mashable.

Figure 10.10 Example of network sharing buttons on Mashable

Sharing and network buttons are available individually at most of the originating social-network sites used by your audience, but there are also many sites that aggregate a wide variety of sharing and network buttons into one nice little widget. Make it easy for your content fans to share your work with their networks and also join your networks by adding these buttons to your owned assets. In the next sections, I will review both individual sharing buttons and also a few all-in-one button-widget providers.

Individual Share Buttons and Network Buttons

The following section covers a list of some of the most popular share buttons and where to find them directly on their respective sites. Consider using these buttons as your primary social-network set for sharing content.

Twitter Twitter is one of the top networks for sharing links and information. Twitter share and follow buttons are among the most popular types used by content creators across the Internet. View the different sharing and follow buttons for your own content properties at `https://twitter.com/about/resources/buttons`.

Google +1 With almost 100 million users, Google+ and +1s are major platforms for information-sharing. Add +1s to your pages to encourage sharing across this network at `www.google.com/intl/en/webmasters/+1/button/index.html`. Note that +1 buttons override `robots.txt` directives, so if there any pages you do not want indexed in Google, do not add this button to your pages. Figure 10.11 shows the customization widget for creating a Google+ sharing icon for your website. Create it the way you want, grab the code, and add it to your website.

Let visitors recommend your content on Google Search and share it on Google+

Customize your +1 button and +Snippet

+1 button preview

+98121 including You, Jonathan Jeter, Kevin Fox, Joost de Valk

Size: ○ Small (15px)   ○ Medium (20px)
      ○ Standard (24px) ○ Tall (60px)
Annotation: inline ▾
Width: 450
Language: English (US) - English (US) ▾

⊞ Advanced options

Copy and paste the following code into your site:

```
<!-- Place this tag where you want the +1 button to render -->
<g:plusone size="small" annotation="inline"></g:plusone>

<!-- Place this render call where appropriate -->
```

Figure 10.11 The Google+ code widget

Google Badge In addition to helping people circle your profile in Google+, a Google Badge helps create a handshake between your published assets and your Google profile. View and create your badge at `https://developers.google.com/+/plugins/badge/`.

Pinterest Pinterest offers a number of different methods for enabling your audience to pin content from your site, as well as follow buttons to grow your network size on Pinterest. View your button choices at `http://pinterest.com/about/goodies/`.

Facebook Get your Like, Recommend, or Send button code right here: `http://developers.facebook.com/docs/reference/plugins/like/`.

RSS If you have a feed, make it stand out with a standard RSS icon, like the one in Figure 10.12. You can get a copy of this image issued under the Creative Commons license at `http://en.wikipedia.org/wiki/File:Feed-icon.svg`.

Figure 10.12 The standard RSS icon provides a visual cue to where subscribers can grab the feed.

LinkedIn InShare is the sharing button for LinkedIn and enables your audience to share content and show the number of people sharing links and other assets. Get the code at `https://developer.linkedin.com/plugins/share-plugin-generator`. Companies can also use the follow button generator button at this URL: `https://developer.linkedin.com/plugins/follow-company`. Figure 10.13 shows the follow code widget for companies listed in LinkedIn.

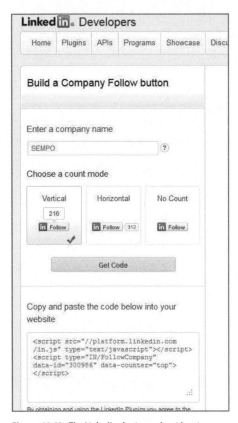

Figure 10.13 The LinkedIn sharing code widget is very easy to use.

StumbleUpon Encourage stumbles on StumbleUpon by placing the StumbleUpon code on your assets. Get it at `www.stumbleupon.com/dt/badges/create`.

Reddit Reddit offers a wide variety of sharing buttons to jump-start your content into a viral sharing frenzy. Find your code at `www.reddit.com/buttons/`.

Multibutton Share Widgets

Using a multibutton widget for sharing can take a lot of the hassle out of maintaining multiple share buttons from various sites. The top button-widget services also keep their code updated and add buttons as other new hot social networks emerge. Adding a sharing widget is as simple as copying the code from these sites and pasting it into the code of your web page. Here are two popular services for share buttons:

ShareThis This service offers many different features and will customize your button code for a number of publishing platforms, including WordPress, Drupal, Tumblr, and Blogger, among many others. You can also choose from a variety of different button styles. Figure 10.14 shows the style selection interface at ShareThis. See `http://sharethis.com/publishers/get-sharing-tools`.

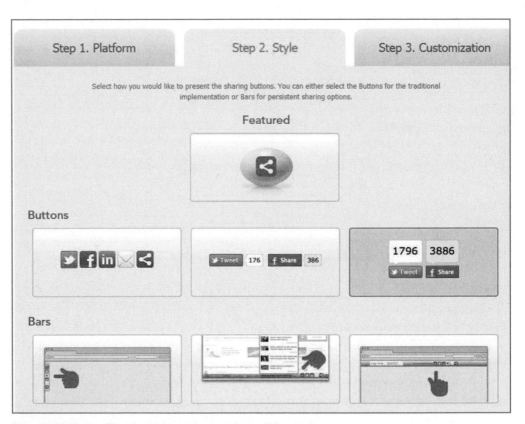

Figure 10.14 The ShareThis widget is very easy to use, with many different options.

AddThis AddThis is another popular multibutton widget. It features a quick interface to select your button style and grab your code quickly. Figure 10.15 shows the code box at AddThis. See `www.addthis.com`.

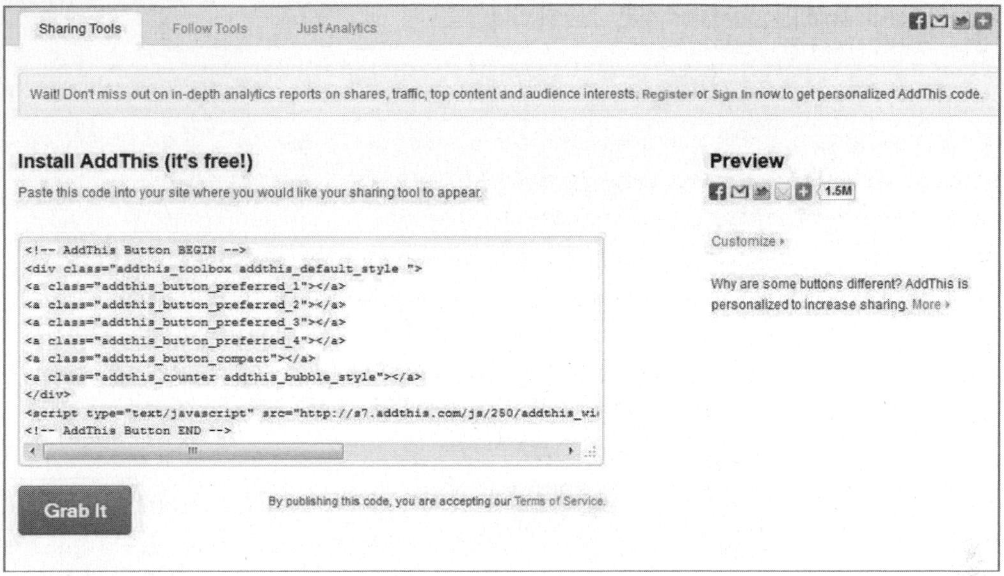

Figure 10.15 AddThis

How to Decide Which Buttons to Use

If you have already installed one of the multibutton sharing widgets like AddThis or ShareThis, then you may have noticed that there are many sharing-network buttons to choose from. These widgets include the top-tier popular networks, as well as smaller, more niche networks. Most publishers don't have a large enough content reserve to cover the complete diversity of the social networks offered in these tools, so it is good to be selective for your site and for your audience.

If you have also performed effective market research, then you already know where your audience likes to hang out, so start by adding buttons for those sites. Then expand to the additional sites that make the most sense for your topic. Twitter, Facebook, and Google+ generally cover a wide range of topics and serve as a core set of buttons for most publishers. If your content has more of a business topic skew, then be sure to add InShare buttons for LinkedIn. StumbleUpon is great for engaging or entertaining content and can deliver massive amounts of traffic. Pinterest skews toward visually based sites with a predominant female demographic, so grab a Pinterest button if this falls in line with your audience target. In short, review the sites suggested in these multibutton widgets, and determine whether they are right for your audience before adding them to your widget or your content pages.

Where to Put Your Sharing and Network Buttons

Think of your sharing and network buttons like a call to action. If your audience likes your content, then you want them to spread it around or become part of your network. To encourage shares, likes, follows, circles, and +1s, ensure that your buttons are in a place on the page where your audience will see them. This means putting them at the top of the page or on the left or right sidebar, above the fold. You may also consider adding a second set of buttons at the bottom of your page for content that goes below the fold in order to catch those consumers who have read all the way through your work. Don't go overboard and put buttons all over your page, but do ensure that your buttons are visible above and below the fold in some way. In Figure 10.16, you can see how Mashable makes it very easy to share and places buttons in a way that serve as a visual cue for their audience to take an action.

Figure 10.16 Mashable is all about connectedness and sharing.

Setting Up RSS Feeds for SEO and Social Spaces

RSS feeds represent a way to *push* your fresh content off your website and into search and social spaces. RSS stands for "really simple syndication" and is a basic feature of sites publishing in real-time or sites that update their content on a regular basis. If you are publishing on your own, there are many easy ways to set up and promote your RSS feeds, and those that will be discussed in this chapter. If you are part of a larger enterprise, consider the items that will be covered in this section, but also plan to go into more detail with your IT team or consultant to implement feeds in a variety of ways. RSS feeds fundamentally provide the following SEO and social benefits for your owned web assets:

- Enables your data to become more portable to places outside your website, for both people and search engines.

- Provides a real-time beacon for your new content, to both people and search engines.

- Syndicate in networks like Twitter and Facebook that create the social signals that search engines look for, based on how much the links are shared or discussed.

- Increases crawlability of your website and freshens up crawl speed by providing more outside points of link access for search crawlers (read more about Google crawling of RSS feeds at `http://googlewebmastercentral.blogspot.com/2009/10/using-rssatom-feeds-to-discover-new.html`).

- Provides a signal of recency to both search engines and social audiences by showing your freshest and newest content first.

- Allows your audience to consume content in a feed reader, without having to constantly check your blog or website for new updates.

- Allows other bloggers and webmasters to post your feed on their sites, which effectively drives more traffic and creates additional accessibility for search engines to crawl. Figure 10.17 shows an example of RSS-feed implementation in the right column of my blog. If the quality of content is good enough, webmasters and bloggers will sometimes pick up your RSS feed and make it part of their blog roll. Sites like Alltop are composed entirely of RSS feeds (`www.alltop.com`).

- Provides an easy automated method for publishing your new content to social spaces like Twitter, Facebook, and LinkedIn.

- Creates your own passive syndication and distribution network through subscribers, which can become active when shared across networks (see Chapter 2 for more on passive and active syndication).

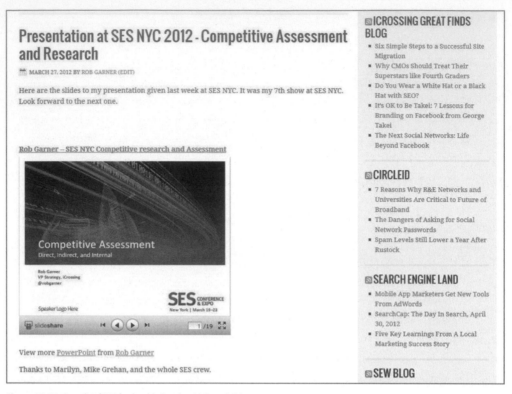

Figure 10.17 Sample of RSS feeds added to the sidebar of a blog

Methods of Implementing RSS Feeds

One of the first questions many marketers have about setting up RSS feeds is identifying the content categories they will create a feed for. The answer to "how many" depends on the categories of content you publish, how often you publish in those categories, and what types of data and content you publish on a regular basis. Also key to this process is determining whether there is an audience for your feed, or, in other words, asking whether your fresh info is really interesting enough for someone to read it on a regular basis without going to your site. Also, remember that feeds are presented based on recency parameters, or "newest first." Here are some of the common content categories that publishers create RSS feeds for:

- Major content categories within a website
- Latest news
- Latest products added
- Updates to keyword searches within databases
- Latest comments
- Latest podcasts

- Latest videos
- Newest press releases
- Freshest blog content
- Current deals and coupons
- Latest ads
- Newest auctions or auctions ending soonest
- Latest job listings

Software with Built-in RSS Feeds

The good news for digital publishers is that RSS feeds are built in to the content-management systems you may already be using. WordPress provides a variety of feeds at the site level and category level, and common forum platforms like vBulletin and phpBB also have RSS feeds or RSS plug-ins ready to go. If this is the case for your content-management platform, then a lot of the hard work is already done for you.

RSS Feed-Creation Software and Apps

Many applications will help you build your own RSS feeds for your content. Two options being used by many marketers are ExtraLabs Feed Editor and Feedity.

Feed Editor is a stand-alone what-you-see-is-what-you-get (WYSIWYG) feed editor for Windows and is fee-based. Using the editor, you can easily define your links, titles, descriptions, and other fields, and the editor will create the code for you. Validate and save your file as XML, upload to your web server, and you are ready to go (`www.extralabs.net/feed-editor.htm`).

Feedity (`www.feedity.com`) is also a fee-based service and enables easy feed creation for your content. Feedity allows you to capture feed items from your existing web pages and has an advanced feature to tell the application specifically where your content starts in the code of your site, based on your source HTML.

How to Create RSS Feeds Using a Word Processor

You can also create your RSS feed in a Notepad document or other simple text editor. First, start your document with the XML and RSS encoding, like this:

```
<?xml version="1.0" encoding="UTF-8"?>
<rss version="2.0">
```

Next, you will need to define the elements of the content you want to display in the feed. Basic elements will include a title (`<title></title>`), date (`<pubDate></pubDate>`), URL (`<link> </link>`), and so on. Other key basic elements can be found on The RSS Advisory Board website at `www.rssboard.org/rss-specification`.

Once you have defined your elements, created your items, and closed your document (</rss>), save it as .xml and upload to your server. Next, validate your feed at http://validator.w3.org/feed/ to ensure that it is readable. Once your feed is validated, it will be ready for RSS feed readers or for use as a link widget for blogs and other websites. Webopedia also has a nice set of additional standard RSS elements listed at www.webopedia.com/quick_ref/rss_02.asp.

If you are publishing a relatively low volume of content, then it is feasible to update your RSS feed manually every time a new item is posted. But if you are dealing with robust feeds from databases or if you frequently publish pages and files, then you will need an automated process for updating your feed or feeds. There is a number of ways to approach automation of feeds, so talk to your IT administrator or consultant to determine the best method for your particular content platform.

Distribute Feeds with FeedBurner

Running your own RSS feeds can often be a "black box" in terms of counting your real number of subscribers and getting useful analytics. One solution to this challenge is to redirect your feeds through a site called FeedBurner. FeedBurner is a feed-distribution platform owned by Google and provides analytics and other metrics for your RSS feeds. FeedBurner is also used by Google to help distinguish good content from the spam by analyzing how many real human users are actually consuming the feeds. Google also uses this data to apply as a social signal to help rank your content.

Once you have established your RSS feeds, setting up your feeds on FeedBurner is quick, free, and easy. To start, you will need to log into FeedBurner with your Google Account at www.feedburner.com. Once you are logged in, you will see a screen to copy and paste your RSS-feed URL (see Figure 10.18).

Figure 10.18 Setting up your feeds in FeedBurner is easy.

After you have entered your URL and the feed has been verified, enter the title of your feed and the name that you want to appear in the URL (Figure 10.19).

The example in Figure 10.20 shows a "burned" RSS feed for my own blog. To obtain your own RSS-feed URL for your own site, click the View Feed XML link in the left corner of the Subscribe Now box. Your audience can choose the format for your feed, including standard XML, Netvibes, Google Reader, and more.

CHAPTER 10: TECHNICAL CONSIDERATIONS AND IMPLEMENTATION

Figure 10.19 Naming your feed in FeedBurner

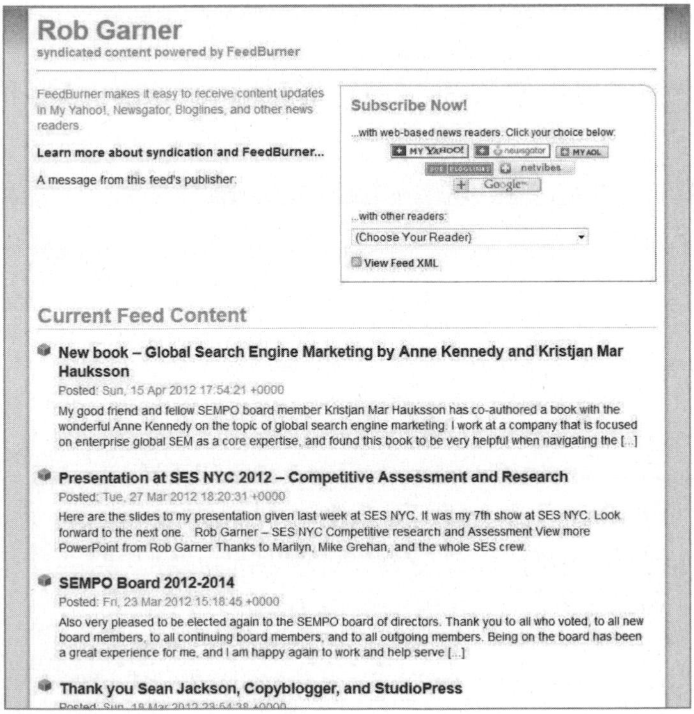

Figure 10.20 A "burned" feed, with various options for sharing in the left corner of the Subscribe Now box.

There is also a variety of ways to integrate a FeedBurner subscription URL on your site, based on some of the popular platforms. In your FeedBurner account, you will see an Options tab, which will walk you through a variety of implementation instructions for many popular platforms.

How to Promote Your RSS Feed

Once you have established your feeds, the next step is to promote them. Use the following promotion examples for either your FeedBurner custom feeds or your basic RSS feeds:

- Ensure that your feeds are prominently visible with other share buttons on your content—use the RSS icon, and add to site maps.
- Use the standard RSS icon to provide a clear visual cue to your audience.
- Use Twitterfeed or a similar tool to syndicate your new content to a Twitter account automatically when it is published.
- Syndicate your feed to LinkedIn on your profile page.
- Create an RSS widget in Netvibes or another feed reader.
- Create a unique page for your RSS feeds on your website or blog.
- Add your RSS feed links to your site map (you should have both a page-based site map and an XML site map).
- Submit your RSS feed to Ping-O-Matic (`http://pingomatic.com`).

As a general rule, it is a good idea to think about promoting your RSS feed URL like you would promote your primary domain. Other methods include adding your feed URL to your email signature, print advertising and print collateral, site headers, footers, and navigational elements.

Google Webmaster Tools and Bing Webmaster Tools Account Setup

As a real-time Internet publisher and social-media marketer, there is one really good reason why you should be concerned about the SEO performance of your website: SEO allows you to extend your message to a greater like-minded audience of *people* that you want to connect to in search and to *people* who search in social settings.

Many marketers scoff at or blow off the search-performance elements of their website, and this is a huge mistake. It's a mistake because they forget about the people using search engines and that search metrics serve as a beacon of content success. It's a mistake because they sometimes have to work 10 times harder than if they had planned for search to begin with. It's a mistake because they have limited their reach and opportunities with their Internet initiatives.

The bottom line is that if you publish online and care about the hygiene of your platform, then you should be using both Bing and Google Webmaster Tools and optimizing your presence for search-engine visibility. These tools will show you how the engines view your site from a performance perspective, how to make a stronger connection between your content and the engines through XML feeds, and overall provide a useful method of increasing the search performance of your content assets.

Google Webmaster Tools

Google Webmaster Tools allows you to sign up multiple sites under one account and view multiple performance metrics. As a real-time publisher, it is very helpful to see Google's SEO perspective of your websites so that you can continue to build up and improve your site where they may need help the most. The features of Google Webmaster Tools include the following:

- Site-link customization
- Change of domain-address instructions
- URL preferences for SERP display
- URL-parameter administration
- Link data
- Search-query data
- Content keywords and theme assessment
- Internal link analysis
- Google+ social metrics (see Chapter 14, "Metrics and Measurement," for more on this)
- Diagnostics

To get started, you will need to log in to Google Webmaster Tools with your Google account info at www.google.com/webmasters/tools/. Once you are in the Webmaster Tools start-up page, start adding websites to your account by hitting the Add a Site button in the upper-right corner of the page. A window will pop up, and you can enter your domain there. Figure 10.21 shows the Add a Site button and pop-up box for entry.

Figure 10.21 Getting started in Google Webmaster Tools

Hit Continue, and you will be taken to the site verification page. Google offers you four ways to verify your site to ensure you are the actual webmaster:

- Upload an encoded HTML file to the root directory of your domain host server.
- Add an encoded meta tag to the home page of your site.
- Use your Google Analytics account.
- Add a DNS record to your domain server.

To validate with an HTML file, Google will provide a link to download a special file with a unique identifier. Copy this file to your computer, and upload it to your web server using a File Transfer Protocol (FTP) program, with your site's login credentials. If you do not have an FTP program, you can download a free client called FileZilla at http://filezilla-project.org/. Another free FTP program is called Core FTP and can be downloaded at www.coreftp.com. Figure 10.22 shows the validation screen at Google Webmaster Tools.

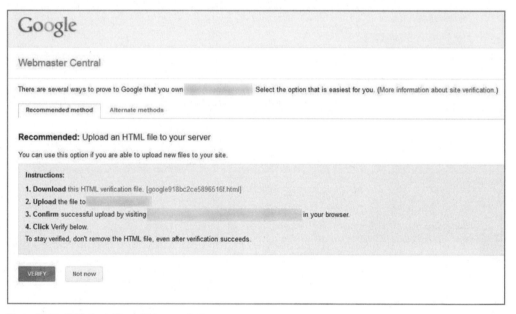

Figure 10.22 Validation in Google Webmaster Tools

Once you have uploaded the file to your root directory, go back to your screen and click Verify to complete the process. Upon successful verification, you should see your site listed in your main Google Webmaster Tools dashboard.

There is a separate tab for the other methods of verification listed previously. One other method shown on the tab is to use the Google meta tag, which is encoded with a unique identifier. Place this meta tag in the head area of your home page, and upload the file via FTP. If you are on a WordPress blog or other content-management system that allows you to change head elements, then you can add the meta tag in your WordPress admin panel and save it. Once you have saved the meta tag, go to the Google page and click to verify the link.

Figure 10.23 shows the Alternative Methods menu for validating your site in Google Webmaster Tools. Once you are verified, you are ready to start managing your site.

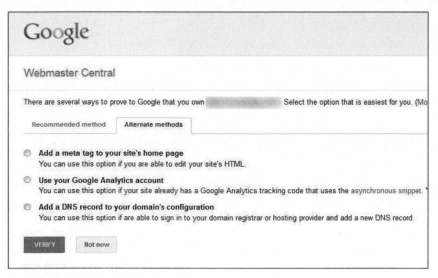

Figure 10.23 Alternative methods of site validation in Google

Bing Webmaster Tools

Bing has its own free and robust website-management center also called Webmaster Tools. It has many of the same features as Google Webmaster Tools, and the verification process is very similar to Google's. Bing Webmaster Tools offers the following features:

- Traffic data
- Crawl data
- Keyword data

To get started, you will need to register for a Windows Live account at `http://login.live.com`. Once you have verified your ID, go to `www.bing.com/toolbox/webmaster/` and sign in. Here you will be directed to the main Bing webmaster dashboard and prompted to add your site URL. Once you have added your site, you will need to verify it by uploading an XML file, uploading an encoded meta tag, or entering a modification to your domain server. Figure 10.24 shows the Bing screen for grabbing the meta-tag code for placement in the head of your home page, just as described in the Google instructions.

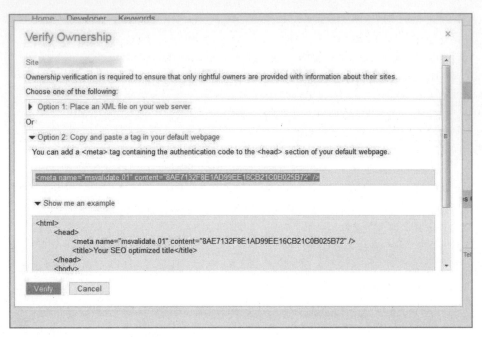

Figure 10.24 Verifying site ownership in Bing

Once you are verified, you are also ready to start managing your site or sites in Bing Webmaster Tools.

Google and Bing XML Site Map Feed Setup

One other important aspect of managing your websites for search-engine performance is to create and submit an XML feed of your site content directly to Google and Bing Webmaster Tools. This exercise does not guarantee inclusion or visibility, but the engines have stated publicly that site feeds help them improve their crawling performance of your website assets, and they highly recommend that webmasters submit feeds directly. Both Google and Bing allow for direct submission of XML feeds and have also teamed up for a standard site-map protocol, outlined further at www.sitemaps.org.

A key reason for producing an XML feed is that online content publishers can no longer expect to pull in their audience directly to their websites. Using feeds allows your content, or notifications of new content, to be pushed out in a way the engine's audience can find it. Using feeds also contributes to the element of *recency*, in that the engine can determine when new content has been published.

To create an XML feed for your website, you can use one of many free tools listed at http://code.google.com/p/sitemap-generators/wiki/SitemapGenerators. This list includes a wide variety of services to meet specific needs. If you are running WordPress, then a simple method of site-map creation is to use the Google XML

Sitemaps Generator plug-in (http://wordpress.org/extend/plugins/google-sitemap-generator/), which will produce a feed that works for both Google and Bing.

For smaller sites, less than 500 pages, I have found the free site map tool at www.xml-sitemaps.com to be effective. Simply go to the home page of your site and submit your URL (make sure that all feed content you want added links contiguously to the home page of your site in order to crawl all pages for the feed). This tool will automatically crawl all links from the home page (and subsequent links of links) and produce a file in a variety of forms. XML-Sitemaps also offers a fee-based service called Pro-Sitemaps (www.pro-sitemaps.com) for sitemaps over 500 URLs, including a standalone sitemap generator that resides on your website server, and also a hosted sitemap service. This service also generates XML sitemaps for news, images, and video.

Another good XML feed generator is the A1 Sitemap Generator by Microsys, which is designed for sites that contain up to tens of thousands of pages. This desktop-based software is fee-based, but it offers a 30-day free trial. Learn more at www.microsystools.com/products/sitemap-generator/.

Submitting Your Feed URL to Bing

Once you have set up your feed and your Bing Webmaster Tools account, submission is easy. Use the following steps to complete the process:

1. Click your website name in the main dashboard page of Bing Webmaster Tools.
2. Scroll down and click the Crawl Summary link.
3. On the next page, click the Site Maps (XML, Atom, RSS) link.
4. A pop-up window will appear. Add the name of your site-map file in the appropriate box. If you are using a subdomain, make sure you also edit this part of the URL (see Figure 10.25).

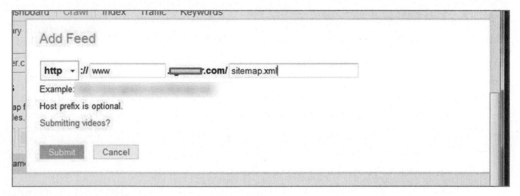

Figure 10.25 Adding an XML site-map file to Bing Webmaster Tools

Submitting Your XML Site-Map Feed URL to Google

Submitting your feed to Google is also very straightforward once you have created an account and feed.

1. Log in to your Google Webmaster Tools account.

2. In the left navigation menu, click the Site Configuration link, and then click Sitemaps.

3. In the top-right corner of the Sitemaps page, click the Add/Test Site map button, and a pop-up submission form will appear (Figure 10.26).

4. Submit your site map file's URL, and you are done.

Figure 10.26   Adding a site-map URL is also a cinch in Google.

Depending how nimble you or your organization is, some of the sections in this chapter may take weeks, months, or years to complete. Be sure to manage your time and resources appropriately in the context of the opportunity. Don't let one technical element be a showstopper; instead, focus on what you can get accomplished. In this chapter and all others in this book, there are always quick wins, short-term efforts, and long-term projects.

In the next chapter, I will discuss some of the search and social aspects of video and images and how you can get the most out of your optimization and content strategies for these efforts.

Video and Images

Video and images make up a major segment of all search-engine referrals, as well as a major share of social-network interactions. Think about your last few interactions on Facebook, and at least one of them probably involved viewing, sharing, or commenting on a video or image asset. Conversely, search-engine results have become much more visual in the past five to six years. No longer satisfied with retrieving search results containing just 10 blue text links, the engines have pushed video and image thumbnails into the prime-time space of their results pages. The impact on your marketing efforts is that you should strongly consider visual elements as part of your overall your strategy.

11

Chapter Contents
How to optimize video assets for search
How social signals contribute to search visibility for video assets
How to increase social signals for video assets
How to optimize image assets for search
How social signals contribute to search visibility for image assets
How to increase social signals for image assets

In addition to emphasizing visual assets in this chapter, you will be learning about the essential textual elements that help search engines and networks find and share your content. Remember that search and social networks are essentially blind when it comes to reading and understanding your visual assets, and the accompanying text, links, and social-signal context will be critical in how your visuals resonate in search and social channels. Also, remember that *keywords are connections to people* in both search and social channels. Don't blow them off. Do thorough research, follow through in the language you use socially, and label your digital video and image assets accordingly.

Video and Image Strategy Development

Before diving into some of the deeper aspects of video and image optimization, let's review these key considerations for beginning an image or video strategy or developing your existing one:

Topic and Theme The first question about your video and image strategy involves determining your topic focus and theme. You don't have to get a million views to be successful—you just need to be relevant to the right person and audience. Look for themes where there is little or no competition, or jump in and start competing with the most visible and popular competitors in your theme space. Also, remember that you don't have to sell a product or service in all of your video content. Video helps your branding and puts the thought of your company in the mind of the viewer. Sales occur later in the buying process of your audience, when they are ready to make a transaction.

Focus Your company can be visually relevant to your audience in a variety of ways. Focus on aspects of your products, show your services in action, and document the places of interest to your audience. One of the most universally relevant visuals to almost all businesses is *people*. People have a natural inclination to read and view information about themselves and the people they know, and by covering the people in your business or industry, you will certainly grab their attention. Even if you offer an abstract product or service, ultimately it is people who consume your product.

Assessing Competition A key element of image and video optimization is assessing your competition. There is no set amount of optimization or promotion for your visual strategy, because every area is different and has a different set of competitors (direct and indirect). Upon determining your competition, you will have a good idea of how visually competitive your keyword space is, as well as the number of players in social spaces.

Market Research Don't start a visual optimization and engagement strategy without first examining your audience, what they like to consume, how they search and converse for this content, and where they like to consume it. Go back to Chapters 3 through 5 for more information on identifying your audience.

Determining the Depth of Your Strategy In Chapter 5, "Content Strategy: Auditing, Assessment, and Planning," I wrote about thinking about content like a forest, not a weed. The same information applies here. The size, quality, and reach of your content are directly proportional to the volume of high-quality content you produce.

Publish and Share It should be very clear by now that passive publishing gets you only so far, so you will need to build up your network visibility, engage and participate in the social channels you publish to, and always share the good content you are providing when it is relevant to your audience.

One word of caution before engaging in any visual-asset strategy: it is essential that you read the terms of service for each social network you plan to publish to before uploading your work. Both Google+ and Facebook have clauses on licensing that you must be aware of. Many professional photographers, videographers, and marketers refuse to post their images on these services because of the "perpetual" licensing terms claimed by some networks.

There is a strong case to be made that search results featuring an image thumbnail gain more attention from searchers than just text-only links. Gord Hotchkiss, SVP of Mediative, is a noted authority on search marketing and user behavior in search engines, as well as my fellow columnist for MediaPost. Along with Ian Everdell, Mediative's manager of user experience and research, they frequently study the impact of user behavior in search engines using eye-tracking research technology. Figure 11.1 shows an eye-tracking heat map for a Google search for *2011 new cars*. Notice that the area containing the most focus is the text result immediately to the right of the top thumbnail image. Their findings further revealed that while the image was not the direct point of focus, images contribute to what Everdell calls an *anchor point* for scanning and reading of textual objects on the search-results page. This means that while the image itself is not always attracting more eye-scanning activity, there is a correlation in that it attracts more interest to the textual search result. The overall implication is that results with images may correlate to increased attraction to your search-result listing.

Video Optimization for Search and Social Channels

Video search is a major segment of web search. In 2007, universal search put video assets front and center in all major engines, and now video is a major segment of all search results. I believe every content marketer should heavily weigh the potential for video content for their business, even if it first seems that video doesn't fit. Carefully looking for the right opportunity in your business space could just as well end up one of the most effective earned-marketing approaches you engage in. This section will cover the key considerations for a video strategy and how to optimize your presence for both search and social channels.

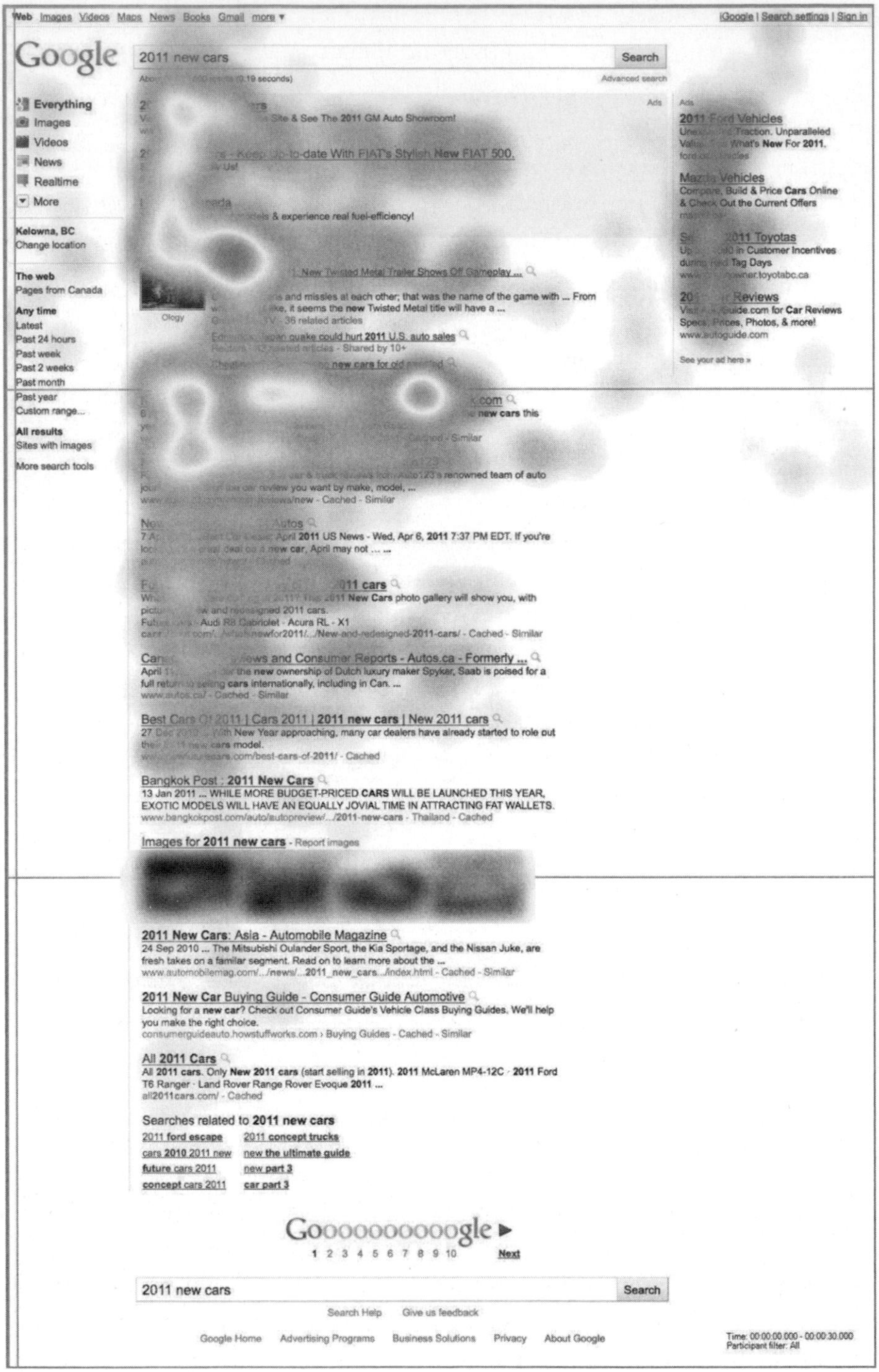

Figure 11.1 Heat map of a Google search-engine results page showing eye-tracking behavior around image icons

The Real-Time Elements of Video

While it can be said that the real-time aspects of video are as old as the television broadcasting medium itself (one-to-many), online video takes on a more interactive real-time component (one-to-many *and* many-to-many). Here are a few of the key real-time elements of online video:

- Videos are one of the most compelling real-time assets for breaking news and topical events.
- Like television, live online video is one of the most engaging forms of content on the real-time Web, and it is shared in real-time.
- Social users broadcast and upload video from anywhere, with mobile devices.
- Once videos are live, commenting systems and other feedback mechanisms kick in, requiring the creator or social-media management to engage in a timely manner.

Compelling and engaging video can create immediate feedback and social signals and start an upward velocity chain upon release. Sharing and feedback can be directly proportional to the interest, information, and entertainment level of the content.

The Interdependent Search and Social Elements of Video

Again, the many-to-many active sharing chain that results from engaging video is the conflux of many different integrated search and social elements. Here are a few of the main interdependent elements of search and social in video distribution:

- Videos can be optimized just like any other web page or text article.
- Social signals for video help increase visibility in search results and within the search results and discovery streams of a social network.
- Communities and social networks are built strictly around video assets, and these networks have internal search capabilities.
- Because it is owned by Google, YouTube takes a very algorithmic approach to social distribution of assets and to how it makes videos more visible within a network.
- Videos can be shared and embedded in social networks, which create additional social signals for search engines.

Video profiles and pages also provide second-tier SERP visibility because videos may be embedded into blogs, forums, social networks, and other web properties. These pages get picked up in search and drive more traffic and exposure for your business, as well as the platform that hosts your video assets.

Creating and Distributing Video Assets

In addition to the optimization aspects of video that will follow, there are several important considerations for getting started (or even revamping your existing presence), and they include the following:

Creating a Video Channel Don't think about just one video at a time—think about what your channel will look like as a group and recurring series. Thinking as a channel involves the development of a theme, understanding your audience, and building up subscribers and followers.

Using Video Assets as Part of Your Overall Sharing and Publishing Strategy (Adding to Blogs, Tweeting, Liking, Sharing) While your current social strategy may involve sharing your existing text-based content in social spaces, also consider how your current audience will react to *video* sharing in your current networks.

Video/Photography Gear and Software Depending on your approach, you will need to choose the right gear and editing software for your video-channel efforts. Your gear can be as simple as a smartphone camera with no editing to more sophisticated gear and editing software.

Also, remember to place a key emphasis on building up an audience for your video channel. Building up your network is both a social strategy and an SEO strategy. Produce quality video content that is so good you will want to promote it on all marketing materials, on your website, in offline advertising, and in all other media you use to market your company.

Video-Optimization Elements

When approaching a video strategy, you are going to face a decision of whether to host your own videos, whether to use a service and social network like YouTube, or both. Every business is different, so carefully consider the right balance for your company. The following sections cover optimization for both approaches.

Optimization for Videos Hosted on Your Own Website

Optimizing videos for search and social should be a regular part of the production process. When uploading to third-party videos sites or to your own site, consider the following areas of optimization for video assets:

Title The title is the single most important optimization element for your video. Be sure to include a relevant keyword in this title. Don't stuff keywords in this area—just stick to accurately describing your content. In most video-site content-management systems, this title will also transfer as an <H1> page heading (read more about the significance of the <H1> heading and title element in Chapter 6, "Creating Effective and Engaging Content").

Description The description is also one of your main opportunities to provide keyword reference and accurately describe your content. This description, no matter how short, often reinforces your titles in search results, especially when it matches a searcher's query.

Tags Tags are on-page keywords that serve as a form of external metadata. Label your tags accordingly with the right keywords. Remember, keywords are connections to people.

Transcriptions and Caption Files Providing a textual layer can help search engines better understand the content of your video in a literal sense. If your videos contain spoken-word audio tracks, then either transcribe them as text or use a service that will perform this function for you. YouTube will use Google services to create captioning for your video, and it is considered a good practice to provide text files of video on your video assets when appropriate. Captioning tools still need to be edited, but doing so can provide a lot of useful information to search engines.

Filenames Use keywords to describe your video in the filename.

Ensure Each Video Has Its Own URL Make sure that each of your individual videos is accessible by a direct URL. This will ultimately allow search engines to create a profile around your video asset, make it linkable from other websites, and also make it shareable in social activity streams. If you are embedding your videos in Flash or dynamically delivering them with asynchronous JavaScript and XML (AJAX), you are effectively hiding your video from both search engines and social networks.

Embedding in Feeds Allowing for your video to be embedded on outside sites allows for the creation of pages and links back to your original video. Enable embeds in your YouTube video, and create embed links on your own hosted videos as well.

Schema.org Definitions for Video For your hosted videos, mark up your links and video code with Schema.org vocabulary. Read more about Schema.org in Chapter 10, "Technical Considerations and Implementation," and on the page for video-object vocabulary at `http://schema.org/VideoObject`.

Create and Submit a Video Site Map for Hosted URLs Google recommends that video producers submit an XML feed to ensure faster crawling and indexing of your videos, especially for Google News. Watch a video and read a helpful tutorial on creating and uploading your video site map to your Google Webmaster Tools account at `http://support .google.com/webmasters/bin/answer.py?hl=en&answer=80472`.

YouTube Optimization

While there are many excellent video sites—Vimeo, Metacafe, and others, this section of the chapter will focus on YouTube because of its deep connections between search and social. YouTube is the world's second biggest search engine next to Google, is owned by Google, and is also one of the largest social networks for video in its own right. YouTube buzzes in real-time, and because of its relationship to Google, properly optimized and socialized videos rank well in Google web search and increase their visibility within the YouTube network. Optimizing for YouTube mirrors many standard optimization techniques discussed in Chapter 6, though it also incorporates many social signals. Developing trust and authority on a social and algorithmic level is also critical for success in YouTube. The following are among the many SEO and social factors that help determine visibility in YouTube and in the search engines:

- Text transcripts
- Number of subscribers
- Number of views
- Age of account or channel
- Quantity and quality of external links built into account channel and individual videos
- Number of likes and ratio of likes to dislikes
- Whether the asset has spam flags or not
- Number of embeds
- Quality and trust of site embedding the video
- Number of comments
- Number of favorites
- Tone of comments and video
- Theme and keyword area
- Number and theme of playlists

The implication for YouTube marketing success is that you need to grow your network of subscribers, promote your channel and videos, and produce highly engaging content.

When optimizing your YouTube videos and channels, here are some additional points for optimization:

- Use a keyword or keywords in the title.
- Use keywords in the description.
- Tag and categorize your videos.
- Add your URL to the beginning of your description.
- Create playlists.
- Fill out as much of your YouTube profile as possible.

Advanced Settings

When uploading videos, YouTube also offers an Advanced Settings tab for a number of key features. Here you can allow or disallow comments and voting and determine whether your videos can be syndicated to mobile phones and TV. You also have the option to turn off the embed feature if so desired, as shown in Figure 11.2.

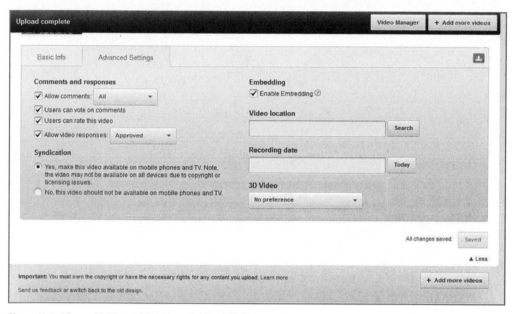

Figure 11.2 Advanced Settings tab for video uploading in YouTube

Other Considerations for Video Optimization

In addition to the specific optimization elements for hosted and nonhosted channels and assets, here are several other key considerations for video optimization:

Syndicating Videos on Various Sites vs. Focusing on Developing a Channel TubeMogul makes it very easy to send out your video to a wide number of video sites. This can be helpful when you want to increase the number of sites in the search results, but it can split your search and social audience among different providers. For most situations, consider focusing your efforts on either a hosted channel or a single channel to develop a deeper network and subscriber base.

Avoid Spammy Keywords *Viagra*, *free*, *webhosting*, *apply*, and calls to action can have a negative effect on your visibility because they are flagged as a potentially negative signal (because they are used so often by spammers). Even if your video is "free," it may benefit you to leave this word out of the title and other optimization elements.

Key Metrics Expand your thinking about the way you measure video results. Views, comments, engagement, and channel views per session are all ways to understand the value and reach of your video efforts.

Optimizing Video for Google News If you are a news provider, ensure that you are following the Google News optimization tips highlighted in Chapter 8, "Blogs, Google News, and Press Releases."

Using Live Video Live video is about as real-time as it gets, and many media providers are going the extra distance to incorporate live video into their overall social and hosted web presence. If live video fits your business model, check Ustream for live broadcasting and also Google+ hangouts for live meetings.

Interview with Greg Jarboe

To provide some added insight into video optimization, I interviewed Greg Jarboe, the president and cofounder of SEO-PR. In addition to being a pioneer in the digital public-relations field, he is the author of *YouTube and Video Marketing: An Hour a Day* (Wiley, 2011). Read more about Greg Jarboe's background in his Chapter 8 interview.

How much impact do social signals (comments, ratings, embeds, and so on) have on the visibility of video assets in Google search results?

Social signals—including likes, shares, embeds, comments, and video responses—all have a significant impact on the ranking of videos in Google search results.

What are some of the key considerations for video optimization in Bing?

The Bing-Facebook integration just went live. The new Bing search results haven't changed much. Social results are in a sidebar, so look there to see new considerations for video optimization in Bing. They are human, not technical.

What social signals does Bing look at to help rank videos?

When you search in the new social Bing, instead of showing videos that your friends have seen or liked, it highlights the people who you know who might have knowledge about the topic you're interested in. So, your outreach should focus on these key influencers.

How do you promote your videos internally on YouTube?

Respond to comments in the first few hours after you publish a video. And use TrueView ads to promote your videos internally on YouTube. With TrueView, you pick the audience you want your video to reach. Then you pay only when those viewers choose to watch your video.

What are some of the keys ways to promote YouTube videos outside of YouTube?

Embed your YouTube videos on your website. Announce them in your email newsletter. Share your content with relevant blogs, sites, and online communities. Reach out to other social media, especially Facebook, Twitter, and Google+. And promote your videos offline.

Interview with Greg Jarboe *(Continued)*

What are the three best ways to get other people to subscribe to your YouTube channels?

First, create great content that is unique, compelling, entertaining, or informative. Second, include specific calls to action in the video or through annotations. Third, set a recurring schedule for your channel and maximize how often you release content.

Do you recommend that your clients host their own videos, start a YouTube channel, or both?

For most clients, I recommend starting a YouTube channel and embedding their YouTube videos on their website. The exception is large media companies, which are able to monetize the video content on their website without sharing 50 percent of their ad revenue with YouTube.

Are there any special considerations for video-based keyword research?

Yes, people often use different search terms on Google than they do on YouTube. So, conduct keyword research using both the Google AdWords Keyword Tool and the YouTube Keyword Suggestion Tool to identify search terms that are used in both the largest and second-largest search engines.

What are your thoughts on using video site maps for hosted videos?

For large media companies that are hosting lots of their own videos, using a video site map is essential. For everyone else, you don't need to create a video site map to give Google information about your video content on YouTube.

Interview with Tarah Feinberg

In addition to serving as the head of the Live Media Studio at iCrossing, Tarah Feinberg is a veteran indie-film producer and strategist, having previously worked at HBO and helped found NBC Universal Digital Studio. He has created, developed, and overseen various video, interactive, and social engagements for brands including Purina, Lipton, Colgate, and AOL, and he blogs about video and social at www.tarah.me. In this interview, Tarah talks about success metrics, creating compelling and engaging video assets, and the biggest opportunities for marketers in video strategy.

How would you describe the importance of storytelling as part of online video strategy, and how can businesses make this work for them?

It is important for businesses to develop multiformat, multiplatform campaigns and ongoing content programs, but video stands out as a deeply influential, shareable, and attractive medium to engage audiences. Technological developments and the evolution of human behavior online have created opportunities to listen and react, informing more iterative storytelling through an ongoing cycle, rather than a finite, linear process. This allows us to continually improve, change, and optimize our brand story—our content and conversations—in real-time, as we monitor, learn, and define new insights. The result: the most contextually relevant and effective content possible, at any given moment.

(Continues)

Interview with Tarah Feinberg *(Continued)*

The opportunities for businesses to innovate and engage audiences, on an ongoing basis, are truly exciting. Some of the basic ideas include creating a series (not one-offs), connecting video themes to other marketing communications, and encouraging collaboration and creativity with your audience in the form of mash-ups.

What are some of the greatest untapped opportunities in online video?

Video is an extremely flexible and dynamic medium that can be used for a variety of purposes beyond passive entertainment. Most businesses that use video still approach it with a broadcasting mentality: we make things for you to watch. However, video can be immensely conversational and interactive. Some of the greatest opportunities include live streaming, gamification, featuring influencers and audience members, and crowd-sourcing.

What are some of the key metrics you consider in measuring the success of online video initiatives?

There are a number of metrics that can be measured for online video, but it is important to develop a focused and deliberate measurement strategy that aligns directly with the business objectives.

In general, I tend to prioritize metrics that demonstrate engagement and immersion in the content, such as percentage of the video that is viewed, comments, and shares. These indicate [the degree to which] viewers find the content valuable and are taking actions to interact and amplify. However, in certain cases, total views and other more passive metrics will be important, such as product launches and brand-building initiatives.

I find it helpful to categorize video (and often other categories) metrics by these overarching goals: community, content creation, awareness and reach, engagement, and advocacy. Within each of these, we can place available metrics, from which we can prioritize those that drive the desired business results. Community includes metrics such as the number of subscribers vs. unsubscribers, volume of viewers from a geographic area, and other demographic factors. For content creation, the number of uploads, velocity of uploads, and number of comments are factors. Awareness covers total views, unique views, and completion rate or percentage of the asset that was viewed. Comments can also be considered for engagement metrics, along with likes, +1s, favorites, and playlist additions. Finally, advocacy includes areas such as shares, embeds, and influence of advocates based on views and shares.

Image Optimization for Search and Social Channels

Images are one of the main content types shared around the Internet, in a wide variety of real-time and social content -management systems. Like most other asset types, images go live in social and search engines in seconds and are often quickly shared around topical events or breaking news. Most people carrying a mobile phone have a real-time camera capability, and apps like Twitpic (www.twitpic.com) and Instagram (www.instagram.com) make instantaneous image-sharing easy for the average user. In this section, you will learn about basic search and social elements of images, the key social networks for image hosting and sharing, and image optimization for both search and social networks.

The Search and Social Elements of Images

Like video, image assets serve as the sole focus for some vertical search engines, as well as the nucleus of several key social networks. Similar to web pages, images can be optimized for extended visibility in both search engines and social networks, and they require both digital-asset optimization and engagement optimization to increase the social signals that search engines look for. The main search and social elements of images include the following:

- Entire social communities are built around image assets and image distribution and sharing (Flickr, Twitpic, Instagram, and so on).

- Image sites can quickly index in engines like Bing and Google, and they appear in the top web-search results depending on the velocity of query interest and relation of the image to the topic.

- Images can refer a substantial amount of search traffic to your site and represent one of the most popular search verticals.

- Image visibility on the main web search-results page provides a more captivating listing and can grab more visibility over text-only results.

- Social interaction around an image or image channel can increase visibility within that channel or in search results (number of comments, views, and so on)—push into popularity streams, keyword streams, and so on.

Key Image Social Networks and Hosting Sites

Images can rank easily in search engines when they are hosted on your own website, but placing your images within a social community can greatly extend sharing and social visibility. As you expand your image strategy, consider the following networks for hosting and sharing your images:

Flickr One of the original social image communities, Flickr (www.flickr.com) is owned by Yahoo! and has a variety of features for sharing and conversing around your image content. Flickr is also a sort of image search engine, in the sense that images can be tagged and also searched by license type. Flickr will allow you to set your license type, including the Creative Commons license (see Chapter 12, "More Considerations for Real-Time Content Marketing, Search, and Social" for more information on Creative Commons). Images can be sorted by recency, interest, and relevance. Use higher resolution for your uploads, and Flickr will also pare them down for you. You can also start a group or network around a topic and use feed URLs for embedding on third-party sites.

Pinterest Though it first appeared in 2010, Pinterest (www.pinterest.com) has become all the rage for social image sharing on the Internet in 2012. Pinterest is a site for bookmarking and sharing images and can potentially provide a lot of traffic to your site.

Picasa Picasa (http://picasa.google.com) is Google's default image site, so when you get a Google account, you also have a Picasa account. Uploading images into your Google+ profile will also translate to a Picasa account.

Twitpic Twitpic (www.twitpic.com) is a popular vehicle for sharing real-time images on Twitter, and one of the most popular methods is by posting on a smartphone. A photo can go from your phone to your Twitter followers in seconds, making it one of the key image-distribution systems for real-time content marketers.

Instagram Instagram (www.instagram.com) is a highly popular real-time photo-sharing app and site with a wide audience. It was acquired by Facebook and should be a serious consideration for your image-sharing strategy.

Facebook Perhaps the most popular activity on Facebook (www.facebook.com) is sharing and commenting on visual assets. Publishing images on Facebook helps you build a substantial audience, because the audience is already there, though you have to earn your network of friends to get the images out there.

Google+ Like Facebook, Google+ (http://plus.google.com) is a highly visual medium, and it also has tens of millions of users at this writing, which is nothing to scoff at. Consider this network as a key distribution point for image sharing.

Photobucket Photobucket (www.photobucket.com) is another popular image service that also has commenting features enabled. Photobucket offers storage, filters, and editing tools, and it is used by a wide audience.

Optimization for Images

Images can be optimized just like any other text asset. Google and Facebook have rolled out technologies that can actually speak the object, place, person, or text included in an image. While Google may be using this technology to varying degrees in its results, images should still be optimized using standard search-engine-optimization best practices if you want the highest possible visibility for your image assets.

Google has suggested its own Google "Glass" may be released in the next year (www.wired.com/gadgetlab/2012/05/sergey-brin-finally-lets-someone-else-wear-google-glass/), and Google Goggles (www.google.com/mobile/goggles/) has the ability to read and provide search context to images you view in the physical world, in real-time. Facebook also has technology that will automatically identify faces in images uploaded to Facebook (http://blog.facebook.com/blog.php?post=467145887130) and will automatically tag them with the person's name and account if they are already a member. Overall, expect these technologies to "optimize" images on their own in the future, but remember that human optimization and social signals will always be a factor. With this in mind, pay close attention to the textual and keyword elements of the following aspects of optimizing your images:

Filename Including descriptive keywords in the filename can help an engine determine what the image is about.

Alt Text The alt text attribute allows for a text description of the image. It is important to describe this image exactly as it relates to the image, and it is generally acceptable to use six to ten words, or less if needed. For more information on writing alt text for images, see the section "Alt Text Attributes" in Chapter 6.

Text Description Surrounding Image Location When placed on a page, the descriptive text surrounding an image can be used by search engines to apply contextual information.

File Size Google prefers larg high-quality images and will cut down the size accordingly for search results.

Location of Image Files Keeping your images housed in a separate folder labeled as `images` serves as another signal to these assets.

Building Pages Around Images and Galleries Including images in blog posts and pages provides additional content to help rank your images and also these pages.

Geotagging Photos are becoming more and more relevant to location or the place that the image was taken. Many smartphones with cameras already apply GPS data to image metadata, and these photos can be plotted on a map. There are also GPS-enabled cameras that automatically geotag your pictures as you shoot them.

Social Signals All of the standard social-optimization elements for video apply to images as well. Commenting, liking, retweeting, linking, and sharing all create signals that both the engines and networks use to determine relevancy and visibility.

Inbound Links Linking both to the page or folder where an image is hosted and to the image can increase visibility in image search.

Interview with Michael Dorausch

Michael Dorausch is a chiropractor in California who gained some serious search and social chops through the process of marketing his own practice online. In addition to being a photographer, he is well-known in many SEO and social spaces as "chiropractic" (@chiropractic on Twitter) and is proficient at optimizing images for news sites in real-time. In this interview, Michael discusses real-time image optimization, keyword research for image optimization, and the benefits of real-time image marketing for businesses.

(Continues)

Interview with Michael Dorausch *(Continued)*

What three things do you recommend for a sound real-time image-optimization strategy?

The first thing I'd recommend is building up a large enough image archive that you can quickly go to when a particular photograph is needed. That might seem complicated or a lot of work, but having the correct image at the right time can pay off handsomely, since you won't have to scramble to get photos taken or waste time searching for images.

Also, choose your top keywords/key phrases and build a set of "go-to" images around those terms. It's better to prepare in advance whenever possible. Many events are predictable and recurring, and image optimization is far too important to be left as something to do as an afterthought.

Finally, it's important that optimized images grab the eye's attention when shown in small formats like 100×100 pixels, since this is the size most images will be when indexed by search engines. Crop images accordingly so that when they are resized, they still convey your intended message.

What types of businesses are suited to a real-time image-optimization strategy?

The most obvious businesses would be those that post news on a regular basis, but that could be summed up to include anyone posting content on a regular basis, which covers many business categories. Businesses that are already indexed by Google News are missing out on opportunities for increased traffic and awareness if they are not optimizing images. Whether a site is indexed or not shouldn't be the determining factor for real-time image optimization. Images are showing up in blended search and are appearing (oftentimes as thumbnails or resized images) across numerous social networks.

How do you perform keyword research for real-time image optimization?

Real-time image-optimization keyword research is somewhat similar to doing standard keyword research. I like to see what images are already appearing in search results for any given keyword or phrase. Using Google, I pick random categories of keywords and search to see what images blend best in search results.

Look at the image before clicking through; does it convey the message? If so, what is it about that image that attracted your attention? Make notes on what images stand out most and work to duplicate that approach for your own needs.

What benefits can a real-time time marketer expect to achieve from real-time image-asset optimization (from a traffic, awareness, link-building, trust, and ROI perspective)?

The benefits I've seen from image-asset optimization have been increases in traffic (sometimes quite significant increases in traffic), better brand awareness, improved trust, and an increase in external linking.

Quality optimized images tend to get shared more, which further increases sources of traffic and opportunities for building brand awareness, as well as an increased potential for inbound linking.

We are at the end of another chapter. As I mentioned in the first chapter, think about how images and video can best fit your business strategy. Many marketers write off the potential for a visual strategy because their business may be service-oriented or more abstract, and they don't think that visual applies. I have almost always found an application for video and image strategies for these types of marketers, for businesses as diverse as home services, B2B verticals, finance, and more. Do your research, and you just might find that a huge opportunity exists for you to seize. In the next chapter, I will cover a combination of things to consider for your real-time content strategy.

More Considerations for Real-Time Content Marketing, Search, and Social

12

By now I have covered strategy, tactical development, platform strategy, research strategy, and content development, among many other areas. This chapter will cover some of the additional important aspects of real-time content marketing and search and social that can be applied to various stages of this book as needed.

Chapter Contents

Social linking

Social bookmarking

Utilizing alerts as a real-time intelligence tool

Establishing Creative Commons licenses for content

Making your website come alive

Social Link Signals for Search Benefits

Links have long been a cornerstone for assessing the theme and authoritativeness for search-engine results. The new link frontier for search-conscious marketers is how to master the art of social link development, because the major search engines have declared that social links are increasingly becoming a critical signal in how digital assets are retrieved and ranked. To go even deeper with the concept of social signals, Copyblogger's Sean Jackson says that reciprocating in social spaces creates a natural effect that benefits both your search and social presence.

"One of the best ways to get social links from social-media influencers is to contribute to their efforts. Commenting on their blogs, providing a guest post, helping connect them with other influencers, and interviewing them are just a few ways to open a line of communication," he says. "Reciprocity is a very powerful motivator and by helping them, you, in turn, will find that they will want to help you."

It really does not matter whether you call this new concept of social signals *social link development*, *networked links*, *social linking*, or some other term you prefer. The bottom line is that there has been a shift in the way that search engines process network signals to help inform their search results. For this discussion, I have loosely chosen to refer to this concept as *social linking* in order to better illustrate the concept.

In a way, this entire book is about social linking. Whenever you publish or engage in social spaces, a trail of new links (and also pages) is created wherever the conversation goes. Your social footprint ultimately leaves signals for search engines to use as a potential beacon for relevancy.

I hope by now you have gathered that social signals are creating new links and that having a positive social presence creates positive search visibility. I've talked a lot about the ways that social creates links for search, so in this section I will also ping some of the smartest minds in search and social to weigh in with their thoughts and help provide a more collective view on what social linking really is.

This section will better explain how your social efforts are helping search visibility by creating social-linking signals for search engines. This section will also help search-engine marketers make a stronger case for integrating search and social efforts, especially because social has become integral to the bottom-line returns from the natural-search channel.

Good links come and go, and many social networks that were once the darlings of link-builders have fallen out of favor. Overall, the most sustainable approach to social link development is to create engaging content that people will want to link to and share in social spaces, without your having to ask or beg for a link.

There is a variety of links produced naturally in the major social networks (regardless of whether they are nofollowed). These include +1s, likes, retweets, shares, profile links, and networked links (top tweets, top shares in LinkedIn, and so on). Other link types include bookmarking sites, links mentioned in blog posts, links used in guest blog posts, enabling linkability by suggestion, and RSS subscriptions in Google feed readers.

I have spoken on a number of panels with noted search and social marketer Eric Enge, and he has kindly allowed me to use the chart in Table 12.1 that shows his analysis of the social signals that engines pick up in various networks (note that these change periodically because of permissions and deals for direct access).

▶ **Table 12.1** Key social actions, as captured by Google and Bing to inform their search algorithms

Social Signal	Bing	Google
Facebook Like/Recommend	Yes	Crawl-Based
Facebook Shared Link	Yes	No
Facebook Mention	Yes	Crawl-Based
Facebook Comments	Yes	Crawl-Based
Twitter Tweeted Link	Yes	Crawl-Based
Twitter Retweet Link	Yes	Crawl-Based
Twitter Mentions	Yes	Crawl-Based
+1	Crawl Based	Yes
Google+ Shared Link	Crawl Based	Yes
Google + Mention	Crawl Based	Yes

SOURCE: ERIC ENGE OF STONE TEMPLE CONSULTING (WWW.STONETEMPLE.COM)

Bing has direct access to Twitter and Facebook data at this writing, so they notably have exclusivity to the social signals in these networks, measuring velocity, trust, and link associations between users and shared content on this network. As a result, they leverage these signals to impact the Bing social search experience and inform results based on the actions of people in your network. In cases where Bing does not have direct access (for example, Google+ social data), the signals are gathered from crawled pages and by identifying the data structure.

Google obviously has direct access to Google+ social data and uses it to inform the Google search results for its users. In other cases, Google is blocked from seeing some social content in both Twitter and Facebook, where Bing has direct access.

More on How Social URL-Sharing Democratizes the Link Graph

In Chapter 2, "Understanding Search and Social," I covered how social media and networking has changed the way we link and the way we seek out links for greater search and social visibility. One of the key evolutionary aspects from a basic linking approach to a social linking approach is that the influencers in link and share graphs were traditionally more technically inclined than the average Internet user. In social, links can be created easily by novice users without using a File Transfer Protocol program or knowing any HTML. In short, a tweet, retweet, or share of a URL can provide some impact as a link.

By extension, a social linking approach also democratizes your approach to link-building and in the way that you naturally attract links and external signals. Before, you might have contacted a webmaster looking for a link citation, or you might have performed blogger outreach to get blog and link coverage. But in social-linking efforts, social sharing in status networks provides the same influence. It changes the approach, in the sense that you should be appealing to the tastes and interest of your audience so that your link is worthy enough to be shared by like-minded audiences. In this sense, your social-linking signals are directly proportional to the interest and engagement level of your content.

Interviews with Other Search and Social Experts on Social Link Development

As previously mentioned, this section on social linking includes several interviews with some of the top search and social marketers in the industry. As you read them, notice the similarities in the responses but also in the nuances of what they say. Overall, with this book and these interviews, you can start to gain a deeper sense and consensus on what social link development is really all about.

Interview with Eric Enge, President of Stone Temple Consulting

In this first interview, I talk with marketer Eric Enge about his approach to search and social, and he provides some valuable tips for readers. Eric is the owner of Stone Temple Consulting, speaks at many major marketing conferences, and is one of the coauthors of the book *The Art of SEO,* (O'Reilly Media, 2009).

"Social linking" is perceived in many different ways, by many different marketers. How do you define it?

There are two different types of meaning you could have when you talk about social linking. The most common meaning is the actual implementation of links on a social site; for example, including a link to an article in a Facebook update or tweet. This is a signal that search engines look at, and they do add value.

The other type of social linking relates to creating great relationships in the social media community by sharing great stuff, promoting the articles of others, interacting with them, and other social behaviors. The existence of these relationships makes it more likely that others will share and promote your content to their audiences. This often leads to people with blogs becoming aware of that content and linking to it in posts on their blog. This is one of the most powerful methods for getting truly organic links to your site.

You have stated in the past that your approach to social connections focuses a lot on offline and on influencers. How does this approach translate to link development and connectedness in the digital realm?

I am a big fan of influencer marketing. In a social environment, influencers can greatly amplify your message. If you tweet your own article on your own site and you have (using Twitter as an example) 10,000 followers, that's great. If it gets picked up by another influencer that has 100,000 followers and they tweet your content as well, that's even better. Participating in the community in a way that causes you to be noticed by influencers is one of the most impactful ways there is to create a great link campaign for your site.

Once you buy into this concept, you then start to think about what is involved in building those relationships. Nothing beats face-to-face interaction for doing that. That is where a willingness to include offline behavior can be very powerful. One way to get face-to-face with an influencer is to go to a conference they are speaking at and go up and introduce yourself.

Of course, that is not always possible, but the basic concept is that the most important relationships are worth more effort. The communications used in building those relationships should be as personalized as possible. To do that, see what they have published online and learn about their interests, and invest the time to see how you can add value to them. Once you have that mastered, your chances of success in building that relationship are greatly increased.

What is the impact of social links with nofollow attributes? If these links request that engines ignore them, how do they create a signal?

These are nofollowed, but they still add value. In general, people exaggerate the impact of nofollow. If Google or Bing perceives the link as a legitimate indicator of the content being valuable, they are going to associate value with it. The definition says that the person implementing the link is not endorsing the site it links to. So, the fact that Twitter, Facebook, and Google+ nofollow their links means that the social-media site does not endorse the content.

The author of the update or tweet, however, may well mean to endorse the content. The search engines can combine this with the "author authority" of the person writing the update or tweet and decide that it is meaningful and still value it.

Twitter applies nofollow attributes to all links, but in what ways do you believe that it provides linking value for search-engine visibility?

There are many possible ways, but here are two examples:

- Certain types of news become well-known on Twitter faster than anywhere else. The classic example is the Mexico City earthquake. CNN had it on its site three hours after it happened. It took the U.S. Geological Society one hour. Twitter had it in five minutes. Search engines cannot ignore this environment as a source of news.

- Identifying high-quality content. As mentioned in the answer to a prior question, if an authority on a topic tweets about a given article, that is a pretty good indicator that it is a pretty important piece of content.

(Continues)

Interview with Collin Cornwell, CollinCornwell.com

Collin Cornwell has led natural search and social strategies for many of the world's largest enterprise companies, and writes his own blog at `http://collincornwell.com`. He is a longtime time advocate of integrating search, social, and content and has continuously taken this approach with his ongoing client strategies. In this interview, he discusses the definition of social linking, effective approaches to social linking, and how to measure its effects.

Are social signals having an impact on the search visibility of your clients?

Social inclusion into the SERPS [search engine results page] is continuing to revamp the search user experience. If we're talking about social's impact on the core natural algorithms and the traditional SERPs, yes. But, primarily they are having a stronger impact on longer-tail queries that aren't very competitive. There is obviously a snowball effect that social can bring in the form of "traditional" links because they spread compelling content that builds off-site equity to a site over time.

How do you define "social linking"?

First you need to define what social is. This might include social bookmarking sites (Digg, Reddit, StumbleUpon, etc.); social platforms such as Twitter, Facebook, Google+, and Pinterest; and user-generated content such as product reviews, forums, etc. All of these are potential spaces for most SEOs [search-engine optimizers] to look for opportunities. Just because you can get links in these spaces doesn't mean you should. Contributing to existing conversations within social spaces may make sense, but only if you have something meaningful or useful to add. If that so happens to include links to targeted URLs, awesome. If that link is shared over and over again, even better. These same social spaces are great vehicles to help spread "new" content and to help spark buzz and conversations that eventually contribute to a client's link graph. Social linking needs to be defined on a per-client basis because some clients have more potential to engage in these spaces than others.

What are some of the most effective ways to build links socially?

Some of the most effective ways to build links via social spaces are to ensure that your social evangelists understand basic SEO [search-engine optimization] best practices, to ensure that everyone understands what URLs and keywords matter, and to ensure that both teams are marching toward the same or shared goals.

How do you measure social's impact on SEO efforts?

Most SEOs measure at the keyword level. To measure the impact that social may have on SEO, it's much easier to measure at the URL level. Measure how many likes, shares, tweets, +1s, etc., that individual URLs receive. I then trend those numbers at the URL level and the change in rank for targeted "head" or "torso" keywords. Marketers should also trend the number of keywords that drive natural search visits to those URLs and really should be doing this regardless of whether it is for search or social. Social signals tend to have more influence on longer-tail queries that you may not even be aware of. Once you start looking at traffic by URL, you can better understand the true impact of social.

It's also important to track the social spaces themselves. Most brands are looking to dominate the SERPs for branded queries, and optimizing a client's domain won't get you there. Keeping track of how your social spaces rank for brand is a no-brainer and does bring an increase in downstream traffic to the client's domain.

Interview with Lee Odden, CEO of TopRankMarketing.com

In my years of speaking at industry conferences on the topic of search and social, Lee Odden has always been there to blog about the conference circuit, in addition to being a noted speaker and author on the topic of search, social, and content. His long-running blog Online Marketing Blog (`www.toprankblog.com`) is also one of the leading blog resources for all things "search and social." In this interview I conducted with Lee, which was first published on Lee's Online Marketing Blog (`www.toprankblog.com/2012/07/social-media-links/`), he talks about his view on how search engines process social signals and how marketers can begin to approach this new cornerstone of search optimization.

How do you define "social linking"?

Social linking most often means using social-media channels to promote content that inspires social shares with links. A tweet, Facebook status update, or Pinterest pin that includes a link to the content being promoted are all examples of social links. Social shares with links = social links.

It's worth considering that social channels are also used to promote content to communities that include bloggers and journalists who may notice and link to the promoted source. Those are not social links per se, but they are inspired from content promoted through social channels.

The advancement of social media and SEO integration has created a shift from seeking links purely for the potential impact on better search visibility to a content-focused approach that emphasizes the impact that promoted and optimized content can have on attracting traffic directly. Social links achieved as a result of promoted content are an equal objective.

How do you define the key types of social links?

I think social links have different characteristics, so the definition depends on what you're after.

One marketer might look at links within social shares and discern value based on nofollow vs. those that pass PageRank because of a primary focus on traditional SEO. Another marketer might evaluate links based on how much traffic was sent in a particular timeframe, additional levels of shares of the link, and overall propagation because of a focus on awareness, branding, and reach.

(Continues)

Interviews with Other Search and Social Experts on Social Link Development *(Continued)*

Other basic social link characteristics or types might include the following:

- Content shared on social channels that includes a link (temporal and permanent)
- Links contained within feeds (RSS, fire hose, syndicated)
- Links contained on social-profile web pages
- Clean links that pass PageRank
- Nofollow or crawler-"unfriendly" links
- Shortened links/URLs

With so many social networks using the nofollow attribute, do you see any indirect search benefits from sharing in these networks?

The most important value from content promotion through social networks is to create awareness, interest, and consideration for people who interact with the information. People who are empowered to publish through blogging, commenting, or other social content-sharing may decide to act on content they've been exposed to through social channels in the form of a link to it.

It's completely up to the discretion of search engines to adhere to nofollow or not. Search-engine policies and terms of use are not something we can control, so approaching direct and indirect benefits from links within social channels should focus on the ability to affect a target audience first and foremost. Doing so in a search engine—friendly way can make that effort even more effective.

If nofollow social links are of little SEO value now, who's to say search engines won't value them in a different way that could become an SEO or social SEO asset in the future? If the links provide value to the influencers and followers we're trying to reach and they act on those links in a meaningful, measurable way, then the most important objective is achieved.

How much of an impact do you believe social linking is having on search-engine algorithms for non-logged-in and nonpersonalized users?

The links contained in the millions of social shares that happen on a regular basis are too rich (in my opinion) for search engines to ignore completely. If content resonates with a community and they actively share that content at an accelerated rate, I can't imagine why a search engine would not factor that signal for generic searches. It might not be a signal with substantial influence now for logged-out users, but I suspect it will grow proportionate to the growth of social-network usage.

It's important not to forget the ancillary impact of social shares with links that surface interesting content to people who decide to create "follow" links from their blogs, in comments or from other content sources that are outside of social networks. That's an example of social linking that can impact search, albeit indirectly.

Interviews with Other Search and Social Experts on Social Link Development *(Continued)*

How do you view the measurement of social links vs. traditional links?

Social shares with links are important for driving traffic and creating awareness of content. The extent that they can be a signal for generic search or logged-in search is a value too. The authority of authors who share the links, the rate and quantity of social shares, and the topics associated with source and destination are all worth considering when evaluating social links.

The reason why the link is created, the context, is as important as the distinction of social vs. traditional. A blogger might link to another web page or blog within an article that contains hundreds of words. A link within a tweet might involve only a handful of words. But that same link could be retweeted hundreds of times in a very short period of time. It's less likely that hundreds of bloggers would write blog posts including hundreds of words within a similarly short period of time.

The anchor text and page/domain authority of the source are important values for traditional links. The annotation (since there is no anchor text with a social link) and rate of link duplication/propagation are important values for a social link. I think there's still value to the cumulative number of social links, but not in the same way as traditional page-to-page links.

Is there an ROI on social linking, or should marketers approach it the same as link-building, in the sense that it is known to be a cornerstone for achieving higher visibility?

I would evaluate based on determining whether social linking is contributing to identified goals. Social linking purely for achieving higher search visibility is a narrow view and leaves a lot of value unrealized. Inspiring social shares of relevant and optimized content can drive direct traffic, produce additional waves of awareness, and provide longer-term benefits for visibility through search. New content discovery through social media often motivates a search. Brand awareness when searching can result in greater click-throughs in the SERPs, even if the position is beyond 1, 2, or 3.

Social Bookmarking

Social bookmarking sites have long been a cornerstone of the Internet. A social bookmarking site is essentially based on a network of users who collect content, share with others, comment, and tag or further identify it in some way. Bookmarking allows users to easily remember their favorite content but also enables the serendipitous process of discovering new and interesting content. In this sense, many social bookmarking sites have become known as *discovery engines*, leveraging the power of search and keyword principles, combined with social-network and community sensibilities. Social bookmarking sites represent a truly unique form of the interdependent search and social experience.

Tips and Considerations for Bookmarking Sites

While I have outlined some of the nuances of the top social bookmarking sites in the following pages, these tips are common to all sites mentioned in this section and can help guide your optimization and engagement strategies:

Enable Sharing and Building Your Networks by Adding Buttons to Your Content By now this should be a no-brainer, but it needs to be stated again. Every one of the major bookmarking sites has its own buttons for sharing, and this is a key spark for allowing and encouraging your content to spread through these networks. You don't have to place every button for every social network on your sites. Pick the sites that are right for you and your audience target, and display them prominently, as outlined in Chapter 10, "Technical Considerations and Implementation."

Create and/or Share Compelling Content Don't go into social bookmarking sites with the intention of gaming the system. The sustainable path for your business and content strategy is to produce incredible content and share content that will delight and satisfy others in your network. Every content item does not have to be a home run, but you should always be looking to your next big idea, because the competition is nothing short of fierce in many areas of business, news, and entertainment. Refer to Chapter 3 ("Ramping Up for a Real-Time Content Marketing Strategy") through Chapter 5 ("Content Strategy: Auditing, Assessment, and Planning") for more information.

Get Out and Participate in Each Network First Jumping in and promoting your own content on any network without first seeing how it works is a setup for disaster. Take time to learn how these sites work and how they complement your other Internet habits, such as email or web browsing. Whether it takes you days, weeks, or months to get comfortable, remember that understanding the user is key to knowing how your content will eventually become popular in bookmarking sites.

Observe the Written and Unwritten Rules of Each Community As stated in previous chapters, in every social community there are written and unwritten rules that need to be observed. When I say to potentially take months of observation in the previous point, I am not kidding. Spending the time to learn the community is appreciated by the audience and will make you more effective in your efforts. You might notice that while the rules say to "be courteous to your other community members," cliques have formed, and you could be shunned for making an otherwise-innocent mistake. If it sounds like a junior-high or high-school problem, it is to a certain degree. People sometimes do strange things when they are given a perceived cloak of anonymity and a social-media account, and you don't want yourself or your business to get caught up in a mess that could have been prevented by simply observing the rules.

Optimize Your Profile In most of the social networks, you have the opportunity to optimize your profile page. Make it count by adding an image if there is a spot for it, using keyword descriptive text, and filling out as much of the profile page as possible.

Don't Be Overly Salesy or Self-Promotional These are discovery networks for interesting and useful content, not sales channels. If you run a business that participates in a social network, you eventually expect some sort of positive business outcome. It would be an insult to your audience to say that your business doesn't want to make money. A little bit of promotion in terms of saying who you are, what you do, or what you are selling is a form of transparency. But when that is all you have to say, it is *highly annoying* to your audience. Observe both the written and unwritten rules for every network in which you participate, because each may have some tolerance for businesses *or no tolerance at all*. Evaluate and participate accordingly.

Use the Toolbars Many of these sites use toolbars to encourage sharing and participation as content is consumed across the Web. Download these toolbars for yourself to better understand the user experience for each bookmarking site and also to help your own experience as a member of these sites.

Remember That Bookmarking Sites Attract Backlinks to Your Content by Osmosis The more visibility that your content gets, the more likely it will be linked to and absorbed by bloggers and other social content–creators who create a variety of social signals. Don't expect direct backlink juice from these sites, because they are all nofollowed. The repetition of creating a *high quantity* of *high-quality* content assets over time will naturally attract many of the backlinks and social signals that you need to help build your link graph, social graph, and share graph.

Also, remember that keyword research is critical. Keywords are connections to people, so keep your primary keyword lists handy, and describe content in a relevant way so that other audiences can find it in the way that they seek it out and would describe it themselves.

Delicious

Delicious (www.delicious.com) is one of the early social-bookmarking communities. Users tag and identify content at the keyword level and can subscribe to individual keyword RSS feeds to read new compelling content surfaced by the community.

There was a time when Delicious was all the rage for search-engine optimizers, because creating and tagging content would help create additional visibility in Google. But because it was overly gamed, this visibility waned over time. This is something of a continuous cycle in the sense that once people go around bragging about their new SEO trick, the engines go back and dial those communities down in the search results. The end goal here is not to get pages and links from Delicious but rather to increase the visibility of your content to like-minded audiences in the networks, using basic search principles. Figure 12.1 shows the most recent results for the tag *socialsearch* in Delicious.

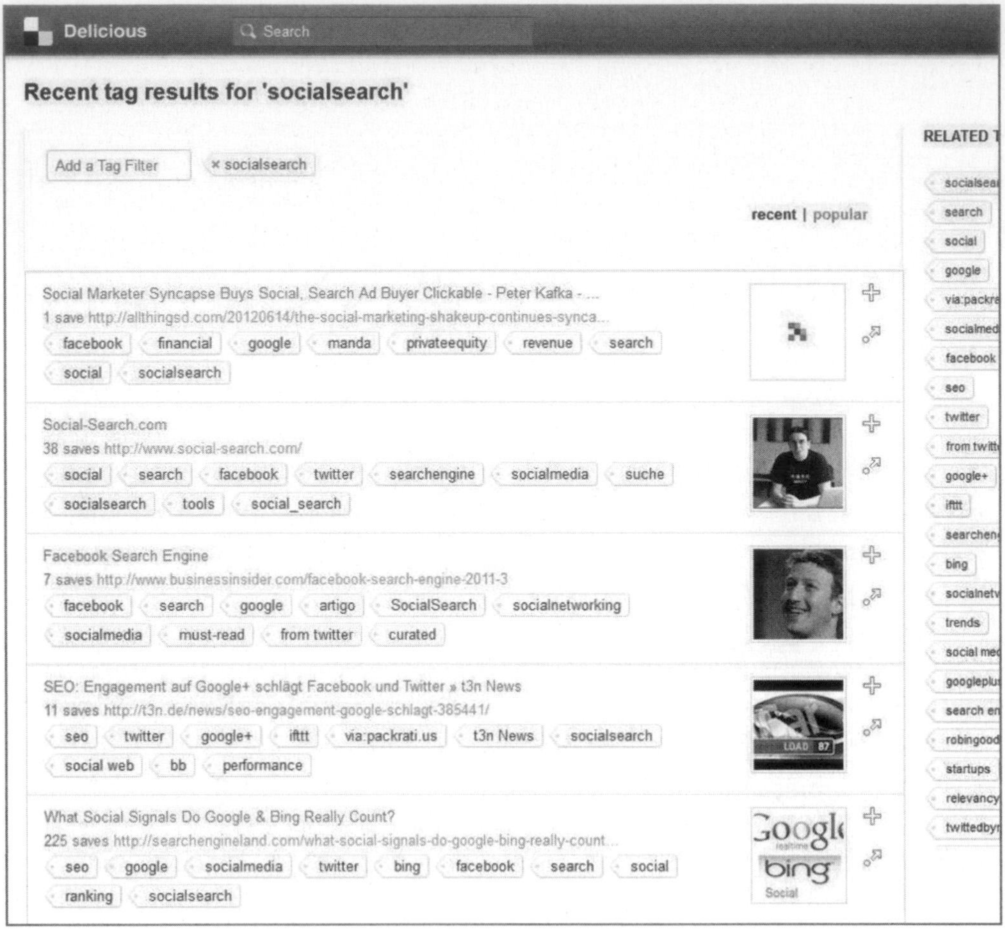

Figure 12.1 Delicious tag search results, sorted by recency

Pinterest

Though it began in 2010, January 2012 was the time that Pinterest exploded in popularity. Pinterest is an image-bookmarking site that has previously skewed toward a female demographic but is quickly gaining an extended audience of men, marketers, and businesses. Like other bookmarking sites, Pinterest is a great way to provide excellent visibility for your content and website assets.

Flickr has implemented a quick and easy way for image owners to set usage rights and to quickly pin images to Pinterest. This is a great way to drive traffic to your Flickr account, increase your footprint in image circles, and have greater control over the rights to specific images and how you would like them to be used. Check out Flickr at www.flickr.com, and go to www.pinterest.com to learn more. Also, see Chapter 11, "Video and Images," for more information on image optimization for search and social.

Reddit

Also in the category of link submission, bookmarking, and discussion is Reddit (`www.reddit.com`). Reddit is a community that shares links to interesting content and asset types and is sortable by recency (newest), rising popularity, category, controversial, and saved. Like in Digg, shares and comments in Reddit build a social conversation around the content.

Like the other sites in this section, Reddit is a great place to research new content ideas that resonate, or hot topics. Don't plan on doing any business here, but if you have content that fits the profile of the site and is also used by your own audience, and reaches an audience that can help propel visibility to other channels, enable sharing buttons for this site on your own content.

Digg

Digg (`www.digg.com`) of is one of the earliest bookmarking and social news sites, and though its traffic has come down from its peak in years past, it still serves as a useful place for many people to consume and find new content. As mentioned in Chapter 8, "Blogs, Google News, and Press Releases," I have had some of my own content go to the first page of Digg, and the subsequent cascade of backlinks, traffic, and new pages created was phenomenal. Digg also has a close-knit community of voters, so key influencers can help push your content over the top.

One of the main elements of getting to the front page of Digg is being able to identify the rising velocity of votes for your content. Stories on Digg go to the home page based on popularity within a given timeframe, so your real opportunity to gain front-page exposure is within 24 hours from the first Digg. Figure 12.2 shows the home page of Digg, featuring the day's most popularly voted social news headlines.

StumbleUpon

StumbleUpon (`www.stumbleupon.com`) is a network of site and content recommendations based on personal preferences, demographic data, and community voting. Many marketers have received massive amounts of traffic coming from StumbleUpon for their catchiest content, with some reporting that StumbleUpon traffic often exceeds Google and other major social networks combined for their period of high visibility.

To get involved in StumbleUpon, sign up and then begin to immerse yourself in the experience of what it is like to discover new content and also to bookmark or "stumble" new content as a user. The point for doing so is not to game StumbleUpon but rather to get inside the mind of the user who shares content and the mind of the user who discovers content.

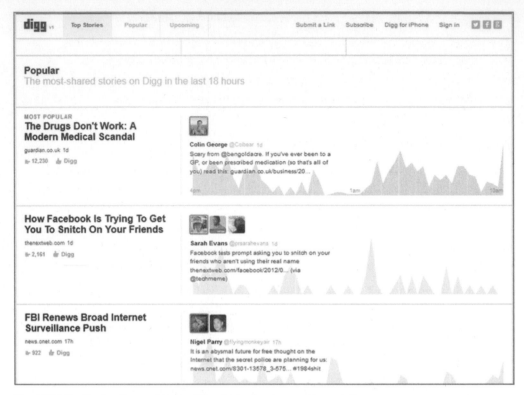

Figure 12.2 Top Digg headlines, as determined by social signals and community popularity.

You will quickly learn that StumbleUpon is popular because it surfaces amazing content that you may have never found otherwise. One of the biggest benefits of StumbleUpon to publishers is that it also offers numerous examples of highly engaging content that should inspire and inform your own content strategies. Study what resonates well in StumbleUpon at the category level, and you will quickly see what it takes to compete, in terms of quality, asset type, tone, and approach.

Simply put, your content efforts need to be unique and brilliant to perform well. This may sound hard for some publishers, but the bottom line is that the rewards are directly proportional to the quality of your content.

Here are a few other key tips and considerations for developing content that resonates in StumbleUpon:

- Use the StumbleUpon short-URL service at `http://su.pr`.

- Download the StumbleUpon toolbar to understand what makes people "stumble."

- Don't recommend your own pages; focus on content creation.
- Enable people to stumble your digital assets by enabling share buttons.
- Create compelling content. Really good content. *Brilliant content.*
- Build up your StumbleUpon network by connecting with others, and encourage follows by placing network buttons on your own content.

How to Set Up and Utilize Alerts

Search-engine alert systems developed as one of the first bona fide *real-time* search engines. Alerts render through a reverse search-engine retrieval process, in the sense that the keyword is first initiated by the recipient via subscription, and the result then appears only when the Web is subsequently crawled and a new match is found by the engine. Search is, of course, not the only form of alert, and there are different ways of configuring social alerts as well, which will be discussed at the end of this section.

How to Use Alerts for Your Real-Time Search and Social Strategy

Alerts can be used in a variety of ways to help you with strategy, planning, and every-day management of your digital presence. Here are some of the key ways that you can use alerts to help inform your digital strategy:

- Getting fast updates on the latest news on hot topics
- Identifying new content ideas
- Receiving real-time alerts for competitive research
- Monitoring brand keywords in real-time
- Monitoring your personal name in a timely frame of recency
- Monitoring buzz about your company
- Identifying potential reputation-management issues
- Identifying hot questions and conversations to be addressed by social-media managers in various social spaces

Google Alerts

Google Alerts (www.google.com/alerts) has long been one of the leaders in real-time alerts services. Over the years, Google's results were adjusted from as recent as an hour to a "last-minute" version. One of the options to receive your alerts is "as it happens," which is close to real-time, though the actual amount of time to receive these alerts is more often within 10 to 20 minutes after it happens. Here are a few key considerations for setting up Google Alerts:

Get Alerts via RSS Feed One of my favorite ways to use alerts is through RSS feeds. Set your alerts and configure your feed in an RSS reader, and you can monitor multiple feeds in real-time.

Note That the Maximum Number of Alerts Allowed Is 1,000 The maximum number of alerts at this writing is 1,000, and that is more than enough for most businesses or individual social-media managers.

Use Advanced Search Operators in Your Alert Using advanced operators helps you hone in on the info you are looking for. Essentially, you can use many of the search operators available in a standard Google search, so don't forget helpful searches for *site:*, *intitle*, *filetype*, and so on. Check out http://support.google.com/websearch/bin/answer .py?hl=en&answer=136861 for a full list of advanced Google search operators.

Yahoo! Alerts

Yahoo! (http://alerts.yahoo.com) is another long-term player in alert services and provides a nice variety of alerts at both the keyword and category levels. It offers specific alerts for breaking news, health news, snowfall, sports, stocks, airfares, and weather, among others. With its legacy in search technology, Yahoo! also offers robust keyword-level subscriptions. Yahoo! sends alerts to your email address or via instant message, pager, or SMS. The maximum number of alerts is 100, batched as "daily delivery" or "immediate delivery," depending on how you prefer to monitor them.

Social Alerts Using Email and Private-Message Systems

Of course, many other types of alert systems are available in forums, blogs, and social networks. If you already use these networks, then you know most rely on email to update you with the latest changes or interactions. While it sounds like common sense (and it is), marketers do not always take advantage of the advanced alerts features of various networks and forums.

Email alerts can get overwhelming if you interact on a number of networks, forums, and blogs. Prioritization is key. When monitoring alerts via email, focus on the most important conversations, such as a thread you may have started or responses to questions you may have posted.

How to Make Your Website Come Alive

As the Web has become more synaptic and real-time, audiences have come to expect publishers to present their content in a real-time mode, in a way that is as easy to share as it is to find. But building and maintaining a web presence is not an easy task. While the monetary costs range from very low to very high, the time-resource costs often preclude many marketers from updating their sites in a way that keeps up with escalating audience expectations.

Making your site come alive doesn't mean that everything has to flash or blink; rather, it should show that you are producing content on a timely basis and that you have a fresh presence, based on what is happening now rather than what has happened during the history of your entire business. The difference is trying to make your site presence be more alive like TMZ, rather than, say, an old dusty library. As mentioned throughout the entire book, the biggest difference is highlighting that you are active and participatory. So, the next time you go to design or redesign your web presence, consider the following elements for making your site have a live feel for your content:

Push Feeds into Site Navigation Add RSS or XML feeds of updated data into the side, top, or bottom navigation pane of your site. Focus on data or content that is updated periodically so your regular site visitors can expect something new and fresh every time they come back to your site.

Take a Modular Approach to Design Undergoing a customized website design or redesign is a major undertaking and can take months or even two or more years to complete. Because the Web is changing so quickly, consider a modular approach to design that allows you to update parts of the page or architecture without having to overhaul the site. Make it easy to enable feeds, update news, or add video or image objects. Overall, taking a modular approach means not locking down your site so tightly that it can't be easily updated to roll with the constant changes in online marketing.

Pull Your Social Feeds into Site Elements Utilize your external social feeds with status updates in your own site presence. If you are tweeting or updating your status regularly, a social feed shows your site users that you are active in social spaces and creates extended visibility for engagement with your audience.

Create Live-Data Apps for the Web Any type of data that is updated with some frequency or is relevant to a timeframe (last hour, last day, last week, and so on) can potentially make an interesting application or interesting reason for a user to come back to your site on a regular basis. Pricing updates, added inventory, weather updates, news, and other data can be mashed up in a variety of ways that interest your audience.

Enable a Live-Chat System As long as you have a human behind the chat screen who is able to respond quickly, live chat is a great way to give your web presence an in-the-moment feel. Chat works for a wide variety of roles within a business, including social-media managers, customer-support representatives, content curators, and researchers, who can all help your site visitors solve a problem or answer their most frequent questions.

Promote Your Phone Number, and Be There to Answer It Making it easy for someone to pick up the phone lets your audience know that someone is right there with them on the other side of the screen. If your site or business is set up with phone support as a primary part of your business, then promote your phone number visibly throughout your site.

Push Analytics, Stats, and Other Quantifiable Data onto Your Pages (Share Data, Following Data) Consider publishing your statistical and analytics data live to your pages and site. Discussion forums are prime examples of real-time content communities that use this data to their advantage, showing who is currently online, how many members have signed up, the total number of comments and threads, and the number of page views for each thread.

Many share buttons will also display the number of social interactions that have occurred around a particular asset and give your pages more of a live feel, or at least serve as an indicator of the amount of social activity going on.

Implement Video and Audio Assets Video and audio assets are a great way to put your website in motion and offer a more active approach to content. Embed video and audio feeds into pages from external sources, or create your own video or audio sections of your site.

Update Your Site to Show Most Recent, Shared, or Emailed Content If you are an active content creator and publisher, then you will likely always have something new cooking or ready for release. Make your new and popular content highly visible by featuring it in the navigation, front page, or an RSS feed from your site. "Most recent" content might include latest news, latest articles, newest video, last product additions or featured products, and latest sale items, among other types. "Most shared" or "Most emailed" would feature these content types as well.

Create an Active News Section News is a staple of real-time content, and providing a newsfeed with your own reporting or from other sites can give your site a livelier feel and add a fresher recency timeframe to your site.

Utilize Asynchronous JavaScript and XML for Real-Time Updates (Ajax) Website experiences are slowly evolving from "pull" experiences (the user searches a database or visits a site) to more "push" scenarios (data is pushed out live as it is updated, without reloading the page). Fundamentally, it represents a shift from page-based websites to *pageless* experiences or Internet applications. Ajax combines JavaScript and XML to update on-page data without reloading the page. Consider the existing use cases for your website and how current forms of data pulls could be updated for push instead. Be careful with how you implement Ajax for both users and search engines—*rich Internet applications* (RIAs) can greatly inhibit your search presence if they are not designed and implemented correctly.

Create a Blog If your website serves as library of information, then add a blog to give it a livelier feel. Talk about how to use your site, call out interesting info, cover news and topical events, or put a new spin on some of your older content.

Using the Creative Commons License to Distribute Your Digital Assets

One of the best ways to distribute your content assets in search and social spaces is to give it away for free and let your audience and communities do the distribution for you. As part of the "you give and you get" principle, creating and distributing assets for others to use without copyright restriction is a great way to earn goodwill from your audience and spread your message and moniker in the process.

Free content and free sharing are among the foundations—if not *the foundation*—of the open Internet. Pioneers in open source like Richard Stallman and Larry

Lessig have paved the way for the Internet as we know it through the sharing and propagation of free software and other digital assets. The playing field for both individuals and large enterprises has been leveled in this sense.

For content creators, the Creative Commons license (www.creativecommons.org) offers a method of open-source distribution for your own content. Once you have created your own content (images, video, text, and so on), you can assign it to a type of license for open distribution. This means that once you have established a Creative Commons license for your content, you have granted open use of your content for distribution. Specific limitations can be set to include use for different types of business or nonbusiness purposes, with or without attribution.

Content under the Creative Commons license will often end up in search engines and social spaces and be used as supporting content for blogs, applications, databases, and even entire sites dedicated to mashing up different types of open-source content. One of the most popular sites under the Creative Commons license is Wikipedia. I have even used image assets in this book under the Creative Commons license, with proper attribution and follow-up to verify the origin of the source.

One example of a marketer who used a limited Creative Commons license to impact their business is the Arkenstone, a fine-mineral gallery owned by Dr. Rob Lavinsky. Dr. Lavinsky has achieved massive visibility online and offline in the area of fine-mineral collecting and geology, and he credits his donation of more than 60,000 images to the Wikimedia Commons repository as one of the key reasons for his success. These images are used as reference all around the Internet on the topic of mineral collecting and study, including in many Wikipedia entries, and Dr. Lavinsky's name and business are attributed directly in many of these images. He financed production of the images himself and just gave them all away for limited free use for educational purposes, though by permission only. Simply put, you can't buy the type of visibility he has gained from the social distribution of his images. It can only be earned.

Dr. Lavinsky cautions that maintaining an archive under the Creative Commons license still requires some maintenance. "While the images are free to use under some restrictions, I have to police how they are used," he says. "I am currently dealing with a company that copied a large number of my images and is selling them on a stock-photo site. My license does not allow for this kind of use, so it takes up time and resources to get them removed and to make sure that the photos are not being misused in other ways. But overall, the image archive has been well worth my time and effort, in terms of the impact it has had on my business."

Dr. Lavinsky also incorporated a community element for sharing his images through a partnership with Mindat.org, a popular community and database for mineral study, and utilized this "niche" social-media network to help expand his audience.

Since Dr. Lavinsky came online as one of the first mineral dealers on the Internet, he has gained a reputation as one of the top authorities in his field, supplying institutions such as the Smithsonian, the Mineralogical Museum at Harvard, and the American Gallery of Natural Sciences, as well as many other thousands of collectors worldwide. He is also widely regarded as an Internet pioneer in the mineral field for having expanded interest in collecting through the Internet since 1996.

The archive has landed his images and citations in many offline publications and books as well, including a Bolivian geology textbook and many scientific reports and journals. Figure 12.3 shows a photo of the January 2011 issue of *Rock & Gem* magazine, a popular magazine for rock and mineral collectors. The gold-nugget photo on the cover was taken from Dr. Lavinsky's archive and used by *Rock & Gem* magazine under the Creative Commons license, with a citation provided back to the Arkenstone. It certainly doesn't hurt that the Arkenstone's images often feature highly intriguing subjects. This gold nugget weighs 51 pounds (23.1 kilograms), and according to Dr. Lavinsky it is the largest gold nugget in private hands.

Figure 12.3 Dr. Rob Lavinsky's Wikimedia Commons image of a 51-pound gold nugget, featured on the cover of *Rock & Gem*

Read more about the Creative Commons license at www.creativecommons.org. Also learn more about the Wikimedia Commons at http://commons.wikimedia.org/wiki/Main_Page.

Email as a Real-Time Marketing Function

Though this book has largely focused on search, social, and web publishing, email marketing still remains the original and fundamental form of online marketing, and parts of it have always been "social" and "real-time," even by today's definitions. If you think about it, most of the largest social networks were built on email. LinkedIn grows its network by automating connection requests through your personal email lists, as would other networks. Twitter and Facebook still send email updates based on your latest social activity, in real-time. In the earliest days of the Internet, email discussion groups were among the most popular forms of real-time and social discussion.

Email is also a critical part of your content and outreach strategy in terms of sending automated responses, status updates, one-to-one outreach, or other types of information updates. Of course, you need user permission to send this kind of communication, but no matter what real-time strategy you take, always consider how you can use email to its fullest potential within every approach.

Now that I have covered this laundry list of important search and social topics, it's time to get more focused on the engagement aspects of real-time content marketing again. So, in the next chapter I'll move along to social-media management and what it means for your search and content-marketing strategy.

Social Media
Management

Hundreds of books have been written on social media engagement, but very few illustrate the dynamic interdependencies between search and social efforts in any great detail. So, in this chapter I am going to show you how to think about social media management in terms of its holistic impact on your content marketing and SEO programs, emphasizing a real-time approach.

13

Chapter Contents

Social interactions help your search efforts in many other ways. Building up your networks provides distribution and signals for SEO. Making friends and interacting with fans and followers show appreciation and that you are present. Being "real-time" doesn't mean you have to panic or scramble to become active. It just means that your company is present and active in the places where your audience is active, too. Remember that recency is the new relevancy, and being present and alive in your social presence provides an automatic advantage in search-engine and social-network visibility.

Considerations for Integrated Search, Social, and Real-Time Content Strategy

I have created this chapter to focus on some of the specific nuances of social with a search frame of mind. But please keep in mind that this entire book is about a new synthesized approach to social-media engagement that incorporates the elements of SEO, content marketing, and an "always-on" presence. Before we get into the multiple new implications of real-time content marketing on social media, let's explore the somewhat new concept of social keyword research to keep top of mind as you proceed throughout the remainder of this chapter.

Keywords Are Connections to People

You may have noticed that I have referenced the phrase in this heading many times throughout the book. I encourage you to make it your mantra for thinking about search and social strategy and to consider this as one of the "simple truths" of search and social, though it is one that many marketers have yet to understand in a meaningful way, let alone embrace. Recalling the "natural language" discussion in Chapter 2, "Understanding Search and Social," and the "conversational demand" discussion in Chapter 5, "Content Strategy: Auditing, Assessment, and Planning," taking a social view of keyword research helps you extend your communications to audiences by shared language and listen to your audience in their own language. TweetDeck, Twitter hash tags, Radian6, or other popular social programs use *keywords* or other *language triggers* to identify audiences, topic, sentiment, and conversation. The methods of traditional search-based keyword research apply but often for a shorter frame of recency and for a conversational purpose or *even paid media* purpose. No matter how you try to divide it, the role of social media manager relies on the use of shared language. Within this shared language there are common triggers, and within these triggers there is keyword and linguistic research to be done.

Keyword research is largely perceived by the social-media marketing community to be a "search thing," but this is far from the truth. I would posit that keyword skills are one of the things that separate the *great* social marketers from just the *good* ones. It is up to you to determine which kind of social media manager you want to be. Read the following sections for a deeper dive into how to think about keywords and natural language to better connect with your audience through content and conversation.

Specific Considerations for Your Real-Time Social Content Approach

In consideration of social engagement and its interdependence on search, and vice versa, here is a recap of some of the major themes interspersed throughout this book for you to apply to your social media management strategy and tactical execution:

Be Strategic, and Answer the Question of "Why?" As a rule of thumb, always ask the question of "why?" when setting your engagement strategy. Make your purpose known to your teams from the very beginning of planning and execution.

Embrace the Natural Language of Your Audience Your audience talks in a natural way, and you should as well. Embracing the natural language of your audience allows you to connect at a deeper level and engage them as part of your brand conversation. Embracing language enables the spirit of the audience to become part of your brand and voice and helps balance your business identity toward your audience. As discussed in Chapter 1, "Real-Time Publishing and Marketing," it also helps fulfill your obligation to listen to your data and act upon.

Work Within Your Primary Publishing Platform, but Also Monitor "Transient" Conversations Publish and converse on your primary networks, such as Facebook, Twitter, and other niche networks of your choosing, but also monitor and engage "one-off" conversations as required on smaller forums, comments of blogs, and other user-generated content communities. The sum of those smaller conversations can often exceed that of the larger networks, and your consideration shows that you and your business value your audience no matter where they may congregate.

Consider the Real-Time User Experience and Your Role Remember that a major part of engaging in off-site conversation is that you are identifying a problem, question, or conversation opportunity. Don't make the assumption that your audience will come straight to your blog or website and that you control the experience. Find the people who seek answers outside of your bubble, and take the experience to them, in real-time. Use the tools listed in Chapters 4, "Market Research and Content Types," and 5, and use search skills to reach your audience in spaces outside of your blog or web presence. This isn't a new concept either, as it was first suggested by Regis McKenna back in 1995.

Remember That Every Social Interaction Leaves a Digital Trail and Is a New Type of Publishing Likes, votes, shares, views, and comments all leave a digital trail. These actions leave a digital record in the form of a linked connection or a page of information. These connections are linked to your profiles in many cases and constitute a digital record that is used to calculate the visibility of digital assets in both search and social channels. As discussed in Chapter 1, marketers must re-examine the definition of "publishing," and gaining a sense of your digital trail will bring your strategy into the modern publishing era.

Know Which Social Signals Drive Search As an active real-time publisher, your social footprint creates signals that result in deeper exposure in both search engines and social networks. Know how your social media management efforts impact search visibility, as they have been outlined throughout the book. Remember that searchers are people too, and your social efforts help to extend your message into search areas where people are also seeking out information and intelligence.

Know the Keyword and SEO Tactics That Help Improve Your Effectiveness in Social Channels As stated at the beginning of this chapter, keywords are not just an SEO tactic—they are connections to people in social channels. Having good search chops can also help you find deep conversations in social, as well as new networks and audiences. Having clean SEO and tech hygiene on your own blog and website also help your content reach other people via automated processes, such as social sharing and search crawling, indexing, and retrieval.

Enable the Spirit of Your Audience into Publishing Efforts Listen to your audience to inform your content strategy. Know where your audience congregates and join the conversation. If necessary, hire the authentic voices to join your company and engage on your behalf (in a transparent way). As previously mentioned, simply embracing the natural language of your audience in search and social spaces is a key method of enabling the spirit of your audience.

Be Authentic This is a form of enabling the spirit of your audience and communicates that you are listening and understand what they want to hear from you.

Strive for Consistency It is not always possible to be consistent in all channels because of different ways of speaking and different usability and creative approaches. But make it a priority to be as consistent as possible with visuals, voice, and tone, as it fits each individual social space.

Empower Your Internal Networks Remember that your key influencers aren't just outside your company—they are inside as well. Find your key social users and company advocates and make them part of your strategy.

Use Your Tools and Use Your Brain There are plenty of tools for social media management, but your brain is still the best tool. Use common sense, know the written and unwritten rules, and treat your audience as they would like to be treated.

Apply Informed Keyword Research to Your Daily Social Media Management Strategy Because keywords are connections to people and content, pay close attention to the keyword language that your audience is using. The language of your audience is a *living* concept, and being present will help you stay on top of current trends. This may include emerging trends, slang, or even the news in your area of business.

Remember That You Are Part of a Shared Conversation About Your Company Engaging in social spaces is a two-way street. You will be able to speak on behalf of your company, but respect the fact that there may be a separate conversation about how your audience perceives your brand or business. Your online presence is a reflection of your company itself. You don't *own* this conversation, you can't *buy* it, though you may be able to *earn* the right to have the conversation. Your business is part of a *shared* conversation, and always will be.

Make It an Obligation to Study Your Data Don't wait six months to a year to find out what your audience is doing and thinking. Instead, make analytics a regular part of your approach to help influence your iterative and ongoing strategy. Social media managers and strategists have access to analytics logins so they will know what is going on with your site, from a macro to a micro level. For more info on what your "obligation to data" means, refer back to Chapter 1.

Engage One Bird to Attract Whole Flocks Engaging with your audience and key influencers can help extend your messaging and communications from one-to-one, to one-to-many, to *many-to-many* when those influencers share and converse.

Give a Lot, and You Get Back a Lot Most businesses are competing with "free" in some way, so one of the best ways to give is with your time, content, and digital assets. To quote Copyblogger's Brian Clark again, "If you feel like you are giving too much, *then you are on the right track*." It works for businesses of all sizes.

Encourage and Demonstrate Trustworthiness with Your Audience and with Search Engines Trust is a social thing and a search thing, too. Build trust with your audience, but also build trust with search engines by policing spam, providing good content, and keeping good SEO hygiene with your digital assets. You need this trust to resonate with velocity and in real-time across networks and search engines.

Find Conversational Demand in Social Spaces Study in-the-moment conversations to discover the evolving and living language and triggers of your audience. Use this language to engage with your audience and inform your content strategy. Conversational demand is findable by keyword triggers and by human review.

Take a Factual Approach to Social You don't have to address a crisis to be active in social spaces or let the PR elements of social become a showstopper for social content marketing. Consider the real-time user experience and those people who may not go to your site for the information that is already there. If your site content is compelling enough for someone to want to read it on your site, then there is likely topical interest outside of the site in social spaces.

Listen to Your Audience Get feedback to inform future and current content—inform your business approach, inform your products and services; share accordingly with the right people in your organization.

Remember That Marketers, Brands, and Business Owners Are Now Publishers If you publish a website or in social spaces, you are now a publisher. If you have a website, blog, or social presence, then you are publishing. It can be done very well or poorly. The choice is up to the business owner.

Remember That the Share Graph Is the Social Marketer's Parallel to the Link Graph in SEO Creating content that is interesting, engaging, and shareable will create more social signals for search engines and help extend your visibility in both search and social spaces. The share graph emphasizes relevant segments of sharing throughout the social graph, in a many-to-many method of distribution. As demonstrated in Chapter 2 with RadiumOne's complementary explanation of the share graph, this concept is very deep, and expands beyond search signals into interest segmentation, theme segmentation, network segmentation, common keyword triggers within a network, and ad targeting, among many other applications.

Know That "Recency" Is the New "Relevancy" Live participation brings a sense of immediacy to your online marketing efforts. Recency is a factor in both search and social, so being participatory makes a huge difference to your audience, which is already engaged in a synaptic way. In social streams and current search streams, *being there* in the form of fluid publishing, real-time research, and live presence is the best way to capitalize on this element.

Understand the *Velocity* of Content Distribution and How to Make It Work for You Simply *being present* will help you know when your content is on an upward velocity trend and will allow you to further promote and send your content over the top in terms of sharing and traffic. Being present will also put you in the right place to identify trending content opportunities as they happen in order to react quickly enough to take advantage of a fast-moving topic. Refer to Chapter 2 to read more about content velocity in search and social spaces.

Understand Passive and Active Distribution Flows Your networks are passive (one-to-many) until the sharing of your direct subscribers and followers becomes active, meaning that your followers and subscribers share with their networks based on how interesting the content is (many-to-many). Refer to Chapter 2 for more information on passive and active distribution flows.

Don't Forget That Smaller Social Spaces Can Often Have a Bigger Impact on Your Business than the Facebooks and Twitters of the World While the major networks should be a key part of most social-media strategies, I believe that there is a highly disproportionate amount of attention focused on Facebook and Twitter, compared to other great opportunities in smaller communities. Find the niche networks and discussion forums that are applicable to your business, and you may discover an untapped gold mine. For a great case study on how a business literally tapped into a huge gold mine on a niche social space for geologists and mineral collectors called Mindat.org, see the Creative Commons discussion in Chapter 12, " More Considerations for Real-Time Content Marketing, Search, and Social."

Know That Your Social Interactions Will Have an Impact on Your Search Visibility to Some Degree, Whether You Foster That Intentionally or Not Social interactions have an impact on SEO visibility, and this fact can no longer be ignored by social marketers or SEOs. How you engage in social now has a correlation to search results and will continue to increase in influence for the foreseeable future.

Remember That You Are Never Done Social media management is not a campaign-based initiative. It is a manifestation of your business in the digital realm and requires a significant live presence. This can be an exhausting thought as you ramp up for a real-time presence. But once you get going, it becomes a lot easier, especially when you set your expectations accordingly.

Know That the Power of Search and Social Is in Understanding Their Interdependencies Keep in mind that social is becoming more algorithmic, just as search is becoming more social. Pitting one against the other misses the point entirely and is like comparing apples and oranges. As a social media manager, use search tactics to fully extend your opportunities in social and show the value of your efforts on search programs.

Remember That Search Users Are People Who Also Use Social Networks and Media If you start to view searchers in a human light, then you will quickly realize that many of the rules of social engagement apply to these users as well. If you still have doubts about this, review Chapters 1 and 2.

Recognize That Optimizing for Search Engines Is an External Usability Issue, Not "Gaming the Search Engines" If you are promoting a sustainable search and social marketing approach for your business, then advocating for your visitors through optimization can help them find what they are looking for more quickly and help solve their problems or query. Reinforcing keyword language is a *usability* and *findability* issue and ultimately is a way of advocating *for your audience* through relevancy, and not a search-engine or social network. If optimization satisfies their intent, then it is successful on a search engine level and a marketing level. If you are a social-media marketer who thinks sustainable SEO tactics are gaming the search engines, get over it. It's a two-way street.

> **Note:** Refer to Chapter 3, "Ramping Up for a Real-Time Content Marketing Strategy," for more information on choosing the right social networks, bringing consistency to your strategy, finding niche networks, and identifying your audience. Also look to Chapter 3 and Chapter 14, "Metrics and Measurement," for more information on social-media measurement.

Using Common Sense in Social Spaces

Marketers and business owners can come up with all of the rules and scenarios in the world for interacting in social spaces, but the bottom line is that common sense most often trumps the rules. Whether you are managing a community or interacting and engaging in another community, you have to put yourself in another person's shoes and consider how they would like to be treated. They would probably expect common courtesy, no name-calling, allowance for reasonable misunderstandings, and general consideration. You still need rules, especially if you have a team or group that is involved in social spaces on behalf of your business, but common sense will take you a long way on its own.

Social Media Managers Are the Curators of the Living Keyword Language of Their Audience

In contrast to a paid or natural search marketer who focuses more on the somewhat *static* keyword lexicon of your audience, a social media manager is often on the front lines with their audience and knows the real-time lexicon firsthand, because they interact and consume the content that surfaces in their like-minded networks. The key to capturing this living language of your audience is *being present* in your marketing efforts. In other words, if the language is alive, then as a real-time content marketer you need to be alive and present as well. As a front-line social-media or audience manager, you know what topics resonate at a given moment or what news is tracking within your area of business. This means you should be tracking new words, adding the dates they appeared, adding notes about their significance, and mining real-time tools and your internal analytics programs for similar trends. Monitor and track this language, use it with your audience, create content using the language, and use these keyword triggers to find new audiences in different spaces using popular search engines. Share this data with other groups in your company, such as customer service, product management, IT, sales, and so on.

Keyword History vs. Keyword Recency, and the Balance Between the Two

I mentioned the "static" and historical keyword lexicon in the previous section, as opposed to the "living language" lexicon. This juxtaposition essentially compares search history over longer periods of recency (think many months or years) vs. shorter frames of recency (last week, today, and so on). Recalling the statistic presented in Chapter 2 that 15 to 25 percent of daily searches in Google have never been searched before, this language doesn't just reflect what people are searching for in search engines but rather what is parallel to discussions in social spaces at a given time. At this rate, the entire search-keyword lexicon changes and regresses within a relatively short timeframe, at least compared to all history of keyword search that is tracked by search engines and social networks. It also reveals that a good chunk of what is being discussed in social turns over at a fairly rapid rate, at least in terms of the descriptive or identifying language used.

As a social media manager, you have an opportunity to manage this cutting-edge keyword language as it appears right before your eyes. It might render itself in the form of new topics, new hash tags, variations of existing topics or themes, and new people coming in and out of the keyword limelight, among many other situations. Your job is stay on top of the language, using your brain power, analytics tools, and keyword tools, among the many other concepts presented in this book.

The Role of Social Keyword Research in Paid Media

Social media managers are beginning to experience the sort of same "paid vs. organic" dichotomy found in search-engine marketing. While "earning your way in" has been the main mantra for "organic" social-media marketing to this point, pressure for the major social networks to show a profit has rendered increasing opportunities for advertisers to buy paid placements. A first-quarter 2011 report by SEMPO reported that many paid-search marketers were driving ad buys in social spaces. It is fair that search marketers would be taking this approach, because many paid social-media placements are based on paid search–management processes, in that they require knowledge of auction-based bidding, keyword triggering, detailed analytics, and measurement skills.

Keyword triggering takes on a different light when it is viewed in social spaces in real-time. It is this area of real-time keyword management and triggering that social media managers can help develop. But "organic" social media managers will still need to step up to the plate and gain the skills of traditional paid search managers if they want to become effective in paid-social-media management.

Think and Act Like a Human Social Search Engine

One major aspect of real-time social media management is in utilizing search principles to find your audiences and relevant conversations. As these considerations are interspersed throughout the book, search should be considered an integrated function of social media management. This means thinking like a search engine in the sense that you are not only talking to real people but also have a sense for how social users find and discover content. Use keyword searches, know the various social user experiences, understand how new content surfaces, and think of different ways beyond direct conversation to reach your audience.

Here is another way to think about real-time customer engagement. If the phone rings at your place of business, you answer it. On the Internet, the "phone" is always ringing *somewhere*, but you have to use search and social techniques to find out where it is ringing before you can answer it. When someone asks a question on a forum or an answer site, the phone is ringing, and someone should answer it. When someone makes a point about your business or area of service in the comments of an obscure but relevant blog, the phone is ringing, and you should answer it. If a customer has an issue with your business and turns to Twitter to seek out help, the phone is ringing, and it should be answered. The difference is that the phone doesn't have one line to your business. It has millions of lines in a fragmented web space, and social search techniques and technologies are the only way to cut down the noise to find them.

By acting like a human search engine, you should be ultimately concerned with being found in social spaces and finding other like-minded audiences and individuals to share content, share conversation, and build your network. It takes a social mind-set, with a knowledge of search tactics and tools, to get the job done.

Amplifying Content: Developing Your Distribution Network and Influencer Network

If you remember the description in Chapter 8, "Blogs, Google News, and Press Releases," of how to start an avalanche of traffic and sharing for your content by throwing a lot snowballs, you know that you need to produce content consistently and spread it through your own networks and the networks of influencers. So, if content is the snowball, then your networks and social platform are the top of the mountain that the snowball starts rolling down. Depending on how good or interesting your content is judged to be by your audience, it will gain velocity by rolling faster down that mountain, through the many-to-many flows of sharing from networks of networks.

Your primary network of people—be it your Twitter followers, people who have circled you on Google+, your email subscribers, your RSS-feed subscribers, or people you are connected to in LinkedIn—serve as your front line of passive distribution. Your network likely includes a number of people exhibiting different social-media behavior types. Your shared content goes through an active distribution phase when these influencers start sharing your assets in a many-to-many way.

Forrester's Social-Media Behavior Types in the United States and Europe

Forrester Research has created a helpful definition of common social-media behaviors that help instigate an *active* or many-to-many approach to distribution, so in this section I will explore these types further (see Figure 13.1). The Forrester classification includes Creators, Conversationalists, Critics, Collectors, Joiners, and Spectators, and Inactives. While these types reveal independent social-media behaviors, they also overlap with each other in some way.

A Creator can also be a Critic and Conversationalist, a Joiner is also a Spectator, and so on. The survey is helpful in understanding your audience and the impact of your content and engagement strategy in social spaces. While the types shown were created by Forrester, here are some other considerations, as they relate to the concepts I have presented throughout this book:

Creators This segment can be considered a primary influencer group, because they create blog posts, publish websites, or create in user-generated content communities. This group creates two-tier SERP [search engine results page] visibility and is often the catalyst for one-to-many and many-to-many active distribution.

Conversationalists This group is also influential in a many-to-many sense and helps propagate your content through networks. They are also a key link in the share graph chain, because they spread links and keyword language in real-time. Talk directly with them, engage where they engage, and chime in on content they are interested in.

Critics This audience types comments in blog or social threads, votes, and reviews, among other activities. This is the group that helps define a key part of your business conversation outside of your owned digital presence.

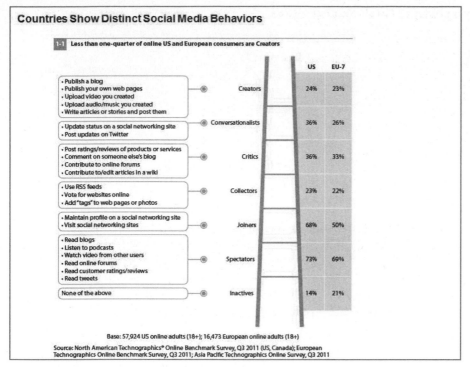

Figure 13.1 Countries show distinct social-media behaviors.

Collectors Collectors vote on content, write reviews of products and businesses, and help categorize and tag content. They also use RSS feeds, use social bookmarking sites such as Digg or Pinterest, and personally aggregate content for their own consumption.

Joiners This group stays connected in social networks, sets up profiles, and gets connected. They might like your company, circle your business, or follow you, as well. They are a key element in building your network and can be influencers in terms of the sheer size of the network. They don't have to create content to be effective—all they have to do is share to help disseminate your messages to a wider range of audiences.

Spectators As the largest segment of the group, spectators are the mass consumers of online content. They read and scan, watch video, and listen to podcasts. They consume both your direct content and the content of all other behavior segments listed previously.

Inactives Not applicable due to non-participation.

Use these segments to help identify influencers and consumers in your own efforts and evaluate the degree in which they might impact your online presence and social-content reach. It is also helpful to better understand the different modes of interaction within various networks. Using the chart as a guide should make it easier for you to segment various types of people and behaviors that you currently observe in the main social networks. Knowing who the key social influencers are can help you focus your efforts in terms of promoting a good piece of content, determining when it is relevant to a conversation, or identifying a conversation that is of keen interest to those influencers.

Beyond identifying influencers, it is also critical to frequently or periodically update your social status with content updates in your networks. This helps you gain social signals that search engines use to rank content and increases the distribution reach for your content. Content amplification is not a one-time deal but rather an ongoing process of outreach and promotion. Over time, your audience gets to know you better, and the increased visibility in search and social spaces helps build your network to even greater levels. Start building today, and measure the effects of your efforts in network size in one to two years or longer.

Internet Fragmentation: Social Media Management Across the "Splinternet"

If your definition of "social networks" is limited only to Twitter and Facebook, then one of my basic hopes is that this book will help you expand your horizons to include the many other niche networks around the Web. This expanded definition of "social" should also include bookmarking sites, forums, wikis, obscure blogs, and answer sites, among many others. While many social media managers focus only on the top networks, you should now also be aware that social conversations exist all across the Internet in a variety of forms, and they still require a human touch. In effect, to fully reach your audience, you will need to address them equally in these areas.

Through my own marketing efforts, I have witnessed the Internet breaking up into many pieces firsthand, in the sense that an audience may prefer to get its information and conversation in different places and delivery methods, though the conversation often remains the same.

Forrester Research also created a term for this rapid fragmentation of the Internet and social spaces the *Splinternet*. Just as it sounds, it means that the Internet has splintered into different forms of communication, where in the past; Internet marketers may have just focused on a website, search, email, or a combination thereof to reach a vast majority of their audience. Social media management and marketing requires quite a bit of juggling across many different spaces to be effective. In addition to promoting and engaging on your key profiles and spaces in Twitter and Facebook, consider the following areas where your audience may like to congregate or the method in which they like to receive information:

- Subscribers to email lists
- RSS-feed subscribers
- Short Messaging Service (SMS) –update recipients
- Visitors to your blog or website
- Press-release readers and subscribers

- Forum members
- Users on LinkedIn, YouTube, Google+, or Facebook

You will eventually find the right combination and mix to reach your audience, one that is manageable on an ongoing basis. Be sure in the beginning to identify the potential areas and ways that your audience likes to communicate, and then determine the approach that best suits your audience.

For more information on the concept of the Splinternet, refer to "The Splinternet Engagement Index," Forrester Research, Inc., on February 6, 2012 at www.forrester.com.

Integrating Your SEO and Social Teams

One of the first successes you can start to cultivate right now for your real-time content marketing platform and outreach plan is to get your social and SEO teams talking and working together on a regular, if not daily, basis. As the previous chapters have explained, search and social are interdependent, and communication is not an obligation—it's mandatory, at least if you want to maximize the impact of your strategy. You may want to consider integrating the search and social teams and integrating roles to involve a mixture of both search and social skill sets. With this approach in mind, here are some ways your teams can help each other extend the opportunities of your real-time content marketing efforts, right now:

Train Social Media Managers on How SEO Works So many of the basic principles of sharing and network behavior are rooted in traditional SEO. Your SEO team or expert should be able to provide your social teams with info on the basics of SEO in fairly short trainings and also leave them with key things to consider and practice in their own outreach and engagement efforts. This aspect should focus on items such as how search engines crawl, index, and retrieve and how linking affects search results, among many other basic points. This book will serve as a training manual for many other aspects that apply directly to the daily duties of an integrated search and social approach.

Train Social Media Managers on Basic SEO Copywriting Principles Teaching your social media and outreach managers how machines read copy is one the quickest ways to start getting more out of your social-media efforts. Writing with the right keywords in mind (in a human way) increases visibility, increases traffic, builds up your networks, and extends the shelflife of your content for years to come. Refer to Chapter 6, "Creating Effective and Engaging Content," for a quick-start SEO copywriting guide.

Train SEOs on How to Write for Humans, Not for Robots Search-engine optimizers are often very good at creating content that resonates well with search engines, but they often do it at the expense of the humans reading the content. A good social media manager will help search-engine optimizers better understand the balance of writing for people just as much as search engines, especially when search-engine optimizers may be on the front lines of real-time marketing communications.

Train Social Media Managers on How to Research Keyword Data Keyword research is a basic search-engine optimization principle that every social media marketer should know about. Choosing the right word can mean the difference between being found in a search engine and being found in a social network, because other network users use keyword triggers to find and engage with new content. Remember that people connect via language, and both search and social experiences rely on keywords and natural language to connect. This training should provide sources of keyword-research data, show how to perform keyword research, and show how to use it for content and conversation ideas.

Show Social Media Managers How Keyword Triggers Work Simply publishing a piece of content with the right triggers can push your content directly to consumers via an alerts system and subscribed keyword lists. It is sort of like a reverse SEO process for a completely hidden audience. Understanding how it works is critical for social media managers. For more information of keyword alert systems, refer to Chapter 12, "More Considerations for Real-Time Content Marketing, Search, and Social."

Blog Optimization Having an unoptimized blog can mean the difference between not being found at all and having your social media managers work 10 times harder to get only half the traffic of an optimized blog. Have your SEO team optimize your blogs using the latest SEO plug-ins, keyword-friendly architecture, and reduction of duplicate content (there's more on optimizing and setting up a blog in Chapter 8).

Show Social Media Managers How to Optimize Common Social Spaces Like Google+, Twitter, LinkedIn, and Facebook While social networks are covered in more detail in Chapter 7, "Social-Network Platforms," each individual social space mentioned earlier can be optimized for both increased internal visibility and increased visibility in search engines. This involves using the right keywords, the right links, and the right anchor text, among many other elements unique to each network.

Show Social Media Managers How to Read Your Analytics to Determine What Resonated with Your Audience (in Both Search and Social) Most seasoned SEOs are skilled at reading and interpreting analytics and log files, and this data can be utilized to gauge overall reaction to and performance of real-time media programs. Training social media managers on analytics programs can help them determine their most successful content ideas and strategies, determine the most successful conversations, and show directly how their social efforts sent traffic back via search engines. Social media managers can also help search optimizers to better understand the current real-time keyword language of their audience to inform other optimization efforts.

Train SEOs Not to Appear Spammy or Over-Optimized in Social Networks The bottom line is that appearing overly optimized or robotic in social networks is a huge turnoff to social users. Remember that social users help propagate content by sharing, which in turn creates more links and social pages for the engines. So in effect, turning off humans in your networks is akin to turning off a search engine to your social signals.

Show Social Media Managers How to Use a Search-Friendly Short-URL System, and Explain Why It Is Important Because social managers will be communicating and sharing much of your content by using short URLs like Bitly or Goo.gl, it is important to know that some of these shortened URLs can translate into valuable backlinks for search. This is why it is important to use a search engine–friendly URL shortener that utilizes a "301 status" permanent redirect (as opposed to "302," page temporarily moved) to tell search engine to give credit to your final landing URL. Short URLs are discussed in more detail in Chapter 10, "Technical Considerations and Implementation."

Train Social Media Managers on How to Avoid Duplicate Content and Why It Can Be a Very Bad Thing for Search Duplicate content can make or break the search engine effectiveness of your social assets, so it is imperative that social media managers understand this concept, because they will likely be repurposing content. There is nothing wrong with repurposing content per se, but it must to be done in a way that doesn't harm your search visibility.

Perform Periodic Content Reviews As a standard rule, social media managers should bring in the SEO team to review content on a regular basis to ensure that the opportunities are extended for both search and social.

Engagement Strategy

Developing your community- and audience-outreach strategy may very well be one of the toughest things you do in real-time content marketing. It takes a lot of planning, lots of careful practice, and development of your business voice and style. As you start to engage in social spaces, ideally you will find yourself becoming more comfortable with network interaction and training others to do so. You may still seek outside help from an agency or consultant. Again, this is an iterative process of constantly developing a relationship with your audience (either passive or engaged), building up a network, identifying new opportunities, and publishing within your defined objectives. And, it is also important to understand that *you are never done*. Community outreach is not a campaign-oriented initiative. It is an ongoing conversation between your business and your audience.

Here are some key considerations as you begin to assemble your real-time social media strategy and plan:

Resource Commitment Be prepared to allocate plenty of time with your real-time engagement and content staff. It is not realistic to expect social media managers to juggle multiple tasks and be expected to respond live online at all times. As you determine the size of the opportunity, you will begin to see the amount of dedication that is required, both on human-resource and budgetary levels. You can go for part of it or all of it, but make sure you have enough resources to properly swallow the chunk that you plan to bite off.

Thought-Leadership Drivers While you may have multiple thought leaders, it is important to keep your messages consistent while still allowing for the flexibility of natural language and conversation. Work toward consistency of your messaging across all networks.

Internal Technical Capabilities and Execution If you haven't already done so, start to get a handle on the technical capabilities of your organization. This will help you determine how much technical implementation will be done in-house, outside your company, or both.

Outside Resources and Tools As presented in earlier chapters (and also in Chapter 14), you should prepare to consider both free and paid tools for real-time content marketing. Become familiar with the basics now in order to understand them more subjectively later.

Audit, Research, Strategy, and Execution Timelines While real-time marketing is an ongoing process, ramping up is not. Set dates, times, and other expectations for completion, or else it will never happen.

Key Events Use this book to help define the key events and milestones in the planning and execution process. Not all of the items described here may apply to your situation, so isolate the ones that do, and set firm expectations and times for an outcome.

Commenting Strategy

One of the core activities in daily social media management is commenting. While this may seems obvious, good commenting requires a social media manager to be an excellent writer, and in most cases their words become part of the public conversation about your company and should not be taken lightly. With this in mind, here are some key considerations for your business commenting strategy across multiple commenting platforms:

Be Attentive When someone writes a comment, they usually have an expectation or desire to be answered in a prompt manner. Respond accordingly, especially when they are addressing you directly. Many blog platforms have comment RSS feeds, and setting up your feeds into an RSS reader can help you monitor dozens of comment feeds at once in real-time.

Be Fast, and Try to Be First Many popular commenting sections get as many as 50, 100, or even a 1,000 comments or more, and the early commenters are the ones who are in the first position as others scan a post, video, or other digital asset. Good first comments are often quoted sporadically throughout the list of remaining replies and help set the tone for the conversation that follows. Don't make silly comments like "first," but do make a well-thought-out comment in a timely manner. It is the difference between being seen by a large audience and getting buried deep in a list of other comments that may never be seen.

Consider Using Your Real Name or Real Business Name When going out into social spaces, avoid using a pseudonym or made-up handle. This increases the transparency of who you really are and increases trust with your audience. It also keeps people honest. People act quite differently under the cloak of perceived anonymity than if they were using their real names, and this is even more apparent if you engage in social spaces with anonymous usernames on a regular basis. In short, real names (your name or the name of your business) help keep the conversation honest.

Add Photos and Icons In places where you post regularly, add your photo or appropriate icon to your profile. This will help your comments stand out on the page and let other users know that you are interested enough in the community to dress up your presence a bit.

Don't Leave "Link Droppings" If It Doesn't Contribute to the Conversation Dropping in links can often make your posts look out of context or make your participation appear self-promotional. This is often a huge turnoff to social users across a wide variety of user-generated content types. Focus on engaging with community for a sustainable strategy, and the links will come later. Considering that most blogs are using nofollow links to deter spammers, links dropped into comments do not even help with search visibility.

Don't Drop in Spammy Links Nothing is more annoying to a social reader in a legit social conversation than coming across gratuitous link spam. There are plenty of scripts that go around planting links on blogs, and there are more than enough humans that do it as well. If most marketers spent a fraction of the time creating good content that they do on dropping links, they would likely get more than what they are looking for. We're talking about producing a sustainable online marketing strategy here, and quick-hit link-spamming just won't cut it for your business—that is, if your business plans on being online for a while. Again, most comment sections have nofollowed links, so it is pointless to spam for link-development purposes.

Stay on Topic Sometimes comments take a detour on new topics that spring from an original article, blog post, or other digital asset. The key thing to remember is to stay on topic of the comments and help guide a conversation.

Use Common Sense The Internet is the World *Wild West*, and nothing will likely ever change this. In the comments sections of various networks and assets you will likely meet and talk with people from all walks of life, with a variety of experiences that are not like yours. Be respectful, but also use your common sense when engaging with people. A general common-sense rule is to treat people the way you would like to be treated.

Target the Right Communities and the Right Content If you are hanging out in a particular social space for any length of time, make sure it is relevant to the audience you are trying to develop. You should still target the "tangential" conversations that may exist outside of your concentrated social spaces, but just remember to stay focused on the top networks in your respective space.

Observe the Written and Unwritten Rules I have mentioned this a few times in this book, but it is worth repeating. If possible, it is a good idea to observe the comments section of a particular social space well in advance of making your first comment in order to know the "house rules," written in the terms of service or FAQ. You may not always have this luxury, but do your best. You will often find that using common sense and treating others the way you would like to be treated will take you a long way to understanding the basic rules. Read for a while to understand the community's most frequent commenters, their history, and their online demeanor.

Don't Be Salesy—Be Conversational and Earn Your Network of Influence If you are turning off people in a network by being overly salesy, then you are not helping your goals. Provide consistent value to your audience in order to earn the attention of your audience.

Interview with Tarah Feinberg

In addition to having skills in film and video, Tarah is an expert in real-time social-media strategy, and in this interview he shares his thoughts on managing social spaces in real-time.

How do you view the social media manager's role in ensuring that their efforts are maximized in both search and social spaces?

The most effective social media manager is a force of integration—integrating priorities from PR, marketing, sales, strategy, creative, paid media, SEO, and other groups—to design a program engineered to drive the specific, desired business results that have been agreed upon by the decision makers at the brand organization. In order to maximize the effectiveness of the efforts, they should work as a facilitator across the entire brand organization as much as possible.

What are the top three key considerations for managing social spaces in real-time, as opposed to viewing social as a "channel?"

The most important considerations for managing social spaces in real-time are aesthetics, content, and engagement.

Aesthetics relates to brand identity and consistency across social spaces. It is vital that brands adhere to their style guides wherever they are, including social platforms. This means that logos, voice, syntax, and other established standards should be followed closely. Consistency greatly increases credibility and visibility across networks, ultimately leading to greater engagement and reach.

Content relates to the importance of following established and evolving best practices for social media. Brands should carefully consider their content-mix model to determine the right proportions of branded and/or product vs. unbranded content, formats (for example, video, photo, text, and so on), posting schedules and frequency, and the mix of topics and themes. By developing an editorial strategy and program, as well as detailed monthly content calendars, brands will be able to monitor the effectiveness of their approach, conduct optimization tests, and iterate on a regular basis. Setting a strong foundation of ritualized and evergreen content while leaving openings for timely, real-time content will greatly drive positive results.

Interview with Tarah Feinberg *(Continued)*

Engagement relates to how active a brand's community is on its social spaces and how effectively that brand is interacting with its audiences on an ongoing basis. It is important to consider more than top-level audience numbers. For example, the percentage of daily or weekly active audience members is much more important than the total number. It is also important to weight different types of engagement. For example, on Facebook, a like is the easiest and least visible; a comment is a bit deeper and a bit more visible on that person's News Feed; a share is extremely valuable because the participant is expressing advocacy and making the brand content as visible as possible to his/her own network. It is important to consider the business objectives and identify the social tactics and content types that drive the most effective types of engagement to achieve those goals.

How much SEO do you think a social media manager should know to make their efforts more effective and help out search performance? Should SEOs be skilled in social strategy as well?

It is essential that social media managers have at least a basic working knowledge of SEO best practices, in addition to their required deep understanding of social-media best practices. Valuable insights can be garnered from search data, including information about the topics, keywords, and trends in which the target audience is most interested. It is also important to consider how social can impact a brand's search results, because the search engines continue to develop their algorithms and feature social content more prominently.

It is likewise important for SEO professionals to have at least a basic understanding of social-media best practices. Just as social professionals can garner insights from search activities, there are valuable learnings that can be yielded from social audiences. As people spend more time on social platforms and share more and more content there, they are becoming invaluable search engines, in their own right, as that data becomes more discoverable.

How should companies approach defining their voice in social spaces?

To effectively define their voice in social spaces, brands should aim to balance their existing style guide with a deep understanding of the way that their audience communicates and the content they consume. Sometimes, it will make sense for a brand to develop an actual persona—a character that speaks on behalf of the company—but it is essential that this is done with extreme attention to authenticity and that it strike a genuine tone. The approach to the brand voice in social should be flexible so that the team can learn and evolve this voice, based on its effectiveness and real-time feedback as the community reacts and interacts. As with all areas of social marketing, it is essential that the voice, or voices in some cases, be tied closely to specific business objectives so that their effectiveness can be assessed and optimized over time.

Empowering Your Networks, Both Internally and Externally

While much of this book is focused on outreach to external networks like Twitter, Facebook, Google+, or any other place where your audience may congregate, there is one other important social network you address: your own networks of the people you work with. Whether acknowledged or not, the people in your organization are acting on behalf of your company if they engage in any public social network, even for personal use.

Social-media participation within your organization is a sort of double-edged sword. Checking out the *public* interactions of your employees online is a good way to identify potential advocates for your brand. On the flipside, those who choose to use their social-media profiles for both personal and work use are still making a representation for your brand. So, by default, the people in your organization are representing your company.

When getting started with a social-media outreach and engagement strategy, your internal network can be extremely valuable for helping spread your content, interaction, and network development. As you begin to plan for building out your social-network platform, consider these ways to build up your internal network as part of your overall strategy:

- Use internal email lists to help enlist your co-workers to join your key networks.
- Distribute a set of guidelines for interacting with your business content, and tell your networks exactly how they can help.
- Hold internal education sessions on the "dos and don'ts" of social media.
- Solicit your colleagues, co-workers, and employees to submit content for publication or offer their expertise.
- Identify groups of people you can count on to answer questions for areas of specialty when needed, or to help spread content.

Internal business networks are becoming increasingly popular in businesses of varying sizes. Email is the default "social" communication for most businesses, and other common methods of internal communication include intranets and chat programs. Twitter-like internal activity-stream software is also becoming popular. Salesforce has its own business-based activity stream, and Microsoft purchased Yammer in 2012. Each of these systems offers similar functionality to Twitter and allows following, followers, and real-time status updates to help increase internal outreach and communication flow.

How to Determine the Authentic Voices in Your Organization

Along the same lines of empowering your internal networks, there is also a deep imperative to identify the key voices within your company. If you are a sole proprietor, then congratulations, you are likely that *key voice*. But as you consider the relative size of a business compared to the potential social conversation at large, there may be a greater need to have multiple advocates, or *teams of advocates*, acting on behalf of your business and reaching out to your audience.

As mentioned in the first chapter of this book, there is no getting around the fact that your business is a combination of both *what you say it is* and *what other people say it is*. You must speak the truth and be sincere and earnest in your interactions and expertise. The best way of doing this is by utilizing the talents of your best brand advocates who are *digitally literate*. You can identify your internal talent by evaluating and asking the following questions:

- Does the person use industry forums or social networks regularly?
- How long has the person been active in social networks or any areas of user-generated content (UGC)?
- How often do they use social media and create content?
- Do they already converse about your general area of business, or do they use it for personal use?
- Does the person publicly promote their social profiles for other people in your company to view?
- Does the person have a blog, or do they create content in any way?
- Are they considered influencers in any particular network, particularly those in your core area of business?
- Are they considered subject-matter, product, or service experts in your area of business?
- Do they frequently tout the positive values of your company?
- How is their online conversational style? Is it amiable, or confrontational?
- Does the person have a well-worn copy of Dale Carnegie's *How to Win Friends and Influence People* on their desk?

To the last point, it is also very important that your voice embody the spirit of your company and audience, but in a sincere manner. Following Carnegie's basic lessons and using common sense will go a long way to helping you become successful in social spaces. Of course, they don't really need to have a copy of Carnegie's book on their desk. But if you think they embody some of the qualities expressed in his book, then they are on the right track to becoming a sincere voice for your organization in social spaces.

Use this set of questions to help identify people who will ally with you on your strategy. You must also have reasonable expectations for participation, because the spectrum ranges from just a little bit of help to full-time social media manager and content creator. If you really think they have the goods, then consider them for a full-time role on your team.

Defining and Developing Your Voice

If you are just starting out with social media management strategy and outreach, then you may find that those first posts, conversations, and content pieces may be a little bit awkward, but that's OK. At this point, you are establishing your voice, your tone, and your content strategy, among many other things. Developing your voice is an iterative process that can take months or even years. While you may rely on some prescribed elements for developing your voice, other aspects are iterative and can't be dictated in a rigid fashion. The unpredictability of social spaces will not allow it. As you develop your voice, here are some basic considerations to allow it to evolve:

- Determine your basic goals.
- Determine whether your goals for voice are attainable and reasonable.
- Define what it means to communicate with people rather than at them.
- Learn as you go, build upon successes, and learn from mistakes.
- Determine the ideals that you or your company represent.
- Determine how each platform (Twitter, Facebook, blogs, and so on) shapes the way your extend your voice.

Also work to develop consistency across multiple networks in your platform. While there are different nuances to each social-media platform, there are also ways to maintain consistency in the way you speak to your audience from place to place. As you develop the previous points, also determine the ways that your voice can overlap in each relative social space.

Personality-Driven Media: Developing Social Personas to Inform Your Voice and Reflect Your Audience

I previously mentioned the use of personas in Chapter 3. The use of personas goes beyond targeting audience types for web design and search and may extend to social audience types as well. A *persona* is a fictionalized characterization of an audience type or person you are trying to reach, for a variety of business purposes. The development of a persona (or personas, if you are seeking multiple targets) is informed through market research, including focus groups, internal data, surveys, and other research mechanisms. An amalgam of the tastes, wants, desires, habits, and conversation style of your audience is created as a model to be communicated to in various channels.

Again, while this process can be used to identify your key audience types, it can also be identified to help inform your own social-media voice in an authentic way. In Chapter 1, I described how enabling the spirit of your audience into your company dialogue is a core tenet of real-time marketing, and using personas is one of the best ways to accomplish this with real-time content. In essence, it is authentic because you are allowing the voice of your customer to reflect the people who represent your brand.

This doesn't mean you should try to force internal personalities to project in ways that are not natural. Instead, it means you should look more closely for the people in your organization or agency that possess the most characteristics of your persona. If your company is already talking closely with your audience, then you will likely find that these people already exist in your company. If they are not currently working for your organization, find them and hire them. Agencies and consultants can also help in this area.

Several other authors have done a great job of detailing how to develop personas with a search and social frame of mind. One book I recommend you pick up is Vanessa Fox's *Marketing in the Age of Google* (Wiley, 2010, 2012) to use personas to develop your own search and social voice.

Job Description and Skill Sets for the Search-Informed Social Media Manager

The job description of the social media manager is rapidly changing as search and social channels become more tightly integrated. Of course, there are the mainstay aspects of the job. *Develop and execute social-media strategy. Write content, and establish a content calendar. Converse with your audience. Build up networks of followers, friends, and circles*. But when search is added into the mix, the job description takes on a different, if not more *strategic*, approach. Here are a few new considerations to develop for yourself or to look for when hiring a social media manager or similar social role:

- SEO experience
- Paid-search experience
- Demonstrated ability to perform keyword research and identify natural language in social spaces
- Understanding of how *social* signals impact *search*
- Understanding of how *search* signals impact *social*
- Link–development experience and understanding of social link building
- SEO-based copywriting experience
- Experience using various SEO measurement tools to help gauge impact of content strategies
- Analytics experience
- Deep understanding of strategic implications of the overlapping concepts of search and social
- Experience in educating internal teams on the business value of search and social

The progressive search and social media manager should also be able to detail the additional value being attained from an interdependent strategy. With search and social budgets representing a major share of most Internet marketers' overall spend, there is greater pressure to show what you are getting from each of these spaces. When operating in silos, some of the value that a company attains may be missed or improperly attributed. By having an understanding of how the two work, the business case can be made for doing both on a significant level.

When to Bring in Outside Talent

Consideration should always be given to bringing in people from outside of your business to help develop your platform and voice and to engage in social spaces. Agencies experienced in digital publishing and participation, individual consultants, or new hires with a depth of real-time marketing experience can provide a tremendous amount of value to help a real-time content strategy succeed. If you know that the people possessing the required digital literacy, thought leadership, and social-interaction capabilities are not available for a real-time marketing role, then the potential benefits of outside help could well justify your expenses and help scale to the full opportunity.

Considering again that your brand conversation is co-owned by the audience that talks about you, why not hire some of those people directly to help contribute to the authentic voice of your business? If they are speaking out and truly believe in your purpose and possess the right amount of digital literacy, they just might be the people you are looking for.

Agencies and consultants can also be of tremendous benefit to your real-time strategy, if not lead it altogether. Because seasoned digital marketers have been long aware and practiced in most of the areas of this book, you can bring expertise into your team with great speed and get going a lot faster than by starting from the ground up. Experienced consultants and agencies generally know the ropes pretty well and can also help you avoid some of the common pitfalls of real-time content, social, and search marketing and could save you months and years of time.

How Your Internal Teams and Disciplines Can Work Together Through Audience Outreach

Being on the front line of your real-time social and content presence provides a view of audience feedback that can impact many other aspects of your business. As you engage and interact in social spaces, consider how your audience outreach and conversations can help inform other parts of your business, as well as how you can get the following resources active under the right situations:

Customer Service In many situations where a business has a call center, there is a strong case to establish a mirrored presence for audiences seeking out answers online in a social network. In this sense, a company's entire real-time strategy may revolve around solving customer issues through direct content and human interaction online in real-time.

Product Development The Internet is like a constantly running real-time focus group in many ways, and online feedback and suggestions for product and service specialists can be priceless in terms of how it might impact the value and quality of your future offerings. Make sure that whoever is providing your front line for social-media outreach has a regular pipeline of communication going into your product and service teams. Even better yet—get your product managers and specialists out on the front lines of outreach themselves.

Sales Establishing connections internally between your front line of outreach and your sales teams will be critical, especially if one of your key goals for real-time content marketing strategy is direct sales or leads. For small businesses, sales and marketing may all be rolled into one role, and for others, getting the sales team to go social without being too "salesy" will also be a matter question to deal with in your strategy.

PR There is often a push and pull between marketing and public-relations teams over who "owns" the outreach strategy. But the answer is really simple—every discipline in your business owns at least one piece of social outreach. Your real-time marketers who are engaged on the publishing side of digital outreach can also be the "feet on the ground" to help PR teams identify a potential crisis or opportunity.

IT When there is a tech issue with a site or owned asset or there is a desire for a new function, social-media outreach can help inform these aspects of technical development. Maintaining lines of communication between outreach and IT in some way can help solve problems faster internally, as well as help your technology evolve.

Human Resources/Employment Over the last several years, social media sites like LinkedIn have taken over job-listing sites as the key places to find and maintain employment. Social-media outreach for employment is one great method of staying in touch with a group that may want to work for you and also for you to help identify and become aware of key talents in your field. HR departments who aren't recruiting in LinkedIn may be missing a huge opportunity, and at the very least, your social-media outreach teams should be in touch with HR as a source of content in various networks.

Common Types of Social Interaction and Engagement

If you are new to social-media outreach or wondering how you might even begin to start participating, a number of foundational social interactions will help get you going. As noted throughout the book, almost all of these actions have an impact on both your search visibility and helping you reach your social goals. The following items will help get you going or thinking about how to set the foundation of engagement strategy:

Read and Comment on a Writer's Post There is no greater way to get involved in a community conversation than to add your thoughts to a blog post or news article. Even if the writers do not always respond, they often read the comments, and the more you post, the more visibility you gain. Commenting helps you engage with community while leaving a digital trail that will be found in search results as well.

Answer a Question or Help Solve a Problem by Providing Expert Advice Does someone have a question mark at the end of their word string? Acknowledge them and answer their question, if you can help them. Do this on a forum, in a blog post or new article, or on a social network like Twitter or Google+. Answering questions in your area of expertise can elevate your status in a social community and make your company or profile visible in second-tier SERPs.

Share a Link That Will Add Insight into a Conversation or Topic (to Your Own or Others' Content) Find a great article or something that communicates what you are thinking or what you might even disagree with? Forward it along to your network. It may not always count as a link toward your backlink profile, but another persona might find your content interesting enough to promote in a web space that does create a link citation.

State an Opinion or Reaction to a Current Event or Add Insight When a big story breaks, share your thoughts or opinion. Share it with someone directly, or send it out to your network. It doesn't have to be a long blog post—just a short status update is all it takes.

Ask Users for Feedback on a Topic or to Help Inform a Product or Service Did you just launch your life's work online, or do you simply need a quick opinion? Shoot out a link, and ask your friends and followers for their thoughts. In the midst of developing a product and stuck on a key aspect of design? Ask your audience what they think in order to help better inform your product or service development process.

Retweet, Like, +1, or Share Content If you like something and think other people like you will like it too, go ahead and retweet it, like it, share it, link to it, or +1 it. Keep your audience and networks in mind, and avoid inundating them with irrelevant or unwanted content. Sharing helps provide visibility to other content of similar interest and also provides social signals to help those other sites gain search visibility.

Announce Your Newly Created Content Did you just launch a new blog post or even a new website or online application? Go to your online channels such as email, Twitter, Google+, Facebook, LinkedIn, and others, and tell your friends. If they are tuned into you, then they will likely tune into what you are doing from a content perspective at some point. Don't expect a mass response the first time. The benefits of announcing your content start to trickle in after the 40th, 50th, or 100th piece of content you produce.

Vote on a Piece of Content Vote on it, bury it, promote it, thumbs-up it, or thumbs-down it.

Reply to Other Comments About Your Content or Conversation It may be common sense, but it is worth repeating that if others address you directly or ask a question, get in and address them, and continue the conversation.

Thank Your New Followers or People in Your Network Send them a personal (not canned) direct response, an @reply, or a public thank-you in your stream.

Whether you proactively embrace these different tactics or not, think of how you might approach each of them in the context of your real-time content marketing strategy. These approaches can help you define your voice in terms of how you want to engage and how you want to be viewed by others in your networks.

We are at the end another chapter and almost to the book's end. Again, there are many great books on the topic of social media management strategy, and to start, I recommend you check out *Social Media Marketing: An Hour a Day* by Dave Evans (Sybex, 2008) and *Groundswell: Winning in a World Transformed by Social Technologies* by Charlene Li and Josh Bernoff (Harvard Business School Press, 2008). In the next and final chapter, I will cover some key considerations for analytics and measurement in the new world of real-time content, search, and social.

Metrics and Measurement

Although this may be the last chapter in this book, the subject of measurement is certainly not the least important one in establishing and executing your real-time content marketing strategy. In fact, the concepts and considerations explained here should be among your first and most important considerations when developing your content-marketing strategy. There have been plenty of great books written on the subject of web analytics and measurement, so instead of retreading over well-documented and established topics, I will dedicate this chapter to discussing key considerations for metrics and measurement as they relate to the search and social nuances of real-time content marketing.

14

Chapter Contents

Considerations for Measuring Content Success in Search and Social

The subject of metrics and measurement is one of the most critical areas to your ongoing strategy and tactical development. This chapter will serve as an overview to learning how to apply measurement considerations to some of the different search and social elements throughout this book. As a foundation for any meaningful discussion of measurement analytics, I highly recommend you also pick up and read Avinash Kaushik's two best-selling books of the topic: *Web Analytics: An Hour a Day* (Sybex, 2007) and *Web Analytics 2.0* (Sybex, 2009). One other highly recommended book is Brian Clifton's *Advanced Web Metrics with Google Analytics* (Sybex, 2012) for those using Google Analytics.

There has been something of an explosion of real-time-analytics providers in the last few years, particularly as the need for measurement of marketing efforts has evolved with the real-time aspects of the Internet. Major providers like Adobe and Google Analytics are providing more social data and even correlating it with search data. Many smaller companies have emerged to provide real-time insights in the form of on-page heat mapping, demographic reporting, and trending conversation analysis in real-time. Some of these tools will be covered later in the chapter.

The Business Effects of Real-Time Content Marketing Are Long-Term

It is important to understand that the positive business effects of real-time content marketing are long-term and are the sum of many connected moments. By acting in a participatory manner toward search, social, and content marketing, your business gains equity in visibility, trust, authoritativeness, direct revenue generation, and awareness, among many other factors. When measuring the effect of your efforts, it is important to focus on the sum of positive effects that lift your business over time. The bottom line is that this type of measurement can sometimes be more art than science.

When metrics, business intelligence, and goals are established carefully, you may also find that there are other ways to measure the lift and return on effort and investment by isolating specific events that are important to you and your business. It is also imperative that you establish a monetary value for your business goals across a wide variety of metrics. The bottom line is that you are spending the money, and you must place a value on business actions. Otherwise, you are spending your marketing and ad dollars blindly, and this also holds true for TV, radio, yellow pages, billboard, and all other types of traditional efforts.

Also, remember that maintenance costs for search, content, and social are a realistic expense. Don't be disappointed when a content freshen-up or technical search engine optimization expense comes up and nips at your gains. In fact, you should embrace these types of expenses, because they help ensure the long-term benefits of your program. Read this chapter for more information on the importance of establishing monetary value for a variety of actions.

Setting Up Measurement Early On Prepares You for Sound Business Decisions in the Future

As I mentioned on the first page of this chapter, measurement is one of the most important foundations of your overall strategy. Many business and marketers become impatient waiting to implement measurement tools or even to provide benchmark reporting, and this is a tremendous mistake. Not knowing what you are getting from your marketing efforts means your ship doesn't have a rudder, and you drift wherever your short-term whims will take you. Conversely, if you establish benchmarks and gain a picture of your business history, then you will see clearly where you have been and where your efforts are taking you. You are spending money on your marketing efforts, and proper measurement helps guide you to make better business decisions in the long term.

I know this may sound like common sense to many marketers, but the truth is that many businesses skip over this important measurement step for short-term gain. Unfortunately, these marketers miss the greater opportunity of understanding the business impact of their efforts and are unable to apply business lessons and intelligence accordingly. Don't be impatient—spend the time to establish the right metrics, to benchmark, and to set a baseline for where you have been in order to understand where you are going and how much it will cost to get there. Real-time content marketing is a long-term effort, with long-term gains. Measuring right the first time sets a path for real sustainability.

Tony Wright, principal of WrightIMC in Dallas, Texas, strongly believes that benchmarking is a key element on the path to success: "Real-time analytics is difficult, and the math doesn't always produce an answer as to how you should change something. That's why it is important to benchmark everything." He adds, "I've actually learned more from many of my failures than some of my successes. Don't stop trying just because you don't get it right the first time."

A Few Key Considerations for Search and Social Measurement

It can be very easy for marketers and analysts to get overwhelmed with all of the data presented in modern digital marketing channels. In wading through so much data, the potential for true wisdom and insights is often lost. Here are a few additional things to consider when developing your measurement strategy; they will bring all of the numbers back down to Earth for you:

View People as *People* Rather Than as *Data* One of the worst sins of modern Internet marketing is that people are commonly viewed as data points. This might involve cornering a person into a spreadsheet as a unique visitor, a keyword referral, or other traffic stat. While I describe these metrics later in this chapter, it is important to remember that your visitors and audience are *people* (you can ignore the robots for now), and in many cases they have a search intent or a problem they are trying to solve. This is often a problem in the way analytics providers are set up, but the good news is that some providers are trying to tell you more about who your audience really is, and this will be discussed later in this chapter. Try to look for the person, the user experience, or the thinking behind the data, and it will guide your audience strategy.

Remember That Real-Time Data Means Nothing Without a Knowledgeable Human to Translate It into Action If you are checking out your data within a relatively short frame of recency, then it is important that it be seen by the right people—those who write content, those who interact in social spaces, and those who optimize content, as well as key decision makers. These roles should have at least some direct access to data, because gatekeeping the data only prevents them from doing their job in a timely manner.

Use the Best Analytics Tool of All—*Your Brain* For all of the talk about analytics and measurement in this chapter, there is no greater tool than your brain. Your brain contains the key link to interpreting data into actionable insights and is the connective element between your business intelligence, goals, execution, and data.

Remember Avinash Kaushik's 10/90 Rule Just as your brain is the most important tool of all, Kaushik recommends spending 10 percent of your analytics budget on tools and *90 percent on the brains* that you will need to make sense of it. Even if you believe that your expensive and shiny new analytics widget is the best thing that ever happened to you, you will not be able to use and interpret it properly without the right amount of brainpower to translate it into business intelligence.

Distribute Your Data and Insights Throughout Your Organization Be sure to spread your findings to other parts of your organization. In some cases, you might not have the direct knowledge to properly interpret the data, so forwarding it to someone with more specific knowledge can help turn the data into an actionable insight. Consider forwarding relevant data to product managers, sales associates, customer-service representatives, hiring organizations within your company, and your IT and creative teams, among many others.

Consider the Metrics of *Stress on Your People* and *Time Lost* as a Fundamental Measurement of Your Efforts Two of the most forgotten or unspoken metrics in all of analytics are the amount of stress put on your organization and how much time might be lost if you go chasing down the wrong metric. As you prioritize your metrics, make sure you strike a realistic balance between the juice you're going to get vs. how hard you have to squeeze to get it. This is the difference between focusing on the right areas and going off on a tangent that yields no positive results.

It is also important to use a variety of sources to measure what you are getting. A single tool or analytics provider will not cut it anymore. Use your on-site analytics as a foundation, but utilize quantitative measurement tools on third-party social sites. SEO-tool providers such as SEOmoz, Majestic SEO, and Raven all provide great tools and reporting to help maintain the SEO and social health of your digital assets and provide key indicators and trends on the effectiveness of your content-marketing efforts. Proprietary agency or consultant tool sets are also very effective at monitoring ongoing SEO performance.

Thinking About Data from Both a Quantitative Aspect and a Qualitative One

There is often a lot of confusion around measurement of many aspects of SEO and social, in the sense that they are a combination of qualitative and quantitative measurements. For example, the number of new backlinks toward a website can be measured quantitatively (453 backlinks last month). But backlinks are still qualitative in that they are only as good as the site that sends the link, which is a highly qualitative judgment—that is, if you are not running the search algorithm. So, measuring and judging the performance of links gained by number alone is not an effective method.

The same is true for some social metrics. In essence, retweets, followers, friends, +1s, circles, and shares are not all alike and are relative to both the authority and influence of people in networks. Again, the measurement of "how many" is quantitative, and the measure of influence is also based on volume and qualitative considerations. Accurate measurement of network reach and individual influence is still a work in progress by most social and search publishers and analytics platforms.

There are many different search and social measurements that follow this combined pattern of both qualitative and quantitative elements. It is important to make sure you clearly understand what this means to avoid applying impossible or useless expectations for yourself, your agency, your consultant, or your business.

Your Data Is a Reflection of the Content and Activity on Your Site and in Social Spaces

Recall the section titled "Think Big: Approach Content Strategy Like a Forest, Not a Weed" in Chapter 5, "Content Strategy: Auditing, Assessment, and Planning"; you can also think about content as a reflection of what you are seeing in your analytics reporting. In effect, the numbers you see at a high level are proportionate to the quantity, depth, and quality of content you have. Also, remember the section "Auditing Your Domain for Optimized Pages"; it explains that your overall unique page content is going to be a signal of how much to expect in your measurement and reporting.

Scaling up your returns from search and social means you will need to scale up your content accordingly, because your efforts and content depth are somewhat proportional to the returns. This may require you to create new individual sections of content and create some of the content types listed in Chapter 4, "Market Research and Content Types," on a regular basis. If your goals are lofty, you may need to scale up in a major way. As a basic tenet of content marketing, your measurement and business goals will increase only if your content is also increasing regularly.

The matter of scale also relates to the way you measure returns in social spaces. Generally speaking, you will see higher returns from Twitter, Facebook, Google+, and others, related to the frequency with which you engage, publish, and converse in those spaces. So, if you are wondering why you may not be getting as much as your competitors or as many returns as you think you should, remember that to a certain degree "what you get" is proportional to "what you give," at least in the content sense.

Why You Should View Certain Metrics Within a Short Frame of Recency

Measurement of real-time content is not so much about real-time as it is about measuring within a tight frame of recency. Many marketers think that acting and measuring in real-time means taking on a harried and almost panicked approach, when this is far from the case. Remember that it is the medium that acts in real-time, but people themselves always need time to think and react. Though it is very quick to publish, even a tweet takes some time to create. A longer blog post may require more thought, and therefore it takes some time. The Web is real-time in its *potential* to resonate instantaneously, but it doesn't mean that all your actionable analytics and data will be instantaneous. It just means they should be monitored in a timely manner. Waiting a week to six months for a report is not going to cut it. If you are monitoring buzz in various social, search, and content spaces, sometimes even a day isn't going to cut it.

The point is that I am not just talking about "right now" when it comes to measuring your real-time performance. The last hour, last day, last week, and last month also provide seed for insight into what is *currently* happening with your content-marketing efforts.

Taking a real-time view of analytics also means you will need to strike a balance with how you measure more current flows, as opposed to historical flows. Most marketers are heavily focused on historical data—what they have received over longer periods of time and data that may be a month old or older. But in focusing on the history of keyword returns and the history of traffic flow, they miss out on the bigger picture of what is buzzing around their beehive right now. Remember that a significant percentage of searches in Google have never been searched before, and the only way to capture some of this action is to monitor within a tight frame of recency. And this type of measurement doesn't just benefit search; it benefits social interaction and helps you find more current connections to your audience. Remember, keywords are connections to people, and knowing the current language through analytics (both on-site and off-site) helps you reach them.

Using Real-Time Data to Measure Lift from Planned and Serendipitous Events

One other great way to utilize real-time data is for measuring the effects of an *event* or a *current happening* in your business space. An event is something that happens, either planned or serendipitous, and causes increased traffic, engagement, conversation, user-generated content, and search referrals. It may be planned in the sense that you are launching a new piece of content or research, or it may be serendipitous in the sense of a breaking-news event that causes a commotion in news, search, and social spaces.

Real-time tools can show spikes across various metrics, and if you are present and in the moment, you are able to apply insight and synthesize real-time actions into business intelligence. Real-time analytics are also useful for viewing the immediate performance and lift of new efforts and implementations. For example, you might push out a new section of 100 pages, some of which you share socially. You can use real-time analytics to gauge how well the content is performing and how quickly it is starting to progress in search engines. Isolating events in search and social and comparing in real-time analytics can also help to directly tie lifts and increases in metrics, especially when you have a large site and many other metrics tend to remain more constant. So, by isolating the event, you are able to see more in the context of the recent impact rather than just seeing it as a small blip on a monthly or weekly report, and you can apply your business insights accordingly.

How Timely Data Can Inform Your Strategy for Actionable Response

As I wrote in Chapter 2, "Understanding Search and Social," *recency is the new relevancy*, and the best way to take advantage of this from a social perspective is by participation in search and spaces and monitoring conversation and trends and data in real-time, or at least in a very timely manner. By taking a *timely* approach to analytics, the data itself is often the signal for taking action, and little additional analysis is required where the implications are otherwise self-evident. Monitoring real-time data is especially useful for social content creators. Frontline social-media managers can offer the data needed by real-time optimizers to stoke the social signals that search is increasingly looking toward to provide search visibility. Here are a few of the key actionable uses for timely data:

- Seeing what is trending on your site in order to react with additional content, conversation, or updates
- Providing additional posts or insights to content with rising interest
- Identifying content that is not trending as well and modifying it accordingly
- Identifying content with higher engagement in order to respond, interact, and share accordingly
- Tracking how well your content is doing right now
- Identifying whether your site has a pulse in the synaptic web landscape
- Managing social interaction in real-time
- Enabling real-time marketers to react to the living language and content demands of their audience in real-time
- Revealing your data as a reflection of the *current* content and conversation footprint for your business

Fresh data is not just for organic-content efforts, and it can also be integrated into paid-media efforts. My longtime fellow MediaPost columnist Aaron Goldman believes that integrating findings from real-time data is a great way for marketers to stay on the cutting edge of their paid campaigns. "Applying real-time analytics to paid search can give marketers a huge advantage," he says. "One way to do this is to look at all actual consumer search queries related to keywords that earn clicks. Any such term or phrase that earns or influences a conversion should be added to the campaign as an exact-match keyword."

Of course, real-time bidding and media is a huge topic and practice in and of itself, but one of the quick ways to play that game is to leverage your research and apply it to your paid-search and paid-social campaigns.

The Importance of Assigning a Monetary Value to Various Actions and Events

Internet marketing has long been touted as being "totally measurable," down to the penny of an advertiser's spend. But there is a problem with measurement when it comes to branding or other direct-response goals. Marketers typically hold Internet marketing channels to higher standards of measurement than TV, radio, and print advertising and marketing. But when pressing for online measurement, remember that the medium does not perform in a vacuum. For activities that don't generate revenue and events such as social engagement, generating awareness, and other branding goals, the marketer needs to place an educated dollar value on each action. This helps the marketer know how their spend is performing, and it also helps them know that they are not spending their money blindly. *Not knowing* the value placed on major actions means that you may be spending money recklessly and simply throwing mud at the wall in the hopes that something will stick.

If you are not measuring various actions down to a specific event, consider these typical offline actions and what they are worth to you in order to help place a specific monetary value on a variety of social and search actions:

- How much is a person walking into your store worth? How can you tie this value to a person on your website?

- What is the cost of hiring someone at your company, and what would it be worth for them to be hired through a lead online?

- How much do you pay for leads? What is the conversion rate for leads through your site? How much does the average converted lead generate for your business? What is your cost-conversion rate for leads received through offline channels?

- What is a branding impression worth to you in radio, TV, or print? How much do your relevant media outlets charge for this kind of exposure? Do you consider branding and impression value in digital spaces as well? What is the value of an engaged visitor?

- What is the value of a returning customer?

- What is the lifetime value of a customer? How much does a repeat customer spend, and are you attributing this back to online channels?

Not only will applying a monetary value to business actions help you figure out what your content strategy is worth to your business, but it will also help you manage other parties who may be providing services or additional support. This can be a difficult exercise for most businesses, and it does not happen overnight. But start right now so you will have enough insight to calculate these costs in the coming months and years.

Establishing a Media Value to Both On-Site and Off-Site Traffic

One of the most common misconceptions about "earned" or "organic" media is that it is *free*. As a business, you have monetary costs, resource costs, and time costs. When your business takes on a real-time content marketing strategy, there is a cost involved. While the cost of content marketing is apparent to many marketers, they often lose sight of one of the main values of their efforts, and this is in the media value of traffic and other gains from earned media.

Establishing the media value for your organic efforts is the process of determining what you are willing to pay for paid-media traffic that may convert to your various business goals or *what you are actually paying* for traffic in similar online marketing channels.

When you are able to establish what you are currently paying or willing to pay for qualified traffic or engagement, then the business case for earned- and organic-media value becomes much clearer. Remember, media value is in addition to what you may be getting in terms of leads, sales, and so on.

If you are engaged in a paid-search marketing program, then you are already placing a monetary value on what a click is worth to you. Take your average cost per click and extrapolate that to new traffic gained from content, search, and social, both on-site and off-site. If you are operating in a socially relevant way, then your traffic may be comparable to the media value of what you are paying in paid search, or paid social-media channels. Use your average paid-click value as a gauge for how you value the traffic from your real-time content marketing program in order to make better business decisions.

So, if your earned-content efforts yield an additional 5,000 visits or sessions per month, multiply that times your average CPC (or blended average across multiple media buys) that you are paying, and you get a directional media value for traffic. Since content efforts typically have long-term traffic benefits, you may also extend that value to potential future gains, over the coming three, six, or twelve months, to determine the potential long-term value of the traffic.

Also consider the value of traffic and engagement in your off-site search and social spaces, and apply a dollar value for branding and engagement in addition to the media value of the traffic, or the exposure. In my experience, earned traffic can come at a fraction of the cost of paid traffic when executed properly, even in competitive spaces.

Veteran content marketer Dan Sturdivant even goes to greater lengths to place a media value on content. "I always recommend that my clients think of content as if it was a "discreet ad unit," he says. "This allows you to place a direct ROI to each content piece, therefore content becomes an asset and not an expense."

Establishing a Monetary Value for Search and Social Equity

One other key value that is often overlooked by marketers and businesses is the value of the earned search equity and the social equity of your efforts. Just as the term implies, *earned* means that your existing presence in search and social spaces has some value, based both on what you might be currently getting and on what it would cost to replicate your existing program based on time, monetary value, and other resources.

If you have an existing search program, then you already have some equity established; that is, unless blackhat or questionable tactics have previously been used, and then you may have a search-optimization or social *liability*. Don't discount what you already have, and perform the audits described in Chapter 5 to fully understand the value of your digital assets from a search perspective. Gaining trust and authority in search engines is worth a gold mine in and of itself and should be considered a marketing asset worth protecting and maintaining. Costs of maintenance are a reality for search, just like any home or car needs maintenance to perform in top shape and extend its useful life.

Equity is also gained in social spaces. You work hard to build up your networks, to produce content, and to engage with your audience, and the value of your efforts extends beyond any immediate returns. You are building a relationship with your audience, and it takes time and money. Take care of it, do no harm, and recognize this value in order to understand the bigger picture of what real-time content marketing brings to the table for your business.

Here are some of the aspects of search and social equity that should be recognized and protected:

- Dollar value of historical investments (cost of search optimization, social-media management, and so on)
- Value of average earned traffic
- Backlink-profile value
- Value of existing content libraries that have been online
- Length of positive search-optimization history, and the irreplaceable time value involved to replicate
- Age that a domain has been hosted with a live working site that provides a value of search-engine trust
- Costs to fix any technical errors in web design or IT that may erase existing search or social equity
- Costs for re-creating content containers that are not search-friendly, social-friendly, or shareable
- Value of "trophy rankings" (e.g., "LED tvs," "Chicago real estate") and the cost to replicate what it took to get the high rankings
- The sum of long-tail traffic from search and social channels

- Your list of followers, friends, likes, and so on
- The sum and history of earned social signals for assets, such as comments, favorites, views, +1s, and retweets

Key Performance Indicators and Metrics

Before I get into some of the detailed key performance indicators (KPIs) that you should be evaluating as a potential gauge for your strategy and tactical plan, I will first go over several top-line considerations for analytics at a very high level.

Divide Metrics Between On-Site, Off-Site, and Where Off-Site and On-Site Connect and Overlap When measuring the effects of your publishing efforts, it is important to distinguish between your owned assets (such as your website or blog) and off-site assets (areas where you interact but do not control at the domain level). Remember to tag your off-site assets when appropriate. Measure the overlapping areas as well, such as traffic from social spaces and reciprocation between social and search returns.

Be Creative There is just as much art to analytics as there is science, so you and your teams need to be creative in translating your data into actionable insights for your business. Don't get stuck in a rut of churning the same old data over and over again. Challenge yourself and your team to think differently about your data and how you can apply your data insights in different ways.

Take Action Remember that data is useful only when you apply insight and take action. Your insights show you where a problem or opportunity might exist, and when you take action, you go and solve that problem or seize the opportunity.

Use Common Sense Plain, old-fashioned common sense will help guide you to the most viable or feasible solution. With any type of data, you will most often find short-term, medium-term, and long-term issues. And those require an appropriate solution as it relates to your own business situation and resources.

Look at Macro Trends, but Also Study the Weeds It is important to know the big picture for your website and overall content performance, but don't skip out on measuring the details either. For all of the current focus on "big data," the "weeds" can tell you how much a particular page or keyword idea is generating and whether it is a good idea to pursue further. Detailed data can also serve as a radar for identifying emerging trends as they are happening. As Collin Cornwell mentioned in Chapter 12, " More Considerations for Real-Time Content Marketing, Search, and Social," getting your data down to the URL level can be a beacon for how well your content efforts are resonating, especially when those page-level efforts are reasonably extrapolated to wider sections and themes of your digital assets.

Create "Events" That Can Spark a Measurable Activity As mentioned in the previous section, having a lot of different things going on with your site can create noise for your analytics signal. To focus in on the signals that matter most, consider your major interactions and content pushes as "events." This may be something that does not currently exist on your site (a page, a section of your website, a keyword phrase, a whole keyword theme) or a content or technical implementation. Once your event is marked, you can hone in and measure all of the new things that come to you in the form of search traffic and social engagement. As you create successful events for positive ROI, reinvest and replicate those events that align with your business goals.

Don't Over-Obsess About a Single Data Point

Internet-marketing measurement can be very complex, and it takes a lot of time and patience to build the big-picture view for your business, as well as a real-time view. Because you will be dealing with data points from many varying sources, it is important to approach analytics with the right balance of effort and insight.

A problem often occurs when marketers or business owners get overly obsessed with a signal data point, to the extent that all resources are focused on a problem or solution that is not proportionally important to your overall goals. The bottom line is that if you are generating a positive return on investment for your spend using either direct response or branding metrics, then you are generally in a good place, especially when compared to many other forms of advertising and marketing.

This does not necessarily mean that efficiencies in spend toward various online activities shouldn't be optimized. To the contrary, they should be optimized but by maintaining a balance within your overall program. Don't take away from resources in content production, social-media management, or search optimization in order to go *chasing ghosts*. Focus on what is real and on generating positive ROI, and keep reinvesting in those areas.

Don't Hold Your Branding and Direct-Response Goals to the Same Standards

One of the biggest pitfalls of analyzing the benefits of search, social, and content is when business owners and marketers try to apply direct-response metrics to branding. If you are trying to measure branding goals by the same standards as direct monetary return, then you are doing it wrong (that is, unless you have strict monetary values applied to each branding goal and action, as previously described). But remember that not all branding goals should have a monetary value assigned. These goals are more qualitative.

I believe that branding is one of the largest untapped areas in all of online marketing. Marketers are obsessed with the online channel as a direct-response medium, while largely saving their brand budget for more traditional areas like the aforementioned TV, radio, and print. By doing so, they have ignored the massive exposure that can be obtained in online channels, beyond banner ads and rich ad placements. It is very possible that the "traditional" branding ad platforms of the future—even in TV, radio, and print—will be run by a robust technology company like Google, Microsoft,

Facebook, or even Apple. But before we get there, marketers will need to change their perceptions about direct response and digital branding. As you begin to establish metrics, be careful of the goals you assign to different directives. If you are not fair in your comparisons or expectations, then you will essentially be holding back your content-marketing strategy from ever performing as well as it could.

Common Metrics and KPIs

In the following sections I will be listing some of the common metrics and measurements of online marketing efforts, as well as some of the social, search, and content measurements. Be careful in how you prioritize these metrics as they relate to your goals, and note that not all of these metrics will necessarily apply to your specific business or goals. And as mentioned previously, don't get hung up on any particular data point unless you have thoroughly answered the question of "why." Not "why" because *it's the way we have always done it*, but "why" as it relates to the level of importance toward your various business goals.

Standard Metrics

While there are many nuanced metrics for measuring the benefit and life of search and social efforts, there are also many standard metrics that you will need to use to guide your insight and decision making. Some of the standard and most common metrics include the following:

- Visits
- Page views
- Number of pages per visit
- Bounce rate
- Time on site
- New visitors
- Returning visitors
- Top pages
- Page load time
- Revenue generated
- Leads generated
- Downloads generated
- Inquiries generated
- Other events generated
- Lifetime value of a customer

Basic Search Metrics

Search metrics are indicative of how well you are resonating with search engines and show what you are getting from your efforts from search channels. Some of the following items include very specific search indicators, and others apply standard metrics to these search indicators. Remember that just because it is listed doesn't mean you have to make it a top priority. Review all metrics, and determine which ones are most appropriate based on your specific business and channel goals.

- Revenue from search channel
- Traffic
- Visits/sessions
- Return visits
- Unique visitors
- Traffic at keyword level
- Page-level traffic, at keyword level
- Conversions at keyword level
- Conversions with most-common words
- Internal site-search keyword data
- Revenue generated by page, from search
- Lifetime value of a customer (LVC) from customers who first entered or attributed from search
- Return on investment (ROI) for various actions or in aggregate
- Rankings, average position
- New backlinks—link trending
- Link growth, from unique domains
- Media value of the traffic, compared to paid search costs
- An event or other action that does not produce immediate revenue (number of inquiries, leads, and so on)

Basic Social Metrics

There is a variety of different social metrics you can measure that show the impact of real-time content marketing efforts and provide an indicator of the social signals created that may contribute to search-engine content performance. Table 14.1 shows a table created by the iCrossing analytics practice, and provides a variety of basic measureable actions for Twitter, Facebook, YouTube, Google+, and blogs.

	Twitter	Facebook	YouTube	Google+	Blogs
Social Graph	followers, unfollowers, follow:follower ratio	fans, unlikes, friends of fans	subscribers, unsubscribers	circles, circled, uncircled	subscribers
Posts	direct messages, tweets, retweets, @reply	posts, comments	uploads, comments	posts	posts, comments, responses
Impressions	accounts delivered to (reach), impressions (exposures)	impressions, page views, unique page views, organic reach, viral reach, total reach, photo views, external referrals	views, unique viewers, mobile, external YouTube views, referred views, viral views	views, photo views, video views	visitors, views
Engagements	favorites, clicks, user replies, retweets, direct messages	responses, comments, clicks, comment rate, video views, interactions, people talking about this	comments, likes, dislikes, favorites, popularity	comments, clicks, video views	comments, likes, views, likes/post
Shares	retweets, mentions	shares, likes, shares/post, shares/impression, likes/post, likes/impression	embeds, shares, shares/view, shares/post, shares/impression, likes/post, likes/impression	+1s, shares, shares/view, shares/post, +1s/view, +1s/posts	shares, shares/view, shares/post

The metrics are categorized in the following ways:

Social Graph This focuses on metrics that contribute to building your networks, increasing your basic reach for conversation and passive content distribution, and providing a graph that social networks and search engines can use to measure social relevancy, trust, and authority.

Posts This provides an indicator of engagement, of increased volume of content in social spaces, and of interest level of your audience in terms of the volume and quality of their responses.

Impressions Once your content is propagated through networks, metrics in the impressions category can provide an indicator of how your content may have been actively distributed and consumed. It also provides an overall indicator of reach and should be monitored on an ongoing basis to ensure that your reach is constantly expanding.

Engagements These metrics also reveal a strong indicator of how well your content is resonating with your audience, in terms of the satisfaction and qualitative reaction to your content. These reactions and responses can also be measured quantitatively.

Shares This category is strong reflection of how well your content is resonating as it relates to the share graph (refer to Chapter 2 for more information on the share-graph concept). Interactions measured on the share graph provide signals to search engines to help them rank content in personalized and social search.

Remember that many real-time tools will allow you to measure the *velocity* of some of these metrics as it relates to monitoring your content performance in real-time. Remember that catching the *rising velocity* of content metrics can help you understand where to focus your promotion efforts to push your content over the top into mass consumption.

Content Metrics

There are additional metrics to be aware of as you are building up your content bank for the long-term benefit of your program. Keep tabs on the following metrics from time to time to ensure that you are tending well to content development and measuring signals that may indicate audience satisfaction:

- Increase in unique pages.
- Increase in unique pages for a particular keyword theme or targeted keyword sets.
- Increase in backlinks, both at the page level and to the home page.
- The ratio of incoming links to your home page vs. the sum of all the other deeper pages within your domain. If your home page dominates, work on enabling links to your deeper site pages.
- Bounce rate.
- Page-level keyword referrals.
- Link-traffic referral.
- Time on site.
- Number of page views per visitor.
- Media value of the traffic to the content.
- Top consumed pages on the site and percentage of overall site traffic to those pages.
- On-page social metrics, such as the number of shares, tweets, likes, or +1s initiated from your original content, rather than being shared within a network.

Insights

Since your brain is the most important measurement tool of all, you will need it to turn data into insight and ultimately turn insight into business intelligence. It is not always easy to cull insights, and you will often find yourself having to push hard to find new things. To help spark new ideas and provide some basic questions for developing insight, study the following questions and determine whether they are relevant to your situation or whether they can help you think about your measurement in a new and creative way to drive your business goals:

- What has changed since your last data pull or last view?

- What events have occurred on your site or in social spaces during this time, and did they cause any of these changes?

- Did you have control over the events, are they beyond your control, or both?

- Are you measuring performance based on branding goals, direct ROI goals, or both? Are your tools comprehensive enough to measure the performance that your goals depend upon?

- Are any of the new changes positive, and if so, how can they be replicated? How long would it take? Is the re-creation of your current success a short-, mid-, or long-term win?

- Is any data missing that could otherwise provide a key insight? If so, why? Do you have the proper tools and analytics in place to measure what you need? If not, why? And what will it take to get what you need?

- What does your keyword data tell you about the living and evolving language of your audience? Are you comparing new keyword appearances in reports against last week, last month, and last year?

- Overall, are your efforts generating positive returns for your business, from either a direct monetary or a branding perspective?

- What are the areas that are providing the highest returns for your business? Are you reinvesting in these areas to build and grow your business? Why or why not?

- What does your audience search for once they get to your site? Are you helping them find it in a real-time setting? Does your site have the right content or feedback mechanism to help them find what they are looking for? If you currently don't have what they are looking for, is there an opportunity for creating new content around this theme?

- Did you have a solid benchmark you are measuring against? Does your benchmark data go back at least one year? How far back does your general history date?

- Are you accounting for seasonality and real-time trends in your data, either on the plus side or on the minus side?

- Are you leveraging any lessons from the past to help capitalize on seasonality in a future real-time scenario? Are you preparing for seasonality in content and conversation in order to react in real-time?

- Are you seeing any correlations between the impact on business goals and any other areas of search and social?

- Are you measuring and quantifying the term benefits of content-marketing initiatives dating back one year, three years, or five years? If not, why? If so, what have you learned, and how can you apply it to new content strategies?

- Are you able to tie in various analytics to show a pattern of success? For example, are you marrying gains in backlinks to increases in content production? Are you comparing the level of live participation and content creation on your blog with trends in audience participation and traffic?

- Did you have major negative changes to any of your key metrics? If so, what events happened to your site during this period?

- Who else has access to your website and social spaces, and did they make any changes during the last reporting period?

- What are your recommendations for changing or updating your business during your current reporting cycle?

- Are there any current keyword or conversation trends that can help inform your existing content and social strategy? What is the context of those changes, and how can they be best addressed?

- What are your top entry pages on your site? Are these pages optimized to match the intent of the user? What feedback mechanisms do you have in place for measuring audience satisfaction with these pages? Do you enable any areas for real-time interaction with your audience on these pages?

- What is your overall percentage of traffic that comes from natural search? Is it higher or lower than previous periods? Why?

- How does your overall percentage of natural-search traffic compare with your top direct and indirect competitors?

- Do you notice any correlation with social interaction driving additional search traffic? Why or why not?

- How much revenue is generated from natural-search on a daily, weekly, monthly, and yearly basis? Is it steadily increasing?

- Are you measuring ranking visibility for your targeted terms and applying the data directionally?

- Are you making gains in search traffic and visibility for your targeted keyword vs. your competitor's keywords (single keyword or keyword groups)?

- Do you see any spiking interest in keyword terms at the hourly or daily level? Why or why not? Where is the traffic coming from? Can you identify inbound link-referral traffic to locate social spaces that may be talking about your company? Are you engaging in conversations on the linking sites?

- What is the monetary value of a like, tweet, retweet, circle, +1, or share? Is your overall footprint with these social metrics growing steadily larger or not? Why or why not?

Analytics and SEO-Tool Providers

Two of the most popular analytics tools used by a wide audience of marketers are Google Analytics, which is a free analytics tool provided by Google, and Adobe Digital Marketing Suite, which is a fee-based suite of tools used by many marketers and businesses. Yahoo! Web Analytics is also another popular choice. As mentioned at the beginning of this chapter, you will need a robust analytics tool as the foundation of measurement of your content strategy, but this section will focus on some other tools to measure the performance of content, search, and social efforts, and it will provide data for your real-time efforts.

Using SEO Analytics for Measuring Content Performance

Many marketers don't think of SEO tools as a way to measure content or social performance, but the fact is that these tools offer some unique insights into the ways your content resonates in both search and social channels. You do not have to obtain all of these tools to be effective, but you can use this section as an introduction to some of the most popular tool and service providers. I also recommend you do further research in social spaces to get feedback from other business owners about their own experience before making a selection for your business. The good news is that most of these paid services offer free trials so you can play around with them and determine which tool is best for you.

SEOmoz

The SEOmoz PRO tool set (www.seomoz.org) offers many great features for managing content performance and technical issues within your website. Figure 14.1 shows a Competitive Domain Analysis report, which compares common search factors between similar sites of your choosing. Figure 14.2 shows reports measuring crawl errors, on-page SEO factors, duplicate content, and other technical considerations. SEOmoz PRO is a fee-based service, though it offers a free trial.

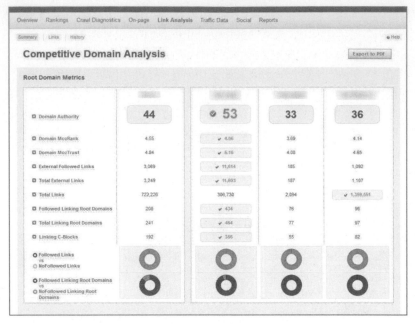

Figure 14.1 Competitive Domain Analysis report from SEOmoz

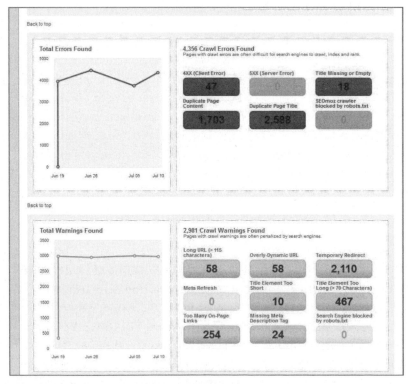

Figure 14.2 A technical diagnostics dashboard from SEOmoz

Majestic SEO

Majestic SEO (www.majesticseo.com) is also another popular web-marketing tool set and features a number of performance reports, including robust link reports, link-volume trends, and domain-based link trends, among many other reports. Figure 14.3 shows the link-report summary page.

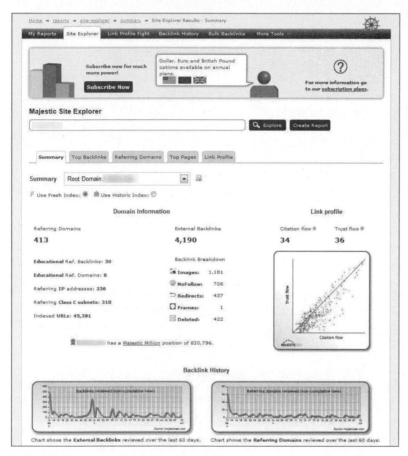

Figure 14.3 The summary site report from Majestic SEO

Raven Tools

Raven Tools (www.raventools.com) is one of the most popular SEO, social, and content tool sets available. Raven Tools offers a wide variety of reports and diagnostic tools, including the Social Stream report that monitors more than 20 different networks by connecting your own social accounts into the Raven system. The Raven Research Assistant tool also integrates access into SEMrush, Wordtracker, and the AdWords tool, and it offers robust ranking reports. Figure 14.4 shows the Twitter Metrics report, and Figure 14.5 shows the SERP Tracker report, featuring bundled Google Analytics data and AdWords statistics at the keyword level.

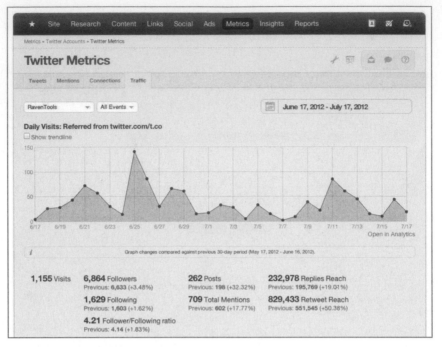

Figure 14.4 The Twitter Metrics report from Raven Tools

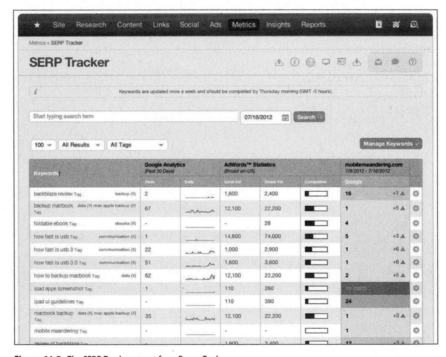

Figure 14.5 The SERP Tracker report from Raven Tools

There are many other great tool sets to choose from, and many agencies and consultants use their own in-house or preferred tool sets, which are not shown here. So, in addition to the previous SEO tool sets, also strongly consider evaluating and using those tools. Of course, don't forget Google and Bing Webmaster Tools mentioned in Chapter 10, "Technical Considerations and Implementation." Each of these tools provides helpful data direct from the search engines themselves and reveals an excellent angle on how well your site is performing from a technical and content standpoint.

Other Real-Time Analytics Tools

Because of the rapid pace of development in the real-time marketing space, there are many great tools that are available that you may or may not be using, because new tools and data providers are coming available every week. Here are some that you might find useful, depending on your particular goals and objectives.

Google Analytics Real-Time Reports

Before I discuss real-time reporting features, it should be noted that Google Analytics is one of the most popular analytics choices by online marketers. Google Analytics is free, and you can establish an account at www.google.com/analytics/ using your Google Account login. Once you have established an account, your login panel features a new section on real-time reporting and focuses on the current statistics of your website and content performance. Figure 14.6 shows a sample of some of the real-time data views, and the data updates within seconds.

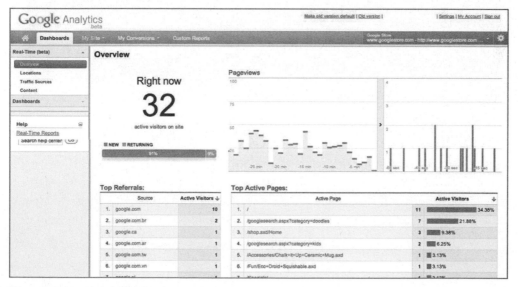

Figure 14.6 A sample real-time report from Google Analytics

The Archivist

This is a service (www.tweetarchivist.com) created by Microsoft professionals and features a nice way to research and trend specific keywords on Twitter. Figure 14.7 displays tweet vs. retweet ratios, volume over time, sources, and top URLs.

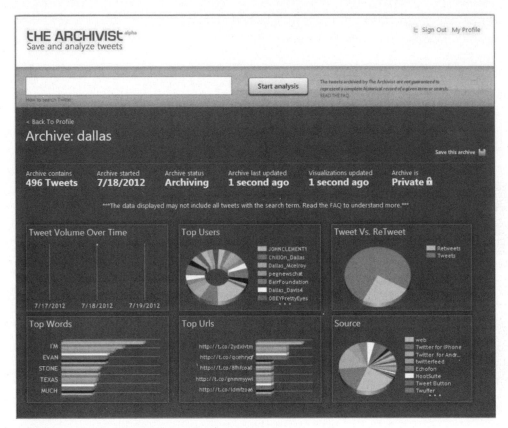

Figure 14.7 A sample results page for the term *dallas* at the Archivist

Social Mention

Social Mention (www.socialmention.com) also offers real-time reporting at the keyword level, showing top keywords, influencers, sentiment, and reach. This is a great way to research the impact of your own content and track the current linguistic trends of your audience. Figure 14.8 shows a sample search for U.S. President Barack Obama and the keyword *obama*.

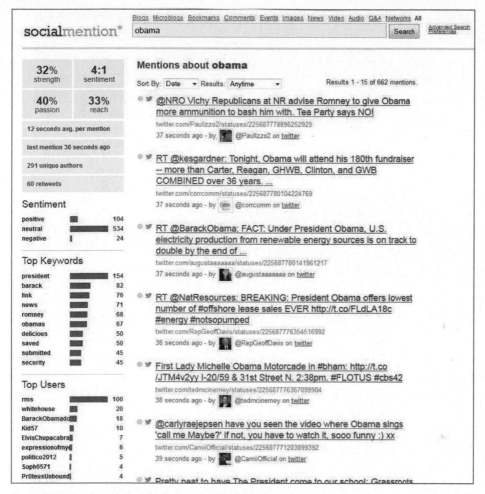

Figure 14.8 A sample results page for the term *obama* at Social Mention

Netvibes

Previously, I mentioned a way to use Netvibes (www.netvibes.com) to monitor conversations through RSS feed monitoring (Chapter 9, "Developing and Engaging in Real-Time Communities"). Netvibes has a free service that I have personally used to monitor my subject-matter space almost every day since 2007, and it also offers an enterprise service for monitoring real-time content and conversation spaces. Figure 14.9 shows a dashboard with content types, content volume, sentiment, and keyword analysis.

Chartbeat

This measurement provider (www.chartbeat.com) offers a number of different real-time reports that provide a pulse for what is happening on your owned digital assets. Figure 14.10 shows reports with concurrent visits, top pages, traffic sources, and top current search terms.

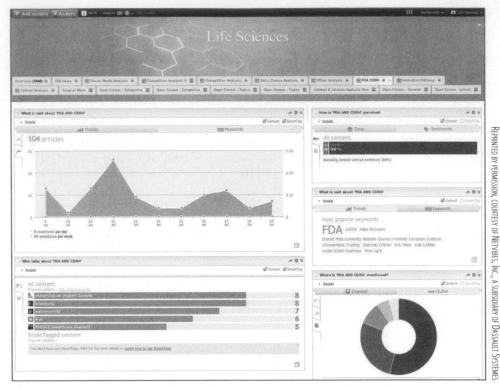

Figure 14.9 The enterprise dashboard at Netvibes

Figure 14.10 A dashboard from Chartbeat

Facebook Real-Time Insights

Facebook also offers a detailed real-time analytics service called Real-Time Insights. This view shows network reach called Friends of Fans and essentially provides a gauge of active reach (many-to-many) and other reach metrics. Figure 14.11 shows a dashboard for Real-Time Insights, focusing on key real-time trends for engagement and content performance.

Figure 14.11 A real-time dashboard from Facebook

Data-Management Platforms

Data-management platforms (DMPs) are systems that allow business and marketers to aggregate their audience data into a single source. They allow data to be managed across multiple platforms and help cull insights for multiple actions, segmentation, engagement, and attribution.

The results of this approach to data management allow for better ad targeting, better intelligence on return on investment, better understanding of audiences, cross-channel analysis, multitouch attribution modeling, third-party integration, secure data collection, and other forms of audience intelligence.

Audience-Management Platforms

Audience-management platforms (AMPs) are an extension of DMPs that are moving marketers away from publisher-owned and third-party data to enabling the business marketer to fully own their own data. Hearst Corporation's Core Audience (formerly Red Aril) service (www.coreaudience.com) is one of the products in this new category and provides data in real-time. The result is that it allows marketers to make more-informed decisions based on real-time data and analysis. The AMP approach extends beyond making digital decisions and can impact other areas of business as well, such as product development and planning, language and positioning, emerging sales channels, and more. The Core Audience AMP also enables multitouch attribution modeling in a way that highlights and targets the highest-value audiences for business marketers. Figure 14.12 illustrates the Core Audience platform approach as an AMP.

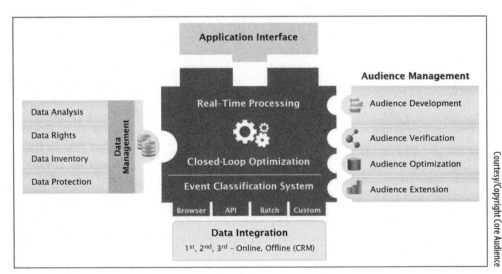

Figure 14.12 The Core Audience real-time audience-management platform

Interview with Doug Bryan

Doug Bryan is considered by many to be one of the foremost experts on ecommerce and retail "long-tail" data-mining applications. Prior to joining iCrossing, and later Core Audience, Doug managed the team responsible for recommendation data in the Data Mining and Personalization Group at Amazon.com.

How is real-time marketing, search and social changing the way marketers are viewing analytics data?

The customers are in charge now, and new technologies like mobile search and social platforms allow them to express their preferences immediately. For example, when an artist like Michael Jackson dies, it becomes a global, shared event, and people turn to Google, Twitter, and other technologies to learn more and to participate. Marketers need to understand when preferences change suddenly and react appropriately for each event.

How can marketers measure the effects of personalization, or can they be measured at all?

Absolutely they can be measured, through flow analysis and through A/B testing. Personalization is a conversion optimization tactic similar to landing-page optimization, and landing-page optimization has one of the highest ROIs of all digital tactics. Both are easily measured using A/B testing.

There is a shift occurring in the way some analytics providers are moving from just showing people as data to a more specific identification of audience type or persona. What do you think is driving this change?

ROI is driving the change. A big part of marketing has always been getting the right message to the right person at the right time. Segmenting the audience into multiple groups allows us to use different messages for each group, thus increasing the chances of getting the right message to a person. For example, if you're selling patio furniture, then you may want to segment by climate since you can sell patio furniture in February in L.A. but not in Chicago.

How do you characterize the difference between a data-management platform and an audience-management platform?

"Data-management platform" is a very generic term that could be used in any industry. Years ago Andy Grove, the CEO of Intel, said that soon every company will be in the IT industry because of their growing dependence on computers. Now that everyone has computers, we compete on data; soon every company will be in the data-science industry. What differentiates an audience-management platform is how its data is used. Audience-management platforms are used to inform and optimize bought, earned, and owned media channels in real-time.

(Continues)

Interview with Doug Bryan *(Continued)*

Which SEO and social metrics do you recommend measuring and monitoring as a key indicator of content success?

Sooner or later we need to get to cost per order or ROI (revenue/cost) so that these tactics can be compared to other marketing tactics. Of course, these metrics should be based on good multitouch attribution modeling, not just last-click winner-take-all. There are many levels of granularity to consider, but this should be measured, at least for SEO as a whole and for social media as a whole. More-granular levels of measurement to consider include brand vs. nonbrand, social-media content theme, search platform (Google, Yahoo!...), and social platform (Facebook, Pinterest...).

What are the real-time metrics that a marketer should be measuring?

Real-time metrics can help you identify what's trending, what's hot. Key metrics include conversion rate by SEO and SEM keyword, engagement rate on social media by post theme, and share rate (also called *amplification rate*) by social-media theme.

What is the right balance for marketers to strike between historical data and analysis vs. real-time data? Should an organization be focused on 50-50, 80-20, 90-10, or some other breakout?

There is no one best answer for all brands and products. The best breakout for an iconic automobile brand will be different from the best breakout for a consumable good like ketchup. Test-and-learn methodologies may be used to discover which breakout is best for your brand and your budget.

What areas of an organization should be monitoring real-time data?

Consumers are in charge now, so any part of the organization that wants to listen to the consumer or authentically communicate with them should consider real-time data. These areas include marketing to determine which messages best turn visitors into buyers, public relations to understand how the public views a brand, market research to understand shifting market trends, and customer-relationship management to understand how your current customers perceive the brand.

Appendix: Additional Reading and Resources

Conferences	
Pubcon/WebmasterWorld	www.pubcon.com
SEMPO Local Groups	www.sempo.org/?page=local_groups
SES	www.searchenginestrategies.com
ad:tech	www.ad-tech.com
South by Southwest	www.sxsw.com
SMX	www.searchmarketingexpo.com
WordCamp	http://central.wordcamp.org/
MediaPost Search Insider Summit	www.mediapost.com/searchinsidersummit/
MediaPost Events: OMMA	www.mediapost.com/events/
OMS	www.onlinemarketingsummit.com/
eMetrics	www.emetrics.org/
Shop.org	www.shop.org
Blogworld & New Media Expo	www.blogworldexpo.com/
BlogHer	www.blogher.com/conferences
Internet Retailer	www.internetretailer.com/conferences/
Content Marketing World	www.contentmarketingworld.com/
Social Media Club	http://socialmediaclub.org/
Search Congress	www.search-congress.com/
Econsultancy Events	http://econsultancy.com/us/events
Affiliate Summit	www.affiliatesummit.com/
Association of National Advertisers	www.ana.net/events

Industry Blogs and Bloggers	
John Battelle	www.battellemedia.com/
Charlene Li	www.charleneli.com/blog/
Great Finds	http://greatfinds.icrossing.com
Marketing Pilgrim	www.marketingpilgrim.com
TopRank Online Marketing Blog	www.toprankblog.com/
Copyblogger: Brian Clark	www.copyblogger.com
SEOmoz Blog	www.seomoz.org/blog
SEO by the Sea: Bill Slawski	www.seobythesea.com/
Harvard Business Review Blog	http://blogs.hbr.org/
SEOBook Blog: Aaron Wall	www.seobook.com/blog
Bruce Clay	www.bruceclay.com/blog
Stone Temple Consulting: Eric Enge	www.stonetemple.com/blog/

Industry Blogs and Bloggers *(Continued)*	
Matt Cutts	www.mattcutts.com/blog/
Rohit Bhargava	www.rohitbhargava.com/
Smashing Magazine	www.smashingmagazine.com/
Compete Pulse	http://blog.compete.com/
eMarketer	www.emarketer.com/blog/
Hitwise	http://weblogs.hitwise.com/
iCrossing UK Blog	http://connect.icrossing.co.uk/
Domain Name Wire: Andrew Allemann	www.domainnamewire.com
CircleID	www.circleid.com
Josh Bernoff	www.bernoff.com
Boing Boing	http;//www.boingboing.net
Content Marketing Institute Blog	www.contentmarketinginstitute.com/blog/
Convince and Convert: Jay Baer	www.convinceandconvert.com/
Brian Solis	www.briansolis.com/
Duct Tape Marketing Blog	www.ducttapemarketing.com/blog/
Tipping Point Labs	http://tippingpointlabs.com/blog/
The Conversion Scientist: Brian Massey	http://conversionscientist.com/
ReelSEO	www.reelseo.com/
Vertical Measures	www.verticalmeasures.com/blog/
Seth Godin	http://sethgodin.typepad.com/seths_blog/
Occam's Razor Avinash Kaushik	www.kaushik.net/avinash/
Techipedia: Tamar Weinberg	www.techipedia.com/
Yoast	http://yoast.com/
aimClear Blog: Marty Weintraub	www.aimclearblog.com/
Forrester Research Blog	http://blogs.forrester.com/
Dan Zarrella	http;//www.danzarrella.com/
Bryan Eisenberg	www.bryaneisenberg.com/
Chris Brogan	www.chrisbrogan.com/
Marketers Studio: David Berkowitz	www.marketersstudio.com/
Eric Ward	www.ericward.com
Gartner Blog Network	http://blogs.gartner.com/
Outspoken Media	http://outspokenmedia.com/blog/
Vanessa Fox	www.ninebyblue.com/blog/

Forums	
WebmasterWorld	www.webmasterworld.com
High Rankings Forum: Jill Whalen	www.highrankings.com/forum/index.php
Cre8asite	www.cre8asiteforums.com/forums/index.php
Digital Point	http://forums.digitalpoint.com/
Search Engine Watch Forums	http://forums.searchenginewatch.com/

Online News Resources	
WebProNews	www.webpronews.com/
MediaPost	www.mediapost.com/publications
Search Engine Land	www.searchengineland.com
Search Engine Watch	www.searchenginewatch.com
ClickZ	www.clickz.com
MediaPost Search Insider	www.mediapost.com/publications/search-insider/
MediaPost Search Marketing Daily	www.mediapost.com/publications/search-marketing-daily/edition/
Mashable	www.mashable.com
Social Media Examiner	www.socialmediexaminer.com
AllFacebook	www.allfacebook.com
Social CMS Buzz	http://socialcmsbuzz.com/
ReadWriteWeb	www.readwriteweb.com/
Search Marketing Standard Magazine	www.searchmarketingstandard.com/
Search Engine Roundtable	www.seroundtable.com/
TechCrunch	www.techcrunch.com/
Lifehacker	www.lifehacker.com
AdAge	http://www.adage.com
Adweek	www.adweek.com
Adrants	www.adrants.com
Wired	www.wired.com/
iMedia Connection	www.imediaconnection.com/
Social Media Today	http://socialmediatoday.com/
Alltop	www.alltop.com
Social Media Explorer	www.socialmediaexplorer.com/

Official Search Engine and Network Blogs	
Google Webmaster Central Blog	*http://googlewebmastercentral.blogspot.com/*
Bing Webmaster Center Blog	*www.bing.com/community/site_blogs/b/webmaster/ default.aspx*
Bing Search Blog	*www.bing.com/community/site_blogs/b/search/default.aspx*
Facebook Blog	*http://blog.facebook.com/*
Twitter Blog	*http://blog.twitter.com/*
LinkedIn Blog	*http://blog.linkedin.com/*
Google Official Blog	*http://googleblog.blogspot.com/*
YouTube Blog	*http://youtube-global.blogspot.com/*

Other Useful Links and Resources	
CoTweet	*http://cotweet.com*
TweetDeck	*www.tweetdeck.com*
HootSuite	*www.hootsuite.com*
WeFollow	*www.wefollow.com*
Twitpic	*www.twitpic.com*
WordPress	*www.wordpress.org*
StudioPress	*www.studiopress.com*
iThemes	*www.ithemes.com*
Basecamp	*www.basecamp.com*
Dropbox	*www.dropbox.com*
Evernote	*www.evernote.com*
Prezi	*www.prezi.com*
Foursquare	*www.foursquare.com*
Tumblr	*http://tumblr.com*
Wibiya	*www.wibiya.com/*
PubSubHubbub	*http://code.google.com/p/pubsubhubbub/*
Scribe	*www. scribeseo.com/*
TouchGraph	*www.touchgraph.com/seo*

Index

Note to the Reader: Throughout this index **boldfaced** page numbers indicate primary discussions of a topic. *Italicized* page numbers indicate illustrations.

meta data
  All in One SEO Pack, 178, *179*
  consistency, 123–124
  description tags, **125–127**, *127*
  Google tags, 256–257
  Google+ tags, 147, *147*
  images, 84–85, 275
  keyword tags, 43, **128**
  nofollow tags, 107–108
metrics and measurement, 101, **329**
  analytics and SEO tool providers, 332, **347–356**, *348–356*
  Bryan interview, 357–358
  considerations, 330–332
  content and activity, 333, 344
  early setup for, **331**
  insights, 345–347
  KPIs, 339–344
  lift events, **334–335**
  long-term business effects, 330
  marketing strategy, 49
  media value, 337
  monetary value, 336–338
  quantitative and qualitative aspects, **333**
  recency frame, 334
  timely data, 335–336
  video, 270
microdata for persons, 237–239
microformats, 231
Microsoft Advertising Intelligence plug-in, **73**, *74*
Microsoft Live, 14
Microsoft PowerPoint, 87, *87*
Mindat.org community, 297
moderation of blog comments, 177
modular design, **295**
monetary value of actions and events, **336–338**
monitoring
  answer sites, 219
  for hot topics, 120–121
multibutton share widgets, **246–247**, *246–247*
Multiple Authors tool, 242
multiple platforms, delivery frameworks across, 15

N

names
  answer sites, 217
  blog logins, 175
  domains, 100
  internal links, **130–131**, *130*
  real, **44**, 316–317
  search and social, **44**
  Twitter profile pages, **157–158**, 160
natural language
  audience, 303

keywords, **140**, 302
  search and social, **25**
Netvibes tool, 217, *218*, **353**, *354*
network analysis, 11
network buttons
  individual, **243–245**, *244–245*
  locating, **248**, *248*
  vs. sharing buttons, **242–243**, *243*
network flows, 13
network of influence, 318
networked link effect, **167–168**, *168*
networked links, 37, *38*
networks
  active and passive distribution in, **40–42**, *41–42*
  answer sites, 217
  audiences, **101**
  content, **13–14**
  early maps, **11**
  empowering, **320**
  of networks, **12–13**
  for platforms, **62–63**
  trust and authority in, **17**
  velocity for publishing in, **140–142**
New York Times, 177
news, **185**
  evaluating, **187–188**
  Google. *See* Google News
  interdependent search and social elements, **186–187**
  optimizing, **189–192**, *190*
  personalizing, **187–188**, *190*
  real-time elements, **185–186**
  resources, 362
  in site design, 296
  site maps, **191**
newsmasters, 185
niche communities, **63–64**
nofollow links
  blogs, 177
  duplicate content, **107–108**
  Twitter, **153**
noindex tag, **107–108**

O

Odden, Lee
  DAO, 15
  social-links interview, **285–287**
one-to-many connections, 13
one-to-one connections, 13
OneRiot search engine
  social-network links, 30
  Twitter, 153
OneRiot study on recency, 34